a delicate balance

Constructing a Conservation Culture
in the South Carolina Lowcountry

Angela C. Halfacre

THE UNIVERSITY OF SOUTH CAROLINA PRESS

a delicate balance

© 2012 University of South Carolina

Published by the University of South Carolina Press
Columbia, South Carolina 29208

www.sc.edu/uscpress

Manufactured in the United States of America

21 20 19 18 17 16 15 14 13 12   10 9 8 7 6 5 4 3 2 1

Library of Congress Cataloging-in-Publication Data

Halfacre, Angela C.
  A delicate balance : constructing a conservation culture in the
South Carolina lowcountry / Angela C. Halfacre.
      p. cm.
  Includes bibliographical references and index.
  ISBN 978-1-61117-071-9 (cloth : alk. paper)
  1. Historic conservation—South Carolina—Atlantic Coast. 2. Cultural
property—Protection—South Carolina—Atlantic Coast. 3. Nature conservation—
South Carolina—Atlantic Coast. 4. Environmental protection—South Carolina—
Atlantic Coast. 5. Historic conservation—Social aspects—South Carolina—Atlantic
Coast. 6. Historic sites—South Carolina—Atlantic Coast. 7. Natural areas—South
Carolina—Atlantic Coast. 8. Atlantic Coast (S.C.)—History, Local. 9. Atlantic
Coast (S.C.)—Environmental conditions. 10. South Carolina—Cultural policy.
I. Title.
  F277.A86H35 2012
  975.7'6—dc23
                              2011050453

This book was printed on a recycled paper with 30 percent postconsumer
waste content.

Title page: detail, lowcountry landscape with rice trunks.
Courtesy of David Soliday.

To the Halfacre family

CONTENTS

When Hurricane Hugo battered coastal South Carolina through the night of September 21, 1989, its winds and waters swept beach houses off foundations, damaged 80 percent of the homes in downtown Charleston, and uprooted oaks that had survived the Civil War—becoming the costliest storm in U.S. history up to that time.

Americans watched on television as tens of thousands of coastal residents discovered their homes crushed, bridges toppled, barrier islands drowned. A massive clean-up followed, with victims struggling in the muggy southern heat with no electricity and little water, food, and fuel.

What happened after the lights came on and the TV crews went home shapes one of the many surprising stories in political scientist Angela Halfacre's *A Delicate Balance: Constructing a Conservation Culture in the South Carolina Lowcountry.* As many shell-shocked locals sold their homes to flee the risk of another storm, many more newcomers—large numbers of whom had first glimpsed its indigenous beauty during the extensive media coverage of Hugo—flocked to the lowcountry.

Not splintered frame houses and forests, rising insurance premiums, or the danger of future hurricanes weakened the lowcountry's pull, strong as the tidal force along South Carolina's coastal shoreline and half-million acres of golden salt marsh. Halfacre captures the allure as both storyteller and academic, weaving oyster-briny memoirs from local voices such as novelist Pat Conroy seamlessly with ethnography and history.

But her foremost contribution is identifying and detailing the "conservation culture" that emerged in the lowcountry during the building/rebuilding boom that Hugo triggered. The conservation culture is atypical of environmentalism, shepherded with the help of some of the most conservative residents in the region and grounded in traditional property and hunting rights. It is sensitive to not only land and water proper, but land- and water-based livelihoods and traditions such as African American sweetgrass basket making.

The most remarkable story may be how, more than two decades after Hugo, the conservation culture continues to flourish. While parts of the lowcountry have succumbed to sprawl as willingly as the rest of the United States, the region has done a better job maintaining its distinctive place and ecology than most have. Historic Charleston is one of a kind. Few other Atlantic coastlines remain contoured with sand dunes and maritime forests. Other ports of southern history are more likely to censor the slave past than to honor its heritage artwork in roadside stands.

For any special place, the ultimate risk is to be loved to death: loved by more and more people bringing even more of what they were used to somewhere else—a corporate drugstore on every corner, Kentucky bluegrass on every lawn—until the special has dissolved into the common. Halfacre explores how one special place has refused to let it happen. Her book carries rich lessons for other distinctive places seeking sustainable ways to grow and prosper that maintain respect for the environment as they preserve a distinctive quality of life and cultural heritage.

The wisdom in *A Delicate Balance* could not be timelier for the United States in the early twenty-first century, a country paralyzed by uncompromising divisions between political parties, between cultures, between classes. The preservation of one of the largest undeveloped estuaries on the Eastern Seaboard, the Ashepoo, Combahee, and South Edisto Basin provides an invaluable habitat for endangered species such as woodstorks and loggerheads as it continues traditions including farming and commercial fishing. The effort here is an inspiration for other special places, such as the Everglades recharge area in Central Florida. South Carolina's conservation culture offers hope that practical consensus among committed private landowners, environmentalists, and sportsmen may yet overcome extremist rhetoric surrounding the proposal for a new Everglades Headwaters National Wildlife Refuge.

The lowcountry's conservation culture is not always harmonious. *A Delicate Balance* shows how its political, social, and cultural threads have become woven so tightly around common goals that it can endure—much like a unique coiled basket woven from historic memory with grasses harvested from the region's singular marshlands.

Cynthia Barnett

ACKNOWLEDGMENTS

I have enjoyed a lifelong love affair with the lowcountry. My own introduction to the region began at the age of two; our family vacationed each summer at Litchfield Beach and Pawleys Island throughout my childhood. We still do. Over nearly forty years my annual visits to Litchfield Beach and surrounding areas nurtured my curiosity about the coastal region. During those four decades I witnessed the dramatic changes described in this book and accumulated a wealth of memories. I am both at home in the lowcountry and aware of changes there in a way that I could never be in less familiar places. While my childhood recollections mostly involve typical vacation experiences with my family, my adult involvement has merged my professional and personal goals. In 1998 I joined the political science department at the College of Charleston. A year later I was appointed director of the master's degree program in environmental studies. During ten years at the College of Charleston I focused my research and teaching on aspects of the lowcountry's culture of conservation. My collaborations with students and faculty members deepened my understanding of the dynamics of change in the region—residential and commercial development, environmental degradation, and the maturation of a culture of conservation.

Like the culture of conservation, this book is a collaborative effort. Any errors are my own; my debts are to others. Directly and indirectly, the ideas and information contained in this book arose from many sources—my students, colleagues, staff members of environmental organizations, government agencies, elected officials, and many residents across the region. My students have been a constant source of inspiration and insight, especially those whom I supervised while they were completing undergraduate research papers and theses or master's theses and internships. The following undergraduate and graduate students developed research projects that directly informed this book: Brian Ballard, Megan Barkes, Alicia Carvajal, Tracy Duffy, Ana Emelianoff, Brian Grabbatin, Zachary Hart, Lucie Hartley, Adrienne Mojinik, Alan Moore, Katherine Owens, Reggie Reeves, Jessi Adair Shuler, Stephen Schabel, Marissa Stern, Allison Turza, Aaron Voelker, and Katie Zimmerman. Since joining the faculty at Furman University in 2008, I have benefited from the conscientious assistance of several students:

Jenni Asman, Lubiana Balasinorwala, Brittany Berger, Courtney Devoe, Anne-Marie Melief, and Anna Strick.

Faculty members at the College of Charleston provided steadfast support and beneficial feedback. My Department of Political Science colleagues—especially John Creed, Lynne Ford, Phil Jos, and William "Bill" Moore—encouraged my initial research efforts. John Rashford in the Department of Anthropology and Sociology improved the accuracy and quality of several chapters, and he has been of great help in understanding the connections between plants and place in the region. Close faculty friends Mitchell Colgan, Marian Currinder, Deborah McCarthy, Martin Jones, and Brenda Sanders bolstered my determination to complete this project. Mark McConnell, the Master of Environmental Studies program coordinator at the College of Charleston, helped my graduate students collect valuable data. Samuel Hines, former dean of the College of Liberal Arts and Sciences at the College of Charleston, and President Emeritus Alex Sanders offered much-appreciated encouragement over several years.

Other research collaborators in the lowcountry, especially Marianne Burke and Cassandra Johnson with the U.S. Forest Service, and Danny Gustafson of the Citadel, expanded my understanding of the multidisciplinary nature of sustainability. Caroline Lee of Lafayette College's Department of Anthropology and Sociology provided richly informed feedback at a crucial stage. Her own articles about the conservation coalition in the lowcountry have been essential resources for my research. Other readers of the book manuscript helped identify my errors and sharpen my analysis: Brad Wyche (Upstate Forever), John Tibbetts (South Carolina Sea Grant), Christopher Morgan (City of Charleston), Elizabeth Hagood (Lowcountry Open Land Trust), Albert Matheny (University of Florida), Larry Dodd (University of Florida), Robert Halfacre, and Sandra Tice-Wright.

My research efforts over the years have been supported by grants from several sources: Arthur Vining Davis Foundations, the College of Charleston, Furman University, the South Carolina Sea Grant, Margaret Cargill Foundation, South Carolina Department of Health and Environmental Control, Urbanization and Southeastern Estuarine Systems (USES) Project supported by University of South Carolina (USC)/National Oceanic and Atmospheric Administration (NOAA), and U.S. Department of Agriculture (USDA) Forest Service. Middlebury College's Writing Beyond Borders Project, funded by the Andrew W. Mellon Foundation, provided encouragement for the development of the book.

Even more substantive, the Andrew W. Mellon Foundation's support for Furman University's David E. Shi Center for Sustainability has been critical in the completion of this book. The Mellon funding enabled students and staff to contribute to the book at various stages. My resilient colleagues on the staff of the Shi Center have helped shepherd the book along in a variety of ways, large and small, not the least of which has been through their willingness to take on important responsibilities so as to enable me to take crucial research trips. Shi Center associate director Brittany DeKnight, program coordinator Katherine Kransteuber, administrative coordinator Cassie Klatka, and former faculty sustainability liaison Frank Powell have been gracious colleagues.

Hundreds of lowcountry residents shared their time and opinions in numerous interviews and focus-group surveys. Many regional researchers were extremely helpful in providing opportunities for data collection about the region. Special thanks go to Chris Marsh of the Sustainability Institute, Ed Pappas of Callawassie Island, Daniel Hitchcock of Clemson University, and Roger Francis of Clemson University Extension Service. Sam and Nan Welch and Derk Van-Raalte provided particularly important insights on the impact of Hurricane Hugo. My experience helping them deal with the devastation of their property and lives after the hurricane deepened my own understanding of the storm's impact. Key interviews provided me with rich data to analyze; in particular I am deeply appreciative of time and insights shared by Dana Beach (Coastal Conservation League), Chip Campsen (South Carolina State senator),Vince Graham (I'On Company), Elizabeth Hagood (Lowcountry Open Land Trust), Charles Lane (ACE Basin Task Force chair), Joseph P. Riley (mayor of Charleston), Mark Sanford (former governor of South Carolina), and Thomasena Stokes-Marshall (Town of Mount Pleasant Council). Cathy Forrester (Lowcountry Open Land Trust), Rita Bachman (Rita's Roots), Kate Parks (Coastal Conservation League), and Lisa Jones Turanksy (Coastal Conservation League) provided valuable data and insights. I am also appreciative of able and helpful assistance from the University of South Carolina Caroliniana Room staff and administration, especially Beth Bilderback. Images from local photographers grace the pages of this book; I offer my appreciation for the sharing of their work. Jeffery Allen (Clemson University), Jovian Sackett (Southern Environmental Law Center), Suresh Muthukrishnan (Furman University), and Lisa Shealy (Lowcountry Open Land Trust) carefully crafted the maps used in this book.

Patrick T. Hurley of Ursinus College deserves special acknowledgment. Our joint research projects while colleagues at the College of Charleston generated the idea for this book. I am deeply indebted to him for our collaborations and friendship. Alex Moore, my acquisitions editor at the University of South Carolina Press, has been a patient listener and steadfast advocate. His enthusiastic support enabled me to meet my deadlines while retaining my sanity. Bill Adams, the press's managing editor, has been a critical and helpful shepherd of the production of the book.

Other close friends have also been steadfastly supportive and helped encourage my own balance: Kathryn Johnson, Elaine Nochs, Bobert Hallford, and Sally Sarratt. My beachcombing dogs—Daphne, Earle, and Winston—provided much-needed, fun-loving distractions over the years in the lowcountry and now in the upstate of South Carolina.

The administration at Furman University nurtured this project. Furman faculty colleagues, particularly those in my departments, supported the effort. Brannon Andersen and Bill Ranson of the Earth and Environmental Sciences

Department and Donald Gordon and Danielle Vinson of the Political Science Department have been especially encouraging.

My most helpful reader has been David Shi, a distinguished cultural historian who is president emeritus of Furman University. His book *The Simple Life: Plain Living and High Thinking in American Culture* (1985) helped inspire my own interest in and approach to environmental stewardship. In addition, his commitment to sustainability as a university president and national leader enabled the creation of the academic center where I work. Most important, his remarkable talents as a writer and editor—as well as his willingness to edit multiple drafts of each of my chapters—have polished my prose without bruising my ego. His stylistic improvements and analytical insights enhanced the manuscript, buttressed my confidence, and helped me navigate some complicated issues. That such a busy person would invest so much attention in my book-in-progress testifies to the generosity of his spirit and the sincerity of his commitment to a more sustainable society.

This book is dedicated to my extended family—Gordon Halfacre; Carolyn and Larry Sheriff; Robert, Lara, Blake, and Addison Halfacre; Harvey and Lela Mae Halfacre; Charles and Elizabeth Folk; Marion Sieffert; and Adrienne Gerus. They first helped excite my fascination with the lowcountry years ago, and they have given me unqualified love and steadfast support ever since. Sustainability is fundamentally about taking a long-term view of happiness—for ourselves and for the benefit of the planet. My family has modeled this ethic for me. Over two generations, it has been the sustaining force in my life. And for that, as well as for so much more, I am eternally grateful.

1862 The Penn Center founded

1932 Cape Romaine National Wildlife Refuge established on 66,267 acres

1934 Santee Cooper electrical power-producing utility approved

1936 Francis Marion National Forest established on 250,000 acres

1937 MeadWestvaco paper mill opened on the Cooper River

National Ducks Unlimited founded

1942 Santee Wildlife Refuge established on 15,000 acres

1951 Nature Conservancy national office founded

1956 Sea Pines Plantation (now Sea Pines Resort) established on
Hilton Head Island

1969 Federal Environmental Policy Act

1970 Proposal of BASF petrochemical plant near Victoria Bluff denied

Nature Conservancy South Carolina office founded

1971 Beaufort County Open Land Trust established, the first Land Trust
organization in South Carolina

Clean Air Act

Occupational Health and Safety Act

1972 Federal Coastal Zone Management Act

Federal Noise Control Act

Federal Clean Water Act

South Carolina Pollution Control Act

1973 Federal Endangered Species Act

1974 Federal Safe Drinking Water Act

1976 Beach Restoration and Improvement Trust Act

Federal Toxic Substances Control Act

Federal Resource Conservation and Recovery Act

Federal Solid Waste Disposal Act

Federal Conservation Act

South Carolina Heritage Trust Act

South Carolina Groundwater Use and Reporting Act

South Carolina Water Quality Revolving Fund Authority Act

South Carolina Sea Grant Consortium

South Carolina Stormwater Management and Sediment
 Reduction Act (amended 1985)

South Carolina Coastal Tidelands and Wetlands Act

South Carolina Water Resources Planning and Coordinating Act

South Carolina Water, Water Resources and Drainage Act

South Carolina Pollution Control Facilities

South Carolina Soil and Water Conservation Districts Law

South Carolina Environmental Awareness Award

South Carolina Mining Act

South Carolina Surface Water Withdrawal and Reporting Act
 (amended 1985)

State Grants for Water and Sewer Authorities, Districts or Systems

Watershed Conservation Districts Act (amended 1992)

1983 Erosion and Sediment Reduction Act

1985 Lowcountry Open Land Trust founded

Alge Island protected by the Lowcountry Open Land Trust

Interbasin Transfer of Water Act

1986 Southern Environmental Law Center founded

1988 Ashepoo Combahee Edisto Basin Task Force established

South Carolina Beachfront Management Act (an amended portion
 of the Coastal Tidelands and Wetlands Act)

1989 South Carolina Coastal Conservation League founded

Hurricane Hugo

High Point, a portion of Wadmalaw Island, donated to the
 Lowcountry Open Land Trust as its first conservation easement

South Carolina Scenic Rivers Act

1990 Ernest F. Hollings ACE Basin National Wildlife Refuge established

Spring Island smart-growth development initiated

State Recreational Waters Act

1991 The Gregorie Tract protected as the first easement property in
 the ACE Basin

Sullivan's Island protected through the Lowcountry Open Land Trust

South Carolina Easement Act

South Carolina Solid Waste Policy and Management Act

1992 Lord Berkeley Conservation Trust founded

1993 Center for New Urbanism founded in San Francisco
Environmental Protection Fund Act

1994 South Carolina Local Government Comprehensive Planning
Enabling Act
South Carolina Reconstructing Act: Department of Natural Resources

1995 Kensington Plantation and Middleburg Plantation protected through
the Lowcountry Open Land Trust, a first
The Lowcountry Open Land Trust's process of protecting
Winyah Bay initiated

1996 The Audubon Society's South Carolina office established in July
Joint Planning Committee formed in Charleston, South Carolina, to
oversee future development of the city

1997 Dewees Island opened as an environmental community

1999 Charleston County's Urban Growth Boundary created, the first
in the lowcountry

2000 South Carolina Conservation Incentives Act
South Carolina Landowners Association formed

2001 South Carolina Smart Growth Initiative formed

2002 South Carolina Conservation Bank Act
Mackay Point Plantation now the Lowcountry Open Land Trust's
largest easement

2004 Lowcountry Open Land Trust partnership with Audubon South
Carolina for donation of Four Holes Swamp and Francis Biedler
Forest as easements
Charleston County half-cent sales tax approved

2005 Arthur Ravenel Jr. Bridge opened
Sweetgrass basket making designated the state handicraft by South
Carolina Legislature

2006 White Tract development near Awendaw proposed

2007 South Carolina Priority Investment Act (a revision of the Local
Government Comprehensive Planning Enabling Act)

2008 Land Use Planning Task Force formed by Governor Mark Sanford
Brosnan Forest donated by Norfolk Southern to the Lowcountry Open
Land Trust, making it one of the largest easements in the Southeast

2009 Community Supported Agriculture (CSA) emerges as a grassroots
movement in the lowcountry

2010 I-526 debates

a delicate balance

Introduction

At the end of the seventeenth century, John Archdale, the governor of the Province of Carolina, described the British colony's southern coastal region as a "fertile and pleasant land." The "fertile and pleasant" lowcountry has since become a storied and culturally significant place buffeted by ironic undercurrents. A history-drenched land whose backwaters remain primeval is also clogged with automobile traffic and awash in sprawling commercial and residential development. Residents cherish their natural heritage—and their valuable beachfront properties. The lowcountry is justly famous for its broad scenic expanses, semitropical climate, lush vegetation, undulating tidal rivers, freshwater wetlands and salt marshes, fast-growing pine forests, moss-draped oaks, historic plantations, vulnerable barrier islands, shell-strewn beaches, swarming mosquitoes, and abundant shore birds and wildlife. Of course, coastal South Carolina is also known for its flourishing tourism industry, abundant golf courses, ubiquitous motels and condominiums, and, as the *New York Times* reported in 2000, the unrelenting "creep of urban growth, suburban sprawl, and industrial expansion in and around Charleston and ports nearby." As of 2011, the "Holy City" of Charleston is Conde Nast's number one tourist destination in the United States. Less well known to the millions of annual tourists are the lowcountry's isolated inland towns and hamlets, rural poverty, and racist legacies.[1]

The perennial tension between preserving the lowcountry's beauty and exploiting its bounty has defined the region's history. It still does. During the last thirty years or so, the coastal region of South Carolina has experienced a land-use crisis. Haphazard residential and commercial development has been transforming wetlands and rural lands into subdivisions, strip shopping centers, and roadways at an unsustainable rate. In 2010 the "growth crisis" prompted the Historic Charleston Foundation and other civic and municipal organizations to convene a forum titled "A Delicate Balance." The conference was intended to help the Charleston metro area better manage the tensions and trade-offs between the imperatives of population growth and commercial development and the health of the environment.[2]

That "delicate" balancing act has actually been occurring for at least three decades. Until the late twentieth century, people had largely assumed that the

Lowcountry landscape with rice trunks. Courtesy of David Soliday.

region's abundant natural resources were limitless. With every passing year that illusion has been punctured. Managing the pressures of growth on the environment and the region's cultural heritage has become more challenging, more contentious, more comprehensive, and more imperative. In the lowcountry the environment and human activities have been inextricably intertwined. The *social* experience of nature—how people have perceived and related to their physical environment—is perhaps the defining element of lowcountry culture, and the cultural dimension is the crucial element in environmental studies.

My interest is not so much in nature itself as it is in the region's symbolic ecology: I am intrigued by how people experience and perceive their physical surroundings and seek to incorporate nature into their quality of life. People and place in the lowcountry are distinct but overlapping partners. As the Kentucky farmer-poet Wendell Berry has emphasized, "our problem, exactly, is that the human and the natural are indivisible, and yet are different."[3]

The delicate balance explored in this book hinges on a fundamental question: how can the lowcountry achieve a sustainable pattern of growth that promotes prosperity, protects the environment, and preserves the coastal region's distinctive quality of life and cultural heritage? In the following pages, I examine how a multilayered culture of conservation has emerged in the lowcountry since the late 1980s: what were the factors that spawned it, sustain and threaten it, help and hinder it. The conservation coalition includes a diverse yet overlapping network of private citizens, advocacy groups, and public officials animated by different motives, all woven together into a complex pattern of formal alliances and informal relationships. Its members act both individually and in concert, often in highly visible ways, and often out of sight. Because of the close-knit nature of the major actors, most of whom know each other and many of whom are close friends, the conservation coalition is remarkably agile. It can respond quickly to threats—and to opportunities. And it is adept at using a variety of techniques and tools. Depending on the issues, it can rally, react, plan, inform, persuade, compromise, cajole, threaten, lobby, or litigate.

A conservation culture necessarily involves a dynamic constellation of ideas, values, organizations, policies, and people. It is concerned with protecting human well-being while preserving environmental quality; it is as much about nurturing people as it is about preserving fragile yet enduring places. Such a conservation culture emerges when a critical mass of citizens and organized groups come to view growth management (often called smart growth, reasonable growth, or sustainable development), land-use planning, environmental protection as well as social justice, ecological integrity, and cultural preservation as urgent community goals. The sense of urgency must be great enough to prompt the formation of informal and formal networks to implement ongoing conservation initiatives. And, in the case of the lowcountry, the conservation coalition must devise both tactics and rhetoric that accommodate the region's powerful and deeply rooted conservative ethos.

The forging of such a conservation culture—its origins, goals, programs, leaders, tactics, and effectiveness—forms the centerpiece of my analysis. This book shows how growing numbers of lowcountry residents, bolstered by substantial political, corporate, and media support, have fought to sustain the rapidly growing region's distinctive sense of place as well as its fragile ecology, natural beauty, and traditional land-based livelihoods. Of course, sustaining the quality of the environment while accommodating growth is not easy; there are few simple issues or easy solutions; it is a balancing act fraught with contradictions and compromises. Yet achieving a sustainable balance has become the foremost societal challenge of the twenty-first century.[4]

The complex dialogue in the lowcountry between economic development and environmental conservation, past and future, has crystallized into an identifiable conservation culture. My use of the term *conservation culture* in this sense carries a subtly different meaning from *environmentalism*, which historically refers to a political and social movement originating in the late 1960s. It is important to distinguish among the terms as interpretive labels. A state or region has always had a physical "environment" and a social and political culture. The term *conservation culture* merges those two realities. Like the concept of environmentalism, a conservation culture encompasses the intangible yet powerful notion of an emotion-laden place. But a conservation culture is much broader in scope and more deeply textured than an environmental movement. It includes efforts to preserve historical artifacts and land-based livelihoods as well as efforts to protect the natural environment. It encompasses more than just a love of the land; it also represents a living legacy of a place's cultural heritage and social dynamics.

The Lowcountry—A Beloved Place

The lowcountry is easy to love but hard to grasp; its essential spirit eludes precise description, for it is a place as well as an image, a geography as well as an ideal. The coastal region has always manifested a seductive charm and a powerful sense of stewardship. Its languid beauties have inspired in both visitors and residents a sense of expansiveness and freedom, an almost primordial innocence and optimism about a region blessed with such abundant natural resources and biological diversity. Even amid the profound changes wrought by rapid population growth and sprawling residential and commercial development, the lowcountry remains a beguiling landscape. The roughly 50-mile wide strip of land stretching inland from the shore some 150 miles along the Atlantic coast from Myrtle Beach south to Hilton Head Island is one of the most ecologically distinctive regions of the United States. Coastal South Carolina is defined by the centrality of water. The lowcountry is a fluid region; it borders on the sea and is crisscrossed by rivers. It features 40 barrier and sea islands, 2,876 miles of tidal shoreline, and a half million acres of salt marsh, wetlands, and watery savannas, more than any other state along the Atlantic Coast. Water defines and nurtures the region—and at times submerges it. Water is the opportunistic lifeblood of the lowcountry; it flows wherever it can—as do water-borne pollutants.

The lowcountry's inviting waters, palpable grace, and stunning views generate tenacious loyalties among residents ambivalent about growth and change. "Our love of the land is fierce," explained writer John E. Davis in 2000. "We are eager to bask in the wealth of development, yet desperate to hold onto our Southern roots—*our sense of place*." Of course, pride of place is a universal phenomenon, but the lowcountry has long excited especially intense loyalties. Many South Carolinians share the sentiments expressed in the motto for the azalea festival in one of Flannery O'Connor's fictional towns. It says, "Beauty Is Our Money Crop." In fact, the state's campaign to promote tourism and investment trumpets the slogan "Smiling Faces, Beautiful Places."[5]

The alluring beauty of the lowcountry has been largely responsible for the region's phenomenal growth and feisty loyalties. In the movie version of Margaret Mitchell's novel *Gone with the Wind*, Rhett Butler, played by Clark Gable, announces at the end of the classic film, "I'm going back to Charleston, where there's a little bit of grace and charm left in the world." The lowcountry's grace has long charmed writers. John Leland, a fifth-generation lowcountry native, describes the Carolina marsh as being "intimate and voluptuous," a "living, decaying seductress" tempting "you ever farther up her devious course."

Likewise, the outspoken novelist Pat Conroy explains his lifelong affection for his native region in *The Prince of Tides*: "To describe our growing up in the

Skimmer in flight. Courtesy of David Soliday.

View of traffic through oak trees, Litchfield Beach. Photograph by Angela C. Halfacre.

Lowcountry of South Carolina, I would have to take you to the marsh on a spring day, flush the great blue heron from its silent occupation, scatter marsh hens as we sink to our knees in mud, open you an oyster with a pocketknife and feed it to you from the shell and say, 'There. That taste. That's the taste of my childhood.'" Conroy speaks of the lowcountry "religiously." His heart "belongs in the marshlands."[6]

Conroy and Leland, like many others, fret about the environmental future of their beloved lowcountry. Leland mourns the "marauding bulldozers" and million-dollar homes in gated communities that have ravaged the landscape and changed its social texture by creating physical barriers between the classes and races. "Strangers possess the land now," he lamented in 2002. Similarly Conroy, in his memoir *The Water Is Wide* (1972), described how the region's "profound and infinite beauty" was being threatened every day by the "soulless and faceless" engine of human "progress" and the destruction wrought by industrial pollution and sprawling development. Writer Josephine Humphries, a Charleston native, shares Conroy's concerns. A dominant theme of her novel *Rich in Love* (1987) is the urban-industrial transformation of the lowcountry. Elsewhere she mourns the "physical destruction of our places," a destructive process that people ironically call "development." It "is the dirty family secret of the South, and, like most dirty secrets, it is known to everyone." Humphries insists that it does no good to blame "outsiders" for the devastating overdevelopment of the lowcountry. "We have done it to ourselves."[7]

Cherishing a Changing Lowcountry

The lowcountry is no longer pristine, but it never has been untouched. By their very nature human beings are agents of change. All landscapes are constructed—by human hands and minds as well as by natural forces. "This is a shared place, porous yet interdependent," says the Beaufort-based writer Teresa Bruce. The human transformation of the lowcountry has been proceeding at a breakneck pace. Over many years, but especially since 1945, lowcountry farms and forests have been converted into urban and suburban communities, commercial development, and industrial parks. In the process the impervious surface area within coastal watersheds has grown exponentially and water quality has deteriorated, thereby generating a profound impact on coastal ecological health and integrity.[8]

Embedded in the lowcountry's long-standing pride of place is a more recent but equally intense ethic of place. This conservation ethic is rooted in a growing recognition that the coastal region's distinctive allure is dependent upon the subtle, intangible mix of landscape, habitat, climate, and folkways that have combined over the centuries to create a cherished homeland. In its essence the culture of conservation began as a protest against the destruction of the land and has evolved into an ongoing effort to accommodate the intersecting needs of the environment, population growth, economic development, and seasonal tourism. The ever-deepening sense of environmental stewardship in the lowcountry grows out of an equally widespread anxiety about the changes wrought by relentless growth. Changes in the ecological landscape have altered social and economic relationships—and vice versa.

The challenges involved in balancing sustainable development and environmental health are not purely ecological, economic, social, or political. They are a combination of all four major systems. Maintaining an equilibrium among them has shaped a culture of conservation marked by a sophisticated pragmatism. Promoting conservation in such a conservative region necessarily requires trade-offs and compromises, persistence and resilience. In comparison to similar coalitions across the United States, the lowcountry conservation culture is most often led by centrist, middle-class, practical people who seek consensus and avoid extremes. Above all, however, the "delicate" balancing act requires that people take the long view of the region's welfare rather than allow shortsighted profiteering to run amok. The lowcountry is "like no other place in the world," says Patrick Morgan, a former director of the South Carolina chapter of the Nature Conservancy. "It needs to be nurtured and managed to maintain its natural processes."[9]

The Coast as a Growth Machine

Over the past fifty years the lowcountry has become one of the ten fastest developing areas in the nation. The coastal region has long welcomed newcomers and visitors, all of whom have contributed to the process of dynamic development—and environmental degradation. A perennial influx of retirees and newcomers from other states has spurred growth in the lowcountry at a rate almost twice that of the national average. Since 1990 more than five hundred thousand people have moved to South Carolina from outside the state, and most of those newcomers have settled in the lowcountry. During the final decade of the twentieth century, the state's coastal population grew by 30 percent. Even more worrisome than the fast-growing population is the rate at which acreage is being developed and habitats are being degraded. From 1973 to 1994 the greater Charleston metropolitan area, the most densely populated in the state, saw the amount of developed land increase to one hundred sixty thousand acres from forty-five thousand acres—a rate six times that of the population increase.[10]

Coastal communities throughout the United States have witnessed similarly mushrooming growth rates during the last fifty years. The population along the Atlantic coast increased from 47 million people in 1960 to nearly 90 million in 2010. The population along the South Carolina coast has grown at an even faster rate, from 403,667 in 1960 to 900,000 in 2010—a 124 percent increase from 1960 to 2010. The 2010 U. S. Census reported that Summerville in Charleston County experienced a 59 percent growth rate during the first decade of the twenty-first century; Bluffton in Beaufort County grew by a whopping 218 percent. Dorchester County alone grew by 42 percent from 2000 to 2010. Housing units in coastal South Carolina increased from 118,333 in 1960 to 500,000 in 2010, an increase of 318 percent (only Florida and Alaska had greater percentage increases). Such patterns of growth are unsustainable if the region hopes to retain its cherished landscape, vital cultural heritage, and "leisurely" pace.[11]

Slowing the Growth Machine

Over time the juggernaut of lowcountry development created a deeply entrenched progrowth regime—business boosters, real estate developers, and their political allies—focused on the commodification of place. They rarely questioned the ways in which they were exploiting, distributing, and consuming the region's natural resources. The growth machine flourished in the second half of the twentieth century, dominating the lowcountry's development until a potent culture of conservation crystallized in the late 1980s. During the 1990s and since, more and more people—as well as local governing bodies and the local media— have called into question the claims and consequences of unchecked development.

Since the end of the 1980s the culture of conservation has blossomed into a powerful force counteracting the progrowth regime. Its basic goals are straightforward: reducing the environmental damage caused by development; strengthening governmental support and statutory protections for the environment (including air and water quality); increasing public awareness about the need for sustainable development and environmental protection; preserving "special" tracts of land in perpetuity; developing large ecological corridors and buffer zones to protect biodiversity and facilitate wildlife management; and preserving the region's land-based livelihoods. At times the conservation community in the lowcountry has organized complex alliances to promote long-range strategic land-use planning at the regional level. At other times the conservation coalition has been more fragmented and reactive, focusing on site-specific issues, particular projects, and immediate threats.

The culture of conservation has come to include concerned citizens and robust conservation organizations, proactive municipal planners, engaged newspaper editors and reporters, committed politicians representing both major parties, and active civic organizations, progressive developers, and committed philanthropists. Collectively they have become powerful enough to exert sustained counterpressure on the progrowth energies of conventional development. At times the conservation coalition has been highly visible, at times it has operated behind the scenes and out of sight. Whatever its methods, the lowcountry's conservation culture has become a vital influence on public policy and public attitudes. Every proposed development project or rezoning proposal is now scrutinized —and often rejected or modified—because of environmental or ethnocultural concerns. Numerous undeveloped areas in the lowcountry have been set aside to preserve and maintain biodiversity, wildlife habitat, and open spaces, as well as environmental and recreational resources.

A Land-centered Strategy

Each region of the nation has a distinct culture of conservation reflecting its peculiar dynamics. Conserving "special" parcels of land has become the centerpiece of lowcountry conservation efforts. Land, of course, is a distinctive commodity. It is bought and sold, rented and leased, subdivided and built upon, but it is also nurtured, planted, lived on, loved, walked upon, fished and hunted, and passed on. It also plays a significant role in a region's ecology—and its economy. Love of the land unifies the diverse residents and organizations promoting environmental conservation: sportsmen and women and other outdoor recreation enthusiasts, environmental organizations, government agencies, political leaders, and private philanthropies. Environmental management protocols and government zoning regulations and building codes have been continuously revised— and more consistently enforced—to address the negative effects of accelerating development.[12]

In large part the conservation culture has been so preoccupied with the preservation of land because of the area's powerful conservative social and political heritage. The single most important distinguishing trait of the lowcountry when compared to other regions is the long-standing sanctity of private-property rights and the equally entrenched culture of social and political conservatism. Conservation efforts in other regions of the United States have often focused on mandated protectionism (the regulation, for example, of air and water quality and regulatory compliance related to endangered-species laws). In the lowcountry, by contrast, the cultural heritage of private-property rights and the predominance of the hunting/fishing culture have led the conservation culture to focus on the protection of land through "voluntary" tools such as land trusts, designated preserves, and conservation easements. As Elizabeth Hagood, executive director of the Lowcountry Open Land Trust, has emphasized, the region's "most ardent [land] conservationists tend to be our sportsmen" who "tend to be ideologically conservative."[13]

The region's conservative ethos has also shaped the rhetorical strategy of the conservation culture. The coalition avoids charged words such as *environmentalism* and shapes its narrative to highlight conservation as a deeply embedded local value, even a public duty. As sociologist Caroline W. Lee recently noted, the lowcountry conservation community has quite consciously—and successfully— portrayed conservation as a "palatable—and even passionate—issue for conservative southerners who treasure their closeness to the outdoors and their sense of independence from state oversight and liberal meddlers."[14]

Civic Conservation

What is often ignored in studies of environmental advocacy is the crucial role played by citizens who nurture a conservation culture at the grassroots level. Media attention highlights the role of policymakers, developers, and spokespersons for environmental organizations. But common folk across the lowcountry have been essential actors in promoting the conservation culture. For centuries, people have been the key element in shaping and reshaping the lowcountry environment. They still are. What is especially remarkable about the region's culture of conservation is that it has forged an effective coalition of such varied stakeholders. Its variety of people, groups, motives, and methods has enabled it to flourish within a region that historically has been defined by its social and political conservatism, its devotion to private property rights and lust for economic development, and its slowness to regulate the environmental impact of businesses and industries.

Conservation efforts in the lowcountry have taken many forms, including the designation of strategic parcels as state forests, nature preserves, or conservation land trusts, the tightening of local land-use policies (zoning ordinances, building codes, comprehensive master planning), the promotion of smart-growth principles and the development of conservation-oriented communities, and participation in grassroots efforts to thwart haphazard development (sprawl). At the same time the culture of conservation has expanded over the years to include efforts to conserve the rich ethno-cultural heritage of the coastal region, including land-based livelihoods such as farming and basket making. For centuries low-country people have transformed the physical landscape and natural resources into communities and livelihoods. Yet the social and cultural dimensions of environmental conservation have not been adequately explored. Many of the low-country's ideas, values, and practices have been derived from the heritage of people earning their living from the land. Preserving the cultural dimensions of the region's environment has become as important as conserving the land and waterways.[15]

How to sustain the distinctive texture and heritage, pace and grace, of the lowcountry amid inevitable commercial and residential development is the region's defining challenge. The alternatives to the growth machine are neither easy nor inexpensive. The tension between human-generated development and fragile ecological habitats, the paradoxes between new commercial enterprises and cherished cultural traditions, the trade-offs between the jobs and revenue generated by tourism and its attendant traffic congestion and hidden costs, and the conflict between the public good and private-property rights have sparked a growing conversation—usually civil but at times acrimonious—about the role and nature of environmental conservation in the lowcountry. "Development is coming like a tsunami," predicted a land surveyor in Jasper County in 2007. The lowcountry has long been viewed as one of the nation's most attractive retirement regions. The population of the Charleston area has been growing at twice the rate of the national population and is forecast to increase by 250,000 through 2030. Such projected growth would consume an additional 37,357 undeveloped low-country acres (assuming that the ratio of population growth to land use remains constant). In 2001 the U.S. Forest Service released a two-year study that identified urban sprawl as the greatest threat to the South's woodlands over the next four decades. The threat is even greater in the lowcountry.[16]

The lowcountry's accelerating growth since 1989 has provoked ferocious debates about the benefits and consequences of development. "I despise developers," Flossie Mills, a resident of James Island, declared in 2007. "I *hate* what I see" happening to the lowcountry. There is something especially significant about a place that arouses such emotions—among both natives and newcomers. Philanthropist Charlotte Caldwell, a Boston transplant who chose to move to the South Carolina coast in the mid-1990s because of its coastal landscape and growing conservation culture, explained in 2000 that "a sense of place is very important to me. It is an insult to see a place [the lowcountry] bulldozed that I chose [to move to] for its beauty, for enjoyment, and even for spiritual benefit." People, she added, "move here because they fall in love with the place. They're interested in making an already great place even better."[17]

Mixed Methodology

To understand the dynamics of the conservation culture in the lowcountry, I have incorporated a variety of intellectual, social, political, economic, and demographic factors and perspectives. This book provides a record of the disparate voices that have converged to form the culture of conservation. It is in part an ethnographic study of how quite different people in the lowcountry perceive, preserve, and reshape the natural environment so as to sustain the region's traditional folkways and beauty. Ethnography is a multidisciplinary field that examines the cultural outlooks of contemporary social groups. In this case my ethnographic approach centers on the disciplines of history and the social sciences —anthropology, economics, geography, political science, public policy, and sociology. The complementary perspectives and methods associated with these disciplines enable this first analysis of the different ways in which quite varied people and groups in the lowcountry have come to view the role of cultural preservation and environmental conservation. In the following pages I assess one of the most distinctive examples of the rise of a conservation consciousness in modern America: how people along the South Carolina coast have assumed greater responsibility for being stewards of the land, cherishing and protecting it, preserving and nurturing it, so as to shepherd more sustainable development, restore degraded landscapes, achieve environmental justice, and protect human well-being.[18]

In studying the variety of environmental perceptions among lowcountry residents, I have employed various methods—historical analysis, field research, and participant observations and surveys, as well as individual and group interviews. I have especially relied on twenty focus-group interviews with lowcountry residents (181 people) as well as individual interviews with representatives of various groups: sweetgrass basket makers, farmers, real estate developers, elected officials, municipal planners, staff members of conservation organizations, volunteers, and board members of nonprofit environmental organizations. I also circulated surveys among a representative sample of both local elected officials and citizens. As a longtime lowcountry resident (until 2008) whose research has focused on the region, I also incorporate participant-observation experiences and the results of several multidisciplinary research projects conducted with my students and colleagues. Such data, coupled with a systematic analysis of the documentary record provided by newspaper articles and editorials, published reports, and legislative studies, allow for a more nuanced examination of the lowcountry's conservation community.[19]

Environmental Perceptions

Gauging how members of a community view their environmental quality of life is not easy; it is largely a function of perceptions, images, and attitudes. Environmental perceptions can be spoken, written, imagined, felt, and embodied. They can reflect carefully reasoned or spontaneously visceral beliefs; they can express well-considered ideas or inherited cultural prejudices. Their tone can be practical, poetic, passionate or polemical. In some cases environmental issues are so contentious and politically charged that people are reluctant to express their true feelings to outsiders or in public settings. Yet however problematic it is to collect and analyze environmental perceptions, such mental maps are crucial elements in a community's effort to balance growth and development with preservation and conservation.

The term *growth management* has two meanings: to manage growth to promote community well-being or to manage the dynamics of the real estate industry so as to promote growth. The latter has tended to be the norm in the lowcountry, and as a result economic development long trumped environmental stewardship. That has changed since 1989. Economic development and ecological health had long been in conflict; now they are more often considered in tandem.[20]

The most emphatically shared "environmental perception" among virtually all of the lowcountry's varied stakeholders is the need to manage growth more wisely, to strike a better balance between bulldozers and beauty. The shared challenge is to balance the demands of population growth and economic development, the rights of private-property owners, the needs of nature, and the value of the region's cultural heritage. Sustainability—ensuring that the distinctive texture of the lowcountry is preserved for generations to come—is the region's challenging goal; community-wide awareness, persistent engagement, and the ability to transcend immediate personal gain and short-term benefits in order to promote the long term welfare of the region are the keys to achieving it.

Varied Voices

Like most regions, the lowcountry displays quite varied perspectives about the quality and role of the environment. Nature has always been, as the environmental historian William Cronon has observed, a "contested terrain" involving conflicting interests, competing plans, racial and class tensions, and diverse policy choices. Commercial developers often view nature as first and foremost a commodity to generate profits, while ecologists view the environment as precious habitat to be protected and preserved. Some of the most preeminent lowcountry conservationists are from prominent, affluent, multigenerational families, while others are wealthy transplants from other parts of the country. Some embrace environmental preservation for ecological or aesthetic or even spiritual reasons. Still others are committed to conservation because they have grown up loving to hunt and fish, while others intersect with the culture of conservation because of long-standing economic ties to the land and its surrounding waters.[21]

The differing motives for conserving the environment resemble the parable of the blind men who each touch a different part of an elephant—leg or trunk or tail or tusk. They then violently disagree about the identity of the animal. Likewise, each interest group and individual in the lowcountry has a different perspective on the role and importance of the environment. Such varied perceptions are best understood when viewed in the context of the differing cultural,

Wicker chair in the marsh, Francis Marion National Forest. Courtesy of Robert Donovan.

historical, and economic factors influencing such social groups. Doing so provides an opportunity for a community to begin developing a more holistic perception of the environment's value. The survival of the lowcountry's natural environment and cultural heritage depends upon the ability of its residents to balance the inherent tensions between preservation and development.

Many South Carolinians view the "great outdoors" as one of their most precious assets for what might be called atmospheric or aesthetic reasons. It is the essential element of the often mentioned but rarely defined lowcountry "way of life." As one resident explained, "every time you drive over the marshes and creeks, you look out and there's a very good chance you will see wood storks or herons on the edge feeding, and they do it because they are healthy creeks, and things can live there. Very often, you will see otters. You drive over the Ashley River bridge, and you can see dolphins playing in the creeks, so we don't just want to protect the landscape, we want it to be healthy and thriving, and the living natural thing that it is, because there are a lot of landscapes that look sterile."[22]

Such atmospheric perceptions and symbolic values can influence the development of environmental policies and the emergence of more sustainable environmental practices. And they help explain a variety of key issues: What do such perceptions of the environment reveal about the formation of a community's attitudes, behavior, and policies? What do they mean for conservation efforts? When has a viable culture of conservation emerged in a community? What are the trends and factors that encourage a conservation culture itself to be sustainable?

Environmental perceptions in the lowcountry are neither uniform nor predictable. Instead, they are socially constructed phenomena, created by people and groups with very different perspectives—and motives. What the varied conservationists share is a desire to have a voice in bringing better balance to the future development and preservation of the distinctive lowcountry environment. George Weathers, an African American minister who helped organize the Sandy Island Community Action Club to protect the Waccamaw River island and its Gullah community from being displaced by upscale residential development, spoke for many marginalized residents when he announced in 1996 that "we have a voice now, and we will speak up about our future."[23]

Such disparate—and at times conflicting—voices have intermingled to create a distinctive conservation ethic—as well as a shifting conservation coalition. The threads contributing to the conservation culture have been woven together into a complex pattern. From those who make their living from the land, such as African American basket makers and multigenerational farmers, to those who own, manage, and develop the land, to municipal planners, environmental groups, civic leaders, and home owners' association members, such distinct voices, at times harmonious, at times dissonant, combine to create a dynamic culture of conservation that is constantly being reconstructed.[24]

This book is an incomplete account of a complex phenomenon: the emergence of a culture of conservation and its ongoing activities. By necessity I have selected particular topics and themes to emphasize and left other topics and issues unexplored or understated. Likewise, in profiling leaders of the conservation coalition I have dealt more with some than with others. A quintet of quite different leaders appears often in the following pages: Dana Beach, cofounder and director of the Coastal Conservation League; Elizabeth M. Hagood, the founding executive director of the Lowcountry Open Land Trust; Charles G. Lane, lowcountry executive, plantation owner, and conservationist; Joseph P. "Joe" Riley, the long-serving mayor of Charleston; and, Thomasena Stokes-Marshall, the first African American member of the Mount Pleasant Town Council and the founder of the Sweetgrass Heritage Preservation Society. Although diverse in background, temperament, and personality, these five leaders have played disproportionately important roles in shaping the culture of conservation.

Another limitation of my research is geography. My working definition of the lowcountry includes nine coastal counties. Yet much of my research and analysis is focused on the Charleston metropolitan area—especially Berkeley, Charleston, and Dorchester Counties. This reflects the fact that those three densely populated counties exercise disproportionate influence on the coastal region's economy, culture, and politics.[25]

The Lowcountry as a Learning Laboratory

My immediate motives for undertaking this study were focused on concerns about the physical environment and efforts to exploit, conserve, and preserve it, but they also belong to an older tradition dating back several centuries, a tradition that views the preservation of nature as a way of preserving physical and mental well-being. Human development, in other words, is as important as physical development. The lowcountry's evolving attitudes toward conservation have been forged through a rich history of conflict and compromise that has most recently crystallized into a fragile consensus committed to sustainability.

A more sustainable civilization depends upon a community engaging in a continuous, conscientious conversation about conservation. This book is devoted to that goal. My hope is that the following pages both inform and enliven the dialogue about sustainable development along the South Carolina coast. In promoting an ethic of sustainability in the lowcountry, most of the region's stakeholders have begun to move beyond the conventional—and often paralyzing—polarity between conservationists and developers. People are increasingly aware of how the quality of their lives is inextricably related to the ecological systems that sustain their lives. Few regions of the United States offer a better learning laboratory about the centrality of conservation concerns than the lowcountry. Even fewer regions' habitats are more immediately threatened by development or more passionately defended. Lowcountry novelist Mary Alice Monroe, a Chicago native, gave voice to the coastal region's increasing determination to manage growth in 2005: "When you come from somewhere where you've seen destruction, and you come to a place that's paradise, you don't take paradise for granted. 'Once it's gone, it's gone.'" Monroe and others are aware that our sense of place is forever informing and shaping us, for our environment is forever in process as both a common space and as a private possession, as a physical landscape and a mental image, forever astir, powerfully fragile, and surprisingly resilient.[26]

ONE

The Lowcountry Environment—
Past and Present

The South Carolina lowcountry is hard to leave and even harder to define. It comprises an irregularly shaped area stretching approximately one hundred fifty miles along the Atlantic coast from Myrtle Beach southwestward to Hilton Head Island and extending some fifty miles inland. The term *lowcountry* derived from comments made by the first Europeans to visit the region in the seventeenth century. As one of the early British colonists wrote, the Carolina coastal area is "soe plaine & Levyll that it may be compared to a Bowling all[e]y." For the purposes of this study the lowcountry region includes nine "saltwater" counties, moving from north to south: Horry, Georgetown, Williamsburg, Charleston, Berkeley, Dorchester, Beaufort, Jasper, and Colleton. These counties are situated from the highly developed Myrtle Beach area in the north down to the Savannah River and the Georgia border.[1]

Along the Coast

The lowcountry is one of the world's most complex coastal ecotones (an area of great biological diversity where two or more distinct habitats adjoin). It hosts six different ecosystems. The mainland features upland forests and mossy swamps (wetlands with more trees than marshes). Freshwater rivers and streams comprise a third ecosystem. A fourth ecosystem consists of hundreds of mostly small barrier islands and mainland coastal fringe, or "strand." Finally, two coastal wetland ecosystems include the shallow marshes near the seashore and the deeper estuaries lying between the marshes and the barrier islands, where the mouths of freshwater rivers intermingle with the saltwater from oceanic tides.[2]

Moving southwest along the coast from Murrells Inlet, salt marshes and barrier islands dominate the landscape. The channel running between South and North Islands creates Winyah Bay, home to the port city of Georgetown. The coastline between Georgetown and the greater Charleston area hosts the Francis Marion National Forest as well as Cape Romain National Wildlife Refuge. These large preserved areas are protected by numerous barrier islands (named such because they shield the mainland from storm damage), most of which are owned and managed by the U.S. Fish & Wildlife Service (USFWS).

Nestled between the Francis Marion National Forest and Cape Romain lies the village of McClellanville, historically the home of predominantly African American fishers and shrimpers who plied the waters of Bulls Bay immediately south of the community. Bulls and Capers Islands (within Cape Romain) are among the southernmost of the barrier islands in the lowcountry that remain undeveloped. Islands farther south—Dewees, Isle of Palms, Sullivan's, Morris, Folly, Kiawah, Seabrook, and Edisto—help create the channels forming Charleston's harbor. Several of the region's thirty-five barrier islands are intensively developed and represent some of the most valuable real estate in the nation. Charleston remains the vibrant hub of lowcountry urban life, as it has been since the eighteenth century. By far the most populous city on the coast, it is has long been a tourist mecca renowned for its history, culture, and grace, as well as a self-confident charm and, at times, a defiant insularity. It has also been a bustling port, long dependent upon the crops and commerce of the inland counties and beyond.[3]

The final segment of South Carolina coast from Charleston southwest to the mouth of the Savannah River is sometimes called the "true" lowcountry because it is so wet. Much of the land in Beaufort and Jasper Counties is covered in water that supports abundant marshes and forested wetlands. Hilton Head Island is the largest and most intensively developed island in the southern area of the lowcountry. Since the 1960s it has been a primary tourist destination, blessed with impressive beaches and numerous golf courses.[4]

The lowcountry has always been defined by its stunningly lovely physical landscape. It has a distinctive look and feel, almost Old Testament–like in its intensities. From its northern boundary at Little River Inlet southwest to the Savannah River, the region attracts large numbers of new residents and millions of tourists eager to enjoy its water-based activities, mild climate, prolific beaches, scenic vistas, historic sites, and forested landscapes. Yet for all of its natural beauty and alluring amenities, the lowcountry has also harbored an abundance of natural hazards: sweltering heat and humidity, malarial mosquitoes, and devastating hurricanes. Such hazards help make the lowcountry such a dynamic and even dangerously wild place. It is unpredictable: always changing, always in motion, always becoming. Every day, the tides reshape the beaches and drain the marshes. The lowcountry is fungible, adaptive, resilient and self-renewing—even in the face of unprecedented human-induced changes.[5]

Flowing Water

Water is the defining feature of the lowcountry. The region's dynamic ecosystem is centered on fluctuating levels of water. Wetlands predominate. As one scholar has said, the area is a "half-drowned coast country." A web of meandering rivers, nutrient-rich estuaries, tidal creeks, alluvial swamps, and golden marshes surround, infiltrate, and drench the land. Over the centuries the lowcountry has been constructed through the perennial layering of eroded soils deposited from upstream. Complex ecological communities have emerged through this fluid process of sediment layering. In turn, the abundant rivers and marshes have furthered the subtle accretion of new lands through riverine interactions. In the process the water from these shifting rivers creates deltas and floods lowlands to form marshlands. Fresh water from springs and rivers often mixes with seawater to form brackish transition zones. These coastal waters and the diverse habitats they help shape are, in large part, what has created the lowcountry's storied appeal: the region's abundant flora and fauna are nourished by the flowing and ponding of plentiful water; the productivity of land and forests in the region depends upon these hydrologic interactions.[6]

Lowcountry rivers, tidal creeks, lakes, lagoons, ponds, and the ocean create a colorful pattern of dyed soils and lush vegetation whose bounty has supported peoples and cultures for centuries. Descendants of the African slaves who constructed enormous impoundments during the eighteenth and nineteenth centuries to produce the agricultural wealth (cattle, rice, indigo, cotton) that helped build the flourishing Charleston economy continue to sew their distinctive coiled sea grass baskets and thereby retain their cultural ties to Africa.

There are more than a dozen lowcountry coastal rivers, most of which flow southeastward from the Carolina piedmont to the coast. As they near the coast, the rivers form a network of estuaries connected by a web of creeks and sloughs (marshes, swamps, bogs). Three rivers stand out for their size and volume—the Santee, Cooper, and Edisto. Each enters the Atlantic near Charleston, and they collectively drain much of the lowcountry region. The Santee River is formed by the confluence of the Congaree and Wateree Rivers at Lake Marion. From there it flows southeast into the ocean between Georgetown and Charleston. The Santee lies north of the urbanized area along the Cooper, while the Cooper River and its tributaries drain most of the central lowcountry. As one of South Carolina's most urbanized waterways, the Cooper River borders North Charleston, Mount Pleasant, and Charleston. At its end the Cooper combines with the Ashley to form Charleston Harbor. The Edisto River is the least developed and southernmost of the region's three dominant rivers. It has retained its rural character and is one of the longest free-flowing, slow-moving "black-water" rivers in North America. (Black-water rivers are slow-moving currents stained by tannins leaching from surrounding trees and vegetation in swampy areas.) These three rivers were important resources first for Native Americans, then for early European agricultural settlements, and finally for the modern industrial development of the state.

Gentle Gradients, Subtle Ecologies

The lowcountry ecosystem features diverse, complex habitats that support thousands of plant and animal species. The region is a giant bouillabaisse of fresh, brackish, and saltwater areas containing a rich stew of plants, nutrients, and organisms essential to the lowcountry environment. The Middle Atlantic Coastal

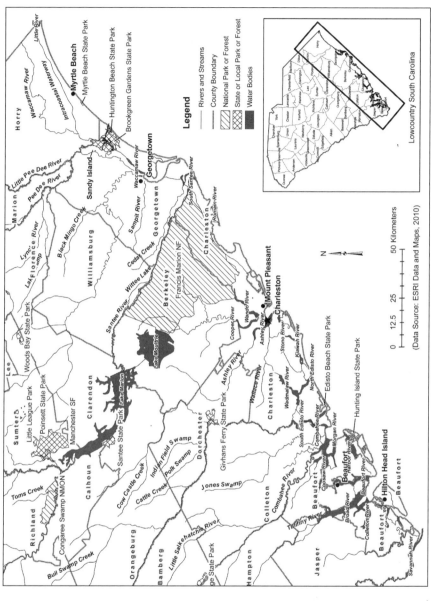

Map of the lowcountry waterbodies. Courtesy of Suresh Muthukrishnan.

Legend

Rivers and Streams
County Boundary
National Park or Forest
State or Local Park or Forest
Water Bodies

Lowcountry South Carolina

(Data Source: ESRI Data and Maps, 2010)

N

0   12.5   25   50 Kilometers

Plain (Inner Plain) in South Carolina hosts significant endemic biota, rare species, and several unique habitats, such as Carolina Bays and pocosins (shrub bogs on elevated land). Savannas (treeless grasslands) and woodlands dominated by longleaf pine were once common, but these habitats have been altered by shifting settlement patterns and associated land uses. The Southern Coastal Plain (Outer Plain) features highly dynamic environments, where river, wind, and ocean actions influence plant distributions. The Cooper River supports flora and fauna common to these ecoregions. The Edisto River Basin's ecology is similar to that of the Santee River, with substantial areas of forested wetlands. Many of the diked wetlands (of the 504,000 acres of wetlands in the lowcountry, 144,000 were once rice fields) are managed to promote commercial forestry and recreational hunting and fishing.[7]

The lowcountry region is a major contributor to the South's biotic diversity. Ninety-four ecological communities call the Edisto Basin home, including twenty-one terrestrial, fifty-seven freshwater wetlands, and sixteen estuarine communities. By their very nature, wetlands host more forms of plant and animal life than most other ecosystems, and they play an especially important role in regulating water levels, trapping nutrient-rich sediments, and consuming pollutants.[8]

Hardwood swamps (forested low-lying wetlands that retain water year round but drain better than bogs), whose flood-tolerant, overstory trees block out sunlight and thereby limit the development of understory plants, are common in forested areas within the flood plains. Such hydric forests are home to diverse species of trees: sweet gum, swamp tupelo, sugar maple, river birch, white ash, laurel, overcup, cherrybark oaks, water tupelo, bald cypress, water elm, water ash, and loblolly pine. The swamps also host large numbers of amphibians, reptiles, and birds, in addition to more common mammals. In drier areas longleaf pine once dominated forests, savannas, and woodlands. Today many of these areas are the site of loblolly pine plantations, several of which are being cleared for new subdivisions.[9]

Marshes (treeless wetlands) are more common in the Outer Coastal Plain and Coastal Zone, with the vegetation reflecting freshwater, brackish, and saltwater conditions. A small number of plant species, sensitive to differences in salinity levels, dominate. In the freshwater areas large stands of giant cutgrass predominate. The freshwater marshes and estuaries (the zone where rivers meet the sea) support numerous shorebirds: osprey, swallow-tailed kites, great egrets, herons, and puddle ducks. Alligators are also common.[10]

In the brackish marsh the dominant grass species are cordgrass and needlerush; bulrush and aster are also prevalent. Nearer the ocean, saltwater marsh vegetation prevails, especially smooth cordgrass and spartina. The South Carolina coast has more salt marsh than any other state on the Atlantic seaboard. The salt marshes constitute one of the world's most productive ecosystems; they serve as abundant nurseries for fish and other aquatic invertebrates, such as blue crab and shrimp. The most characteristic salt marsh residents are fiddler crabs and marsh periwinkles. Maritime forests are also plentiful along the coast on barrier and sea islands. There the typical vegetation includes live oaks, red oaks, palmetto, varied pines, magnolia, holly, wax myrtle, and wild olive.[11]

Humans have long exploited species common to these habitats. In fact, Native Americans collected numerous products from shrubs, trees, and other plants, such as holly berries. Even today these habitats provide important resources for local communities, among which the most famous are the area's sweetgrass basket makers as well as other Gullah (an indigenous African American folk culture that includes distinctive linguistic patterns, religious beliefs, and practices, and kinship ties) communities in the lowcountry.

Besides the collection of longleaf pine needles, palmetto fronds, bulrush, and "blades" of sweetgrass, members of the lowcountry Gullah communities collect other plants, such as snakeroot or life-everlasting, for medicinal purposes and still others, such as magnolia tree blooms, for sale in local markets. Indeed Charleston long has been known for these so-called flower ladies.

The lowcountry's numerous rivers have long been prized by anglers and biologists alike for their abundant fish. Almost ninety different fish species have been collected from the freshwater portions and 120 different species from the saltwater areas in the Edisto Basin. Such biological diversity and the rivers' distinctive geography have resulted from flowing water that has attracted diverse peoples over many centuries. And it is the changing interactions between people and the physical environment that have informed community reactions to a changing landscape.

Native Americans and Land Use

The first people who arrived in the lowcountry began the process of altering its environment. By the time Europeans approached the South Carolina coast in the sixteenth century, Native Americans had been making productive use of lowcountry natural resources for as long as ten thousand years. In those ancient times woodland bison and mammoth still roamed the lowcountry grasslands. Hunting was the primary form of subsistence for what archaeologists call the nomadic Paleo-Indians, but as temperatures warmed and the Pleistocene glaciations came to an end, around 8000 B.C., the region's climate and flora gradually transitioned into what we know today.[12]

Native Americans increasingly relied upon a wide variety of resources from ocean, freshwater, and forest environments. They lived in small bands that migrated seasonally between the coastlines and the hardwood forests, where they subsisted through hunting, fishing, and gathering (fruits, nuts, seeds, and berries). A network of trails crisscrossed the lowcountry. The Native Americans spent spring and summer along the rivers and coastlines, then moved to higher lands in autumn to hunt white-tailed deer, returning to the coast during winter.[13]

Beginning several thousand years ago, Native Americans began to settle along the Carolina coast at the same time that essential food plants—corn, squash, pumpkins, and beans—were spreading from Mexico to the eastern part of the United States. With the advent of agriculture Native American settlements in the lowcountry became more permanent. Garden plots flourished in the region's dark, alluvial soil. Fires were used to clear forests for planting, to remove undergrowth to facilitate hunting, and to clear away crop refuse and weeds for new plantings. Such fires helped enrich the soil with wood ash rich in phosphorous and calcium carbonate. As an English visitor noted, the Carolina Indians "never Dung their Land, but set fire to the Weeds, which makes very good Manure."[14]

Around A.D. 1150 Mississippians entered what became South Carolina and began building settlements in the area's river valleys. The local woodlands tribes resisted the intruders and continued to dominate the lowcountry until European colonization. Among these, the Muskhogean speakers or Cusabos lived south of the Santee down to the Savannah River. The Edisto Basin also hosted Kusso, Etiwaw, Kiawah, Escamacu, Combahee, Ashepoo, Stono, and Yemassee, all hunter-gatherer tribes. Fishing, hunting, gathering, and varied types of farming provided ample resources; there was little need for tribes to compete. Over time the Native Americans altered the lowcountry environment at the same time that they invested it with sacred symbolic value.[15]

Colonizing Land, People, and Trade: 1500–1700

Today's lowcountry culture and landscapes are in many ways still influenced by the actions and interactions of Native Americans, European American planters, and Africans more than four hundred years ago. Through war and peace, as well as periods of great prosperity and times of desperate poverty, their lives and histories blended together to create the lowcountry's unique culture and ecology. Natural factors shape history as much as people do. Climate, geology, and ecology are agents of change and shapers of possibilities. This has been especially true in the lowcountry.[16]

The Spanish were the first Europeans to explore the coast of South Carolina. In 1526 an expedition led by Lucas Vásquez de Ayllón founded San Miguel de Gualdape on the coast, possibly near Winyah Bay. The small settlement, however, was short-lived. It was quickly abandoned after Ayllón died and disputes with the Indians erupted. Frenchman Jean Ribaut led an expedition of Huguenots (persecuted French Protestants) to Parris Island in 1562, where they founded Charlesfort. Yet their settlement also lasted less than a year. The Spanish returned in 1566 and established the garrison town of Santa Elena on Parris Island off the coast of what has since become Beaufort. By 1569 the Spanish population of Charlesfort had grown to more than three hundred and showed signs of prospering. But food shortages, conflicts with Native Americans, and disease led the Spanish to abandon the site in 1587.[17]

English settlement of the lowcountry began in 1665, when King Charles II granted a unique land-grant charter to eight Lords Proprietors, all prominent aristocrats and loyal royalists who were eager to seize profits from America. The proprietors, led by Sir John Colleton and Anthony Ashley-Cooper, named their colony Carolina in honor of King Charles. In 1670 three tiny ships carrying English settlers sailed first to Ireland and then spent forty days at sea before arriving at Barbados. Four months later the expedition headed for Carolina. One of the ships ran aground during a tropical storm; another storm swept a second sloop to Virginia. Only the frigate *Carolina* made landfall at Bulls Bay, some thirty miles north of what came to be Charleston. The 130 English, Irish, and Welsh colonists, some of whom had already been living in Barbados, followed the advice of Kiawah Indians and ventured south to Albemarle Point along what they called the Ashley River. There they created the first enduring European settlement between Spanish Florida and Virginia. They called it Charles Town. The Kiawah befriended the newcomers and developed an extensive trading relationship with them.[18]

The new Carolina colony's reputation for religious tolerance attracted a diverse group of ethnic migrants from Europe—Huguenots and Catholics, Irish, Scots, Scots-Irish, Dutch, Germans, Quakers, and Sephardic Jews. Later, Greeks and Italians would follow. The dominant group in the first years of settlement, however, was made up of aspiring planters from the British West Indies: Jamaica, Antigua, Nevis, Montserrat, and especially Barbados and the Bahamas, many of whom brought gangs of Africans with them. The West Indian Britons set about transforming the lowcountry environment—especially the forests. They raised cattle and hogs and exported forest-based products, such as pitch, tar, turpentine, and lumber.

Charles Town was initially built along the west bank of the Ashley River, but ten years later, in 1680, the colonists moved the settlement to the peninsula between the Cooper and Ashley Rivers. By 1690 Charles Town (the name was compressed to one word after the Revolutionary War) was the fifth largest city in America behind Boston, Philadelphia, New York, and Newport. The first wave of European settlers acquired the most fertile lands close to the rivers. Property along the Ashley River went first, followed by lands on the Cooper River and its tributary, Goose Creek.[19]

European colonists viewed the American environment as a source of profitable commodities. To them nature was to be exploited and subdued, not conserved and celebrated. They described the Carolina coast as a "wilderness"—to them it seemed unknown, disordered, and uncontrolled. Waves of colonists from Great Britain, Barbados, and Virginia, attracted by promotional pamphlets touting South Carolina as a "pleasant and fertile Country," poured into the lowcountry, aggressively competing for the best riverfront land. At the same time white traders traveled well inland to develop a thriving commerce in furs and hides with Native Americans. In exchange for beaver and deer skins, they offered trinkets, cookware, blankets, rum, and weapons. From 1699 to 1715 an average of fifty-four thousand deerskins a year were shipped from Charles Town across the Atlantic. By the mid-eighteenth century that number had more than doubled.

Much more problematic was the Europeans' commerce in Native American slaves. White traders encouraged Indian warfare as a means of purchasing captives as slaves, many of whom were sold and dispatched to Caribbean colonies.[20]

The Europeans brought to the lowcountry more than a lust for land and profits. They also brought infectious diseases that ravaged Native Americans who had never been exposed to such microbes. With no antibodies to ward off infection, the indigenous population experienced devastating epidemics of smallpox, influenza, typhus, and measles. The provincial governor of the Carolinas during the 1690s, John Archdale, declared that it "pleased Almighty God to send unusual Sicknesses amongst them, as the Smallpox, etc., to lessen their Numbers." He was convinced that the "Hand of God was eminently seen in thinning the Indians, to make room for the English." By 1800 what had once been a lowcountry Native American population of 7,500 (estimated) had been reduced to a few hundred.[21]

Over time the white settlers pushed the Native Americans out of the lowcountry. From the Ashley and Cooper Rivers, European settlement spread north to the lower reaches of the Santee River and southward to the Edisto, where the English and Spanish competed for land and trade with warring Indian tribes. Huguenots, who nicknamed the region the "French Santee," dominated the lower Santee River and upper Cooper River Basins, which would become one of the most fertile rice-growing areas in the colony. European settlements flourished first along intertidal rivers and then expanded inland along the Edisto. However, the encroachment of European American settlements along the Cooper, Santee, and Edisto Rivers forced Native Americans to move north. Those who remained faced dwindling game populations, infectious diseases, and difficulty controlling land. By the 1760s coastal and inland tribes were devastated by settler-related violence and disease: most were driven out, killed, or died of smallpox.[22]

Transforming Swamps, Cultivating Rice

The first major European-led transformation of the lowcountry landscape occurred late in the seventeenth century as farmers began experimenting with the growing of rice for world markets. They discovered that the translucent grain was perfectly suited to the growing conditions in the semitropical lowcountry. Rice loves water; it flourishes in warm, moist soils; it thrives when visited by frequent rains or watered by regular irrigation. The control of water was therefore the paramount concern of rice growers, and water is the most abundant lowcountry resource.

The first experiments in rice growing were in the savannas. The yields of the thirsty rice plants were dependent on regular rainfall, however, and the rains did not always come when most needed. By the 1720s planters had developed much higher yields by cultivating rice in freshwater inland swamps, the low-lying lands out of which the streams seeped rather than flowed. Growing rice in former swamps involved backbreaking toil. White planters quickly delegated such "mud

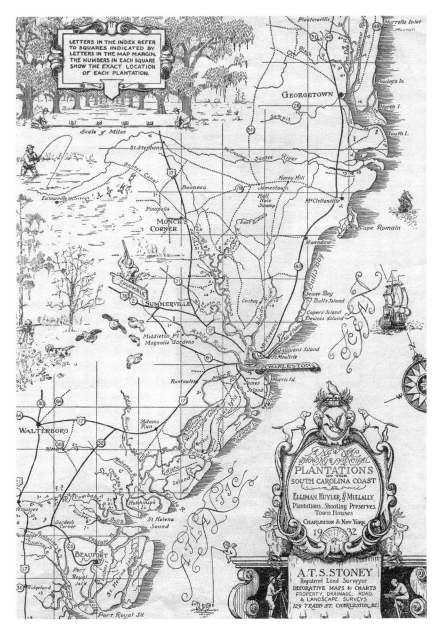

Map of coastal South Carolina plantations in 1932.
Courtesy of South Caroliniana Library.

work" to enslaved Africans. As Jedidiah Morse, a prominent Charleston minister, admitted in the late eighteenth century, "no white man, to speak generally, ever thinks of settling a farm, and improving it for himself, without negroes."[23]

Slaves taken from West Africa, where rice had been cultivated for centuries, were essential to the lowcountry economy during the eighteenth and early nineteenth centuries. The enslaved Africans knew both the techniques and the technologies needed to cultivate the grain, then winnow and pound (de-husk) it. They were also accustomed to the strenuous labor in mucky fields. As Governor John Drayton explained, an enslaved African could "work for hours in mud and water" cultivating rice "while to a white this kind of labor would be almost certain death." Using only hand tools, captive Africans transformed the lowcountry landscape. They first removed massive bald cypress, tupelo, and sweet gum trees from freshwater swamps infested with snakes, alligators, and mosquitoes. They then drained the water, leveled the land, and enclosed the newly squared fields with earth embankments and dikes. Floodgates on the dikes allowed workers to drain or flood the field as needed.

Eventually an elaborate network of bunds and sluices, ditches and dikes redirected water from creeks, rainfall, and springs to water the rice fields. A mid-eighteenth-century British governor of South Carolina, James Glen, marveled at the physical and economic transformation of the colony. He thanked God that South Carolina no longer suffered from "its uncultivated condition, overgrown with woods, overrun with wild beasts, and swarming with native Indians." Thanks to English ingenuity and capitalism, he said with no acknowledgement of the "mud work" provided by enslaved Africans, the colony had become "one of the fairest provinces belonging to our Imperial Crown."[24]

By the 1720s the lowcountry was exporting six million pounds of rice a year—and importing a growing army of enslaved Africans. The profitable, labor-intensive rice plantation system spawned a voracious demand for more West Africans. A Charles Town newspaper in the early eighteenth century announced the arrival of 250 Africans "from the Windward and Rice Coast, valued for their knowledge of rice culture." By the 1720s African Americans outnumbered Europeans in the coastal region. In 1703 there were three thousand enslaved Africans in South Carolina. From 1720 to 1729, when North and South Carolina became royal colonies, the number of slaves doubled, and the port of Charles Town became the primary gateway for enslaved Africans brought to North America.[25]

Wetland rice farming, however, eventually suffered from the fickleness of lowcountry weather patterns. Flooding rains or prolonged drought played havoc with rice. The unpredictable supply of rain water (and occasional destructive downpours that washed away dikes and flooded fields) prompted the wealthiest planters during the second half of the eighteenth century to move their rice-making operations to the lower reaches of the lowcountry's tidal rivers. The ocean tides push saltwater inland up the region's rivers for as much as thirty miles. Several of the tidal rivers, especially the Santee, Waccamaw, Black, Great

Pee Dee, Little Pee Dee, Edisto, Ashepoo, and Combahee, feature a sheet of freshwater on top of a current of saltwater because freshwater is lighter. Planters discovered that they could skim off the tidal freshwater and thereby take advantage of the diurnal rising and falling of coastal rivers to nourish the rice plants, deter weeds, and periodically release nutrient-rich alluvial sediment to replenish the soil fertility. Tidal rice plantations had a much greater "command of water," as Governor Drayton noted, and "the crop [was thereby] more certain, and the work of the negroes less toilsome." The importation of more than fifty-eight thousand enslaved Africans to South Carolina from 1759 to 1775 facilitated the laborious transition of the rice economy to tidal irrigation.[26]

The growing of tidewater rice was much more profitable, but it necessitated profound—and expensive—changes in the landscape. The tidal irrigation scheme was what one planter called a "huge hydraulic machine," a sophisticated, large-scale system of agricultural engineering using floodgates, trunks, canals, banks, and ditches. Fields were flooded at high tide and closed at low tide to trap the water. The gates were opened at ebb tide to drain excess and often brackish water. This complex process of irrigated farming involved a massive earth-moving process (using only hand tools) that transformed the landscape and changed the area's hydrology. The banks enclosing rice fields on the twelve-and-one-half-mile stretch of the east branch of the Cooper River were more than fifty-five miles long and contained more than 6.4 million cubic feet of earth.[27]

As the eighteenth century progressed, planters transformed lowcountry landscapes, from the Pee Dee and Wacamaw Rivers in the north to the Savannah River in the south. By mid-century, for example, the Edisto River was lined with rice plantations. A network of canals and dikes linked newly cleared swamps and the resulting fields and serpentine embankments with tidal freshwater zones in the Edisto River Basin. While the salinity of low-lying wetlands in the lower Edisto prohibited rice production, indigo, the most profitable of all colonial crops, was planted on higher, well-drained land. Indigo produced a deep-blue dye that became so popular in mid-eighteenth-century Britain that the government offered a bounty, or incentive payment, for it. During the 1750s it accounted for one-third of the colony's total export revenues. But once the colonies gained their independence, the indigo growers lost their bounty, and their interest in growing indigo quickly waned. The physician Alexander Garden reported that lowcountry planters "have never made themselves fully Master of any one thing but the Management of Rice."[28]

By the start of the American Revolution, Carolina's hugely profitable "rice kingdom" included more than one hundred fifty thousand acres of tidal swamp and tidal freshwater marsh that had been converted to rice fields. South Carolina rice became the most prized cereal around the globe. Grocers in England praised the quality of "Carolina Gold" rice above all other varieties. From 1768 to 1772 South Carolina planters annually exported sixty million pounds of rice. The Cooper River planters became immensely rich and emerged as dominant social and political leaders. In 1774 the per capita wealth of Charles Town and the lowcountry was four times that of the Virginia planters and six times that of New York City residents. South Carolina had become by far the wealthiest British colony in North America. When Bostonian Josiah Quincy Jr. visited Charles Town in 1773, he was dazzled by what he saw: "In grandeur, splendor of build-ings, decorations, equipages, numbers, commerce, shipping, indeed in almost every thing, it far surpasses all I ever saw, or expected to see, in America." Of the ten richest North Americans at the time of the Revolutionary War, nine were South Carolinians (all from the lowcountry), including Peter Manigault, the rich-est man in North America.[29]

The prosperity generated by the "rice kingdom" was not without cost. Low-country planters accumulated phenomenal wealth and launched an array of eco-nomic activities, only to realize too late that they had unwittingly done grievous harm to the environment. Planters along the Santee River, for instance, discov-ered that their prolonged use of tidal irrigation had made the river more prone to seasonal flooding by scouring the banks. Other "improvements" undertaken to facilitate rice growing and milling had similarly unexpected effects. Efforts to widen rivers to improve navigation allowed for saltwater to migrate farther up river. Dams built to provide water power for rice mills impeded both river-borne commerce and the passage of fish. A Charleston engineer named Charles Hateley warned in 1792 that the actions of rice planters to modify the landscape "may be attended with ruinous effects, which may not be foreseen" until it was too late. He noted that "nature in the formation of her works has acted for the general welfare of man. It therefore behooves us to consider well the conse-quences before we deviate from, or counteract her ways."[30]

The Rise of Cotton

The rice economy modified the lowcountry landscape and helped spur Charles-ton's early development as a port city through the eighteenth century. By the start of the nineteenth century, however, cotton was becoming increasingly important to the region's economy. Like rice cultivation, the cotton culture reshaped land use and spurred economic growth. From 1790 to the end of Civil War, cotton production was the most important economic force in the South and exerted worldwide influence. Many of the swampy lands between the headwaters of the Santee and Cooper Rivers, formerly used for rice, were transformed to exploit the relative profitability of cotton. Other factors also diminished the dominance of rice. The entry of Indonesian-grown rice into the global commodities markets, like competition from international indigo growers in earlier years, helped drive down prices for Carolina rice and thus reshaped planting decisions in the low-country. Lands along the Cooper and Santee Rivers, and their contributing streams, often contained oak and dogwood trees, generally mixed with shortleaf pine, which indicated the presence of limestone near the soil surface. Such lime-stone-rich soil was ideal for the growing of cotton. But the primary spur to cotton production was Eli Whitney's invention of the cotton gin in 1793. It greatly eased the task of separating the seeds from the cotton fiber. Suddenly cotton was the new bonanza crop. In 1790 about ten thousand pounds of sea island (long-staple) black-seed cotton were exported from South Carolina. Just ten years later more than eight million pounds were sold to foreign markets.[31]

The rush to grow cotton had substantial environmental implications. Cotton, like corn, leaches nutrients from the soil. Because land was so inexpensive in the post-Revolutionary era, farmers intensively planted fields with cotton year after year and moved on to inexpensive new lands rather than nurturing the old fields. During the first half of the nineteenth century, the "cotton kingdom" in the South was responsible for some of the worst land erosion in history.[32]

The rise of the cotton culture also required improved transportation networks connecting the inland cotton-growing areas to the port of Charleston. In 1793 more than a thousand slaves began work on the twenty-two-mile-long Santee Canal. Thirty-five feet wide and five feet deep, with ten locks, it was completed in 1800, about the time that cotton production and prices were soaring. The new canal meant that Santee-grown cotton had a direct shipping route along the Cooper River to Charleston and then to the insatiable British textile market. In 1830, more than 1,700 vessels used the canal. By the 1840s, however, a combination of drought, newly built railroads, and the reluctance of farmers to pay tolls dampened interest in the Santee Canal.[33]

The Civil War

That the lowcountry was the largest slave-holding region in the nation helps explain why its white residents endorsed secession with such fervor during 1860. "Slavery with us is no abstraction—but a great and vital fact," Arthur P. Hayne, a prominent Charleston attorney and former U.S. senator, wrote in a letter to President James Buchanan. "Without it our every comfort would be taken from us. . . . *Nothing short of separation from the Union can save us.*" Hayne and other lowcountry planters believed that their way of life was at stake in the aftermath of Abraham Lincoln's election in the fall of 1860. As an Edisto Island planter, Joseph E. Jenkins, told a meeting of secessionists: "Gentlemen, if South Carolina does not secede from the Union, Edisto Island will."[34]

The Civil War, of course, went badly for the Confederacy—and it was an economic catastrophe for South Carolina slave owners. In early 1865 federal troops led by General William T. Sherman pushed north from Savannah into the South Carolina lowcountry. Along the way they destroyed plantations, farms, houses, fences, livestock, and railroads. Of the fourteen plantations along the Ashley River near Charleston, only Drayton Hall's main house was left standing. Federal forces, led by the Twenty-first United States Colored Troops, entered Charleston in February 1865. The African Americans in the city cheered and embraced the soldiers. Enslaved black people quickly exercised their new freedom. With the arrival of Union armies, many African Americans destroyed plantations throughout the lowcountry. "The ex-slaves," a *New York Times* correspondent observed, "have become imbued with a spirit of freedom and are determined to bear the yoke no longer." As the war ended, thousands of lowcountry African Americans who had been taken to the upcountry by their owners during the war returned to the coast, eager, as one of them said, "to get back to their old homes."[35]

Gaining Land, Claiming Opportunity: 1865–1945

The Civil War ended slavery and restored the Union. It also ignited a new struggle over the political and economic future of the former Confederacy. Like the rest of the southern states, South Carolina emerged from the war with a chaotic social structure and a devastated economy. Two-thirds of the South's wealth vanished during the war years. After the war Confederate bonds and currency were worthless. Large-scale commercial agriculture—rice and cotton—collapsed during the war and languished thereafter. Fields went unplanted for years, and tax revenues plummeted. "Clearly we are on a descending scale," sighed a Charlestonian in 1865. "Our merchants are gloomy, trade is stagnant, and every interest is suffering."[36]

The wartime destruction of plantations and livestock, the emancipation of slaves, who made up 60 percent of the state's population, and the acute shortage of labor and capital decimated the economy. Social services, including public schools, were inadequate for white residents and pitiful or nonexistent for African Americans. Even more poignant was the human loss. Over one-third of the state's young white adult men died during the war—of wounds or disease. Thousands more returned home missing one or more limbs. The "war has ruined us" said Charlestonian John Berkeley Grimball. In 1867 a lowcountry white reported that "the old order of things has passed away, never to return." Nearly "every plantation is more or less mortgaged." The "majority of the planters have nothing left but their lands."[37]

With no cash to hire newly freed slaves or to pay overdue property taxes, many planters gave up on agriculture. In part because of the lack of credit, in part because of competition from commercial rice operations in Louisiana and Texas, in part because of hurricanes that devastated the rice fields, no more than half of the planted rice acreage in the lowcountry revived after 1865. In 1866 a journalist reported that the "rice fields in the vicinity of Charleston . . . have been almost entirely neglected." He explained that the freed slaves "will not work in them because the labor is hard and destructive of health and life." Malaria was rampant. After the Civil War lowcountry agricultural life reverted largely to subsistence household cultivation and truck farming.

Of the fifty-two Cooper River rice plantations north of Charleston, only nine were planted in 1866 and only seven the following year. In Georgetown County rice production plummeted 80 percent from 1860 to 1880. As other states, especially Arkansas, Louisiana, and Texas, began growing rice using modern

Farm workers planting Irish potatoes on Edisto Island.
Courtesy of South Caroliniana Library.

technology, Carolina rice lost its competitive edge. After the Civil War most rice fields were abandoned; thereafter, they largely lay fallow or were converted into duck-hunting plantations.[38]

Another factor affecting the lowcountry economy after the Civil War was a spate of ferocious hurricanes and destructive floods. In August 1885 a hurricane swept across the coast, ripping the roofs off homes and churches, destroying shipping, damaging wharves, warehouses, and railroads, and submerging crops. Three years later floods wreaked "incalculable damage" on the cotton, corn, and rice crops. The largest plantations suffered "total loss." The outlook for the region's rice culture was described as "gloomy" and "especially discouraging." An "unprecedented" hurricane in 1893 roared across the sea islands near Beaufort, killing as many as two thousand people, mostly African Americans. Virtually every home was blown down and all of the livestock killed. "In some localities," the *New York Times* reported, "the tidal wave destroyed all the fertile soil." The rice crop was thrown "into complete stagnation" by the "Great Storm of 1893." More hurricanes hit the lowcountry in 1896 and 1898. The last sizable lowcountry rice acreage was destroyed in a 1911 hurricane that devastated not only the plantations but also the docks, warehouses, and rice mill in Charleston.

Hurricane damage to Charleston Ferry Wharf in 1911.
Courtesy of South Caroliniana Library.

House near Beaufort in the late 1800s.
Courtesy of South Caroliniana Library.

The tidal surge in Charleston reached at least six feet above the high-water mark. As Duncan Heyward, a former governor and lifelong rice planter noted, when "I saw the ocean actually coming up Meeting Street. . . . I knew . . . that the death-knell of rice planting in South Carolina was sounded."[39]

Land ownership patterns in South Carolina and the lowcountry were dramatically transformed by the Civil War. "We all know that the colored people want land," said a white delegate to the 1868 state constitutional convention. "Night and day they think and dream of it. It is their all in all." There were three primary ways for African Americans to acquire land. They could purchase newly subdivided plantation lands; they could receive lands directly from the Union Army through "Special Field Orders"; or they could claim properties that were abandoned by the white owners. By 1870 several thousand African Americans were able to acquire through various means a patchwork of landholdings in the lowcountry, in part because of the declining prices for land resulting from the demise of commercial farming and the plantation system.[40]

Today many of the descendants of the freed slaves still live in the small enclave communities that were formed on or near former lowcountry plantations. They continue to own land through the historic title, referred to today as heirs' property. Heirs' properties were (and are) owned not by individuals but by complicated kinship networks without clear title records. Heirs' properties are often located in what originally were deemed undesirable areas—low-lying, mosquito-infested marshlands or swamps—or in areas at some distance from the coast. Ironically these areas today are considered highly desirable for both individual landowners and developers because of their proximity to waterways and their picturesque viewsheds.[41]

The Timber Industry

The post–Civil War South was like an impoverished colony that looked north for capital and entrepreneurial creativity. At the same time that African Americans were gaining access to land, wealthy northern investors and industrial timber companies, especially after 1880, were buying up huge tracts of forests in the lowcountry at low prices. Many southern leaders were eager to see the languishing region create an industrial sector comparable to that in the North. By necessity such promoters focused first on extractive industries. With the depletion of forests in the Northeast and the Great Lakes states, the timber barons headed south.

During the colonial period the lowcountry had become a fertile source for the harvesting of forestry products ("naval stores") from the prolific resin of native longleaf pines—especially tar, pitch, and turpentine. Tar and pitch were used to caulk ship hulls and prevent rigging and ropes from rotting. The pine-based preservatives were so valuable to the British navy that the government provided a bounty for the exports. The naval stores industry was almost as profitable as growing rice in the lowcountry. Timber was also in great demand. The plentiful trees provided wood for fencing, firewood, and the construction of buildings and houses. Wood was also needed for commerce. Tens of thousands of wooden barrels and casks were needed to ship rice, naval stores, and other commodities from the lowcountry. In the eighteenth and early nineteenth centuries, enterprising landowners built small sawmills to cut logs into framing timber and make shingles. Ax-wielding workers laid waste to the cypress swamps. Lumbering in the nineteenth century was an extractive industry at its worst. Loggers presumed that the dense forests were limitless, and they set about recklessly destroying the region's virgin timber resources.[42]

After the Civil War the nation's demand for timber soared. It was needed not only for residential and commercial construction but also for roads, bridges, mines, and rail lines. Commercial lumber companies, mostly from the North, began using powerful new technologies (dredges, skidders, logging railroads, winches, and draglines) to clear timberlands throughout the lowcountry. So many timber speculators rushed south to buy cheap land that the railroads ran special trains from Chicago to accommodate the land boom. By 1887 the *New York Lumber Trade Journal* could report that "northern capital is seeking investment more and more in the pine lands of the South." In South Carolina, a state starved for capital and jobs and desperate for new revenue, dozens of timber companies constructed logging camps, sawmills, and rail lines to harvest the timber. By 1900 they were shipping vast quantities of lowcountry lumber across the United States and around the world—and they were leaving behind a vast trail of destruction. They practiced a "cut out and get out" policy that sought to maximize profits while devastating the forests.[43]

Chicago tycoon Francis Beidler, for example, formed the Santee River Cypress Company and bought more than 165,000 acres of hardwood bottomland along the Santee, Congaree, and Wateree Rivers. Dozens of other northern timber companies made similar purchases. From 1890 to 1910 the Santee River Cypress Company acquired tens of thousands of additional acres, mostly swamp lands filled with cypress, gum, ash, cottonwood, and pine. Every river in the lowcountry became a timber corridor. Up to five miles of timber was clear cut on both sides of the rivers, then floated down for milling. Rail lines were then built to extend the cutting operations, and soon logging railroads crisscrossed the hinterlands. Over time, as the forests were clear cut, the once majestic bottomlands came to resemble a barren graveyard of stumps, slash, and mud. As the woodlands vanished, so too did much of the wildlife and plants and topsoil that depended on them. The clear cutting of forests not only removed the forest canopy but also destabilized watersheds and increased the propensity of rivers to flood.[44]

Profits were more important than posterity in the post–Civil War South. In 1888 another Chicagoan, William H. Harrison Jr. published a book titled *How to Get Rich in the South,* in which he declared that the South offered the best investment opportunities for northern capitalists. The region "possesses greater natural wealth than all the balance of the Union." He highlighted the South's inexpensive forest lands as being especially enticing. "The supply of timber is inexhaustible," Harrison proclaimed, and much of it "is being bought in large tracts by [northern] lumbermen." Nature had bestowed on the South "blessings too bounteous to describe!" He loved "to walk through the virgin forests of the South and see the trees, rearing their heads as if conscious of the great wealth they represent."[45]

By 1900, given the aggressive marketing efforts of Harrison and others, timber had become the largest industry in the South and the second largest in South Carolina (behind textiles). The scale of commercial logging was enormous. The Atlantic Coast Lumber Corporation, formed in 1899 in Georgetown by northern investors, became one of the largest lumber companies in the world. Its sprawling mill covered fifty-six acres and included a five-million-board-foot dock and shed. At one time the company owned 250,000 acres in eight counties and employed 1,500 people. Like all extractive industries, however, lumbering generated terrible side effects. The widespread—and shortsighted—harvesting of timber devastated the region's environment. After clear-cutting a site, the crews would move on, leaving behind a cutover landscape of stumps and slash (limbs and debris). As a professional forester explained, the forty years from 1880 to 1920 witnessed throughout the Deep South the "most rapid and reckless destruction of forest known to history."[46]

The lowcountry's rate of timber harvesting was unsustainable. In 1907 the state agricultural commissioner predicted that the "present wasteful methods of forest utilization will soon exhaust our timber resources." The "very destructive methods" of exploiting the forests reveal that "little regard is had for the future." By 1920 there was virtually no marketable timber left in the lowcountry. All of the major lumber mills in Georgetown County, including the Atlantic Coast Lumber Corporation, shut down by 1932. With no trees left to absorb storm water, erosion spread across the region, carrying topsoil into streams and rivers. "The navigable streams of the state," reported the commissioner, "are being so filled with sediment that they are being closed to commerce." Yet most public officials remained indifferent to the destruction as well as to the possibility of replanting as recommended by the new profession of "scientific forestry." As late as 1922 a South Carolina legislator asked, "What is forestry?"[47]

The Phosphate Boom—and Bust

During the late 1860s a profitable new extractive industry—phosphate mining—generated excited interest in the lowcountry. Phosphate rock, when pulverized, is a crucial source of fertilizer, especially for the red-clay soil in the Deep South where cotton was grown. Large phosphate deposits were discovered in the lowcountry west of Charleston before 1860, but there was little interest in the mineral until after the Civil War. In 1868 two Charleston scientists asked investors in Philadelphia to finance a phosphate-mining industry in the lowcountry. One of the Philadelphians breathlessly reported to a lowcountry planter that "there are large investments [to be] made and *enormous* profits expected." Within a few years dozens of plantations had sold or leased rights to their fields and rivers for mining operations. Thousands of wage laborers, mostly African Americans, were hired to dig and crush the rock. Most of them lived in camps adjacent to the mines. During the 1880s production soared, and the lowcountry became the primary domestic source of phosphate for the nation. But the phosphate boom was short-lived. New discoveries of more accessible deposits in other states and political infighting over river-mining rights led to the collapse of the industry in the 1890s. By the end of World War I South Carolina's phosphate industry had largely disappeared, leaving the region pockmarked with abandoned quarries, pits, and slag heaps.[48]

During the late nineteenth century the destructive consequences of prolonged resource exploitation in the lowcountry fostered piecemeal efforts to conserve the region's dwindling natural resources by promoting "wise use" and preservationist principles. The catalyst for this emerging conservation consciousness was the ecological degradation caused by commercial logging and phosphate mining, an environmental transformation of unprecedented magnitude. The first group of intentional habitat conservationists were largely outsiders.

From 1870 to 1930, with the decline of rice growing, the collapse of land values, and the construction of new rail lines, wealthy outdoor sportsmen, mostly from the northern states, purchased scores of lowcountry plantations and converted them into private hunting and fishing estates and winter retreats. The new owners included some of the nation's richest families: the Cranes, Doubledays, Du Ponts, Guggenheims, Huttons, Kresses, Luces, Pratts, Pulitzers, Roosevelts, Whitneys, Vanderbilts, and Yawkeys. William Bradley of Massachusetts, for example, bought lowcountry land in 1870 and later invested in phosphate mining. His son came to own sixteen thousand acres in Colleton County.[49]

Most of the northern patricians who purchased plantations were primarily interested in fishing and hunting (mostly waterfowl), but they also sold timber, raised cattle, or grew vegetables. Whatever their priorities, they operated on a grand scale. In 1893 sportsmen from New York, New Jersey, and Pittsburgh bought thirty-five thousand acres in Jasper County to create the Okeetee Club, which eventually encompassed sixty-two thousand acres. While building stately new homes and vast estates, several of the wealthy northerners brought with them a hunting ethic different from that of most lowcountry residents.

They did not view game or fish as economic resources; they instead viewed hunting more as a "manly" sport dependent on species preservation. The sport hunters sought to change laws and customs to ban "market hunters" and poachers so as to preserve the declining fish and game populations. In doing so they provided—often unintentionally—"a godsend for land preservation. The new owners wanted most of their land left exactly as they found it: open woods, fields

Successful hunt at Oakton Plantation on Winyah Bay, 1923. From left: Graham Reeves, Foster Bourne, Richard Reeves, Charles Reeves, Richard E. Reeves, Mrs. Richard E. Reeves, and Susie Reeves. Courtesy of Virginia Skinner.

protected for the birds, waters undammed and unpolluted. They were true [land] conservationists, if not environmentalists."[50]

The Cotton Cycles

From 1880 to 1920 the lowcountry experienced cycles of economic expansion and decline that triggered important changes in land-use practices and the health of the region's ecology. The number of white landowners plummeted. While a few African Americans were able to purchase land, most of them joined the swelling ranks of tenant farmers and sharecroppers. By 1890 less than 40 percent of South Carolina farmers owned their own land, and most tenants and "croppers" found themselves perpetually in debt, living from crop to crop, praying for good weather. After the Civil War and well into the twentieth century, hundreds of textile mills were built in the former Confederate states, many of them along fast-running rivers that eventually provided hydroelectric power. Such industrial development helped diversify the region's largely agricultural economy and provide low-paying but much-desired jobs to a region desperate for economic growth. Nevertheless, the South remained tied to the farming of cotton well into the twentieth century—for good and for ill.[51]

The surge in demand for cotton during World War I revitalized commercial agriculture in the South and brought a wave of prosperity to the lowcountry. However, the global demand for cotton and tobacco collapsed in 1921. Cotton brought forty cents a pound in January of that year; by December the price had plummeted to thirteen cents. Tobacco experienced a similar decline. For the next twenty years lowcountry farmers were saddled with chronic agricultural depression exacerbated by a series of droughts. A bad situation worsened with the arrival of an unwanted immigrant from Mexico via Texas: the boll weevil. By mid-1921 the boll weevil (a tiny beetle less than one-quarter inch long) had entered South Carolina and soon began wreaking havoc on cotton plants. The boll weevil proved to be the costliest pest in American agricultural history. In Williamsburg County cotton production dropped from 37,000 bales in 1920 to 2,700 in 1922. By 1930 one-third of the state's farms were mortgaged, and land erosion was rampant.[52]

Over time, as the agricultural sector languished, the lowcountry's landscapes began to revert to their more natural forms. Without regular dike maintenance, former rice fields devolved to tidal marshes and cotton fields returned to forest. South Carolina's prolonged economic doldrums and deeply embedded racial prejudice caused many white and African American residents to leave the state; after 1920, South Carolina no longer had a "black majority." By 1940 one-fourth of the 2,260,000 people born in South Carolina lived in other states. The depressed agricultural economy during the 1920s and 1930s also depressed the value of land. As one desperate plantation owner, Sam Medway, said, "Lord, please send us a rich Yankee." The stagnant lowcountry economy dramatically slowed the region's population growth. In 1790 Charleston was the nation's fourth largest city; by 1860 it was the twenty-second largest; and by 1900 it had fallen to sixty-eighth.[53]

Santee Cooper and the Great Depression: 1921 to 1945

In the wake of the boll weevil infestation and the destruction of much of the cotton economy, the Great Depression of the 1930s brought the state's economy to its knees. With Carolinians literally starving, both white and black voters overwhelmingly supported Franklin D. Roosevelt's attempts to revive the economy in the face of the Great Depression. By far the most expensive economic renewal project in South Carolina was focused on bringing affordable electricity to the state's rural regions. Senator James "Jimmy" F. Byrnes persuaded President Roosevelt that efforts to bring electrical power to the state could generate a sustained economic recovery. In 1934 Roosevelt approved the idea to create a state-owned power-producing utility called Santee Cooper. The new enterprise would be the largest New Deal project in the state and one of the largest in the nation. Santee Cooper (officially called the South Carolina Public Service Authority) would be responsible for providing electricity for the first time to many citizens of a state in which only 2 percent of the 168,000 farms had electricity, developing the

Santee, Cooper and Congaree Rivers for navigation purposes and to minimize natural flooding, reclaiming and draining swamps, and reforesting the watersheds of the state's rivers.[54]

Critics mobilized to stop the project, however. The private utility companies branded as socialistic the government effort to construct and manage hydroelectric facilities. Equally incensed were people concerned about the effect of the project on the environment. They denounced the planned lake's destruction of ancient swampland, virgin hardwood forests, and countless waterfowl and mammals. The state's poet laureate, Archibald Rutledge, warned that the massive federal project would turn the Santee River into a "brackish estuary" and eliminate the major source of winter food for migratory ducks. The reservoir would also "ruthlessly" destroy historic homes and churches. He called upon "every lover of wildlife, every sportsman, everyone who appreciates the charm of the primeval wilderness" to "unite against the perpetration of this crime." Rutledge's quixotic crusade so infuriated one state legislator that he convinced the senate to censure him and strip him of his poet laureate title (the bill failed in the House).[55]

The opponents of the project, however, failed to convince voters that the project would not bring jobs and prosperity to a blighted region. In 1939 construction crews began work on the largest land-clearing and earth-moving project in American history. In the process of constructing the world's longest earthen dam, another dam, and two reservoirs (Lakes Marion and Moultrie), 171,000 acres of swamp and timberland were cleared, 200 million feet of timber cut, 42 million cubic yards of earth moved, and 3.1 million cubic yards of concrete poured. Some 12,500 people, mostly men, were hired to do the work. At its highest point the 26-mile long earthen dike towers 78 feet above the surrounding coastal plain. More than 900 families (some 4,000 people) were resettled, along with 93 cemeteries and 6,000 graves. In the decade after construction of the Lake Moultrie hydroelectric facility, 91 percent of area farms, retail customers, military bases, and industries were directly supplied with electricity.[56]

The completion of the Santee Cooper hydroelectric project in 1942 marked a transition in the function and structure of the Cooper and Santee Rivers. Filling up Lake Moultrie inundated most of the historic plantations along the Cooper and Santee. It also reduced the flow of the Santee River, depriving its delta of a rich source of fertile sediment. At the same time, concern was growing about the health of South Carolina's rivers and their adjacent lands. Policymakers, historians, scientists, and other citizens began to recognize the rivers' ecological and aesthetic significance.[57]

So too did the federal government. In 1936 President Roosevelt designated 250,000 acres between the Cooper and Santee rivers as the Francis Marion National Forest. The forest, about twenty miles northwest of Charleston, has 1,400 species of plants, 300 bird species, and 25 Carolina bays (landform depressions, often marshes or ponds, that are rich in biodiversity). In 1942 Roosevelt created the 15,000-acre Santee National Wildlife Refuge. He had grown concerned about the damage to waterfowl and wildlife habitat caused by the construction of the Santee Cooper dams. These federal preserves and sanctuaries had significant ramifications for the next stage in the region's social and environmental development.

The Perils of Prosperity: 1945–1989

After the end of World War II, the state of South Carolina, desperate again for new jobs, aggressively promoted industrial development. Virtually any new or expanded commercial activity was welcomed with open arms. State officials and business leaders fanned out across the nation and around the world to convince businesses to relocate to the state. In the decades after World War II the low-country—as well as the rest of the Sunbelt states—experienced profound industrial and suburban growth. From 1950 to 2000 the coastal counties grew at a rate of 151 percent, compared to an increase of only 86 percent for the national population. To encourage such growth, they trumpeted the state's cheap land, low wages and low corporate taxes, lack of labor unions and low utility costs, as well as the state's "business-friendly" culture (including minimal regulation of businesses). South Carolina, said Governor James F. Byrnes, "is friendly toward industry. Our government, our communities, and our people want industry and—want to see that it is prosperous and happy."[58]

The Timber Industry—Phase Two

Along with the legacy of ecological destruction, lowcountry lumbering encouraged the growth of a powerful economic sector dependent upon water and trees: pulp and paper manufacturing and related forest industries. The region's fastest growing industry after 1945 was timber for lumber and paper. During the twentieth century new techniques for converting pulpwood into paper led to dramatic growth in the timber industry that, in turn, produced devastating pollution of the waterways and the air. Converting logs (mostly pine) into pulp requires massive amounts of water (about thirty thousand gallons per ton of product in the 1960s) that was then discharged as wastewater into creeks and rivers. Making paper also involved enormous quantities of sulfur, whose pungent fumes blanketed the region. The process of converting pulp to various "white" paper products also requires large amounts of bleach, whose effluents were dumped into area waterways. In the 1970s new filters and "scrubbers" greatly reduced the sulfurous emissions, and by the 1990s many progressive paper companies were substituting ozone for bleach and using recycled paper. By then, however, much of the environmental damage could not be reversed. Out of the huge paper-manufacturing industry emerged an elite class of business and civic leaders who were determined to protect their right to use vast quantities of the region's natural resources.[59]

In the mid-1930s the West Virginia Pulp and Paper Company (later renamed Westvaco and eventually MeadWestvaco) opened a massive paper mill near

Charleston, and International Paper Company began similarly large-scale pulp paper production in Georgetown. The fast-growing industry soon began to dominate—and pollute—the countryside, buying up vast tracts of forest lands, often purchased from the grandchildren of the former plantation elite. By 1953 there were fifty-one pulp and paper mills in the lowcountry; over the next forty years another fifty-four mills were constructed. The rapid development of the paper industry generated unprecedented changes in land ownership and land-use patterns in the lowcountry. Pine plantations for the production of pulpwood now encompass more than three million acres, and renewable forestry has become South Carolina's primary agricultural commodity and number one cash crop. Its statewide economic impact is an estimated $17.5 billion.[60]

The dramatic growth in commercial pine harvesting, however, has often come at the expense of hardwoods, as native forests were converted to large pine farms. In addition, paper mills have often been major contaminants of rivers and streams. Many South Carolina public officials, eager to attract new industries to the state, were willing to sacrifice environmental quality in their quest for new jobs. In 1956, for example, the state legislature exempted the Bowater Corporation, which planned to build several pulp paper mills across the state, from meeting state standards intended to prevent water pollution. A 1972 statewide survey revealed that 65 percent of South Carolinians believed that attracting new industries was a higher priority than protecting the environment. During the 1970s South Carolina joined three other southern states—Texas, North Carolina, and Florida—in attracting the most polluting industries (paper mills). In his 1979 inaugural address, Governor Richard Riley, a progressive reformer, pledged to institute a more balanced approach. "It is not unreasonable," he declared, "to envision a South Carolina of great natural beauty and great economic strength at the same time."[61]

The Military-Industrial Complex

The most important economic development in the lowcountry (and the whole southern region) during and after World War II was the dramatic growth of federal expenditures for military-related facilities and programs. "Our economy is no longer agricultural," the Mississippi novelist William Faulkner observed in 1956. "Our economy is the federal government." By 1973 more southerners worked in defense-related enterprises and facilities than in the textile industry.[62]

Charleston had long been a focal point of the national coastal defense system. From 1878 to 1914 the federal government constructed in Charleston a new harbor, a dry dock and naval yard, a coastal defense installation, and a naval station. By the 1960s the federal facilities in the Charleston area were providing more than one-third of the region's personal income. The lowcountry had become, said journalist Marshall Frady, "one of the most elaborately fortified patches of geography in the nation." The colorful, imperious congressman L. Mendel Rivers, who chaired the House Armed Services Committee during the Vietnam

War, displayed extraordinary success in garnering massive federal appropriations for his lowcountry district. During his thirty-year-long legislative tenure, the pistol-toting Rivers found federal funding for a cornucopia of new military projects: a naval hospital, a U.S. Air Force base, an air force fuel storage farm, an air force recreation center, a U.S. Marine Corps air station, two U.S. Navy Polaris missile facilities, a marine corps recruiting center, a navy supply depot, a U.S. Coast Guard base, and three U.S. Army National Guard offices. Such pork-barrel expertise led one of Rivers's congressional colleagues to quip that if any more defense-related facilities were built in the lowcountry, "the whole place will sink completely from sight by the sheer weight of the military installations." The plethora of new military facilities in the lowcountry soon attracted numerous defense-related companies to locate nearby.[63]

Industrial Development along the Cooper River

During the second half of the twentieth century the Cooper River became the industrial hub of the Charleston (and lowcountry) area. As development spread along the river, idle rice plantations were transformed into housing and industrial sites. During the 1950s and 1960s the U.S. Naval Base, shipyard, and submarine station, all along the Cooper River, grew into one of the nation's largest naval facilities. In the 1950s three multinational corporations—DuPont, Bayer, and Agfa—launched the sprawling Bushy Park industrial corridor near Goose Creek. Over the years more companies, including several pharmaceutical and chemical plants, moved to the four-thousand-acre site. In the 1970s aluminum smelter Alcoa-Mount Holly built a large plant between Goose Creek and Moncks Corner. Since the late 1990s Nucor Steel has operated a mill near Cainhoy that produces three million tons per year; much of its feedstock (scrap metal) is received by ship and barge on the Cooper River. Such rapid industrial development transformed the small rural towns of Goose Creek and Hanahan into heavily concentrated suburbs.

The intensive industrial development along the Cooper River has made it one of the most economically important—and most polluted—rivers in South Carolina. In 2002, in an effort to reverse a perennial decline in the river's water quality, state environmental officials told industries and utilities to reduce substantially the volume of pollutants being dumped into the river. The order from the S.C. Department of Health and Environmental Control (DHEC) resulted from nearly ten years of environmental impact studies, which the affected corporations "challenged virtually every step of the way." Yet in the end the polluting companies were not held to account. The repeated failure of the state's environmental regulatory agency to enforce its own regulations or garner legislative backing led the *State*, the largest newspaper in South Carolina, to run a multipart series in 2008 highlighting the gap between DHEC's mission and its behavior. The evidence led the investigative reporters to conclude that "state regulators have given polluters breaks, withheld information from the public and pushed

A sunny day on the beach, at Myrtle Beach in the1960s.
Courtesy of South Caroliniana Library.

development over the protection of natural resources. Has the agency that's supposed to safeguard the environment and our health lost its way?"[64]

One reason for growing concern about industrial development along the Cooper and Ashley Rivers is that they remain home to the largest number of historic sites in the state. The Cooper River Historic District, a thirty-thousand-acre section centered on both branches of the Cooper River, remains a remarkably intact historic and cultural landscape. Of the ninety-two National Register of Historic Places sites along South Carolina river corridors, twelve are along the east and west forks of the Cooper, including Mulberry, Middleburg, and Medway plantations. The Cooper River also ranks among the state's most popular sites for recreational fishing.

The combination of surging tourism and dramatic residential and industrial development has transformed the lowcountry in the last fifty years. South Carolina, concluded Walter Edgar, the state's preeminent historian, grew more rapidly during the 1970s "than it had in 150 years," and the lowcountry experienced the fastest growth rates in the state. Much of the entire lowcountry beachfront area, from Myrtle Beach to Hilton Head, witnessed extensive retail development.

In the Charleston region the West Ashley area experienced a classic post–World War II suburban boom, and the same phenomenon occurred across the Cooper River in Mount Pleasant beginning in the 1960s. The population of Mount Pleasant increased 33 percent from 1960 to 1970. The 1970s saw an increase of 101 percent, and the population grew another 117 percent in the 1980s. Since then, with the opening of the Mark Clark Expressway (I-526) in 1992, growth rates have increased substantially. As Mount Pleasant and other areas around Charleston grew, many former vegetable farms were converted to suburban tract housing. Today about half of James Island has been annexed by the City of Charleston, while Mount Pleasant, the state's fifth largest city, continues its northward expansion along U.S. Highway 17.[65]

Meanwhile, farther south, in high-visibility coastal resorts such as Hilton Head, Kiawah Island, and in the Beaufort area, developers in the 1960s and 1970s began transforming the lowcountry's signature Sea Islands into affluent gated subdivisions centered on golf, tennis, and tourism. Charles Fraser, a Savannah native and committed conservationist who graduated from Harvard College and Yale Law School, was in the vanguard of what would become a new generation of developers focused on the lowcountry coast. In 1956 he began implementing a comprehensive plan to transform Hilton Head Island (second in size only to Long Island along the Atlantic coast), most of which his lumber baron father owned, into a "conservation" resort, with detailed guidelines for contractors and residents to follow in preserving the island's landscape. But he was too successful—and he did not control the island's developers who followed him or the 2.5 million people who visit the island each year. By 1991 he wanted to stop development at Hilton Head. "If I could freeze Hilton Head today, it would be an extraordinary island," he said. Fraser acknowledged that the explosive development of golf resort communities in the lowcountry was indeed outpacing the region's resources, especially water, and thereby threatening the quality of the environment.[66]

Contemporary Times: Rapid Growth—at What Cost?

Efforts to preserve, conserve, and develop the lowcountry have been locked in an awkward embrace over the last twenty-five years. In the wake of Hurricane Hugo and as a consequence of massive investments in roads by the federal and state government during the 1990s, the lowcountry's population has mushroomed. Much of the growth has come at the expense of agricultural or natural areas. Residents often blame outside developers for the transformation of the barrier islands and coastal areas, turning tomato and tobacco fields and small towns into sprawling suburbs with gated subdivisions, high-rise condominiums, and expensive golf courses. Yet, ironically, many of the newcomers to the region during the past twenty years or so have been attracted by the lowcountry's mushrooming conservation culture. Progrowth and slow-growth advocates have gradually fashioned a tense but workable relationship.[67]

What does the future hold? The comprehensive land-use plan for Berkeley County, completed in 1999, could just as well have been written for the entire lowcountry region. It said: "The County is . . . at a crossroads. Population projections predict that Berkeley County will continue to absorb a significant share

of growth in the region. Therefore, concerns about growth, development patterns, and the future are increasing. . . . Changes in rural areas have triggered
concerns about the future of forestry operations, traffic, and loss of the County's
scenic and historic resources." More population growth, along with new residential and commercial development, will accelerate the conversion of farms
and forests into urban/suburban areas with concomitant increases in impervious
surfaces—changes that can have profoundly negative effects on ecological health
and integrity.[68]

Since the 1990s, the large land-rich pulp/paper conglomerates, desperate for
cash, have been systematically selling off their vast timberlands. As a 2007 regional planning study asserted, "there's no more frightening prospect for Charlestonians than timber companies selling off huge chunks of their land, often far
from urban centers, to developers who'll clear-cut lots, throw up standard subdivisions, and trigger huge new floods of long-distance commuters onto the
region's already overtaxed roads."[69]

By 2030 the seven lowcountry counties— Georgetown, Charleston, Berkeley,
Dorchester, Colleton, Beaufort, and Jasper—are projected to experience a 46 percent increase in population growth, ranging from 20 percent in Charleston
County to 73 percent in Beaufort County. "Our planning models reflected a certain number for growth for the next 10 to 15 years, and we have far exceeded that
in just the past three years," Beaufort County Council chairman Weston Newton
said in 2004. Accompanying this population growth, and perhaps more threatening to the environment, will be the increase in developed acreage. Urban development and conversion to pine plantations are expected to claim 35 percent of
the state's coastal plain forests by 2040, according to a U.S. Forest Service study.
"The development threats that are hitting the coastal plain were probably un-
thought of 15 years ago," said Edwin Cooper III of Ducks Unlimited. Yet "most
people don't want to sell to developers," Cooper adds. "There is tremendous connection of landowners in South Carolina to the land."[70]

The U.S. Department of Agriculture ranks South Carolina among the top ten
states in developed acreage. Land development in the state increased 30.2 percent from 1992 to 1997; however, population increased only 5.3 percent during
the same interval. Growth rates in lowcountry land development follow these
statewide trends. A 256 percent increase in developed acreage occurred from
1973 to 1994 in the greater Charleston area (Berkeley, Charleston, and Dorchester Counties), but the population grew by only 41 percent. From 1960 to 2010
the City of Charleston grew from 6 square miles to 106, largely the result of
annexations.[71]

The lowcountry's economy remains dependent on the quality of its coastal
environment; its most valuable industry is tourism. Myrtle Beach, Charleston,
Kiawah, and Hilton Head draw millions of annual visitors from throughout the
United States and around the world. Visitors flock to Charleston to see its historic buildings and restored plantations. Kiawah Island and Hilton Head Island

are renowned for their upscale atmosphere, prestigious golf courses, and pristine beaches. And for decades the lowcountry has become an ever greater magnet for retirees.[72]

Until recent years the historical theme of the lowcountry was heedless development. Conservationists faced an uphill struggle in convincing conservative people to think in terms beyond their own immediate financial benefit. That has changed. Sustainable development and environmental conservation have become acknowledged goals. In 1999, for example, the Berkeley County Comprehensive Plan stipulated that the county "will strive to protect and conserve existing natural, scenic resources for the benefit of present and future citizens." It likewise pledged "to provide a variety of recreational activities and facilities that attract new residents and economic development while being compatible with the county's existing character and environment." Keeping the lowcountry "a pleasant and fertile land" is not easy. Conflicts and misperceptions still abound—as the following chapters reveal—but so does hope. "The good news," proclaimed Dana Beach, head of the Coastal Conservation League, in 2007 "is that coastal communities are ripe for better growth and more conservation."[73]

TWO

The Emergence of a
Conservation Culture

Ever since the first Europeans encountered the lowcountry in the seventeenth century, the region has been viewed primarily as a commodity, a "pleasant and fertile" place to be exploited—its lands bought and sold, cleared and cultivated, mined and clear-cut, drained and paved. Unsustainable economic development and population growth remained the dominant themes of the lowcountry's history well into the 1980s. During that decade and since, however, an increasingly powerful culture of conservation coalesced to challenge the dominance of unrestrained development. Buoyed by new federal and state legislation, a critical mass of lowcountry residents and elected officials, both Republicans and Democrats, began to see conservation as an essential element of public policy. Former Republican governor Mark Sanford, who owns a lowcountry plantation, declared in 2007: "With the growth that's going to be coming our way over the next ten years, now is the time to make sure our natural resources are protected going forward." He added that a culture of conservation was crucial to the efforts to preserve the state's pride of place, "the unique look and feel of South Carolina." To be sure, there had been sporadic conservation activities in the lowcountry throughout the twentieth century, but they were fragmented and largely peripheral until events in the 1980s and after combined to bring environmental concerns into the forefront of community priorities.[1]

Such an ethic of environmental stewardship and sustainability did not emerge full-blown; it is still evolving. It has benefited from changes in attitudes, leadership, government regulations, and public engagement that were years in the making. Yet by 1998 the conservation culture was sufficiently powerful to generate what the editor of *Coastal Heritage* magazine, John H. Tibbetts, called "a great debate over changing land use." People in the lowcountry, he added, were searching for "innovative methods of economic development that would allow for greater protection of open spaces and rural landscapes." And local governments, for the first time, were "considering innovative techniques to slow down suburban sprawl." Concerns about sprawl and the quality of the environment have come to dominate "civic discourse," which in turn is reinforced by persistent support for environmental concerns among the lowcountry media, especially the region's major newspapers.[2]

Perhaps the most tangible evidence of the depth and influence of the culture of conservation was the opposition it provoked. In 2000 Mark Nix, a veteran consultant for conservative causes, founded the South Carolina Landowners Association, a nonprofit organization spearheaded by Charleston-area citizens concerned about the "negative and intrusive effects of" recent environmental legislation, land-use regulations, and zoning ordinances. Efforts to restrict development, Nix argued, were trampling on property rights, constraining liberty, and inhibiting economic growth. "Land is the foundation of our wealth," he declared, "and we deserve to have it protected. When we stop doing that, we have a problem." That Nix and others felt threatened enough by conservation efforts to create such a progrowth organization testified to the rising influence of a grassroots environmental ethic. Understanding how and why such a culture of conservation emerged—and how its texture and tactics differ from similar efforts in other parts of the country—can inform the national conversation about conservation.[3]

Until the 1990s most scholars assumed that transformations in public policy and social attitudes occurred incrementally and gradually, over long periods. In fact, however, many major changes do not follow such prolonged patterns. Instead they sporadically erupt in staccato bursts of energy and activity followed by periods of relative stability. The development of environmental policies in the United States has manifested this episodic pattern. Long periods of stability have been interrupted by intervals of significant innovation. This was the case on a national level beginning in 1969 with the passage of the National Environmental Policy Act after the oil spill off the coast of Santa Barbara, California. From 1969 and 1976 the Congress passed the Clean Air Act (1970), the Occupational Health and Safety Act (1970), the Coastal Zone Management Act (1972), the Consumer Product Safety Act (1972), the Clean Water Act (1972), the Noise Control Act (1972), the Endangered Species Act (1973), the Safe Drinking Water Act (1974), the Resource Conservation and Recovery Act (1976), the Solid Waste Disposal Act (1976), and the Toxic Substances Control Act (1976).[4]

A similar burst of significant state and local environmental legislation occurred in the South Carolina lowcountry twenty years later, including the Beachfront Management Act (1988), the South Carolina Scenic Rivers Act (1989), the South Carolina Conservation Easement Act (1991), the South Carolina Solid Waste Policy and Management Act (1991), the Environmental Protection Fund Act (1993), the Local Government Comprehensive Planning Enabling Act (1994), and the Land Conservation Bank Act (2002). Such a syncopated process resembles how evolutionary biologists describe the evolution of species. Rather than evolving slowly and uniformly over millions of years, species sometimes change as the result of profound external events "punctuating" what had been a prolonged phase of equilibrium.[5]

The emergence of a discernible conservation ethos in the lowcountry during the 1990s mimicked the dynamics of the "punctuated equilibrium" model. Just as extraordinary events such as meteor impacts and climate change can profoundly accelerate or redirect the speciation of plants and animals, natural disasters—hurricanes, floods, earthquakes, tornadoes, and plagues—can reorient public attitudes and spur changes in environmental policies. For such "punctuating" transformations to occur requires that the essential actors, institutions, and ideas needed to reorient policies and practices already be in place; they simply need a potent precipitant to catalyze them. This is especially the case in the realm of environmental politics. It has been an arena of activity particularly prone to fits and starts rather than a stable process of orderly evolution.[6]

By the late 1980s a multiplicity of factors converged to provide the preconditions for a tangible shift in both environmental policies and public attitudes about conservation and sustainability in the lowcountry. These foundational factors included a proprietary devotion to the coastal landscape ("a love of the land" / "a sense of place") among a growing number of citizens, the process of sprawl reaching a point of crisis, and the emergence of robust regional conservation organizations. That so many people of such varied backgrounds began participating as a conservation coalition was an especially distinctive element of the lowcountry situation. A prominent environmentalist who participated in the ACE (Ashepoo-Combahee-Edisto) Basin Task Force, which focused on a massive area of conserved land south of Charleston, insisted that the lowcountry's conservation coalition is distinctively diverse yet harmonious: "The thing in South Carolina that's unique and it's evolved from this is that we don't have sort of a sportsmen's group, an environmental group, and a forestry group and an agricultural group. They are all in bed together."[7]

Other factors contributing to the emergence of a conservation culture include the earlier passage of important federal and state environmental legislation during the 1960s and 1970s and a growing willingness of local and state officials to use legislative and regulatory measures to protect the environment. In 1972, for example, the U.S. Congress passed the Coastal Zone Management Act, a landmark piece of legislation that has had reverberating implications for the lowcountry—as well as the nation. The act declared that the efforts of most state and local governments to regulate commercial development in fragile coastal ecosystems were "inadequate." It urged local governments to "exercise their full authority" in managing coastal "land and water use decisions." Compliance with the new law, however, was voluntary, and South Carolina was slow to act. Despite the availability of federal financial incentives, state agencies, as well as local government officials in the lowcountry, did not rush to strengthen restrictions on coastal development. It was not until 1976 that the state legislature enacted the South Carolina Coastal Zone Management Act (Coastal Tidelands and Wetlands Act). The language of the new state legislation was especially clear about one essential point: lowcountry development needed to be better regulated. The act acknowledged that "important ecological, cultural, natural, geological and scenic characteristics, [as well as] industrial, economic and historical values in the coastal zone, are being irretrievably damaged or lost by ill-planned development that threatens to destroy these values."[8]

The Coastal Zone Management Act created a new independent state agency known as the Coastal Council to oversee the implementation of new policies related to lowcountry development. The new state agency lacked adequate authority to carry out its mandate, however. As a blue-ribbon commission appointed by the legislature concluded in 1987, the South Carolina "beach/dune system is now in a state of crisis. Over 57 miles of our beaches are critically eroding." The state legislation related to beachfront development "has been ineffective because too little authority . . . was given to the coastal council which is responsible for administering the [Coastal Zone Management] Act." The commission's findings prompted the General Assembly to pass the Beachfront Management Act in 1988. The new legislation highlighted the importance of the beach and dune system in protecting life and property from storms, generating significant economic revenue through tourism, protecting habitat for important plants and animals, and ensuring a healthy environment for recreation and improved quality of life of all citizens. It also noted that "unwise development" had placed houses too close to the beaches and dunes. The act established stricter guidelines for beachfront construction. The Beachfront Management Act helped bolster the traditionally tepid local and state governmental support for conservation efforts. Equally important has been the role played by dynamic corporate and civic leaders sympathetic to environmental concerns. Many of them saw a direct link between environmental conservation and opportunities to generate new forms of "green" economic development.[9]

Still other factors affecting the growth of a conservation culture include the mobilization of conservation activists and concerned citizens into a powerful grassroots movement, including rural residents who make their living from the land. At the same time, and often at the other end of the social spectrum, developers began building upscale, environmentally friendly, conservation-based communities promoting the significance of the lowcountry landscape. Moreover, an important new tool for environmental protection was the growing popularity of conservation easements and land trusts as legal methods to preserve valuable lands.

Finally, the growing influx of newcomers, many of them affluent northerners who brought with them a commitment to environmental activism and grassroots engagement, began to play an increasingly important role in encouraging conservation—and transparency—in their new communities. For example, a staff member working in the City of Charleston's Department of Planning, Preservation and Sustainability explained that "the culture of the 'bubba system' has changed with the influx of people from other places who want to have a look at and be a part of the decision making. So, there's lot more attention to making sure that things are done in a way that can be scrutinized." Newcomers often criticize the "good old boy" political network long prevalent in the region. In some ways, however, this informal system of relational politics has facilitated the emergence of a conservation culture. A handful of conservation-oriented political figures have exercised a disproportionate influence on zoning and regulatory decisions as well as on the passage of key legislation. Some of the "good old boys" have spearheaded the donation of conservation easements to preserve land and heritage.[10]

These and other factors affecting the evolution and effectiveness of the low-country conservation culture are discussed in subsequent chapters. Ethnographic data and fieldwork (focus group interviews, individual interviews, survey data, participant observation, multidisciplinary research projects), coupled with a systematic analysis of the documentary record provided by newspaper articles and editorials, published reports, and legislative studies, revealed that three especially powerful forces served as catalysts in coalescing the factors needed to create a culture of conservation in the lowcountry. They were: 1) "sprawl shock"—a widespread backlash against the unwanted aspects of the region's unsustainable rate of residential and commercial development; 2) the dramatic impact of Hurricane Hugo in the fall of 1989; and 3) the fears generated by the predicted effects of global warming. Concerns about the environmental impact of sprawl and the risks posed by natural disasters served as the catalyst for profound changes in lowcountry attitudes toward protecting the environment.[11]

Sprawl Shock

The very scale and pace of sprawling development along the South Carolina coast provoked a rising chorus of concern during the 1980s and after. Development, of course, is always a mixed blessing. It can bolster tax revenues, provide jobs, services, and amenities, and enhance a community's appeal to new businesses and prospective residents. But unchecked, uncoordinated development can also cause paralyzing traffic congestion and dangerous air and water pollution; it can disrupt neighborhoods, overcrowd schools, accelerate the deterioration of inner cities, and eliminate the open spaces that originally inspired suburbia and exurbia (residential communities in rural areas beyond the suburbs).[12]

These patterns of unplanned development have been the dominant force shaping residential and retail development in the United States since the end of the World War II. From 1950 to 1970 America's cities gained ten million people; in the same period the suburbs added 85 million people. Post–World War II federal policies centered on getting sixteen million military veterans (and their families) educated, housed, and back to work. The acute postwar housing shortage spurred the scrape-and-sprawl suburban revolution, and by the 1970s it had developed a momentum of its own. Home ownership became the almost universal premise of the American Dream. For the first time in history a majority of people gained ownership of a detached single-family home. During the half century after World War II the good life was presumed to be a big home with a big yard on a big lot accessed by a big car—or two. "I think you buy as much house as you think you can afford," said Phillip Ford, the executive director of the Charleston Trident Association of Realtors. "We've always liked big cars. For most people, it's a status thing."[13]

Federal and state tax codes favored home owners over renters, and government agencies such as the Federal Housing Administration and the Veterans Administration provided inexpensive mortgages that enabled millions of homes to be built in the years following the war. People frustrated by the urban housing shortage, inadequate public services, and inferior city schools eagerly populated the new subdivisions carved out of forests and farms. The countryside beckoned, and people fed up with the high cost of living in congested cities rushed to enjoy the sylvan promise of suburbia. In 1950 one-quarter of Americans lived in suburbs; in 1960, one-third; and by 1990, well over half. More than 90 percent of metropolitan growth since 1950 has occurred in the low-density suburbs, where two-thirds of Americans now live.[14]

Population growth, social mobility, the interstate highway system, government-subsidized mortgages, the cult of the car, inexpensive land and gasoline, and general prosperity helped sustain the feverish suburban building boom well into the twenty-first century. Over time the larger suburbs evolved into self-sustaining "edge cities"—complete with industries, office parks, shopping malls, and outdoor recreation. These, in turn, have spawned more-distant suburbs of their own—rural "exurbs"—no longer tied directly to a parent city.[15]

Sprawling suburban growth has been a persistent feature of urban development for centuries, but during the second half of the twentieth century it became the dominant form of community development, a genuine mass movement. It was a rational, if shortsighted, response to a clear social need. After World War II people voted with their feet—and their cars. People moved into subdivisions whose names showcased the back-to-nature urge: Streamwood, Elmwood, Lakewood, Cedar Hill, Garden City, Forest Grove, Park Forest, Oak Park. Millions of Americans during the 1950s and after felt much better off—more status, more security, more privacy—in their new leafy subdivisions than they had been renting increasingly expensive and usually cramped apartments in large cities. But unchecked suburbanization was unsustainable. Feverish suburbanization became the victim of its own success, outgrowing its capacity to maintain its ideal of restoring the delicate balance between the city and the countryside. "There isn't a metropolitan area in the U.S. that has a comprehensive plan to accommodate its growth," lamented the Baltimore developer James Rouse in 1966. Sprawl was turning America "into a nation of Los Angeleses." In noting the massive suburban migration transforming American life in 1969, *Time* magazine warned that the implications of such "sprawl, congestion and the very quality of life are obvious—and appalling."[16]

The suburban revolution also exacerbated the racial divide, especially in the 1950s and 1960s. A disproportionate number of the people migrating to new suburbs after World War II were middle- and upper-class white people. They participated in what one analyst has called the "secession [from the city] of the successful," leaving behind proliferating racial ghettos. Detroit from 1950 to 1960, for example, gained 185,000 African Americans and lost 361,000 white residents. St. Louis lost 22 percent of its white population during the 1950s. Robert Weaver, the Harvard-educated African American appointed by President Lyndon Johnson to head the new Department of Housing and Urban Development, said in 1966 that "we need an open suburbia—not just an upper- and middle-income-class suburbia."[17]

It did not take long for "soulless" suburban sprawl to attract intense criticism from novelists and playwrights, planners and commuters, social critics and inner-city leaders. Andres Duany, Elizabeth Plater-Zyberk, and Jeff Speck, a trio of planners who have become crusaders for the "new urbanism," have characterized haphazard sprawl as being "largely devoid of places worth caring about. Soulless subdivisions, residential 'communities' utterly lacking in communal life; strip shopping centers, 'big box' chain stores, and artificially festive malls set within barren seas of parking; antiseptic office parks, ghost towns after 6 P.M.; and mile upon mile of clogged collector roads . . . ; this is growth, and you can find little reason to support it." By the 1970s an "orgy of land speculation" triggered by profitable suburban sprawl had swept across America as real estate developers extended suburbia farther and farther into the countryside. Rising national affluence translated into the development of more land per person. Americans were spreading "out across our open land like a tidal wave," said a Dartmouth College geographer in 1973. A 1974 report titled "Environment: The Costs of Sprawl," compiled by three federal agencies, pointed out that better planning could significantly reduce the land consumed by sprawl, cut infrastructure costs, generate less air pollution, and reduce the use of automobiles. By the end of the twentieth century, managing sprawl had become one of the most strategic environmental challenges in the United States. In 2000 Maryland Governor Parris Glendenning spoke for many public officials when he stressed that "sprawl costs taxpayers dollars to support new infrastructure, costs natural resources that we know are not unlimited, and costs us as a society in lost opportunities to invest in our existing communities and neighborhoods."[18]

In 1971 the writer John McPhee lamented the irony of Yosemite National Park's being so stunningly gorgeous that it was exercising a "fatal beauty," attracting more people than it could absorb. Likewise, the lowcountry has long been the fastest growing region in South Carolina and one of the fastest sprawling regions in the nation. One writer labeled sprawl in South Carolina "an insatiable paving machine that swallows up the landscape." Ron Brinson, a former editor of the *Charleston Post and Courier*, the lowcountry's largest circulation newspaper, preferred a different metaphor. "Unbridled growth," he asserted, "grips metropolitan Charleston like a swelling anaconda, insidiously choking community values and our region's gold-standard qualities of life."[19]

Interviews with residents of all ages and backgrounds revealed that people commonly link their fears about the pace of sprawl and traffic congestion to the degradation of the natural environment, their quality of life, and the likelihood that property taxes would increase with continuing residential and commercial development. From 1950 to 2010 the population of the state's coastal counties grew at almost twice the national rate. Sprawl has been the engine driving the region's growth. From 1973 to 2009 Charleston's urban area expanded much faster than its population, growing almost fivefold, from 70 square miles to 335 square miles. Long-serving Charleston mayor Joe Riley declared in 2000 that he could not imagine there being a "hotter housing market in America than Charleston." The rapid growth rate was causing all sorts of problems for the region: rising infrastructure expenses, clogged traffic, and damage to the environment: erosion, flooding, altered stream flows, and habitat destruction.[20]

During the half century after World War II, most people embraced low-density, car-dependent sprawl with few reservations. "It was the ascendant, determining place form of our time," recalled Suzannah Lessard in a provocative 2001 essay about place, design, and nature. Suburban sprawl, she acknowledged, was democracy at work on real estate. It was a middle-class phenomenon with its own "fundamental legitimacy." But sprawl seemed to have things backwards. "What was evolving was a landscape in which the built world surrounded and framed the natural world, instead of the other way around."[21]

The 1990s witnessed mounting concerns about "unnatural" suburban monotony, traffic congestion, and the fragmentation of community created by "gated" neighborhoods promoting ever more privatized (and "secure") residential environments. What in part distinguished sprawl in the lowcountry during the late twentieth century was the decision by large pulp/paper conglomerates to begin selling off their vast timberlands for residential and retail development. It was a windfall for sprawl and a nightmare for conservationists. MeadWestvaco, for example, began buying acreage in South Carolina in the 1920s. By the 1990s it owned four hundred thousand acres in the lowcountry. In the Charleston metropolitan area alone, company-owned lands were larger than all of the land inside the city limits of Charleston and North Charleston combined. Most of that land had been preserved over time by the company, sprinkled with hunt clubs, boat landings, historic sites, and nature preserves. As a result, the timberlands served as a de facto "greenbelt" for the lowcountry.[22]

In the 1990s, however, the company started selling large parcels for residential development as a means of generating cash. By October 2001 MeadWestvaco had sold 120,000 of its 425,000 acres, including thousands of acres in the Ashley River Scenic Corridor, a storied district containing twenty-six historic sites (many of them former plantations). The corridor gained listing on the National Register of Historic Places in 1994. The following year it was named one of the

"Most Endangered Historic Places in America" by the National Trust for Historic Preservation. And in 1996 the state legislature officially designated it a "Scenic State River." Working with the state Department of Natural Resources, the Ashley Scenic River Advisory Council drafted a management plan for the corridor, but it had no effect on private development.

The large timberland sales by MeadWestvaco threatened the environmental integrity of the Ashley River Corridor. Two tracts totaling more than ten thousand acres were sold to developers who announced plans for new residential megacommunities called Poplar Grove and Watson Hill that would contain thousands of upscale homes, condominiums, hotels, and golf courses. Longtime residents worked with the Coastal Conservation League, the coastal region's flagship environmental advocacy group, to oppose the developments, and their strenuous efforts paid off. Residents fashioned an unprecedented arrangement whereby the developers of Poplar Grove agreed to downsize the community from the original plan calling for five thousand homes to a few hundred and to create a conservation easement for most of the acreage. The Watson Hill developers eventually abandoned the project because of steadfast opposition.[23]

The successful resistance to Poplar Grove and Watson Hill did not stop the juggernaut of development, however. Mayor Riley declared in 2004 that "we are growing at the fastest pace the state has ever grown in its history." Throughout the lowcountry, sales of huge timberland tracts by MeadWestvaco, Plum Creek Timberland, and International Paper sparked an unprecedented land rush, spurred population growth, and exacerbated suburban sprawl. Conservationists were shocked. "My initial reaction was sheer horror," said Dana Beach, the executive director of the Coastal Conservation League. A 2007 study of the

Traffic on Highway 17, Mount Pleasant.
Photograph by Angela C. Halfacre.

lowcountry by two national land planners expressed the concerns of the community about the disproportionate impact of timberland sales: "There's no more frightening prospect for Charlestonians than timber companies selling off huge chunks of their land, often far from urban centers, to developers who'll clear-cut lots, throw up standard subdivisions, and trigger huge new floods of long-distance commuters onto the region's already overtaxed roads." All of the municipal planners and staff members of lowcountry conservation organizations interviewed for this book expressed anxiety about the impact of large timberland sales to developers.[24]

Long-range projections developed in the early twentieth-first century demonstrated that the rate of growth in the lowcountry was unsustainable. By 2030 the lowcountry counties—Horry, Georgetown, Charleston, Berkeley, Dorchester, Colleton, Beaufort, Jasper, Williamsburg—were expected to experience dramatic population growth, ranging from 20 percent in Charleston County to 73 percent in Beaufort County. "Our planning models reflected a certain number for growth for the next 10 to 15 years, and we have far exceeded that in just the past three years," Beaufort County Council chairman Weston Newton said in 2004. More people have meant more sprawl. Urban development and the growth of commercial pine plantations are expected to claim 35 percent of the state's coastal plain forests by 2040. "The development threats that are hitting the coastal plain were probably unthought-of 15 years ago," said Edwin Cooper III of Ducks Unlimited in 2003. Others saw the frenetic rate of growth in more dramatic terms. "Everything that people come here for in the first place, and the reason they decide to stay, is being destroyed," said Sam Passmore, then a staff member at the Coastal Conservation League. The troubling question facing the lowcountry, he added, is how "do you prepare for and manage this growth without destroying the area's cherished rural and historic resources?"[25]

The U.S. Department of Agriculture ranks South Carolina among the top ten states in the proportion of developed to undeveloped acreage. Land development in the lowcountry since 1990 has been increasing at a rate five to six times faster than the population growth. A 255 percent increase in developed acreage occurred from 1973 to 1994 in the greater Charleston area (Berkeley, Charleston, and Dorchester Counties), while the population grew by 41 percent. Along the South Carolina coast about thirty acres of rural land were being converted to urban use or sprawl each day. The U.S. Forest Service called urban sprawl the greatest threat to the landscape of South Carolina. "Urbanization and development are the single biggest factors in the loss of timberland acreage," said Ken Cabe, a South Carolina Forestry Commission spokesman.[26]

During the late twentieth century the lowcountry's frenzied growth rates began to reach a tipping point of public concern. The progrowth culture had unwittingly created the instrument of its own destruction: a growing public backlash against the excesses of unregulated development. The overdrive pace of development began to frighten planners and frustrate residents as well as visitors.

Map that was critical in gaining public support for conservation issues in this region. Courtesy of Jeffery Allen and the Strom Thurmond Institute of Government and Public Affairs at Clemson University.

Sprawl shock spurred the emergence of a conservation culture. A fundamental shift began to occur in the discourse about the identity and future of the lowcountry. In 1997 the *Charleston Post and Courier* reported that "area leaders have begun to take a harder look at sprawl and its effects." Two years later the newspaper announced that dealing with "rapid growth" had become the coastal region's foremost issue. Hugh Lane Jr., the president of the Bank of South Carolina and a lifelong conservationist, concluded that the sudden awareness of overdevelopment during the 1980s and 1990s "was the single biggest thing that woke people up" about the fragile future of the lowcountry. Lane recalled that influential political leaders and media commentators suddenly acknowledged the urgency of dealing with runaway growth. In 2000, for example, Mayor Riley said, "we don't have much time" to address the threats posed by sprawl. He and others began repeatedly posing the fundamental question: could the region's distinctive natural environment survive the accelerating rate of population growth and economic development? A journalist echoed Riley's sense of concern when he declared that sprawl had become "the biggest issue" facing the lowcountry. The region, said Riley in 2004, "was at a crossroads." If sprawl were not brought under control, he predicted, "the physical beauty, the environment, and the quality of life in the lowcountry would be irrevocably damaged."[27]

Sprawl shock galvanized efforts during the 1990s and after to reduce the rate of development and promote smart growth: economically sustainable, environmentally sensitive, and more socially equitable patterns of development based on more compact developments with higher densities. A committed culture of conservation emerged in a variety of forms. Many lowcountry county governments began countering sprawl with new land-use regulations and zoning restrictions. Beaufort and Berkeley Counties began paying landowners to prevent development on their property. A growing number of developers began promoting ideas such as smart growth and new urbanism, both of which emphasize the importance of planned development, open spaces, common areas, higher densities and more compact structures, diminished dependence on automobiles, and more reliance on current infrastructure rather than on new roads and sewers. Lowcountry legislators endorsed the idea of using state monies to create a "conservation bank" to purchase and protect large parcels of undeveloped land. Beaufort and Charleston Counties mimicked the state program. At the same time lowcountry conservation organizations saw their memberships, budgets, and visibility soar. Public hearings for virtually any proposed new developments attracted larger crowds of concerned citizens. Lowcountry newspapers began devoting regular attention and editorials to issues related to sprawl. "The rapid population growth of Charleston, Berkeley, and Dorchester counties over the last two decades," said the editors of the *Charleston Post and Courier* in 2005, "has instilled in many longtime residents the dangerous notion that widespread, disruptive development is inevitable. If enough people succumb to that defeatist attitude, it could become a self-fulfilling prophecy. But if enough people work together to properly restrict and direct development, much of the lowcountry's precious natural and historic heritage can be preserved."[28]

The celebrated writer Pat Conroy expressed the sentiments of many lowcountry residents when he wrote a biting letter to the editor of the *Beaufort Gazette* in 2006. Conroy, who had attached himself "like a barnacle" to the lowcountry since moving there with his U.S. Marine Corps father and family at age fifteen, furiously denounced efforts by public officials and developers to circumvent efforts to "preserve the rural nature of northern Beaufort County" by allowing for some sixteen thousand new homes. The county's comprehensive land-use plan focused on encouraging development in areas that already had infrastructure in place. Now, Conroy argued, the mayor was promoting megadevelopments in unimproved rural areas of the county, thus necessitating new roads and schools. "Those of us who love Beaufort," he pledged, "are rising up, and, by the grace of the one who made this land, we will be heard." He said there should be "riots in the streets" over such attempts to revive old patterns of unrestrained development.[29]

In 2001 the editors of the Hilton Head newspaper, the *Island Packet*, concluded that the efforts to manage growth in the lowcountry had "overwhelmed county and municipal governments." Public officials had failed to take the long view.

They had approved residential and industrial development projects without adequately appreciating the long-term costs of additional infrastructure expenses (roads, sewer and water lines, schools, and so forth) and traffic congestion. They had failed to require impact fees of new residents or developers and had failed to generate new sources of revenue to pay for additional services. There were not enough members of the planning staff or enough building inspectors to manage the relentless growth. "The minimization of sprawl along main traffic arteries is a must." Protecting the water quality of coastal rivers and streams was equally important. But the editors stressed the most important need: "Explosive, unsustainable growth must be controlled." There was little time to act, they warned. "If we citizens of Beaufort County do not speak up and demand that county and municipal governments do the job they were elected to do—to properly manage the growth of Beaufort County—the quality of life . . . will continue to decline."[30]

In 2000 such concerns about relentless growth led a group of lowcountry officials to travel to Columbia where they pleaded with legislators to pass smart-growth initiatives to help "ease overcrowded schools, traffic snarls, and deteriorating air and water quality." They reported that people on the coast were "fed up" with gridlock traffic congestion and "dismayed that the open spaces around their neighborhoods are being swallowed up by strip malls." Ted Power, a Mount Pleasant Town Council member, told the lawmakers that his community had taken the extreme action of implementing a six-month moratorium on large residential developments. Others expressed similar concerns. The "flood of new people," a journalist explained, "is diluting the unique heritage of the coast [and] slowly eroding a culture developed over four centuries. . . . Entire ways of life are vanishing. Traditions are being forgotten."[31]

Such lamentations appeared with increasing frequency and intensity. "The feeling of community is gone," said a distressed resident of the Isle of Palms. Traffic congestion was "going from bad to worse," said Charlestonian Brian Moody, who chaired a newly formed group called Citizens for Community Improvement. The same outlook led a James Islander to denounce sprawl. "I despise developers," she said. "Too often," she added, "I hate what I see happening to the lowcountry." Many of those suffering from sprawl shock cited the state's reluctance to regulate economic development as the primary culprit. "In a state in which property rights is the law of the land, the legislature is hesitant to restrict development. That is left to local communities." And the citizenry have grown ever more active in engaging the issues created by unplanned sprawl. By the 1990s there had developed a growing consensus that the lowcountry must find alternatives to unrestrained growth.[32]

Elected officials responded to the shifting sentiments in the lowcountry by promoting smart growth, regional land-use planning, new land-use restrictions, and long-term thinking. In 1999 Mayor Riley said that the need to manage growth more sustainably was "suddenly before us." Two years later he told a national environmental conference that rampant growth in the lowcountry had produced chronic beach erosion and pollution, flooding and altered stream flows, gridlocked traffic and disappearing wetlands. It was time, he added, for the public to decide where to draw the line with unregulated development. "It's going to take establishing coastal land management and conservation measures and creating ecological zones to defend against development."[33]

The good news, Riley reported, was that the devastation caused by Hurricane Hugo had led lowcountry cities, counties, environmental groups, and citizens to be more conscientious about environmental conservation: to support new land-use regulations and foster a new awareness that ecological damage also damaged the region's quality of life—and its tourism-centered economy. "Although the problems associated with coastal sprawl are complex," Riley stressed, "the solutions are straightforward. Communities need to make active decisions about where and how to grow if they are going to protect their quality of life."[34]

The Risk of Natural Disasters

Nothing punctuates public awareness like a natural disaster. Calamities remind us of the fragility of life, the resilience of the human spirit, and the inability of humans to control an overpowering nature. The creative destruction spawned by disasters often teaches valuable lessons. In the lowcountry, concerns about sprawl were given new urgency, energy, and momentum by the devastating impact of Hurricane Hugo. On September 21, 1989, the killer storm roared ashore near Charleston at high tide, carried along by 135-mile-an-hour winds and a 10-foot storm surge. The hurricane churned through Charleston Harbor, ripping the roof off the city hall, damaging 80 percent of the downtown houses, and destroying almost 40 percent of the trees. The wind, waves, and flooding rains destroyed lives and livelihoods, property and infrastructure, beaches and habitats. Eighteen people were killed, 70,000 were left homeless, and 225,000 were out of work. Nearly 40,000 homes were damaged or ruined. Hurricane Hugo proved to be the costliest storm in U.S. history up to that point (later hurricanes Andrew and Katrina were even more costly). The psychological trauma was as great as the physical destruction. Marjory Heath Wentworth, a lowcountry resident and the state's poet laureate, remembered her emotional distress: "Your life is on hold for so long. It changes you. It's like going through death or surviving a horrible illness."[35]

As so often happens with natural disasters, those hardest hit were the very poor and isolated, especially those living in already disadvantaged rural communities such as the small coastal villages of McClellanville and Awendaw, northeast of Charleston. Many residents had no electricity or water for weeks after the storm. For them, the Red Cross was the only source of food, water, and shelter—for weeks. In the days and months after the storm subsided, many shell-shocked residents sold their homes or property (often slashing prices for a quick sale) to avoid the risk of future hurricanes.[36]

The rampaging hurricane ravaged the land as well as its residents; it dramatically disturbed the coastal ecology. Once the winds abated and the flood waters

Land for sale along Highway 17. Courtesy of Christopher Bonney.

receded, the lowcountry was a scene of mass destruction. A region beloved for its beauty was left scarred and disfigured. The massive hurricane mowed a path through the lowcountry one hundred miles long and fifty miles wide. Three million acres of timberland were leveled by the massive storm. In the area north of Charleston around Cape Romain and Bulls Bay, the hurricane toppled most of the mature trees—loblolly pine, longleaf pine, oaks, cypress, and tupelo—in the sprawling Francis Marion National Forest. Two-thirds of the endangered red-cockaded woodpeckers were killed. Vulnerable barrier islands were especially hard hit. The hurricane submerged the Isle of Palms and Sullivan's Island and cut Pawleys Island in two. Bridges that connected islands to the mainland were toppled or destroyed. The hurricane was, said a reporter, a frightening "wake-up call after an unusually mild 40 years for natural disasters."[37]

In 1900, in the aftermath of the terrible hurricane that rampaged across Galveston, Texas, the editors of the *New York Times* had described the "reckless defiance" shown by people rebuilding on devastated beaches. Yet such defiance characterized the lowcountry as well. Hurricane Hugo scarred but did not scare the coastal region. Hugo's awesome devastation altered the landscape but did not halt migration into the lowcountry. Despite the risk of future storms, despite rising insurance premiums for coastal properties, and despite new state regulations intended to limit development along the coastline, large numbers of people, many of whom first learned of the area through the extensive media coverage of Hurricane Hugo, flocked to the lowcountry coast in the storm's aftermath. According to a Charleston city planner, the hurricane "really brought a lot of attention to this area because people saw Mayor Riley on the news every night for months talking about what happened. It was really one of the first big hurricanes in a long time, probably in twenty years, that people in the nation got to see on television. They're seeing Mayor Riley and showing the City of Charleston to all of folks in the Northeast quadrant." Many of the newcomers were out-of-state workers needed for the prolonged reconstruction efforts, and many of them stayed once the reconstruction effort ended. Sprawl flourished as never before in the aftermath of the hurricane.[38]

Disasters often produce what scholars call economic "recovery machines." Hurricane Hugo provided such a recovery machine for the lowcountry. Fueled by insurance payments and massive infrastructure investments by the federal and state government during the 1990s, the coastal population mushroomed at the end of the twentieth century. Planners for the Town of Mount Pleasant reported that Hugo's destruction spawned repairs as well as new construction "all over the lowcountry." A Charleston planner mentioned that the prolonged media coverage of the hurricane provided a marketing boon: "Charleston became exposed to the rest of the country. It became discovered after Hugo."[39]

It did not take long for the rebuilding process to spark overbuilding. Six months after the costly storm, the *Washington Post* reported that "the lessons of Hurricane Hugo have been forgotten almost as quickly as the huge storm's flood surge receded." Catastrophe capitalism thrives on what the Hungarian-born economist Joseph Schumpeter famously called "a gale of creative destruction." Natural disasters have frequently been engines of dynamic development and economic growth. Calamities fuel private enterprise as well as government spending, and their economic advantages benefit the affluent residents much more than the working class or the very poor. "It's a perverse thing," explained economist Steve Cochrane. "There's real pain, but from an economic point of view, it's [a natural disaster is] a plus."[40]

The reconstruction of the lowcountry in the aftermath of Hugo provided a boon to the construction industry. In the first two-and-a-half years after the storm, a building boom added some five hundred million dollars in income to the lowcountry economy. Many home owners with full insurance coverage garnered windfalls that enabled them to upgrade their properties as they rebuilt them. One journalist called this phenomenon the "Jacuzzi effect" because "a lot of people had Jacuzzis after Hugo who hadn't had them before."[41]

What the *New York Times* called the "frenetic pace of development" after Hugo's fury was spent exerted more pressure on the region's environmental carrying capacity. One Georgetown resident reflected on the different perspectives among natives and newcomers: "I think for the newcomers, where they're coming from [the urban Northeast], the population is so much less here, than where they're coming from. They can't believe how much open space there is. And the people who have been here fifty years, the population is so much more now, they can't believe how many people are here."[42]

The new Clyde Moultrie Dangerfield Bridge connecting the Isle of Palms, a six-mile-long barrier island, to Mount Pleasant, for example, was a direct result of Hugo's devastations. The construction of the bridge "opened up the floodgates for tourism," according to Mike Sottile, the mayor of Isle of Palms. "There are more people and more traffic." The pace and scope of growth, he added, were "changing the character" of the lowcountry. All vestiges of the island's working-class roots will have vanished in the not-too-distant future." Ironically the surge of growth stimulated in part by the impact of Hurricane Hugo had made the low-country even more vulnerable to future storms. "If a storm as powerful as Hugo were to hit the island today," Sottile predicted, "there would be twice as much destruction as before because of the [additional] development." People readily perceived a connection between the hurricane and the rate of new development afterwards. In an interview for this book an African American resident in the Sewee to Santee area spoke about the rate of growth after Hugo: "So, the developer, . . . that's what it's all about. And South Carolina, since Hugo, has really takenoff running. Have you all noticed? After Hugo went down, they [developers] started getting it together. Mount Pleasant was developed so fast they didn't even have a chance to . . . [construct] the fire departments and schools and what not."[43]

Another African American resident highlighted the challenges of trying to retain ownership of family properties amid the lowcountry land boom and the influx of affluent newcomers:

Going right back into mostly our heritage, this whole area is poor people, white and black. But for the most part, everybody's poor, and everybody did the same thing to earn a living. Economically things have gotten better, but for the most part, there are still some pros and cons. Now, the land is prime [property], everybody wants it. . . . The only thing you could call your own was that land in your family. That's why people work so hard to pay those [property] taxes, because that's the only thing they could say "this belongs to my family . . . ; nobody can take it." Nobody wanted it back then, but now the tables have turned if you've got waterfront property. If you went all the way from, I'd say Mount Pleasant, come all the way to South Santee, everything on the waterfront was all owned by blacks. For the most part, you can see that it's been going, going, going . . . gone [since the land rush after the hurricane in 1989.]

It was not coincidental that lowcountry African Americans were disproportionately hard-hit by the hurricane and that a higher percentage of black people sold their properties after the storm than white people did.[44]

Yet while serving as an engine for new development, Hurricane Hugo also acted as an engine for environmental concern. For everyone living in the low-country, whether natives or newcomers, the pace of sprawl after Hugo profoundly affected the region's quality of life. Jesse Tullos, the editor of the *Georgetown News*, reported that the "red-hot building boom" triggered by "Hurricane Hugo's recovery" had left many residents "road-dazed." Daily traffic had become unmanageable. Since he moved to the lowcountry in 1988, just before the hurricane roared ashore, continuous "growth" had been the region's byword. "More people meant more cars and more of everything: shopping malls, grocery stores, fast-food places, and everything else." Tullos acknowledged the "battle . . . against suburban sprawl" and its destruction of the region's "natural beauty." Although he did not oppose growth per se, for growth "brings prosperity and economic opportunity for virtually everyone," Tullos had become a crusader for planned development. Growth needed to be managed: "The mission of those of us concerned about the changing character of Georgetown County is to ensure that future growth takes the form of real neighborhoods and not uninspiring suburban sprawl."[45]

Others echoed the need for a more balanced approach to the impact of new development on the environment. In 2009, on the twentieth anniversary of the hurricane's landfall, a journalist declared that the terrible storm had changed the lowcountry, "but those changes weren't all bad." In its destructive wake Hugo had provided the galvanizing impetus for profound changes in conservation politics and policy making. Just days after the hurricane battered the lowcountry, the *New York Times* reported that a new storm was brewing over the pace and nature of coastal development. The result was a "significant conflict between private property rights and the public interest," explained Cotton Harness, an attorney for the Coastal Council, the state agency charged with overseeing coastal development. According to one lowcountry white resident, "what happened afterwards is the same thing that happened on Sullivan's Island and everywhere else: the five-thousand- [was] replaced [by] ten-thousand-square-foot homes." Most of the residents interviewed for this book emphasized that Hurricane Hugo was a turning point in the emergence of a culture of conservation. They believe that the national publicity about the hurricane attracted more newcomers to the area—and more sprawl. In addition, the damage wreaked by Hugo exacerbated concerns about the fragility of the lowcountry environment and their sense of community. The rebuilding process created even greater concerns—related to cost, possible future loss, the stress of being dependent on others to assist them in transition, and the associated increased development.

A concrete example of the ways in which the experience of Hurricane Hugo aroused greater environmental concern occurred on Sullivan's Island, the upscale beachfront community across the harbor from Charleston. Like all barrier islands, Sullivan's Island is a dynamic place. The sand making up the beaches, dunes, and maritime forest is constantly shifting as a result of tidal action and storms. During the twentieth century sand had gradually accumulated along the island, widening the distance between homes and the beach. Shrubs also began growing on the "accreted" land. Hurricane Hugo's winds and storm surge completely submerged the island, eroded dunes, and carried over wash into the interior. But the areas of the island most resistant to the hurricane's impact were those protected by the "accreted" natural areas. In the aftermath of the hurricane residents saw that their best protection from another hurricane would be to protect the beachfront natural areas so as to minimize storm damage inland. In February 1991 the Town of Sullivan's Island, working with the Lowcountry Open Land Trust, placed approximately ninety acres of accreted beachfront property into a protective easement ensuring that the property would never be developed or built upon. The easement is composed primarily of a maritime scrub forest and a dune system that buffer the rest of the island. Such a conservation easement of valuable beachfront property, explained Elizabeth Hagood of the Lowcountry Open Land Trust, "might not have happened if Hurricane Hugo had not occurred." The Sullivan's Island community "saw immediately the benefit of mother nature to protect them. . . . It was the most significant conservation of front beach that has ever been done on the east coast."[46]

Conservation efforts occur at the intersection of private rights and public interests. As Cotton Harness elaborated, "Perhaps nowhere in the country do we see those two rights conflict so clearly as on the oceanfront beaches" of the lowcountry. Orrin Pilkey, a preeminent coastal geologist at Duke University, agreed that Hurricane Hugo had become a catalyst for a much more serious conversation about conserving the distinctive landscape of the lowcountry. It was a very "timely hurricane," he said, adding that "if this hurricane doesn't prove that something has to be done [about overdevelopment along the coast], nothing will ever do it." Hugo "re-awakened South Carolinians to the hurricane threat."[47]

The surge of population growth and construction after Hurricane Hugo also brought with it a wave of newcomers from the northern United States, many of whom brought with them an active commitment to environmental conservation. "The people that come here from Ohio and New Jersey," observed Dana Beach of the Coastal Conservation League, "have seen how the places they grew up in have changed, and they don't want to see that change happen here, too." Robert Goldberg, a transplant from Boston living on Dataw Island, highlighted the importance of the lowcountry's beautiful environment in convincing him to relocate to the region. "I moved here from Boston to get away from traffic jams; I love that a traffic jam in Beaufort is made up of about five cars." Such environmentally sensitive migrants became an important component of the region's emerging culture of conservation.[48]

The residue of Hurricane Hugo raised stern questions about the need for stricter building codes, zoning regulations, land-use changes, and environmental protections. So the natural disaster was a double-edged sword: the "miraculous" rebuilding of the shattered region created a watershed moment (a "wake up call," as people termed it) that helped to crystallize what has since become a widespread culture of conservation. The hurricane created what one resident called "an historical marker, a point in time by which we can measure our lives. Because it changed everybody's life. Everybody's." The deadly storm was also a marker in the development of the region's culture of conservation. As Mayor Riley pointed out in the immediate aftermath of the hurricane, the lowcountry needed not only to rebuild. He wanted the community also to learn from the painful event how to be a more sustainable society: "to blossom and grow in beauty and quality."[49]

The Threat of Global Warming

If the combination of sprawl shock and the surge of development and population growth after Hurricane Hugo helped ignite a public backlash, the specter of global warming and its implications has enhanced the region's conservation culture. Warming temperatures are threatening South Carolina's coastlines with rising sea levels. According to the U.S. Environmental Protection Agency, "a significant amount of sea level rise has likely resulted from the observed warming of the atmosphere and the oceans." Over the past seventy-five years, local and global factors, especially melting glaciers at both poles, have led to a "relative sea-level rise" of about a foot in Charleston Harbor. But climate change—and sea-level rise—are accelerating. According to the Intergovernmental Panel on Climate Change (IPCC), global sea levels are predicted to rise between 0.6 and 24 inches within the next century. "There's no question about the direction we're heading," according to Robert Bindschadler, the chief scientist at the National Aeronautics and Space and Administration Goddard Space flight Center in Greenbelt, Maryland. "Every time that the planet has gotten warmer, ice sheets have melted. The question is how much and how fast they will melt." The results of such an unprecedented rise in sea levels would be profound—and expensive. The U.S. Environmental Protection Agency estimates that the sand replenishment that would be needed to protect South Carolina's coastlines from a twenty-inch sea-level rise could cost billions of dollars.[50]

During the 1990s and since, concerns about the effects of climate change on the South Carolina coast have spurred efforts to regulate development and reduce the emission of greenhouse gases. In 1997 the Environmental Information Center in Washington, D.C., predicted that many of the lowcountry's highly developed barrier islands and ecologically sensitive marshlands would be submerged by rising sea levels over the next century. "Oceans will rise, low-lying coastal areas will flood, and huge chunks of Wild Dunes, Mount Pleasant, and James Island will vanish under water if steps are not taken to cool global warming," reported the *Charleston Post and Courier* in 1997. Ten years later a new study by the IPCC concluded that the pace of climate change was quickening. Scientists predicted that parts of Hilton Head, Fripp, and Parris Islands would be under water within a century.[51]

The Beachfront Management Act of 1988 addressed many important issues that relate to the threat of rising sea level. It included an array of regulations intended to limit beachfront development, many of which were controversial. New homes were required to be set back from the ocean, and construction of new seawalls was prohibited. A crucial underpinning of the 1988 state law is a provision that a seawall built before 1988 cannot be rebuilt if 50 percent of it has been destroyed by a storm. The law's intention was to allow the shorelines naturally to migrate inland. This would mean that oceanfront lots and homes would eventually be undermined and topple into the sea.[52]

It did not take long for beachfront property owners to challenge such restrictions. In late 1986 David Lucas, a builder and developer, paid $975,000 for two oceanfront lots in the Wild Dunes development on the Isle of Palms northeast of Charleston. Citing the new regulations in the Beachfront Management Act, the state refused Lucas's request for a building permit. He filed suit, arguing that the state law constituted an illegal "taking" of his property values. A state court ruled in his favor, only to see the South Carolina Supreme Court overturn the decision by a 3–2 vote.[53]

In 1992 the United States Supreme Court heard the Lucas case on appeal and reversed the decision of the South Carolina Supreme Court. In its 1992 opinion the majority ruled that a state land-use policy that effectively prohibits a property owner from building constitutes an illegal "taking" of that person's property—a violation of the Fifth Amendment. The owner must therefore be compensated by the state. Justice John Stevens, who dissented in the *Lucas* ruling, argued that the court's decision would "greatly hamper the efforts of local officials and planners who must deal with increasingly complex problems in land-use and environmental regulation." In 1993 the state paid Lucas $1.75 million for his two lots.[54]

While many beachfront property owners complained about new land-use restrictions and zoning ordinances, others in the lowcountry embraced the emerging conservation culture. In 1999 the *Charleston Post and Courier* observed that "rising sea levels will give an additional reason" for the region to deal more effectively with "new development and sprawl." Soon thereafter, the Charleston Area League of Women Votes partnered with the South Carolina Aquarium and the Coastal Conservation League to host annual public forums dealing with global warming issues. In 2001 the city councils of Charleston and Georgetown passed identical resolutions pledging to begin reducing greenhouse gas emissions. In 2006 Mayor Riley joined the U.S. Conference of Mayors Climate Protection Agreement and pledged to reduce Charleston's greenhouse gas emissions. He did so because of the compelling urgency to begin slowing the rate of climate change. "We did it," he explained, "because we have to think globally and act locally. Every community needs to challenge itself to reduce harmful emissions." In early 2007 the editors of the *Charleston Post and Courier* cited a new report from the 113-nation IPCC that confirmed that global warming was accelerating. What should the lowcountry do? "Expand our use of alternative energy sources (including nuclear power) and make an overdue commitment to conservation."[55]

The prospect of climate change and rising sea levels alarmed governmental leaders. In 2007 Governor Mark Sanford shocked national Republicans by writing an op-ed piece for the *Washington Post* in which he declared that the "climate change debate is here to stay, and as America warms to the idea of environmental conservation on a grander scale, it is vital that conservatives" engage the discussion. At the same time, Charleston's Mayor Riley declared that global warming was among the greatest dangers facing the planet, and the people living

Damage from Hurricane Hugo in 1989, Sullivan's Island. Courtesy of South Caroliniana Library.

House on stilts for flood prevention at Folly Beach. Courtesy of Mitchell Colgan.

in the lowcountry needed to take immediate steps to reduce carbon dioxide emissions. "The science is very clear and exact," he said, "If we don't act, if we don't act quickly, the climate will go haywire." Riley agreed to cochair the newly formed South Carolina Mayors for Climate & Energy Leadership. And he acknowledged the peculiar threats of sea-level rise to the lowcountry. "Charleston, just for self-protection, must take the challenge of sea level rise very seriously."[56]

In October 2007 the South Carolina Department of Health and Environmental Control (DHEC) created the Shoreline Change Advisory Committee. That same year the mayors of Bluffton, Hilton Head, and Beaufort urged the United

States presidential candidates in both parties to pledge to make addressing climate change a top priority. Hilton Head Mayor Tom Peeples said that "it's our duty to minimize impacts to the earth as much as we can within reason." Beaufort mayor Bill Rauch predicted dire consequences if serious action were not taken. "This is the lowcountry here, and if the seas are rising, there's no one that's in more trouble than we are." Two years later the committee issued a comprehensive report titled "Adapting to Shoreline Change." In 2008 the state's governor, Mark Sanford, created by executive order a nine-member advisory commission on climate change that later created more than fifty policy recommendations intended to slow the onset of climate change, including a voluntary reduction in greenhouse gas emissions. Sanford reflected his self-described stance as a "conservative conservationist" when he expressed his concern "that sea levels and governmental intervention may end up rising together. My earnest hope going forward is that we can find conservative solutions to the climate change problem—ecologically responsible solutions based on free-market principles that both improve our quality of life and safe guard our freedoms."[57]

In 2009 a coalition of business leaders, renewable energy advocates, and environmental organizations calling themselves Friends of the Lowcountry launched the Save the Lowcountry Campaign designed to increase public awareness about the probable impact of global warming on the South Carolina coast—and the economy. "Tourism is the engine driving South Carolina's economy," stressed Frank Knapp Jr. of the South Carolina Small Business Chamber of Commerce, "but global warming could cause that engine to break down." Rising sea levels could endanger more than the tourist industry; it could also transform a way of life. As one of the participants in the Save the Lowcountry Campaign explained, "If we don't do something to stop global warming now, our beloved lowcountry could be gone forever."[58]

Conservation as the New Normal

Whatever the motives or precipitants, a culture of conservation was solidly in place in the lowcountry at the beginning of the twenty-first century. People were eager to work together to find creative—and increasingly aggressive—ways to manage sprawl so as to conserve the lowcountry's distinctive environment. In 2000 Governor Jim Hodges called a statewide summit of four hundred real estate developers as well as political, business, and environmental leaders to discuss "how to avoid suburban sprawl" and promote "smart growth." The governor pointed out that South Carolina ranked forty-eighth among the fifty states in protecting or preserving open space, and it ranked ninth in the amount of farmlands and forests being converted into urban or suburban development. Participants noted the frenzied growth across the state but emphasized the especially disturbing trends in the lowcountry, where residents were experiencing the brunt of population growth and development. "The growth issue has arrived," declared Ken Driggers of the Palmetto Conservation Foundation in 2000. "Ignore it at your peril." Four years later Charleston County voters approved a one-half-cent sales-tax increase to fund annual purchases of "greenbelt" properties (or easements) to impede sprawl and preserve wildlife habitats and undeveloped rural lands. (By 2010 the program had acquired fifteen thousand acres).[59]

The conservation culture in the lowcountry region has come to include the following key elements: environmentally progressive bipartisan political leadership in a conservative state; sophisticated regional conservation organizations; transformed land-use planning practices; the emergence of conservation-based residential communities; and organized efforts to sustain aspects of the region's cultural/racial heritage and to nurture land-based livelihoods, including farming. The nature and the mix of these various elements are unique to the lowcountry, but the story of their coming together to form a conservation culture is instructive. Nearly a quarter century ago, these elements emerged to challenge a long-standing culture of indifference to the exploitation of the region's natural environment. How and why that happened is the focus of the following chapters.

THREE

Leveraged Leadership

In September 1989, the same month that Hurricane Hugo roared across the lowcountry, Sierra Club volunteer and former New York City financier Dana Beach founded with his spouse, Virginia, and their friend and fellow bird watcher, Jane Lareau, the Coastal Conservation League (CCL), the first full-time local organization dedicated to preserving—in a comprehensive way—the quality of the lowcountry environment. The three founders were determined that their beloved South Carolina coast not mimic the overdevelopment and habitat destruction that had occurred in Florida. Dana Beach devised the idea for what became the Coastal Conservation League. A native of Columbia who had served as an aide to Republican state legislator Arthur Ravenel Jr., he had spent the previous year traveling along the southeast coast, meeting with local and regional environmental organizations such as the Chesapeake Bay Foundation, the Coastal Federation in North Carolina, and the Georgia Conservancy to gain insights into how to structure and lead such an organization on the South Carolina coast.[1]

Beach's knowledge and determination greatly exceeded his financial resources. With a solid grounding in ecology, economics, and politics, the Beaches and Lareau raised a shoestring budget, rented cramped offices, and launched the CCL to promote "smart growth" in the lowcountry—at the same time that the coastal region was recovering from Hurricane Hugo. The devastating storm, Beach recalled, created a crucial "time-out to think about things rather than the normal trajectory of life and GDP [Gross Domestic Product]." The anxiety and frustration triggered by Hugo's destruction "allowed a conversation [about growth and conservation] to happen "and "gave a period of calm after the storm for lowcountry relief." The weeks and months after the hurricane also encouraged thoughtful responses to addressing the fragility of the coast and a dialogue about what "really matters to the region."[2]

The Coastal Conservation League—An "Eco-Political Machine"

The CCL is a remarkable success story. Since its modest beginning in 1989 it has grown into the largest and most prominent environmental organization in the state—and one of the most respected in the nation. "Around the country [in 2004]," said J. Gustave "Gus" Speth, cofounder of the Natural Resources Defense

Council and dean of the Yale University School of Forestry and Environmental Studies, "you can see a lot of [conservation] groups emerging as leaders, and the Coastal Conservation League is emerging as one of the best." By 2010 it had a staff of twenty-six, two full-time lobbyists in the state capital of Columbia, satellite offices in Charleston, Beaufort, and Georgetown, and a three-million-dollar annual budget. It also boasted five thousand dues-paying members representing what a *New York Times* reporter described as a combination "of old and new landed gentry, some rich, some inclined to preservation for its own sake, and others because they love to hunt and fish." Perhaps most important, CCL has been unrelenting in its efforts to protect the lowcountry environment and raise public awareness about the need for such protection. The tagline for its mission is "nature and community in balance."[3]

The effectiveness of the Coastal Conservation League as the region's flagship conservation organization is largely the result of two strategic emphases adopted in its early years. First, Beach decided that the league's initial focus should be the conservation and preservation of land. "We are one of the most wasteful states in the nation in terms of land," he said in 1999. Yet land-use policies and practices were receiving little attention. Established conservation organizations in the state and across the nation were using regulatory legislation to improve water and air quality or protect endangered species. Beach concluded that the league's niche would be land-use issues and land preservation projects in part because land was the most essential unifying element of a conservation program. It enabled people from all walks of life—and especially political and social conservatives—to embrace environmental efforts. As Cathy Forrester, a former CCL staff member (who now works for the Lowcountry Open Land Trust), said in 2004: "There's a long tradition of stewardship of the land in the lowcountry. We have members who have lived here a long time. They are seeing the changes and are concerned. We also have a lot of people who have moved here from elsewhere—places that have been destroyed—and [they] are seeing the same processes [at work] here and are concerned." Moreover, by protecting land and preserving the lowcountry "way of life," CCL could also indirectly improve water and air quality and wildlife habitat.[4]

The second strategic emphasis was Beach's decision to "leverage" the growing strength of CCL by forming an array of formal and informal alliances. He recognized early on that "we needed a bigger coalition of partners" in order to marshal their respective resources and technical expertise so as to have a regional impact. To that end the CCL quickly developed a tactical emphasis on leveraging visibility, influence, and resources by organizing innovative partnerships with other conservation organizations as well as with local, state, and federal agencies. Over the years the CCL has partnered with chambers of commerce, corporations, the timber industry, trade associations, and churches in dealing with land-use issues. "Everyone's a potential ally," Lareau acknowledged. CCL's political savvy and pragmatic bent led a journalist to call it an "eco-political machine."[5]

Dana Beach, 2010.
Courtesy of Mathew Scott.

Over time the CCL has broadened its scope beyond the initial focus on land-use policy and land preservation. It is much more holistic now than it was in 1989. Beach has developed an "integrative, comprehensive, multi-disciplinary approach" to conservation. Bright, committed, and tenacious, he is a soft-spoken but forceful leader who displays a well-informed fearlessness. As a South Carolina native he understands the peculiar social and political texture of lowcountry thought and culture. While Beach has become famous for his ability to persuade, cajole, push, demand—and even threaten—opponents, the organization has intentionally avoided the "in-your-face" militancy adopted by some environmental organizations across the nation. "We try to build an impression of a group that is very thoughtful, effective, firm but fair," Beach observed in 2004. His longtime colleague Lareau sharpened the point, noting that she "had learned to do environmental activism from the Sierra Club and the Audubon Society. There is a lot of self-righteous indignation in it. Dana taught me to remove the anger and personal emotion, to look at the issue and figure a way to put it forward."[6]

The success of the Coastal Conservation League has not been easily gained, however. The coastal region has long been dominated by a progrowth business climate and a culture devoted to protecting private property rights. Developing a conservation culture in such a bustling region has been a challenge. "For most of our existence," explained Beach, "we have struggled to convince city and county officials, members of the General Assembly, and other South Carolina decision makers of the importance of conservation and smart growth."[7]

Yet the CCL has enjoyed more victories than defeats. Over the years the organization has garnered the support of the local media, especially the *Charleston Post and Courier;* lobbied successfully for more stringent land-use regulations, construction ordinances, and state environmental enforcement efforts; spearheaded resistance to marsh island bridge projects proposed by resort developers; thwarted a new coal-fired power plant to be built on the coast; promoted smart-growth concepts and slowed suburban sprawl; reduced cruiseship conjestion; raised awareness of environmental issues, including climate change and sea-level rise; and helped support numerous conservation land trusts as well as negotiate even more conservation easements. "We became known at first as the group that's going to stop things," said CCL program director Megan Desrosiers. "Now we're trying to effect change to get what we'd like done." Although critics in the real estate sector lambast the CCL for its obstruction of development, even they acknowledge that the Coastal Conservation League is "viewed much more favorably than the development community" in the lowcountry.[8]

The CCL has become especially adept at forging powerful coalitions with other environmental organizations while working collaboratively with local, state, and federal government agencies. In conjunction with the CCL's twentieth anniversary in 2009, the *Charleston Post and Courier* praised the organization for allying so effectively with "other environmental organizations, charitable foundations, and land preservation groups."

The lowcountry media have also been essential allies. Newspapers and television stations have provided regular coverage of conservation-related issues and events as well as editorial support. As a staff member of an environmental organization noted, press coverage of conservation issues and efforts is outstanding: "There are times when we are in the newspaper three times in one day; sometimes we'll be in three times in one week. . . . We are all over the media. . . . The reporters all know us, and we know them. . . . And we're not shy about proposing editorials and drafting editorials for them and doing op-eds. We're very aggressive with the media." The publisher of the *Charleston Post and Courier* acknowledged in 2000 that "this newspaper has editorially supported" the Coastal Conservation League "on many occasions."[9]

Constructive Leadership in a Conservative Region

Creating and sustaining a culture of conservation requires effective and even courageous leadership—on many levels. How Dana Beach and other lowcountry leaders have fostered the culture of conservation in a politically conservative region tells much about the lowcountry's unique heritage and social dynamics.

The ways in which they have worked together to create such a powerful, bipartisan conservation coalition reflect their passion for the lowcountry and its distinctive way of life. As a prominent conservationist stressed, the challenge in the lowcountry is to make its preservation efforts "fit the mindset of South Carolinians." In practice this has often meant focusing the public discourse about conservation more on cultural traditions and quality of life than on ecological concerns. In other words the most effective messaging of the conservation culture has been intentionally conservative. The efforts to protect and preserve natural resources have succeeded to the extent that they have been portrayed as a natural outgrowth of the lowcountry's historic dependence upon and love for the land and outdoor recreation. Love of place remains the most compelling rationale for preservation, and the region's hunters and anglers, most of whom are self-described ideological conservatives, are among the most passionate preservationists. "The environment is viewed nationally as a liberal issue, but in South Carolina, it's not," observed Republican state senator Arthur Ravenel, the former U.S. Congressman who hired Beach as the environmental liaison in his Charleston office in 1987. "Every time you turn around," Ravenel added, when "the polluters, the abusers, and the over-enthusiastic developers want to do something harmful to the environment," the lowcountry conservation coalition springs into action.[10]

Whatever the particular focus or tactical emphasis of the conservation culture's efforts, this much is certain: the quality of its leadership has been a crucial factor helping to punctuate the prolonged dominance ("equilibrium") created by the coastal region's growth machine. The diversity and quality of such leadership—and the ways in which it has accommodated the coastal region's distinctive economy and political culture—have been essential to its success.

Over the years social scientists have identified two primary styles of leadership. The first, called transactional leadership, focuses on the exchanges between leaders and followers, while the second, transformational leadership, highlights a leader's ability to inspire in associates greater productivity, motivation, and integrity. Transformational leadership motivates people to embrace the value and importance of an organization's goals by transcending their self-interest for the good of the enterprise. Such leaders have the ability to encourage others to perform and contribute at levels that transcend what is expected. Transformational leaders, in other words, are more inspirational and educational than simply hierarchical; they *convince* others to perform at a high level rather than simply *direct* them to do so. Transformational leadership is visionary, consensual, ambitious, and energetic. Its goals are often audacious. Transformational leaders are bold; they are willing to take calculated risks; they seek out opportunities for innovation and collaboration. By contrast, transactional leadership is more bureaucratic than bold. It emphasizes authority, power, and control; it asks for predictable levels of performance in exchange for tangible rewards (or punishments). Of course, any particular leader rarely fits neatly into such clear-cut typologies, but the models are useful for making broad distinctions.[11]

For all of the scholarly attention devoted to corporate, military, and political leaders, little has been written about the nature of leadership in the field of conservation advocacy. The lack of scholarly attention is in part a function of the complexity of environmental problems and the administrative and scientific expertise needed for effective advocacy and education. Norman Christensen Jr., the founding dean of the Nicholas School of the Environment at Duke University, argued that environmental leadership must necessarily be multidisciplinary and multidimensional, creative and collaborative: "The solutions to environmental problems (whether climate change, species conservation, or water quality management) demand communication, understanding, and collaboration among diverse disciplines and traditions. The problem solving requires an understanding of basic science-based processes, the roles of humans as problem causers and solvers, and the potential health, emerging and organizational management options that might be applied to a problem." In general leaders of environmental causes have tended to adopt collaborative or "flat" management structures and styles in administering their organizations rather than conventional hierarchical models.[12]

One of the few studies of leadership within conservation organizations was conducted in 2000. The researchers centered their analysis on the degree to which environmental leaders displayed transformational or transactional management styles. "Transformational leaders," the social scientists concluded, "set out to empower followers and nurture them in change. They attempt to raise the consciousness in individuals and to get them to transcend their own self interests for the sake of others."[13]

More specifically, conservation advocacy—especially amid conservative political and social cultures–requires leaders who are passionate but also patient, competent, and resilient. They need to understand the long-term nature of conservation issues as well as the complexity and nuances of environmental challenges. Promoting environmental conservation rarely allows for simple answers or easy solutions; instead it often involves weighing difficult trade-offs. The complexities and compromises embedded in conservation advocacy are often better suited to leaders who are temperate and tenacious rather than strident and impatient, scientific and diplomatic as well as idealistic and militant.[14]

Generalizations about leadership are tricky, however. Leadership effectiveness is an elusive and contextual activity; different situations require different leadership styles. As political scientist Frank Baumgartner recognized, "leadership exists only in relation to the people or organizations to be led; therefore, the understanding of leadership requires an understanding of the range of contexts within which leaders act. . . . The most successful use of strategies depends on the proper fit with the context in which they are being used." The emergence of a conservation culture in the lowcountry has illustrated the necessary relationship between a community's cultural and political context and the style of its conservation leadership. The most successful leaders have practiced what some social scientists have called "master management," a strategy combining the best elements of the transformational and transactional models of administrative leadership.[15]

The example of the conservation culture in the lowcountry, however, also suggests a third type of leadership. Conservation efforts in the coastal region often require cooperation among a variety of local, state, and federal government agencies, elected officials, nonprofit advocacy groups, and engaged citizens. Such efforts involving multiple actors and agencies have fostered what might be called leveraged leadership. Informal collaborations and formal partnerships have been the most effective tools to leverage change in the region. Creating such coalitions has required leaders who can effectively combine both transformational and transactional styles in forming alliances designed to preserve the lowcountry sense of place.[16]

Political cultures often shape the particular tone and texture of conservation cultures. Environmentalism as a contemporary social movement in the United States has long been associated with political liberalism. On one level, therefore, it is surprising to see such an extensive culture of conservation in the lowcountry, a region awash in a social and political conservatism that often drowns out the efforts of environmentalists. In a 2009 Gallup survey South Carolina was rated the sixth most ideologically conservative state in the nation. Yet the diversity of the people promoting more enlightened land-use policies, growth management efforts, and natural resource conservation in the lowcountry defies the conventional association of conservation advocacy with affluent liberals. The leaders of the lowcountry conservation culture encompass a multitude of voices and perspectives. How people coming from such varied backgrounds and representing such different ideological perspectives have coalesced into such an effective conservation coalition illuminates how environmental advocacy can adapt to quite different circumstances. That the environmental advocacy organizations have worked so well together in forging both formal partnerships and informal alliances has been a crucial factor in the success of the culture of conservation. "We all work hand-in-glove," said Elizabeth Hagood of the Lowcountry Open Land Trust.[17]

The deeply embedded conservative culture in South Carolina and the lowcountry has led most conservation leaders to adopt a pragmatic philosophy in their efforts to slow the "growth machine" and to pursue an inclusive strategy in recruiting supporters and forming alliances. Dana Beach exemplifies such an outlook. The man dubbed the "King of Conservation" in the lowcountry has played the role of backroom broker more than public gadfly. While occasionally using lawsuits or organizing public protests, the Coastal Conservation League has spent "more time at the negotiating table than it does on the picket line." Beach has preferred to work with real estate developers, foresters, the U.S. Army Corps of Engineers, and corporations to find creative alternatives to conventional development. In characterizing the approach that he and the CCL have taken,

Beach emphasized that "we promote good development within designated growth areas. We oppose it in conservation areas. It would be profoundly irresponsible of us to oppose all development," Beach said. "We'd lose all credibility." He candidly admitted that "we are unabashedly manipulative. We win. But we certainly do a lot of negotiating. We're realists. We are ultimately strategic opportunists. I would never deny it."[18]

Beach and the CCL have been openly pragmatic in their willingness to work with diverse stakeholders, forge frequent alliances, and embrace necessary compromises. It is for them a delicate balancing act, weighing their ideals and rhetoric against the realities of lowcountry attitudes, traditions, and political and economic power. Beach, for example, has repeatedly emphasized that he is not opposed to economic growth; he instead has stressed the benefits of smart growth. The CCL's official mission is "to protect the natural environment of the South Carolina coastal plain and to enhance the quality of our life of our communities by working with individuals, businesses, and government to ensure balanced solutions." A particularly important factor in the CCL's success has been its ability to bridge the gap between stereotypically "liberal" environmentalists and the more conservative hunting/fishing community in the lowcountry. Both groups want wildlife and "wild" lands preserved, but often for quite different reasons. The balancing act in the lowcountry between development and environmentalism has made the roles and styles of political and community leaders especially important—and even transformational.[19]

Conserving a City

Like Dana Beach, Charleston's Mayor Riley is a dynamic pragmatist when it comes to promoting conservation and preservation in the lowcountry. A Charleston native and former Democratic state legislator, he was first elected mayor in 1975 and has since become widely recognized as one of the most effective—and longest-serving—mayors in the nation. That he was elected president of the U.S. Conference of Mayors attested to his national stature. That he was asked to chair the Berkeley-Charleston-Dorchester Council of Governments (BCD-COG) affirmed his reputation as an elected official capable of transcending parochial interests in favor of regional planning. That he was the first recipient of the Urban Land Institute's J. C. Nichols Prize bolstered his national role in promoting smart growth and environmental stewardship. The Nichols Prize, named for a preeminent city planner and urban developer, is the nation's most prestigious award for progressive land-use planning and community development.[20]

In 1999 the *New York Times* published an effusive profile of Riley by columnist R. W. Apple Jr. It began by saying: "You can't say it about many cities, but you can say it about this one: One man changed its destiny." What distinguished Riley from most mayors, Apple declared, were his integrity and his "genuine passion for his work. He is—dare we use the word in this cynical era?—a true visionary." It was an unflappable, tireless, and innovative Riley who spearheaded

Mayor Joseph P. Riley at the Waterfront Park in Charleston, 2010.
Courtesy of Peter Frank Edwards.

the revitalization of downtown Charleston, led the community's recovery from the devastation of Hurricane Hugo, and creatively accommodated the traumatic closing of the vast Charleston Naval Base. Riley also appointed in 2009 the City of Charleston's first full-time sustainability director to oversee and coordinate all of the city's far-flung efforts to conserve natural resources, farmlands, and waterways.[21]

In his role as mayor for more than three decades, Riley has combined many of the best attributes of transactional and transformational leadership. He is both a visionary bubbling with fresh ideas and a master manager able to implement and oversee complex projects with many moving parts. Inertia is his greatest enemy. "I know my job is to lead" rather than "just to sit around and keep things as they are. It's to make things better." And better things result when a leader sees ways to leverage projects to create multiple benefits. From Riley's perspective the development of the Waterfront Park and the Charleston Aquarium exemplify his effort to help people see the hidden benefits of particular projects. The Waterfront Park, planned and built in the 1980s, preserved a strategic waterfront parcel from commercial development and in the process saved more wetlands from being destroyed.

The park provided a strategic civic space, a public gathering place that celebrates the city's connection to the harbor and entices people to downtown. As Riley explained, "We took the opportunity to restore marsh that had been damaged and recognized . . . that what we were doing was good not only for the environment, but it also brought nature right up to the urban edge." Similarly Riley transformed the effort to construct a downtown, seaside aquarium into much more than a conventional development project. While the city's tourist-dependent business executives promoted the project because of its role as an economic engine, Riley touted its benefits as a community "teaching tool." He helped people see that the aquarium (opened in 2000) would be "a wonderful place for increasing awareness and interest and regard for the environment."[22]

Riley has long believed that enlightened growth management is the most acute strategic issue for Charleston and for the lowcountry region. In a 2000 newspaper interview he said that he most enjoyed "the opportunity to create places of beauty that enhance the quality of life of our citizens and [to conserve] places of beauty that will be around forever." Balancing the forces of economic development with the need to protect and preserve the environment and the region's historical and cultural heritage, Riley believes, requires concrete legal regulations and well-defined boundaries. Vague ideals are not sufficient to control growth. "If you don't have rules," he said in a 2010 interview, and the desire for environmental protection is "purely subjective, development will always win." Precise laws and zoning ordinances facilitate preserving the "balance and scale" of community development. Riley is equally emphatic about the importance of the conservation coalition in the lowcountry being diverse and inclusive. When compared to similar efforts across the nation, the lowcountry culture of conservation enjoys "a stronger consensus . . . that crosses political, philosophical, and party lines." His tactical emphasis on forging innovative public-private partnerships to promote smart growth (new-urbanist design) and regional planning has mirrored Dana Beach's focus on leveraged collaboration rather than ideological/emotional confrontation, even though the two men occasionally differ passionately over particular issues (for example, most recently, the increase in the number of cruise ships making port in Charleston and the proposed construction of new highways). Preservation, Riley insists, is crucial to the community's powerful sense of place, and he is convinced that strenuous efforts to preserve "historic Charleston" and the "lowcountry environment" are essential to the city's flourishing tourism industry and economic development.[23]

Lowcountry Conservation Leadership

Since 1989 Riley and Beach have been the two most prominent leaders within the culture of conservation in the lowcountry. But many others have also contributed to the effort. When residents interviewed for this book were asked to identify the coastal region's conservation leaders, they readily produced a long list of people from all sectors—public, private, and nonprofit. While Riley and Beach were mentioned most often, many other leaders of conservation organizations and allied efforts were frequently cited, including Charlotte Caldwell, a transplant from Massachusetts and former board chair of the Coastal Conservation

League; Emory Campbell, director of the Penn Center on St. Helena Island; James S. "Jimmy" Chandler Jr. (deceased), a tenacious environmental attorney from Pawleys Island who founded the South Carolina Environmental Law Project; Elizabeth Hagood, the first executive director of the Lowcountry Open Land Trust (later serving as a trustee and interim director) and former chair of the board of the South Carolina Department of Health and Environmental Control; Louise Maybank, a Wadmalaw Island resident who helped devise the guidelines for the Charleston County Greenbelt land acquisition program; Coy Johnson, the director of South Carolina Ducks Unlimited; Mary Pope Hudson, former executive director of the Lowcountry Open Land Trust, executive vice president of the Land Trust Alliance, and founder of the South Carolina Land Trust Network; Har-

Elizabeth Hagood, 2010.
Courtesy of Elizabeth Hagood and the Lowcountry Open Land Trust.

riet Keyserling (deceased), a self-described "New York Jewish liberal" transplant to Beaufort who served in the General Assembly and became a dogged advocate of environmental protection; Father Francis Kline (deceased), the dedicated conservationist abbot of Mepkin Abbey, a Trappist monastery near Charleston; Jane Lareau, one of the original and current staff members of the Coastal Conservation League; Mike McShane, chair of the board of the state Department of Natural Resources and chair of the Ashepoo-Combahee-Edisto (ACE) Basin Task Force, and chief executive officer of Nemours Plantation Wildlife Foundation; Chris Marsh, executive director of the Lowcountry Institute on Spring Island; Michael Prevost, the Sewee to Santee Project director for the Nature Conservancy of South Carolina; and, conservation-oriented real estate developers Charles Fraser (deceased), Jim Chaffin, Vince Graham, and John Knott.

Elected officials for whom the culture of conservation has been a priority include conservative Republicans such as former U.S. Congressman and two-term governor Mark Sanford (2002–2010), as well as prominent legislators Chip Campsen, Tom Davis, Ben Hagood, Glen McConnell, and Arthur Ravenel Jr. African American conservation leaders include Thomasena Stokes-Marshall, a long-serving Mount Pleasant Town Council member and Fred Lincoln, the president of the Cainhoy Huger Community Development Corporation.

An especially influential leader in fostering the lowcountry conservation culture was Peter Manigault (1927–2004), an avid outdoorsman who succeeded his father as president and publisher of the Charleston-based Evening Post Publishing Company in 1959. His grandfather, Arthur M. Manigault, was a Georgetown-area rice planter who bought the *Charleston Evening Post* in 1895. The family acquired the *News and Courier* in 1926. The two newspapers were merged to become the *Charleston Post and Courier* in 1991. Under Peter Manigault's leadership the Evening Post Publishing Company acquired ten television stations and fourteen more newspapers, including the *Georgetown Times,* the *Moultrie News* (Mount Pleasant), the *Journal* (James Island and Folly Beach), the *Charleston Mercury,* the *Summerville Journal-Scene,* the *Berkeley Independent,* and the *Goose Creek Gazette.* The company also purchased an international features syndicate as well as large tracts of forest land.

An ardent historical preservationist and environmental conservationist, Manigault grew up in a family "steeped in the history of Charleston and the lowcountry." He was determined to do all he could to preserve the region's natural resources and historic texture. To that end he served on the boards of the National Trust for Historic Preservation and the Lowcountry Open Land Trust. He and his spouse also placed thousands of acres they owned into a conservation easement to preserve it in perpetuity. Manigault also was a major philanthropist, providing significant financial support to coastal environmental organizations and causes.

But perhaps most important, Manigault used his position as publisher of the lowcountry's most influential newspapers to ensure that editors gave steadfast attention—and editorial support—to conservation issues and efforts. "He provided the leadership for the newspapers to make preservation issues important news. He gave ink, he gave space, he gave coverage," Mayor Riley recalled. "Without all that, Charleston would have been a very different place."[24]

Like the Manigaults, many other multigenerational families have committed themselves to preserving the lowcountry's distinctive natural environment. The Lanes of Charleston, for example, have assumed a leadership role in many of the most important conservation efforts.

Charles G. Lane is a founding partner of Holcombe, Fair and Lane, LLC, a lowcountry real estate company specializing in land conservation. He has also served on the boards of virtually all of the region's major conservation organizations: the Coastal Conservation League (chair), Ducks Unlimited, Delta Waterfowl, the Nature Conservancy, the South Carolina Conservation Bank, the Donnelley Foundation, and the ACE Basin Task Force (chair). His brother Hugh Lane Jr., an avid duck hunter along with his brother, is the president and chief executive officer of the Bank of South Carolina, which he helped found. He too is a pillar of lowcountry conservation organizations, having served on the boards of the ACE Basin, the Belle W. Baruch Foundation, the Lowcountry Open Land Trust Board, and the Charleston County Greenbelt Bank Board. That a relatively small number of ardent conservationists serve together on so many nonprofit boards facilitates their taking concerted action on particular projects, threats, or opportunities. As they acknowledge, their "ability to forge consensus and change individual preferences [related to conservation issues] is much easier and less messy in a small, private group than in a large public process."[25]

Charles and Hugh Lane, 2010.
Courtesy of Ben Williams.

The Dynamics of Lowcountry Leadership

Two factors shaped the emergence of the conservation culture in the late 1980s: the quality of environmental leadership in an ideologically conservative region and the leadership's emphasis on the region's peculiar passion for the land. Land—what to conserve/preserve, what to develop—is the fulcrum of the conservation culture. Large national environmental and conservation groups such as the Audubon Society, National Wildlife Federation, and the Nature Conservancy play important roles in the lowcountry. But the more regionally based organizations have been the primary actors shaping the culture of conservation. At the same time, local elected officials, real estate developers, and municipal planners have played important roles. At times their behavior has seemed counterintuitive. For example, individuals who are self-described political conservatives proudly label themselves conservationists when it comes to protecting the land where they were raised and on which they grew up hunting and fishing. Likewise, African Americans, a group that is rarely engaged in conservation efforts in other parts of the country, have become increasingly active in the lowcountry—often for socioeconomic reasons (examples are sweetgrass basket makers and small farmers).[26]

The common thread binding together most of the people leading the culture of conservation is a heritage of outdoor recreation that has blossomed into a passionate pride of place centered on a love for the land. "If we ever did anything right in hindsight," Charles Lane recollected in 2010, "we said that our whole conservation ethic was [centered on] preserving traditional land uses and values. . . . We were pro-hunting, pro-fishing, pro-farming, pro-private property ownership." Mayor Riley likewise applauded the deeply engrained culture of hunting and fishing in the lowcountry for its role in bridging class and racial divisions. The widespread tradition of outdoor recreation has been "very important" to the emergence of the conservation culture because "people are in touch with the land, and they understand the vital importance of the land, and the water, and the air."[27]

Conservative Conservationism

The outdoor recreation heritage has also helped bridge traditional ideological and partisan divides. "The conservation ethic in South Carolina has always been there," explained conservative Republican legislator Chip Campsen. "Most of the people, or many of the people, that are the real movers and shakers in the conservation movement, . . . are hunters and fishermen." Campsen, a lifelong, fifth-generation lowcountry resident who has served in both houses of the S.C. General Assembly and operates a tour boat business in Charleston Harbor, said that whenever he is faced with difficult public policy decisions, he tries to "err on the side of conservation." His efforts led the South Carolina Wildlife Federation to name him Conservationist of the Year, and he has received the Public Service Award from the South Carolina branch of the Nature Conservancy and the Legislator of the Year Award from the Conservation Voters of South Carolina. He described himself as a devoted conservationist and "one of the most conservative members in the General Assembly." He added that the most common theme among the conservation leadership in the lowcountry, white or black, conservative or liberal, "is that all of us live on and work with the land. We are avid outdoorsmen. This is a way of life for us. . . . It is part of the fabric of who we are, Republican or Democrat." Unlike people across the nation who claim the label *environmentalist* by sending a check each year to a national organization such as the Sierra Club, Campsen contended, it is the daily immersion in and "passion for" the outdoors that has shaped conservation leadership in the lowcountry. "It's the folks that are actively involved in the hunting and fishing culture in South Carolina, and the farming culture."[28]

Campsen epitomizes the conservative bent of the conservation culture. Unlike the conservation efforts in most parts of the nation, he explained, where "you usually find environmental policy organizations that are advocating more regulation, more infringement on property rights, more restrictions, that's not the way it is in South Carolina." Campsen was only half right, however. The lowcountry heritage of hunting and fishing—as well as the broader and more intangible "love for the land"—have indeed shaped the culture of conservation.

But, as Mayor Riley pointed out, the region's conservation efforts have promoted new land-use and land planning rules and regulations—as well as direct and indirect limitations on private property rights. Campsen himself acknowledged that growth must be regulated: "At some point, we have to say no to the next subdivision or the next development or the next manufacturer or the next utility or whatever because" there are not "enough natural resources."[29]

Campsen's close friend, two-term Republican governor Mark Sanford, displayed a similar land-preservation-centered conservative perspective. The two men "grew up together, we hunted and fished all our lives" together, and they attended Furman University in Greenville, South Carolina, together. When Sanford served as a congressman representing the lowcountry, the League of Conservation Voters gave him the highest pro-environment voting score of any Republican from the Southeast. "Unfortunately," he recalled, "I was voting against my own party." During Sanford's first term as governor, he appointed Campsen as his chief policy adviser. Over the years they have regularly taken their sons (each has four boys) hunting and fishing. Like Campsen, Sanford is a self-described "conservative conservationist." Although born and raised in Florida, he spent his summers as a youth on the family's three-thousand-acre Coosaw Plantation in what is now the ACE Basin in Beaufort County. Sanford has since inherited the plantation. From his childhood days Sanford was always struck by how different South Florida and the South Carolina lowcountry "looked and felt"—even though they were both coastal communities. He resolved early on to prevent the lowcountry from mimicking South Florida and losing its distinctive sense of place and quality of life. "If we're no more deliberate about anticipating the wave of humanity coming in our direction, then we're going to end up looking just like South Florida. From the standpoint of the conservation movement, I was blessed with a perspective that saw a snapshot of our future, if we didn't do anything to impact what that future would look like."[30]

Although Sanford has long prided himself on being what he called "hard right" or "hard libertarian" on fiscal issues, he explained in a 2010 interview that he has always been "green on environmental issues" because of his family history "on the land" in the lowcountry. "All my life's lessons came from that place," he recalled. "I think to really bond with children to the land, you've got to have them work it." Beautiful land, as in the ACE Basin, he explained, "creates that much deeper bond" between people and nature. Like Campsen, he is a self-described "land-oriented guy" who spent summer days "in a John boat . . . literally like Tom Sawyer and Huck Finn. It was just sort of wondrous, the sense of space and freedom that came with exploring the woods and waters of the lowcountry. I know Chip [Campsen] had some of the same experiences, which is why on conservation issues, I think we've ended up at the same spot." Sanford also believes with Campsen that environmental stewardship is a "biblical principle." So if "one is really conservative, and this is where I would argue that Teddy Roosevelt was a true conservative, you're going to push for conserving financial resources, but you're also gonna' push for conserving land, or air, or sea resources because they are finite in capacity and quantity."[31]

The reverence for outdoor recreation and the primacy of private property rights among so many proponents of the conservation culture helps distinguish the environmental experience in the lowcountry from other regions of the nation. The deeply engrained cultural heritage of fishing and hunting and the reluctance to infringe on private property rights has generated steadfast support for *voluntary* land preservation among otherwise conservative people, many of whom, when asked, view "environmentalists" with suspicion and even disdain. As Sanford stressed, "the conservation movement has its genesis in part in the natural tie to the land, the water." The widespread love for hunting and fishing, reflected in the overwhelming statewide vote in 2010 to protect the right of all people to hunt and fish by a constitutional amendment, has nurtured networks of friendship and shared experiences that have bridged partisan divides. At the same time, the extraordinary dependence of the lowcountry economy on a tourism sector that itself is dependent upon the distinctive quality of the environment has also helped bridge the ideological divide between political conservatives and the stereotypical liberals who have long been associated with the environmental movement. Sanford insists that "the quality of life" in the lowcountry, the "look and feel" of the coastal region, is "absolutely paramount to [the region's] economic success, both from a retirement standpoint [newcomers] and from an investment standpoint . . . [because] in many cases people came here because there was a pretty good quality of life."[32]

Like Sanford and Campsen, many otherwise conservative people see the direct economic benefits of maintaining the lowcountry's majestic beauty. As the conservation-oriented developer Vince Graham explained, the "stewardship ethic" in the lowcountry has obvious roots in the region's love of the land and the religious notion that God created nature to be used—shepherded and preserved. The land ethic also dovetails with the coastal region's conservative heritage. After all, he noted, *"conserve* is the root word of *conservative* and *conservation."* Finally, as Graham explained, conservation in the lowcountry often means good business. The quality of the lowcountry's natural environment is the essential ingredient of its business climate—and vice versa. "If a place doesn't make economic sense," he emphasized, "it will die. If it doesn't meet basic human needs, and I think community is in some sense, for most people, a human need, and then people appreciate beauty."[33]

Still another factor shaping the distinctive coalition making up the culture of conservation is the widespread desire to conserve the lowcountry's heritage of land-based livelihoods because of their centrality to what people refer to as the way of life associated with the coastal region. As Graham stressed, "we've got this wonderful culture and tradition that's born of the blend between African and European heritage, mixed in with food and music and architecture, and farming." He and other leaders of the conservation culture anchor their concept of sustainable development in this desire to preserve the region's cultural heritage and way of life.[34]

Over the years many of the most prominent lowcountry conservationists have self-consciously sought to avoid linking their efforts with the more politically charged term *environmentalism*. As Charles Lane stressed, "all we [the leading conservationists who were born in the lowcountry] talk about is preserving this way of life, this culture, this sense of place." In the promotional materials created for the ACE Basin, for example, Lane and others wanted to avoid or minimize both the ecological rationale for land conservation and the threat of federal enforcement of endangered species legislation. They instead focused on "protecting traditional land use practices, protecting old historic sites, and all these kinds of things" so as to forge unexpected alliances and minimize ideological disputes. Lane and others affirmed that powerful, informal personal relationships undergird the various alliances that have been created to nurture the culture of conservation. As Campsen declared, "you will probably not find another state in the country in which you have land owners and environmental policy organizations working as closely together as they do in South Carolina."[35]

Lane echoed Campsen when he explained that the "formula for success" developed by the lowcountry's conservation culture is both simple and "transportable" to other regions of the country: "You have to have people that live there lead it, and believe in it, and want it, and be passionate about it, and are willing to talk to their neighbors, neighbor to neighbor, and say, 'We live in a special place, these are values we ought to transfer to our children, it isn't our right to destroy these attributes in our lifetime.'" In the ACE Basin, Lane pointed out, large property owners exerted tremendous social pressure on their neighbors to join in the conservation effort. Such a grassroots, relationship-based tactical strategy, he added, constitutes "true conservatism" because it promotes "conservation from a conservative standpoint. If we ever did anything right, it was the decision to promote conservation as an effort to preserve traditional land uses and values. So what we were doing was conserving what we had, the good things that we had, [what] we wanted to preserve and keep." That he and others couched their conservation efforts in language that resonated with lowcountry residents' pride of place and their reverence for outdoor recreation had enabled their success.[36]

The prevailing conservatism among lowcountry conservationists also helps explain the coalition's strategic emphasis on protecting land through purchase or conservation easements. As Lane noted, most of the property owners in the ACE Basin quickly realized "that a conservation easement was the private property owner's right. He always had the right to develop his land; now he had the right not to develop his land. It was sold [by the task force to the property owners] that way. It was never outsiders doing it; it was insiders."[37]

Lane attributes much of his own passion for conservation to his father, Hugh Lane Sr., a prominent Charleston banker and civic leader who owned a lowcountry plantation. The younger Lane remembered that his parents "loved hunting and fishing and the beauty of nature." And he, too, "just fell in love with nature as a young kid" and later grew "interested in land conservation." He has been promoting smart growth long before there was such a term. "My father was a hunter, [and] he would pick me up from school on Friday, and we would drive to the country." Along the way to their country home and a weekend spent in a duck blind, Charles Lane marveled at the relentless suburban sprawl. "I would say, 'Dad, when's this going to stop?'" His father replied: "Your generation is going to figure out how to plan all of this stuff so we can have economic prosperity, but we don't kill the things that made this region so special." Lane's father added that "it's your responsibility when you leave the land to leave it in a better condition than when you found it."[38]

Charles Lane was quick to note that conservation in the lowcountry is not simply focused on the physical environment. It is equally committed to conserving the cherished aspects of the region's distinctive ethno-cultural heritage. He and other conservationist leaders are preoccupied with "preserving this way of life, this culture, this sense of place." And that includes the Gullah-Geechee culture. As Campsen remarked, "I have grown up with that culture around me. I have great appreciation and respect for it. I don't want to lose it. I love places that have not been homogenized by modernity."[39]

Preserving Folkways

The leader who has been in the forefront of the effort to preserve the Gullah culture is Thomasena Stokes-Marshall. Born in the Snowden community outside of Mount Pleasant in 1943, she was three years old when her parents moved the family to New York City. Throughout her childhood, however, she spent the summers with her grandmother back in Mount Pleasant. After a career first as an officer with the New York State Department of Corrections and then as a New York City police detective, she returned to Mount Pleasant in 1993 to care for her ailing mother. Five years later she was the first African American elected to the Mount Pleasant Town Council. Her campaign platform promised that, "if elected, I would work to change the focus of Town Council from making decisions that helped to facilitate uncontrolled growth, to protecting the quality of life for all of our residents. I promised I would work to reduce the Town's growth rate to allow for better management of the Town's resources, address the negative impacts of growth upon our communities, keep our property taxes low, preserve and protect our green spaces, and to expand and improve our roadways and infrastructures."

Once elected, she went to work fulfilling her campaign pledges. Along with three other new council members, she resolved to begin containing suburban sprawl and protecting the town's rural communities from development. "There is a lot of history there [in the black rural hamlets]. Things that are pretty much intact going back 50 years or more," she said. Stokes-Marshall helped implement

Thomasena Stokes-Marshall
at the Mt. Pleasant Sweetgrass Pavilion, 2010.
Courtesy of Ben Williams.

a series of growth-management programs that included limiting the annual increase in building permits to 3 percent for seven years and requiring developers to help pay for the infrastructure expenses of new subdivisions and shopping centers.[40]

Stokes-Marshall admitted that, like many African Americans, she had rarely thought about issues related to environmental conservation—until she moved back to the lowcountry and became a town council member. While living in New York, "I don't think I gave conservation much thought." In Mount Pleasant, however, she began attending zoning hearings at which real estate developers wanted "to turn everything into concrete and mortar." She found that the rural African Americans "who have lived here all their lives, . . . who have farmed the land, who have lived off the land . . . are more in tune with conserving and preserving than those that have migrated from elsewhere." She also discovered that the majority of black people in the Mount Pleasant area, "especially those who have been here all their lives—they would like to keep it like it is, like it was. They are not too keen on all this development. They also feel like outsiders, like others have just come in and taken over their area, and they have had no voice in it." The developers, she stressed, were white, "and they have plenty of money, and they can buy the land and bring about the changes. [With just a few exceptions,] they are not interested in what the people here think should happen."[41]

Stokes-Marshall's election to the town council in 1998 coincided with the town's developing its first comprehensive land-use plan in order to comply with a new state law mandating holistic planning at the local level. "That's when we really started focusing on conservation." She endorsed the elements of the comprehensive plan that required developers to save or replace trees, to create aesthetic buffers, and to provide green space. The developers "raised hell" at such restrictions and mandates, but "we held strong" because "what makes the lowcountry is all the green space, trees, lakes, rivers, creeks—all of those things."[42]

While serving as a town council member, Stokes-Marshall also undertook a conservation project of her own: helping to preserve the Gullah-Geechee heritage in general and the art of sweetgrass basket making in particular. More than three hundred years ago enslaved people from West and Central Africa brought their basket-making handicraft to the lowcountry, and their descendants passed it down from generation to generation. Coiled "fanner" baskets played a critical role in the processing of rice in the eighteenth and early nineteenth centuries. During the twentieth century the intricately woven baskets became popular with tourists, thus providing an important source of supplemental income to many African Americans living near Mount Pleasant in what is known as the East Cooper community. With the dramatic development of the coastal region since the 1960s, most of the natural habitats where sweetgrass flourished were destroyed. Many of the new gated residential communities built during the 1980s and after were constructed in areas where the basket makers had harvested sweetgrass for generations. Basket makers found themselves prohibited from collecting the grass.[43]

Stokes-Marshall became fascinated by the challenges of preserving the distinctive cultural traditions in her community. "One thing that has made me so involved," she recalled, "is it has become a history lesson. I have learned about the basket makers and the Gullah and Geechee people. The more I learn about it, the more I want to hold on to that part of history." To help conserve the region's African American cultural heritage, she became the first executive director of the Sweetgrass Cultural Arts Festival Association (SCAFA), a nonprofit organization founded in 2004. The association orchestrates an annual festival in Mount Pleasant that showcases the basket-making tradition as well as the Gullah cultural heritage. SCAFA also offers programs to educate the public about the heritage of basket making, and it helps coordinate efforts to locate sweetgrass for the basket makers in the lowcountry, including the planting of new stands of grass on both public and private lands. Stokes-Marshall also developed a summer camp for children to learn about the Gullah-Geechee culture and to weave baskets. She said that "the primary focus of holding these camps is to pass on this art form to the next generation. I love that the number of participants has increased, and now there is a nice mix of races and age groups." Stokes-Marshall also took the initiative in getting sweetgrass basket making designated as the state's official handicraft as well as orchestrating the efforts to construct a sweetgrass pavilion at the new Memorial Waterfront Park.[44]

Stokes-Marshall has been relentless in her efforts to preserve key elements of lowcountry culture. Energetic and feisty, she has sought allies and resources from every sector. And she is not easily deterred. "Anyone who knows me will say I'm aggressive," she says. "I have no trouble stepping in when I see a need." The low-country has showered her with conservation awards. Nakia Wigfall, a basket maker and leader of the Sweetgrass Cultural Arts Festival Association, noted that "Thomasena fights hard to help protect and preserve our Gullah/Geechee neigh-borhoods and the materials used to make sweetgrass baskets."[45]

Leveraged Leadership

Whatever their particular motives or goals, the leadership exercised by key low-country elected officials, conservation organizations, and environmental activists has been transformational in its effects. Some of the leaders have operated qui-etly, behind the scenes, in a transactional way; others have developed visible and transformational roles in the promotion of conservation. Whatever their pre-ferred mode, the most prominent leaders of the conservation culture anchor their concept of sustainable environmentalism in their sense of place, and they mani-fest it through powerful personal alliances rooted in their upbringing and con-nection to the lowcountry landscape and residents. Such leveraged leadership is a primary element undergirding the culture of conservation.[46]

The leveraged leadership practiced by so many lowcountry conservationists illustrates what sociologist Caroline Lee has termed the combined power gener-ated by various "conservation coalitions." The conservation coalitions have coa-lesced around the conservative networking strategy adopted by the leaders of the lowcountry conservation efforts: nurturing the widespread support for the idea of preserving the region's cultural heritage, its love of land, history, and culture. The centrality of land preservation cuts across political and social boundaries and accommodates the region's deep-seated commitment to private property rights. It also protects wildlife habitats and scenic beauty. Preserving land from devel-opment also helps protect waterways by reducing runoff. This land-centric em-phasis has enabled the conservation culture to have the widest appeal. Although individual leaders invoke the emotional attachment in the lowcountry to pride of place and the preservation of the region's heritage for different purposes, the result is the same: it enables the conservation coalition to bridge various perspec-tives and particular preservation priorities. By repeatedly talking about conserva-tion as a form of cultural preservation and economic necessity, diverse regional leaders have been able to consolidate their individual priorities into a collective commitment to conserving both natural resources and cultural traditions. Con-servationists in the lowcountry have demonstrated that unlikely allies can in fact become powerful partners. The leverage generated by such coalitions of diverse partners has provided the distinctive energy animating the culture of conservation.

FOUR

The Primacy of Land
and Partnerships

In a 2010 interview Republican state senator Chip Campsen marveled at the burgeoning grassroots involvement with the culture of conservation in the low-country. A generation before, he noted, there had been only a few scattered in-stances of the citizenry engaging issues of land use and environmental quality. Now, he emphasized, civic conservation was intense, widespread, and effective. "If anyone thinks the public doesn't demand conservation," he said, "they need to go to some of these public hearings when some big development is seeking a permit . . . and look at the opposition that's out there. That's the public demand-ing conservation."[1]

Over the centuries the role of natural resources in the lowcountry has shifted from extraction and production to consumption, tourism, and recreation. Land is now used less for husbandry than it is for houses, stores, offices, and motels. How land is used and developed is largely a local issue. Federal and state environ-mental agencies exercise little jurisdiction over land use. Instead such issues are usually left to local zoning boards and planning commissions. It is this localized authority that provides citizens with a chance to participate in decisions affect-ing their immediate environment. However much land-use planning in South Carolina has benefited from greater technical expertise, professionalism, and tech-nological sophistication, it remains an exercise in local political influence and power. Until recent years lowcountry land-use decisions included little public involvement, especially among those who live or work near a proposed project, be it a housing subdivision or a roadway. That has changed as a result of the maturing culture of conservation's influence on public perceptions.

Land is both a form of private property and a public asset; communities as well as individuals have rights at stake where land is concerned. The Cherokee Indian word for land includes many more meanings than simply a reference to a place: it encompasses history, culture, and spirituality. Land in the lowcountry has a similarly holistic connotation. At the same time that land provides a foun-dation for constructing roads, buildings, and homes, it also serves a community by storing, filtering, and purifying water; by providing soil on which to grow food and trees; by creating habitat for wildlife and game animals; by creating aes-thetically attractive green spaces and viewsheds and nurturing mental well-being and spiritual energy. As Aldo Leopold, the preeminent forester, wildlife manager, and conservationist of the twentieth century, wrote, nature "is an interconnected whole; its parts are interrelated. Land is not just a commodity but part of a biotic community." There is "only one soil, one flora, one fauna, and one people," Leopold stressed, which is to say there is "only one conservation problem"—the maintenance of healthy land. A land's health, he said in 1944, "is the capacity for self-renewal in the soils, waters, plants, and animals that collectively comprise the land." How private property owners use their land, he insisted, necessarily affects the surrounding land community. So there is a public interest in how private property is used—and abused. But stern questions arise: how can private landowners be convinced to act in the public interest? What can be done to get people to think in terms beyond their own immediate economic benefit?[2]

Over the years conservationists have employed an array of techniques to encourage and cajole landowners to adopt an ethic of land stewardship. The conservation coalition in the lowcountry has increasingly discussed land not simply as individual parcels of property but as interconnected elements with important ecological connections and ecosystem processes—and historical significance. "Land provides us a common heritage," as Elizabeth Hagood, the executive director of the Lowcountry Open Land Trust, explained in 2011. "It defines what we were and what we will become." The region's intense love of and respect for the land explains, she added, why the lowcountry has developed an "ethic of stewardship that has made us a national leader in land conservation, both private and public."[3]

In addition to ensuring that new residential and commercial development projects integrate conservation premises and practices into their design and governance, the conservation coalition has also focused on the widespread preservation of undeveloped land. For instance, conservation organizations have garnered funds from local and state government sources, as well as from philanthropists and foundations, to purchase many key parcels. In addition, numerous conservation land trusts and easements have added to the growing inventory of conserved land. In 2010 Kate Parks, project manager with the Coastal Conservation League, identified 700,198 acres that have been protected in the coastal counties since 1985 (most of which have been preserved since 1989). That represents a remarkable 16 percent of the total acreage in the coastal counties.[4]

Land as a Cultural Commodity

The land-based emphasis of conservation efforts in the lowcountry reflects the region's distinctive history and culture and especially the long-standing cultural value of private property rights. Land in the coastal areas, explained Dana Beach of the Coastal Conservation League, is viewed as "much more than an economic commodity; it is also a cultural commodity." The lowcountry passion for the land cuts across conventional racial, class, and political divisions. In addition, the coastal region's peculiar historical pattern of land ownership has bolstered a

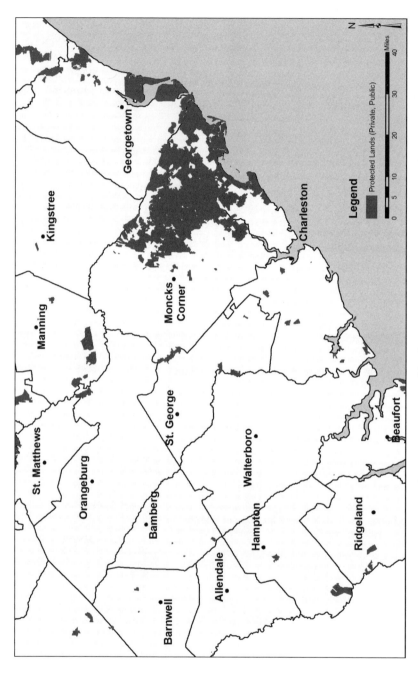

Lowcountry protected lands, 1985. Courtesy of Lisa Shealy and the Lowcountry Open Land Trust.

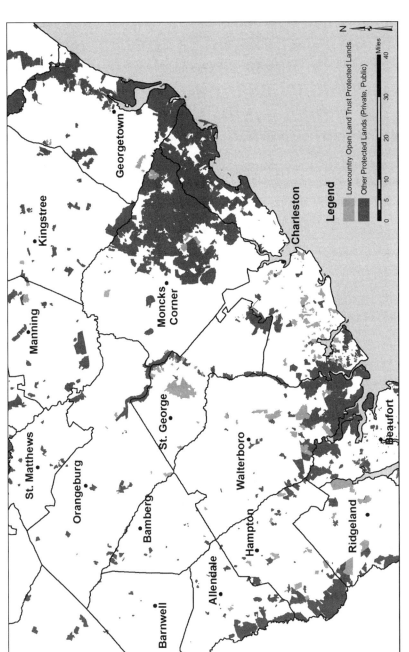

Lowcountry protected lands, 1985–2010. Courtesy of Lisa Shealy and the Lowcountry Open Land Trust.

land-oriented conservation strategy. Because many of the former rice and cotton plantations remained in the hands of a handful of large pulp/paper companies or a small number of wealthy property owners, such as the Atlanta-based media mogul Ted Turner, a few owners of vast acreage can have a dramatic impact by deciding—voluntarily—to set aside some or all of their land as a preserve or trust. These factors, said Beach, "set the stage for a [politically and socially] conservative region to have a discussion about why land conservation matters."[5]

In other regions of the United States, especially in the Far West, environmental activists (to use what is still a highly charged term in the conservative lowcountry) have adopted what might be called a litigious biodiversity strategy. That is, they have repeatedly used the federal Endangered Species Act, signed by President Richard Nixon on December 28, 1973, as their primary tactical weapon in slowing or stopping various development projects. In introducing his comprehensive emphasis on conservation, Nixon told the U.S. Congress in 1972 that the new federal laws, agencies, and programs he would sponsor were intended to generate an "environmental awakening," a "commitment to responsible partnership with nature," and a rejection of the "cavalier assumptions that we can play God with our surroundings and survive." Several conservation organizations in the western states have taken Nixon at his word, using the coercive leverage of federal laws passed in the 1970s and since to force corporations, developers, and federal agencies to abandon or revise projects that would threaten particular species (for example, spotted owls, snail darters, willow flycatchers, wolves, pygmy owls, northern goshawks, desert-nesting bald eagles, and whooping cranes).[6]

There is nothing comparable in the lowcountry to the Center for Biological Diversity in Tucson, Arizona, a small, underpublicized environmental advocacy group with outsized ambitions and remarkable success. Since its founding in the early 1990s, the Center, made up now of fifty-five uncompromising attorneys, biologists, and activists and supported by more than four thousand dues-paying members, has "fashioned itself into the most effective environmental operation you've never heard of." It has used "biological data, legal expertise, and the citizen petition provision of the powerful federal Endangered Species Act" to gain legally binding "protections for animals, plants, and their habitat—first in New Mexico and Arizona, then throughout all eleven western states and eventually into other key areas across the country." On September 6, 1997, the *Albuquerque Journal* reported that "environmental activists in the Southwest, more so than in other regions of the country, are suing to protect endangered species. And they are winning." By 2008 the Center for Biological Diversity had won 90 percent of the five hundred lawsuits it had filed. In the process it had won first-time legal protections for 350 species and seventy million acres of critical habitat. And they had been awarded by court orders hundreds of thousands of dollars to reimburse them for their legal fees. Peter Galvin, a former U.S. Fish and Wildlife Service scientist with a mystical bent who cofounded the Center with Kieran Suckling, calls their take-no-prisoners litigation-centered strategy "going for the jugular."[7]

Effective environmental advocacy, however, can come in many different forms. Lowcountry conservationists, while occasionally resorting to confrontational litigation and militant rhetoric, have taken a different tack from the "in-your-face, take-them-to-court-first" approach of their western counterparts. The South Carolina Environmental Law Project (SCELP), founded in 1987 by the crusading Pawleys Island attorney Jimmy Chandler, has focused its efforts on "forceful legal advocacy" on behalf of an array of conservation groups and concerned citizens. Unlike the Center for Biological Diversity, however, SCELP does not initiate litigation on its own. Instead it provides support to existing environmental advocacy groups.

Similarly, rather than focusing their entire strategy on the adversarial use of federal laws protecting endangered species, the diverse elements of the lowcountry conservation coalition have instead stressed collaborative efforts to protect large parcels of land, often working with individual landowners to arrange voluntary gifts or easements. By designating vast tracts as preserves or by perpetually protecting parcels through land trusts or easements, the conservation community has sought to slow the rate of sprawl, create permanent open spaces, and preserve the region's landscapes and its endangered biodiversity. In doing so they have also become intentional in their efforts to preserve the distinctive quality of life in the lowcountry centered on pride of place, love of land, and the heritage of devotion to private property rights. Hagood explained that her extensive experience negotiating easements or purchases with private landowners in the lowcountry revealed that their primary motivation "is a deep-rooted land ethic indigenous" to the region. "It is unique to the lowcountry in its character and stems from a cultural heritage that values land, family, legacy, and the lowcountry itself." The land ethic is "a stewardship ethic that transcends mere property rights. It encompasses a legacy component that considers multi-generational impacts and responsibilities; it is values-based, placing family, tradition, love of the land and the outdoors on par with or above economic value."[8]

John Rivers Jr., a prominent Charleston corporate executive and conservationist, endorsed the strategy of preserving large parcels when he urged in 2007 that "our political leaders, our conservation groups and our philanthropic organizations . . . as a collective body of unified, concerned citizens, gather our financial and environmental support resources to purchase as much land as possible from willing timber companies and private landowners in order to protect and enhance the quality of life for existing and future generations living in South Carolina." His emphasis on "willing" property owners was an explicit acknowledgement that most South Carolinians—including those sympathetic to environmental protection—would resist any coercive effort by state or local authorities to "take" or "condemn" valued lands.[9]

At the same time that the conservation coalition has adapted its tactics to the prevailing values of the region, it has become increasingly effective at influencing environmental public policies at both local and state levels. The growing visibility and stature of the conservation community have enabled it to challenge the long-prevailing notion that coastal land is simply a commodity to be exploited. Since its emergence in the late nineteenth century, the conservation movement in the United States has professed a simple message: nature is much more than a developable asset; it has many nonpecuniary values. As Aldo Leopold stressed in 1939, a parcel of land is not just a sterile piece of earth to be bought and sold; it hosts a biotic community of interrelated elements; it includes not simply the soil but also encompasses the wildlife, water, ecological dynamics, and human activities occurring on a site.[10]

Another reason why the conservation culture in the lowcountry has focused its strategy on conserving large parcels is because so much acreage was put on the market by pulp/paper and railroad companies during the 1990s and early in the twenty-first century. "Based on market components," said David Liebetreu, International Paper Company's vice president for forest resources in 2006, "our forestlands are worth a lot more to other people than they are to us." Lowcountry conservation organizations, government agencies, philanthropic foundations, and individuals have worked together and at times separately to acquire several large, ecologically valuable parcels, but they are often hard pressed to compete in bidding wars with real estate developers eager to build new golf-centered subdivisions. To take advantage of the opportunity afforded by timber companies selling large swaths of land, the South Carolina General Assembly authorized the Heritage Trust program to issue thirty-two million dollars in revenue bonds to enable it to purchase forest lands put up for sale by timber companies. "This is a once-in-a-generation opportunity to protect thousands of acres of valuable wildlife habitat," stressed John Frampton, director of the South Carolina Department of Natural Resources. The tracts purchased by the state in collaboration with environmental organizations such as the Nature Conservancy, were chosen based on their ecological value (endangered species, stock of hardwoods and softwoods, and proximity to other protected areas.) "It's a great example of private, public, and nonprofit cooperation," said the chief executive officer of International Paper Corporation, John Faraci.[11]

Conservation Tools: Land Trusts, Easements, and Bargain Sales

The conservation coalition has used several methods of acquiring or conserving land. Both city and county governments have purchased land, using general revenues or general-obligation bonds. During the 1990s, for instance, Hilton Head Island raised nearly fifty million dollars for the purchase of green spaces through property taxes, bond issues, grants, and real estate transfer taxes.

Conservation land trusts have become another popular vehicle for conserving land. Land trusts are private nonprofit legal entities created solely for the purpose of conserving land—either by purchase or through donations. Many land trusts are local; others are statewide, regional, or national. The first land trust in the United States was created in the mid-nineteenth century, but there were very few until a century later; since the 1990s, however, the popularity of land trusts has skyrocketed in conjunction with more generous federal and state tax incentives. There were only 53 land trusts in the United States in 1950. By 1980 there were 431, and by 2010 the number had grown to more than 1,700. Almost ten million acres are protected by land trusts nationwide.[12]

Land trusts can conserve all types of land: farms, forests, open spaces, wildlife habitat, urban parks, scenic corridors, wetlands, and waterways. Land trusts typically impose restrictions on the land's access and uses. They can prohibit, restrict, or allow free public access. Many trusts permit limited public recreational activities—hunting, fishing, hiking, canoeing, kayaking, camping, birding, or other environmentally sensitive activities—on the land they own. Some land trust protocols allow for regulated farming, ranching, or logging.[13]

The individuals or organizations that create land trusts often display different motives and use varied methods. Some trusts are created to "preserve" land in perpetuity; others are organized to "manage" the natural resources on the property so as to minimize the environmental impact. Most land trusts purchase or accept donations of land. Landowners may also sell or donate a conservation easement to a land trust. Such easements often qualify for federal and state tax benefits. Easements are an especially valuable tool to preserve and protect property while maintaining the tradition of local control and private ownership. Voluntary easements are less expensive than outright purchases. They involve formal legal documents restricting the property owner's possible uses of all or a part of the parcel. For example, a property owner might formally forego the right to construct additional structures on the property, while retaining the right to plant crops or to hunt or fish on the land. Or an easement can prohibit the property from being subdivided and developed. Such restrictive easements often involve payments to the owners for forgoing their development rights, while enabling them to retain rights of ownership and of farming, forestry, hunting, or other traditional uses. Future owners are bound by the terms of the conservation easement. The nonprofit land trust that brokers the easement is responsible for monitoring the property so as to ensure that the terms of the agreement are not violated. More than forty thousand acres in the ACE Basin were conserved when property owners negotiated easements transferring their development rights to land trusts. In the Charleston and Beaufort areas, however, development rights are more valuable and therefore more expensive to acquire with public funds.[14]

The people who take advantage of tools such as land trusts and easements are often motivated less by profit than by the desire to conserve cherished land in perpetuity. In 1995 Robert Schofield III and his family signed a conservation easement, agreeing not to develop their 762-acre Hasty Point plantation west of Pawleys Island. Schofield explained that the culture of conservation in his family reflected a devotion to the land as well as a sense of spiritual stewardship felt by many lowcountry residents. "The real value of a place is the way it is. We feel like we don't own this land so much as it's been lent to us by the powers that be."

While he could make much more money by allowing his picturesque plantation to be subdivided and developed, "the value to my family would not be there anymore."[15]

Still another land conservation tool used in the lowcountry is called a bargain sale. It occurs when an owner sells property to a nonprofit organization for less than the market price or its appraised tax value. The difference between the market or appraised price and the actual sale price qualifies as a tax-deductible donation to the organization. There are other strategies to conserve land as well—including local, state, and federal government funds earmarked for the acquisition or protection of land parcels. Since the 1980s lowcountry land trusts have taken advantage of all of these resources and methods for conserving or regulating access to hundreds of parcels along the coast.

The effort to preserve huge land areas reflects in part the environmental community's recognition of the state's conservative political texture. Unlike controversial political efforts to impose tighter environmental regulations or zoning codes, land trusts tend to garner bipartisan support because their work is voluntary rather than government-mandated. Willing property owners *choose* to sell their land or restrict its uses through easements. As a reader of the *Beaufort Gazette* declared, "land buying is my favorite method of limiting development. Nobody's rights are violated. No 'taking' [of private property] by zoning." The fact that many land trusts also allow for hunting and fishing also makes them popular among outdoor recreationists. As Hagood acknowledged in 2011, "conservation as a lowcountry ethic is consistent with conservatism. In fact, they both come from the same Latin root, *conservare*, meaning to save or preserve."[16]

Lowcountry Nonprofit Conservation Organizations

Environmental organizations are the foundation of a culture of conservation, for they serve as developers and agents of its identity. They also play the major role in shaping environmental politics and policies as well as mobilizing public opinion and activism. In 2006 the Gaylord and Dorothy Donnelley Foundation funded a study of five regionally focused conservation organizations that had exercised the most significant impact on environmental opinions, policies, and projects in the lowcountry. The data reveal that the growing professionalization, sophistication, and resources of these organizations greatly influenced the development of the region's culture of conservation. But perhaps most important to their success has been their unusual ability to work together on a variety of strategic initiatives and public policy changes.[17]

Staff members of the five environmental organizations interviewed by the Donnelley Foundation highlighted the unique challenges of promoting conservation in a conservative state. Several of those interviewed admitted that they often avoid using the term *environmentalist* to describe themselves or their organization; instead they use the term *conservationist* because it has a more positive connotation in the region. The staff members acknowledged that they cannot afford to be caricatured as "tree-huggers" or "extremists." A Ducks Unlimited staff member reflected the conservative tenor of the hunting/fishing organizations by admitting that he shared the widespread bias in the state against militant environmentalists: "I don't think of anyone good when I think of an 'environmentalist.' I always say that I'm a 'conservationist.' Because a lot of people think, if you're an environmentalist, you want to lock it [the land] up and don't do anything with it, whereas conservation is more about wise use, whether it's consumptive or non-consumptive use." A Coastal Conservation League staff member offered a variation on the theme when he contended that "90 percent of the American public believes that [land-use/development] decisions are made in the backroom, and they're made between dishonest politicians and dishonest developers. They don't like environmentalists, but they don't like developers either. And they think conservationists are a good balance, a necessary evil, a watchdog, and that's the word that came up repeatedly [in public surveys]; you wouldn't necessarily want to have them [conservationists] in your house, but you want them outside barking."[18]

And what is the role of such conservation watchdogs? Coastal Conservation League staff members expressed their desire to "guide growth" in the lowcountry and "to maintain in a meaningful way, where it's real, lowcountry culture, lowcountry [sense of] place. . . . We want [to conserve] our actual lowcountry."[19]

The culture of conservation's encouragement of private property owners to preserve parcels of land voluntarily has helped bridge partisan political differences. Although the rights of property owners and developers have long been considered sacrosanct in South Carolina, lowcountry conservationists have used the court system to oppose or modify residential, commercial, and industrial projects that posed a direct threat to the region's quality of life. But the most distinctive successes of the lowcountry conservation coalition have been outdoors rather than in courtrooms. Over the past quarter century the conservation coalition has focused on preserving land through the use of land trusts and easements—or outright purchases.

The land-preservation-centered strategy has elicited the support of an eclectic network of organizations and activists that span the ideological spectrum—environmentalists, hunters and anglers, natives and newcomers, property owners, and political leaders of both parties. In the spring of 2000, for example, the South Carolina General Assembly, controlled by Republicans, passed the Conservation Incentives Act. It provided tax incentives to property owners who permanently restricted the uses of their lands through conservation easements. In signing the bill, the then governor Jim Hodges, a Democrat, said that such easements would "respect property rights, reduce property taxes, and preserve our environmental treasures—all at the same time." Chip Campsen, who authored the Conservation Incentives Act when serving as a Republican representative in the General Assembly, explained that he and other political conservatives supported such tax breaks because "you can't do this kind of conservation through legislation or zoning ordinances. You need to build incentives for conservation if you are going to conserve big chunks of habitat."[20]

The emphasis on land trusts and conservation easements in the lowcountry also reflects in part the region's textured history and potent pride of place. In 2005 Cindy Baysden, the executive director of the Beaufort County Open Land Trust (the first in South Carolina), revealed that many people decide to protect their land with conservation easements not for the money or the tax deduction but purely out of a desire "to preserve a sense of history and a sense of place." People living along the coast have long viewed land as the region's primary asset and its most cherished amenity. As a staff member with a lowcountry conservation organization explained, "people in this state are [unusually] interested in what happens to the land."[21]

From the first arrival of humans along the Carolina coast, the land has exercised a powerful influence in the lowcountry, often bordering on the sacred. Of course, people over the centuries have focused on the land for different purposes. During the seventeenth and eighteenth centuries the Lords Proprietors managed their Carolina lands solely for the purpose of economic gain, largely from the cultivation of rice and indigo. With the Confederacy's defeat in the Civil War and the subsequent decline of the rice and cotton cultures, lowcountry residents were left with little other than the land. Many residents were forced into subsistence farming, some as owners, more as tenants or sharecroppers. They were "dirt poor" but land rich; they had little money, but they had the land. They had little stature or power, but they had the land. They had little education, but they had the land. It was the land that provided the lowcountry with what Scarlett O'Hara in the classic Civil War film *Gone with the Wind* called "the only thing that lasts."

Staff members of the region's conservation organizations repeatedly highlighted in interviews the powerful love of the land in the lowcountry as the primary factor nurturing efforts at environmental protection. Some noted the centuries-old practice of exploiting natural resources and human beings (slave- and low-wage-labor) that "has shaped the social constitution of this state and still does." Yet over time the land was invested with social as well as economic value. Over many generations people in the lowcountry, especially men, have bonded with their children by participating in various outdoor activities: hunting, fishing, and farming. As a result the allegiance to the land transcends monetary valuations. Dana Beach remarked that "land becomes more than an economic commodity; . . . it becomes a cultural one. This sets the stage for a conservative state to have a discussion about why conservation matters." Elizabeth Hagood agreed. She stressed that the deeply embedded "land ethic" in the lowcountry "is the prime-mover of conservation" efforts. "It is the lowcountry land ethic that has produced a conservation movement in the lowcountry; not a conservation movement that has produced a conservation ethic."[22]

Aesthetic values are also significant factors in stimulating environmentalism. The staff members of conservation organizations universally expressed delight in the variety of landscapes and wildlife habitats in the lowcountry: urban, suburban, exurban, rural, wetlands, and beaches. They also felt affirmed by the growing number of lowcountry residents who support efforts to conserve and protect the environment. And they generally highlighted the coastal region's distinctive texture and history as a factor shaping the culture of conservation. To them the prevailing land ethic is palpably different from that of the rest of the state and of the South Atlantic region. Said a Ducks Unlimited staff member, "South Carolina, to me, comes down to the lowcountry, and the rest of the state just seems to be a different place entirely." Another staffer stressed how many people in the lowcountry had grown up engaging in outdoor recreation: "Among hunters and fishermen, there's a real strong land ethic, whether they own the land or not, people who are tied to the land in that way. There is a real profound community of hunters and fisherman who passionately love their areas. It's as important as the life of their kids."[23]

Connectedness to the land was perhaps the most consistent motive mentioned in interviews with residents as well as the staff members of conservation organizations. An executive with the Lowcountry Open Land Trust explained that "without the connection to the land, people drift away [to other priorities]. There are lots of other technical and scientific reasons to do land conservation, but really the underlying thing is: what is the benefit to the people? And I think the benefit to the people is that it maintains their identity." The sense of identity with the land is indeed powerful, but it also has different meanings for different people. The "reality of conservation," said Beach, "is that people who do it bring their own agenda."[24]

Protecting the land—for biological, aesthetic, historic, cultural, recreational, and economic reasons—has become a deeply felt principle rather than simply a casual preference. Lifelong conservationist Charles Lane views land trusts and easements as the best tools for cementing a family's often multigenerational ties to the land and protecting the region's ecology. "We have a responsibility to be good stewards and pass it on to the next generation," Lane believes. "When families and neighbors get together and make a commitment to keep the land the same time for their children, and their children's children," he explained, "it insures that everyone will have access to the same freedom of open space and nature."[25]

The strategic emphasis of environmental organizations and individual environmentalists on land trusts and conservation easements to mitigate the negative effects of unrelenting residential and commercial development has achieved extraordinary results. Private land conservation has been facilitated both by a growing presence of not-for-profit entities, particularly land trusts, and important new funding sources, largely government-financed, for either land acquisition or the purchase of conservation easements.[26]

In December 2007 the editors of *Bluffton Today* reflected on the modern development of the South Carolina coast and applauded the growing success of the conservation community in preserving large tracts of land. "We've all learned some hard lessons from the lowcountry land boom of the past 30 years. We've slowly come to the realization that the best way to slow growth is to take land out of the reach of developers." They acknowledged that growth was inevitable in the lowcountry. "There's no gate to close or bridge to burn that will keep people away." While the advent of comprehensive long-range planning and zoning restrictions by counties and municipalities was improving the impact of development on the environment, the best solution for the lowcountry would continue to be the "preservation of open space with combinations of public money and private goodwill" facilitated by the earnest efforts of the various nonprofit conservation organizations focused on the lowcountry.[27]

Among the most prominent nonprofit conservation organizations active in the lowcountry are the Coastal Conservation League, the Conservation Voters of South Carolina, the South Carolina Environmental Law Project, the Nature Conservancy, Ducks Unlimited, the Trust for Public Lands, the American Farmland Trust, the Audubon Society, the Lowcountry Open Land Trust, Edisto Island Land Trust, the Beaufort County Open Land Trust, the Lord Berkeley Conservation Trust, and the Southern Environmental Law Center. Of course, there are many other organizations in the lowcountry participating in the conservation coalition. Some of them are quite small; others are large national organizations that, for a variety of reasons, have not developed a significant role in the lowcountry.[28]

Some of the most active conservation groups, such as the Nature Conservancy and the Audubon Society, focus on preserving particular habitats; others incorporate broader elements of the region's natural, cultural, and agricultural heritage. While local conservation groups such as Lowcountry Open Land Trust, the Beaufort County Open Land Trust, and the Lord Berkeley Conservation Trust help protect "natural areas" or "wildlife habitat," their easements also include commercial farms and forests. Such broader conservation efforts emphasize the productive capacity of the land while often regulating farming, ranching, or forestry activities. While each conservation organization has a distinctive mission, there is considerable overlap among the activities of the organizations in that they are all dedicated to protecting significant properties from development (additional or inappropriate) and maintaining the lowcountry's cultural heritage and its landscapes.

The (South Carolina) Nature Conservancy (1978)

Founded in 1951, the Nature Conservancy (TNC) is a national environmental organization with operations in all fifty states. (It also has an international presence.) It calls itself the "leading conservation organization working around the world to protect ecologically important lands and waters for nature and people." Although TNC was involved in South Carolina in the 1960s, it did not charter a state chapter until 1978. Since then it has focused its efforts in the lowcountry on forging partnerships to leverage its influence and its monies. For example,

TNC's first South Carolina project was a collaboration with the Audubon Society. In 1969 they created the 3,400-acre Francis Beidler Forest Sanctuary (since expanded to 12,500 acres) near Harleyville, within Four Holes Swamp, which stretches sixty-two miles from Calhoun County to the Edisto River. It includes perhaps the largest stand of virgin-growth bald cypress and tupelo gum trees in the world. According to TNC, the Beidler Forest project started their "tradition of partnering with other conservationists."[29]

The South Carolina chapter of TNC has since conserved more than 321,000 acres and has grown from 252 members in 1978 to more than 8,500 members. It has played a significant role in the development of several "landscape-scale projects" in the lowcountry, including the much celebrated ACE Basin southwest of Charleston and the Winyah Bay Bioreserve encompassing more than a one-half-million-acre watershed formed by the Black, Pee Dee, Little Pee Dee, Sampit, and Waccamaw Rivers, including the state's largest tidal freshwater wetlands. TNC also helped to promote the passage of the South Carolina Conservation Bank Act (2002).

While active statewide, the South Carolina Nature Conservancy focuses on the lowcountry region. A sense of urgency animates its activities. In 2004 Joe Hamilton, the Conservancy's South Lowcountry (from Beaufort south to the Savannah River) project director, said the coastal region had two choices: "It can preserve land, tens of thousands of acres, from development, or it will change into something else. And you don't want to be here for that something else." The conservancy purchases land directly or, more often, it forms collaborations with like-minded organizations to acquire land. Joseph H. Williams, a South Carolina native and former Oklahoma oil executive who retired to Spring Island and served as a South Carolina Nature Conservancy trustee, said the organization understood the unique political and social dynamics of the lowcountry and adapted its tactics accordingly. Because much of the undeveloped property left in the lowcountry in the 1990s and the early twenty-first century was owned by corporations, especially pulp/paper companies, the state's Nature Conservancy sought to work with them. Collaboration was more effective in saving land than contentiousness. "The Nature Conservancy," Williams explained, "believes that people of moderate persuasions can do radical things in a quiet way without being confrontational." He highlighted the Nature Conservancy's evolving focus on conserving large areas. "Early on," he said in 1998, "they [the Nature Conservancy] made the mistake of saving pretty projects. They discovered that you have to set larger priorities . . . in order not to exhaust your resources. . . . If you are going to make a difference in conservation today, you have to do larger-scale projects."[30]

A prime example of the Nature Conservancy's habitat-size-centered strategy is the acquisition of entire islands—freshwater, marsh, and barrier—so as to create self-contained habitat preserves. In 2004, for example, the Conservancy purchased 1,018-acre Jeremy Island, across the intracoastal waterway from McClellanville.

Lowcountry Nonprofit Conservation Organizations

Organization	Type of group	Region of focus, S.C. office	Staff	S.C. office staff
Lowcountry Open Land Trust	Land trust: voluntary conservation easements on property	Lowcountry of South Carolina	7	4 full-time, 3 part-time
Southern Environmental Law Center	Environmental litigation	South Carolina	Approx. 70	4 full-time
(South Carolina) Coastal Conservation League	Multifaceted advocacy: political, legal, grassroots	Coastal plain of South Carolina	25	25
Ducks Unlimited	Wetlands conservation, land protection, some policy advocacy	South Carolina, North Carolina, Georgia, Florida	Approx. 300	7
The Nature Conservancy	Land management and conservation	South Carolina	Approx. 3,000	27
Penn Center	Historical and cultural preservation	Lowcountry of South Carolina	N/A	21

Established	Budget	Members	Mission
1985	$700,000	500	"to protect and foster voluntary conservation of the irreplaceable Lowcountry forests, farmland, open spaces, wildlife habitat and wetlands, thus helping to conserve forever our community's unique sense of place and quality of life"
1986; South Carolina office 2008	Not disclosed	N/A	"to use the full power of the law to conserve clean water, healthy air, wild lands, and livable communities throughout the Southeast"
1989; South Carolina office	$2 million	S.C. approx. 3,000; 4,000 overall	"to protect the natural environment of the South Carolina coastal plain and to enhance the quality of our life of our communities by working with individuals, businesses and government to ensure balanced solutions"
1937	Not disclosed	U.S. 643,000; worldwide 773,360	"to conserve, restore and manage wetlands and associated habitats for North America's waterfowl. These habitats also benefit other wildlife and people"
1951; South Carolina office 1970	$448 million	More than 1 million	"to preserve the plants, animals and natural communities that represent the diversity of life on Earth by protecting the lands and waters they need to survive"
1862	Not disclosed	N/A	Preservation of the Sea Island and Gullah history and culture

The Conservancy then sold the island to the U.S. Fish and Wildlife Service, which incorporated it into the adjacent Cape Romain National Wildlife Refuge, which it manages.

The Lowcountry Open Land Trust (1985)

In 1985 a group of Charleston-area conservationists, frustrated by the slow pace of governmental efforts to protect and preserve lowcountry habitats, formed the Lowcountry Open Land Trust (LOLT). Founded in 1986, it is a nonprofit organization dedicated to working with private property owners, including corporations, to acquire and protect parcels or to provide conservation easements so as to restrict development in perpetuity. Initially LOLT focused on protecting tiny Parkdale Island (now called Alge Island) along the Stono River, a tidal channel southwest of Charleston. When area residents learned of a plan to build condominiums on the small island, they formed a nonprofit organization and put it under a conservation easement. The nonprofit entity was then turned over to a board of directors formed to create LOLT in 1986. Since then LOLT has expanded its efforts across the entire lowcountry region. LOLT protects one-quarter of all the land on the forty-three-square-mile Wadmalaw Island, south of Charleston, thousands of acres of former rice fields and plantations; it also added thirty-four thousand protected acres to the ACE Basin and helped protect the Ashley River Historical District. By 1995 the number of people interested in conservation easements had soared. "Things are booming here. It's as if voluntary conservation of land has come of age," said then LOLT executive director Megan Gallagher. "It's of extraordinary interest to people." Since 1985 LOLT and private landowners have protected hundreds of parcels throughout the coastal plain representing more than eighty-five thousand acres, from the Savannah River to north of Georgetown. LOLT "has dramatically increased the pace of conservation of our watershed," noted Norman Brunswig, executive director of the state chapter of the Audubon Society. Like the Coastal Conservation League, LOLT is "committed to a collaborative approach to conservation. One of the goals of our land protection program is to strike a balance between resource protection and human (landowner) needs."[31]

Southern Environmental Law Center (1986)

In contrast to many regional conservation efforts across the country, the lowcountry conservation culture has preferred negotiation and consensus over litigation and confrontation. Yet there have been important instances when litigation or the threat of legal action has been used effectively, especially in circumstances involving conflicting interpretations of federal and state environmental laws. The Southern Environmental Law Center (SELC), established in 1986 and headquartered in Charlottesville, Virginia, is the least visible of the major conservation organizations operating in the lowcountry, but it has played an important role behind the scenes in shaping the culture of conservation. Its founder, Rick

Middleton, recalled that the SELC was "born out of a love of the South, its natural treasures, and its strong sense of place." The SELC, which employs forty attorneys (the majority of whom have been with SELC for at least fifteen years), "use[s] the power of the law to protect the environment and health of the Southeast."[32]

In 2006, in conjunction with the organization's twentieth anniversary, SELC revisited its strategic priorities. It thereafter decided to continue to "increase . . . [its] litigation capacity" and added a new priority: "help address global warming and lead the South toward a new energy future." The organization has identified several "greatest hit projects" that include challenging the proposed construction of new highways that could increase sprawl, ensuring the implementation of the Clean Air Act, preserving "special" places, and enforcing water-quality protections. The Charleston SELC office has been quite active in the lowcountry, usually working with local environmental organizations to thwart activities endangering the coastal environment, including efforts to fill in wetlands, build major highways on barrier islands, and construct more coal-fired power plants.[33]

The South Carolina Coastal Conservation League (1989)

Executive director Dana Beach of the Coastal Conservation League (CCL, originally the South Carolina Coastal Conservation League) has practiced what he calls a pragmatic approach to environmental issues that combines public policy advocacy with a passion for land preservation. "There is a relationship between good public policy and private conservation," he said in 2003. "One of the great enemies of private conservation is capricious government." In addition to numerous projects protecting or preserving thousands of acres of rural lands, the CCL has facilitated the passage of progressive, comprehensive land-use plans for various lowcountry municipalities and counties and helped push through new zoning codes designed to combat sprawl. Eric Meyer, a former land-use program director at CCL, explained that the organization favors an "inside-outside" strategy, encouraging growth in already developed areas in order to take advantage of existing infrastructure while restricting sprawl in undeveloped areas. "People want to live on the coast because it offers an incredible quality of life," Meyer noted in 2004. "The Coastal Conservation League is not opposed to growth. We're just concerned with how [best] to accommodate that growth. State and local policies [have historically] tend[ed] to perpetuate urban development, and if that happens we'll continue to see less and less coastline, more urban sprawl, traffic problems and loss of natural habitat."[34]

Thanks in part to the efforts of CCL, a widespread conservation ethic has crystallized in the lowcountry since 1990. Even groups that habitually oppose restrictions on development or private property rights have softened their stance as the result of the growing conservation ethic in the lowcountry. Mark Nix, the executive director of the South Carolina Landowners Association, insisted in 2005 that he was not simply "promoting unbridled growth but rather well-planned growth geared towards the benefit of the entire community."[35]

Ducks Unlimited (1989)

One of the largest and most influential groups making up the lowcountry conservation coalition is made up of people passionate about hunting and fishing. Such outdoor recreation enthusiasts, many of whom represent multigenerational kinship networks in the lowcountry, sometimes make for strange bedfellows with other conservationists whose motivation is centered on ecological or aesthetic concerns. Although they often differ in their political orientation and cultural demography, sports enthusiasts and conservation advocates in the lowcountry have forged numerous alliances to protect coastal habitats, especially the wetlands and waterways frequented by migratory waterfowl.

Ducks Unlimited (DU), having begun its South Carolina chapter in 1989 (the national group was established in 1937), is one of the most important not-for-profit organizations working to enhance the quality of hunting and fishing in the lowcountry by preserving habitats, not just for waterfowl but for all wildlife. Although its fifteen thousand members are primarily hunters, Ducks Unlimited shares a common concern with the lowcountry's other environmental organizations: unchecked development is gobbling up some of the most valuable wetlands along the coast. Members succinctly expressed their concern by creating a popular bumper sticker: "Hunters against Sprawl." Ducks Unlimited has focused its resources on promoting conservation easements. The South Carolina chapter leads the nation in the number of conservation easements it has established or facilitated. The chair of the state chapter stressed in 2006 that the key message of S. C. Ducks Unlimited is: "It is not necessarily about duck hunting. It's about preserving habitat."[36]

The Penn Center (1862)

The most distinctive conservation organization in the lowcountry is the Penn Center on St. Helena Island, near Beaufort. It is the fulcrum of lowcountry efforts to preserve Gullah culture. Established in 1862 by two white women missionaries and supported financially by northern Quakers, it was the first school in the nation to educate freed slaves during and after the Civil War. By 1900 the school had changed its name to Penn Normal, Industrial and Agricultural School, and it had shifted its educational focus to vocational training. African American students from across the lowcountry could receive training as teachers, carpenters, shoemakers, and blacksmiths as well as in the agricultural sciences. When the school closed in 1948 the Penn Community Services Center took its place, focusing its programs on improving the quality of life for lowcountry African Americans. It offered day care programs for island children and also provided health education classes. During the Civil Rights Movement of the 1960s, Martin Luther King Jr. and the executives of the Southern Christian Leadership Conference often used the Penn Center for leadership retreats and strategic-planning sessions.

In 1974 it was named a National Historic Landmark. In the early 1980s it was renamed the Penn Center.[37]

The relentless encroachment of resort developers on the sea islands during the 1980s caused great concern among members of the Gullah community, environmentalists, and historical and cultural preservationists. To deal with the threat the Penn Center joined the Coastal Conservation League in 1992 to launch the Sea Islands Preservation Project. Its mission is to safeguard the Gullah heritage and ensure its sustainability by helping residents become economically self-sustaining. The leadership of the Penn Center concluded that local residents could "no longer sit back to wait for other people to make their decisions for them." It was now imperative for them "to play a part in that decision making."[38]

During the mid-1990s the Penn School for Preservation, a program of the Penn Center, trained property owners and public officials to manage growth so as to preserve Gullah-owned lands while bolstering the traditional livelihoods dependent upon the natural environment: shellfish harvesting, farming, and basket making. The Center created an annual educational and training program for community leaders and public officials, both black and white. The program provided community leaders with the tools needed to protect heirs' property and defend themselves against developers: zoning restrictions, land-use planning, and legal assistance. The culminating project of this leadership program was the creation of a comprehensive development plan for St. Helena Island that would maintain its rural character. In the process of learning how to plan for sustainable development, the participants—retirees, elected officials, government workers, entrepreneurs, and small-business owners, domestic workers, ministers, and grassroots community organizers—formed new social and political networks. For some of the African American residents who participated in the leadership program, it was exciting to learn that "we have a lot of white people on this Island who are concerned about the future of the Island." Other programs hosted by the Penn Center have nourished African American handicrafts through the creation of a Folk Arts School and promoted the preservation of historic structures. Emory Campbell, former executive director of the Penn Center and a native of nearby Hilton Head Island, grew concerned about sprawling development in the lowcountry that had pushed many African Americans from their ancestral lands. To address the challenges posed by profit-centered development, he worked with Beaufort County officials to have St. Helena Island designated a conservation district.[39]

Conservation Partnerships

During the late 1980s and early 1990s the emergent conservation organizations in the lowcountry had more passion than power. None of them had the financial strength, political influence, or technical expertise to carry the movement. To their credit the leaders of the organizations recognized this reality and resolved early on to combine their assets through creative alliances. One of the distinguishing strengths of the conservation culture in the lowcountry has been the extraordinary willingness of conservation organizations, government agencies, corporations, property owners, foundations, and philanthropists, despite quite different missions, motives, and constituencies, to communicate, cooperate, and collaborate. As a staff member of a conservation organization stressed, "When you pull in a network, you maximize the chance that your initiative will succeed." There has been a remarkable "lack of territoriality amongst the conservation people," she added. Diverse coalitions that bring together conservation organizations, government agencies, philanthropists, elected officials, and property owners not only generate social capital and provide opportunities for consensus; they also are politically popular. Another staff member stressed that "when opposed people lobby together, politicians really like it." The ability of partnerships to leverage the resources and clout of the individual participants makes the partnerships worth the effort. As an official with a federal environmental agency in the lowcountry concluded, "'partnerships' is the key word, and the more partnerships you get, the better it is." Charles Lane affirmed that the scope and variety of "collaboration is unique" within the conservation culture. The lowcountry has benefited from a remarkable number of unlikely, complex partnerships centered on particular projects that have changed the face of conservation. Three of these elaborate project-based alliances deserve highlighting: the ACE Basin, Sandy Island, and the crafting of legislation to create the South Carolina Conservation Bank.[40]

The ACE Basin (1988)

A tipping point of sorts in the emergence of the conservation culture in the late 1980s was the ambitious effort in 1988 to create what came to be called the ACE Basin. (The acronym refers to the three tannic tidal rivers—Ashepoo, Combahee, and Edisto—that drain 350,000 acres of woods, swamps, and relic rice fields before forming the estuary between Charleston and Beaufort at St. Helena Sound.) The ACE Basin is a unique public/private partnership that has restricted almost two hundred thousand acres for sustainable uses and preservation; it now has federal conservation status as one of the largest protected ecosystems on the Atlantic coast. The ACE Basin project illustrates the primary strategy of the lowcountry conservation coalition: to counterbalance development by preserving—or restricting activities on—large ecologically strategic tracts of land. These ecosystem-size projects reflect the way environmental organizations, property owners, and government agencies have worked together on complex, signature projects in the coastal region. They also highlight the distinctive blend of motives and methods displayed by the region's conservation community.

The alarming rate of residential and commercial development in the lowcountry during the 1980s sparked numerous efforts to preserve and protect the region's natural areas, watersheds, and cultural heritage. Yet most of those efforts were relatively small initiatives undertaken by individual environmental organizations or state or federal agencies. In 1988, however, that fragmented practice changed when a group of diverse organizations—Ducks Unlimited, the South Carolina Nature Conservancy, the South Carolina Department of Natural Resources, and the U.S. Fish and Wildlife Service—were recruited by concerned property owners to form an unlikely coalition representing conservationists, hunters and anglers, farmers, government agencies, and corporations. They called themselves the ACE Basin Task Force. The vast ACE Basin, named in 1992 by the Nature Conservancy as one of the twelve "Last Great Places in the United States," includes nine marsh and barrier islands, upland pine forests, bottomland hardwood forests, cyprus swamps, and freshwater marshes.

The ACE Basin Task Force greatly expanded the conventional notion of conservation. In the 1930s the preeminent conservationist Aldo Leopold said that the "impulse to save wild remnants [of nature] is always . . . the forerunner of the more important and complex task of mixing a degree of wildness with utility." It was that "more important and complex task" that guided the ACE Basin Task Force members. They did not want to create a tightly restricted wilderness watershed and wildlife refuge in which human access would be restricted; they instead wanted to expand the notion of a preserve to include the conservation of "traditional" human activities (such as farming, shellfish harvesting, hunting, and fishing) and to safeguard the "rural character" of one of the largest undeveloped estuaries along the Atlantic coast and one of the lowcountry's greatest natural treasures. While allowing property owners to continue to farm, log, hunt, and fish, the ACE Basin maintains the area's historical ambiance while restricting the industrial and resort development characteristic of much of the state's coastal zone in the past thirty years.[41]

To halt the encroachment of sprawling development from Charleston and Beaufort, the task force sought to use all available tools—easements, designated federal Wildlife Management Areas (WMA), Wildlife Refuges, federal research centers and reserves, and land donations and purchases—to protect a massive contiguous area of lowcountry landscape. Billionaire Ted Turner was the first private landowner—of many—to place a conservation easement on his property at Hope Plantation in the basin. In 1991 the Westvaco Corporation placed seventeen thousand acres of timberland under the umbrella of the basin's protective covenants. Seven years later the Westvaco Corporation (now MeadWestvaco), the Lowcountry Open Land Trust, and Nemours Wildlife Foundation joined the task force. By then the amount of formally protected land in the 350,000-acre ACE Basin had grown to 128,000 acres, including dozens of private plantations. Today the protected property is almost 200,000 acres, an area comparable to the size of a national park and thereby large enough to protect the region's biodiversity.[42]

Although today the ACE Basin looks wild and pristine, the imprint of human hands remains a vital part of its heritage. During the eighteenth century many of the hardwood forests in the basin were cleared to create rice fields, the remnants

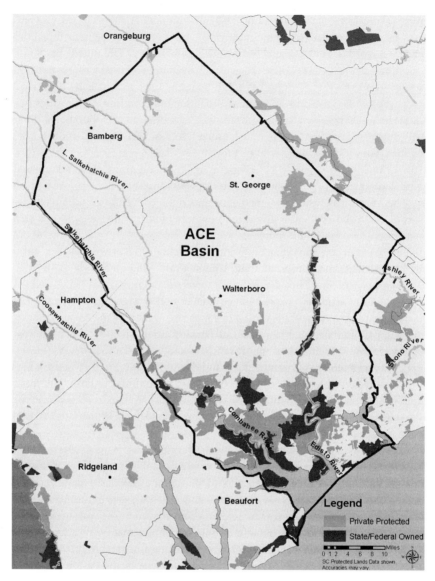

Protected lands in the ACE Basin. Courtesy of
Lisa Shealy and the Lowcountry Open Land Trust.

of which remain visible. When the rice economy died out in the late nineteenth century, many of the plantations were bought by wealthy sportsmen and turned into hunting retreats. "The wildlife of the area is a byproduct of the history of the area," observed Scott Leonard, a veteran outfitter in the basin. "The wildlife would not exist if [the land] weren't kept in large tracts."[43]

Today most of the ACE Basin is made up of privately held lands owned by about 130 families who agreed to conservation easements to ensure that conventional residential and commercial development will never occur on their property. The property owners stretched the concept of conservation to include not just the land, wetlands, wildlife, water, and ecological processes, but also the human folkways that had been practiced in the region for generations. Like their ancestors or predecessors, families owning property in the ACE Basin still harvest shrimp and crabs, hunt game, catch fish, cut timber, cultivate crops, canoe, kayak, and watch birds. "We saw what was coming [development], and that wasn't acceptable," recalled Charles Lane, a founding member of the task force whose family has owned the Willtown Bluff plantation in the basin for generations. The ACE Basin is not simply a preserve, Lane pointed out. "It's a working landscape, where people and nature co-exist." The task force knew that it was trying to do something distinctive. "It was a different way of looking at conservation altogether," Lane said in 2009, on the occasion of the basin's twentieth anniversary. "The basin has a culture, a history and a way of life, and the only tool we have to keep it is the willingness of the property owners" to restrict and regulate the permitted activities. The ACE Basin has become a living testimonial to the pride of place in the lowcountry. Lane stressed that he and his family created the conservation easement for their plantation "because we love the land. We felt ourselves stewards of the land. We're more interested in making sure those experiences we had on that land were passed on to future generations." Lane spoke for many in the lowcountry when he emphasized that "it is loved. It's nurtured. It's full of endangered species, but man is part of the landscape. This is our culture, our way of life."[44]

Two-term Republican governor Mark Sanford highlighted his own love of the land in promoting the ACE Basin partnership: "All my life's lessons came from that place," he recalled. "I think to really bond children to the land, you've got to have them work it. Beautiful land, as in the ACE Basin, creates that much deeper bond."[45]

The ACE Basin epitomizes the collaborative—and relatively conservative—strategy of the conservation culture in the lowcountry. It "is probably one of the best partnerships that has ever been put together," said John Frampton, director of the South Carolina Department of Natural Resources. The wealth and conservation bent of most of the property owners in the basin was a crucial factor in the success of the task force. Deeply embedded issues of race and class were sublimated through the overarching influence of white patrician families in shaping the collaboration and structuring its major elements. Almost half of the people

Sandy Island boat dock. Photograph by Angela C. Halfacre.

living in the ACE Basin are low-income African Americans, yet they were under-represented—and, some would argue, underserved—on the ACE Basin Task Force. But however problematic the racial and class dynamics of the ACE Basin, the ecological result has been universally applauded: the basin remains one of the largest undeveloped estuaries on the Atlantic seaboard. Its diverse habitats include pine and hardwood uplands, cypress swamps, fresh, brackish, and salt water tidal marshes, barrier islands, and beaches. The basin hosts a wealth of wildlife resources, including threatened species such as bald eagles, wood storks, ospreys, loggerhead turtles, and sturgeon. Because of their importance to ducks and geese, the former rice plantations in the basin are protected under the North American Waterfowl Management Plan. The Ernest F. Hollings ACE Basin National Wildlife Refuge, created in 1990, is a twelve-thousand-acre parcel within the basin, about twenty-five miles southwest of Charleston.[46]

A Place Apart: Sandy Island

A quite different but equally illuminating case study of collaborative conservation involving African American property owners, government agencies, and environmental organizations in the lowcountry involves the successful effort to preserve Sandy Island and its small unincorporated Gullah community. Located between the Waccamaw (on the east) and Great Pee Dee (on the west) Rivers along the upper reaches of Winyah Bay in northern Georgetown County, just a few miles south of the hyperdeveloped Myrtle Beach, and across the Waccamaw River from verdant Brookgreen Gardens, the twelve-thousand-acre island was until 1996 the largest privately owned freshwater island on the East Coast, about fifteen times the size of New York City's Central Park.

Quiet and quaint Sandy Island boasts a unique ecology and history that powerfully illustrate the intertwined nature of land and tradition in the lowcountry.

In 1997 an archaeological survey identified fifty-one sites on the island, some dating back ten thousand years, to be considered for addition to the National Register for Historical Places. The 1,100 acres of wetlands on the east side of Sandy Island, along the Waccamaw River, were converted to rice plantations during the 1800s. A few remnant impoundments and water-control structures used for rice culture remain intact.

A place apart in time, Sandy Island is a unique land form in South Carolina. The egg-shaped nine-by-twelve-mile island supports a dozen different biotic communities and contains ecosystems not found anywhere else in the state. Its forested bluffs and cypress-studded creeks nurture tidal freshwater forested wetlands, emergent marsh along black-water and alluvial rivers, and a rare coastal maritime sandhill community that includes some of the oldest and largest longleaf pine forests in the state. In addition to eagles, osprey, bear, deer, and turkey, Sandy Island is home to one of the earth's rarest birds, the endangered red-cockaded woodpecker, as well as the endangered peregrine falcon.

Sandy Island also hosts an endangered human community: the last intact Gullah community in the state. For more than a century several hundred acres on the southeastern tip of the island have supported a tiny, close-knit village made up of about three dozen African American households. Many of the seventy-five full-time adult residents (and another sixty or so extended family member "weekenders" who live nearby) are descendants of enslaved West Africans whose labors had converted the island's distinctive freshwater marshes into nine lucrative rice plantations. In 1878 the Reverend Phillip Washington, a former island slave who prospered after the Civil War, returned to Sandy Island, founded the New Bethel Baptist Church, and eventually, in 1882, gained title to 320 acres on which he established a small self-governing community. He died in 1890, and his property has since been passed down through his heirs over several generations. It has two small churches, a general store, and a cemetery but no paved roads, schools, or police protection. Sandy Island is the only residential community in South Carolina without bridge, ferry, or road access to the mainland. The residents, including children, use small private boats or the state-owned school boat to cross the river to go to work or school along the Grand Strand from Myrtle Beach south to Pawleys Island.[47]

In 1989, the same year that Hurricane Hugo struck the lowcountry, a different storm ensued over the fate of Sandy Island. In that year the Sandy Island Associates, a timber harvesting and resort development company that owned 9,164 acres on Sandy Island (two-thirds of the entire island), submitted a request to the South Carolina Coastal Council to construct a two-lane, 750-foot-long private bridge connecting the northern end of the island to the mainland across Bull Creek, where the associates owned another large parcel. The initial request explained that the bridge was needed for timber extraction, but the cost of the concrete bridge exceeded the projected value of the timber, leading critics to argue that the developers intended to do more with the island than simply harvest logs, especially since barges or a temporary floating bridge could have been used to transport logs. In fact, a revised development plan completed in 1990 included a "conceptual" proposal to create an "exclusive and elite" resort community with equestrian trails, golf courses, a marina, and up to 9,500 townhouses, villas, apartments, and condominiums for as many as twenty thousand new residents. The report insisted that such an upscale resort community was "the use for which Sandy Island is most suitable."[48]

The fact that Sandy Island Associates was owned by two of South Carolina's wealthiest and most politically powerful men, Spartanburg-based textile magnate Roger Milliken and E. Craig Wall Jr., the owner of Canal Industries headquartered in Myrtle Beach, a huge timber and land development company, gave their request added credibility—and notoriety. They garnered the support of the Waccamaw Regional Planning and Development Council, the Coast Guard (which is responsible for bridge permits), as well as Republican Governor Carroll Campbell (both Milliken and Wall were members of the governor's reelection campaign finance committee). When Roger Banks, field supervisor of the Charleston office of the U.S. Fish and Wildlife Service (USFWS), objected to the bridge plan because of its possible negative impact on the red-cockaded woodpecker population, Milliken and Wall asked the regional director of the USFWS to remove him from the case. The regional director refused to do so. The landowners then asked USFWS executives in Washington, D.C., to remove Banks, but they too refused.[49]

The possibility of transforming remote Sandy Island into a densely developed resort community set off a prolonged controversy. Members of the island's black community discovered that the centuries-old tradition of allowing residents access to privately owned lands ended abruptly with the erection of fences and the posting of trespassing signs. They also were shocked to discover that the white developers requesting the bridge were not going to allow the black residents to use it to access the mainland. The "developers," said the Reverend George Weathers, the village's unofficial mayor, "didn't treat us with respect." More worrisome to the black residents was the possibility that they, like their counterparts at Hilton Head and Daufuskie Islands, might be displaced by the higher taxes resulting from high-end homes and golf courses. "My generation is always worried about development," said islander Wilhemena Pyatt. "We feel that if the white developers come, it is going to be bad news." Pyatt and other islanders formed the Sandy Island Community Action Club to protest the proposed bridge. Sixty-five residents signed a petition requesting that the state turn down the proposed bridge. "We have a voice now," said Weathers, "and we will speak up about our future."[50]

Environmental and civic groups mobilized opposition as well. David Farren, an attorney with the Southern Environmental Law Center in Chapel Hill, North Carolina, predicted that the proposed timber harvesting on Sandy Island would in fact "be in the shape of golf course fairways. I find it outrageous on a fundamental level to have a private bridge across a public waterway that will bring development, higher taxes, and degradation of natural resources all at once." The Penn Center worked with Sandy Island residents to avoid the fate of Daufuskie Island, about thirty minutes by boat from Hilton Head. In the 1980s resort developers purchased much of Daufuskie and built golf courses, country clubs, and expensive residential communities, all of which had the effect of raising local property taxes so high that many of the longtime black residents were displaced, just as had occurred earlier on Hilton Head. Now Sandy Island was facing the same threat.[51]

The prolonged Sandy Island bridge controversy generated extensive media coverage, including articles in the *New York Times*, a special series of investigative reports in Columbia's *State* newspaper, and eventually, in 2006, an hour-long SCETV documentary. In a biting letter to the editor of the *State*, Columbia resident Tom Wall summarized the unfolding drama over Sandy Island: "The fate of a number of South Carolina's other sea islands may soon befall Sandy Island. A few powerful people are poised to destroy a human community and a pristine ecosystem." He added that Roger Milliken and Craig Wall (no relation) were officially requesting a bridge to transport timber but "the end result will be permanent destruction." His concluding statement encapsulated the outlook of conservationists: "That Messrs. Milliken, Wall, and others are in an incredibly wonderful position to preserve such a culturally and ecologically magnificent area but choose, instead, to embark on a journey that will eventually disfigure and destroy invaluable human and natural resources is both sad and enraging."[52]

Those opposed to the bridge at Sandy Island took some comfort in June 1993 when the South Carolina Coastal Council's management committee put on hold its approval of the proposed bridge pending required environmental impact studies. Two months later the Coastal Conservation League, the South Carolina chapter of the Sierra Club, and the League of Women Voters of Georgetown County, with the help of the Southern Environmental Law Center and the involvement of other groups such as the Nature Conservancy and the U.S. Fish and Wildlife Service, officially requested that the state deny the request for a bridge to Sandy Island. In explaining his opposition to the bridge, Dana Beach of the Coastal Conservation League stressed that Sandy Island is "culturally, biologically, and geographically unique." In fact, he asserted that it was the most ecologically significant land along the nation's entire Atlantic coast. Any development on the island would have "a dramatic, far-reaching, and long-term effect." Beach added that while he acknowledged that Milliken and Wall owned the island acreage and thereby enjoyed the rights of private property ownership, Sandy Island represented such an ecologically strategic area "that it needs more protection than a [government] regulatory program can provide. It needs to be bought [and preserved]."[53]

In 1995, however, the South Carolina Office of Ocean and Coastal Resource Management (formerly the South Carolina Coastal Council) issued a permit for the disputed bridge, pending more environmental impact studies. Environmentalists appealed the decision, only to see it upheld by circuit judge David Maring in May. An attorney representing the African American island residents and environmental organizations filed an appeal to the state Supreme Court. Meanwhile federal and state wildlife agencies—the U.S. Fish and Wildlife Services and the S.C. Department of Natural Resources—postponed the construction of the bridge until the Sandy Island Associates provided detailed environmental impact plans to protect endangered species on the island during the timber harvest. At the same time a proposal from the U.S. Fish and Wildlife Service for a National Wildlife Refuge that could eventually include Sandy Island further clouded the property's future options. In December 1995 the South Carolina Office of Ocean and Coastal Resource Management turned down the request for a Sandy Island bridge because the Sandy Island Associates had failed to provide the required environmental impact studies.[54]

Meanwhile another possibility for preserving Sandy Island emerged in 1995 when the South Carolina Department of Transportation (SCDOT), in order to comply with federal environmental laws, began seeking wetlands to purchase that would "mitigate"—or compensate for—other federally protected wetland areas in the path of new road construction. In essence SCDOT would buy strategic wetlands properties across the state, protect them with conservation easements, and "bank" them as "credits" to be exchanged for permission to damage or destroy other wetlands. The funds saved by allowing construction through wetlands would be used to purchase or designate other wetland areas as perpetual preserves to be monitored annually.[55]

In 1995 SCDOT appointed the Mitigation Team, a multiagency task force coordinated by the U.S. Army Corps of Engineers. The other federal stakeholder agencies included the U.S. National Marine Fisheries Service, U.S. Fish and Wildlife Services, and the U.S. Environmental Protection Agency, Region IV. The South Carolina agencies represented on the Mitigation Team included SCDOT and the Departments of Natural Resources, Ocean and Coastal Resource Management, and Health and Environmental Control. Two nonprofit environmental organizations—the Coastal Conservation League and the Winyah Bay Task Force—were invited to participate in the team's decision-making process because their missions included the protection of both cultural and natural resources.[56]

Although the Mitigation Team assessed the feasibility of several possible low-country parcels, by 1996 it had fastened on Sandy Island as the most valuable ecological and cultural site to be preserved. The task force faced enormous challenges in deciding how best to structure an unprecedented proposal to purchase the acreage owned by the Sandy Island Associates and convert it into a wildlife and nature preserve. The issues were complex, involving a complicated maze of local, state, and federal regulatory and jurisdictional issues. The diverse stakeholders varied dramatically in outlook, and there was a constant threat of interagency territoriality and bureaucratic inertia. Yet the Mitigation Team succeeded in spite of such challenges. Several factors contributed to its success. That the members of the team already knew and trusted each other from previous projects and interactions helped enormously. As one of them remembered, "there was never really a question of anybody not being trustworthy or trying to pull something." From the start, one of the team members recalled, the task force included middle managers who were all of comparable stature within their agencies or organizations. They viewed each other as equals: "I knew [that I was] dealing with people who had your interest at heart and were trying to do the right thing in terms of building roads and protecting the environment."[57]

In 1996 SCDOT decided to purchase the 9,164 acres on Sandy Island owned by the Sandy Island Associates. Lowcountry environmental organizations heartily endorsed the recommendation. As Dana Beach said on behalf of the Coastal Conservation League, "the SCDOT can save Sandy Island while allowing South Carolina to obey the law." The Sandy Island Associates, however, had to agree to the sale. H. B. "Buck" Limehouse, a prominent Charleston executive and conservationist who was then serving as chair of the SCDOT, volunteered to broach the idea with Roger Milliken and Craig Wall. "The developers [Sandy Island Associates] didn't want anything to do with the other side [environmental organizations], but I had their business background and could speak their language," Limehouse recalled. "I knew I could convince them to do the right thing. It just makes good sense to take advantage of bargain land prices, set aside land in a mitigation bank against future transportation development, and at the same time protect the land purchased as a natural wildlife habitat."[58]

Limehouse championed the preservation of Sandy Island as part of the Mitigation Bank. In March 1996 SCDOT bought most of Sandy Island for ten million dollars (not including the village or several private residences). The Nature Conservancy donated an additional one million dollars toward the purchase, and it agreed to manage and monitor the Wetlands Mitigation Bank properties on Sandy Island to ensure that they were not developed. Efforts to conserve more land in the area around Sandy Island led to the establishment of the Waccamaw National Wildlife Refuge in 1997.

The arrangement that Limehouse negotiated with the Sandy Island Associates to create the Sandy Island Public Trust Nature Preserve was one of the nation's most instructive examples of how diverse public and private interests can form creative partnerships to protect significant natural and cultural resources—and thereby expand the concept of conservation to include historic human cultures as well as the physical environment. "It sounds incredible, but everybody won," Dana Beach observed. "Now a way of life and an entire ecosystem are protected from commercial development." The land purchase ended years of acrimony and litigation over the island's fate. "I think it brings an end to that controversy and everybody wins,'" said Sidney Futch, a vice president of Craig Wall's Canal Industries.[59]

The announcement of the state's purchase and preservation of Sandy Island generated widespread acclaim, and the project has since won numerous state and federal awards. "Sandy Island is South Carolina's own Garden of Eden," said Richard Eckstrom, the state treasurer, at the dedication of the nature preserve in March 1997. And "it will remain so forever." Leon Larson, the regional director of the Federal Highway Administration, added that the Sandy Island project was "the most effective [example of] highway mitigation in the United States." The editors of the *Myrtle Beach Sun News* said SCDOT's purchase of most of "idyllic" Sandy Island was a "victory" for the culture of conservation in the lowcountry, providing a "conspicuous and notable step toward the preservation of habitat and a culture." The beautiful freshwater island "houses an important part of our cultural memory and legacy." The *State* newspaper in Columbia expressed the growing culture of conservation across the lowcountry when they observed that "any time our heritage and our wetlands, so necessary to our state's health, survive even another year, we have cause for celebration." The preservation of Sandy Island constituted "one of those rare moments when everyone worked together for a solution that pleases most and offers benefits to many. We can only wish for more such moments." In 1997 the Coastal America Partnership, a coalition of local, state, and federal agencies and nonprofit environmental organizations gave its highest award to the members of the Sandy Island Mitigation Team.[60]

An essential aspect of the Sandy Island story was the involvement of the black community. The Mitigation Team, much more so than the ACE Basin Task Force, sought to ensure that representatives of the small Gullah community on Sandy Island played an active and informed role in the process of deciding the island's future. "We were very concerned that the community be protected," explained a task force member, "and that they not be patronized. It's a very viable community; . . . they are very progressive and have a very good way of life. So protecting their community, and protecting their life, and protecting the environment on Sandy Island forever [was critical]." The two members of the task force from the Coastal Conservation League and the Winyah Bay Task Force explicitly assumed responsibility for representing the interests of the African Americans living on Sandy Island. The result—converting Sandy Island into a nature preserve and wildlife refuge—was warmly embraced by the Gullah community. "We wanted our life to stay the way it is," concluded the island's "headman," or unofficial mayor, George Weathers. "Now it's going to stay that way forever."[61]

The South Carolina Conservation Bank

The lowcountry culture of conservation originated with environmental organizations and gradually spread to corporations, foundations, and the local and state political network. Conserving "special" lands has been an especially successful example of bipartisan political support for the environment. As a journalist observed in 2000, "the growing support for preserving the state's special places started with private conservation groups. It has spread to the Legislature, the governor's office and state agencies."[62]

The foremost example of the ability of land conservation efforts to bridge conventional political divides in South Carolina was the creation of a state Conservation Bank in 2002 by the General Assembly. Like the ACE Basin and Sandy Island projects, the South Carolina Conservation Bank represented still another example of diverse governmental agencies, environmental and civic organizations, and bipartisan political leadership working together to preserve land through partnerships. Compared to other states South Carolina public officials had been relatively indifferent to large-scale land conservation efforts until the early twenty-first century, when the state government and several municipalities started funding annual preservation efforts. The South Carolina Conservation Bank was established to provide an ongoing source of funds to acquire land or purchase conservation easements. Beginning in 2004, a percentage of the real estate transfer fee (approximately fifteen million dollars per year) would be used by the bank's board of directors to purchase land or conservation easements from willing sellers. The bank awards grants to make such purchases on a competitive basis to state agencies, municipal governments, nonprofit land trusts, and other qualified conservation groups. The South Carolina Conservation Bank owns no properties. Property owners can sell conserved property to an eligible trust fund or sell or donate conservation easements and retain ownership and rights to traditional uses of the land. The legislation creating the land bank was crafted so as to encourage public dollars to be matched by private funds, thereby increasing the amount of protected land.[63]

The idea for such a conservation bank emerged in 1997 when Dana Beach recruited a steering committee for what would become the South Carolina Landscape Mapping Project, intended to identify the highest priority areas across the state to be conserved. The steering committee included representatives from the Coastal Conservation League, Ducks Unlimited, the Nature Conservancy, the Lowcountry Open Land Trust, MeadWestvaco Corporation, the ACE Basin Task Force, and the Audubon Society. Thereafter more than seventy-five of the state's leading botanists, biologists, ecologists, foresters, historians, and conservationists participated in the mapping effort. While they were identifying the most strategic lands to be conserved and sites to be voluntarily preserved, Beach and other members of the steering committee discussed how best to finance such efforts. Charles Lane suggested that the state create an annually funded "land bank" to purchase strategically important parcels. He proposed the idea to Chip Campsen, then a member of the General Assembly from Isle of Palms, who agreed to sponsor such a bill. But it took several years and intensive lobbying to gain passage.[64]

In 2000 Democratic governor Jim Hodges created the South Carolina Land Legacy Initiative to support the South Carolina Conservation Bank Act and to promote voluntary land conservation efforts. The Land Legacy Initiative resulted from a new one-billion-dollar federal program called the Lands Legacy Initiative, launched by President Bill Clinton in 1999, which encouraged states to preserve open space and promote smarter growth. The federal legislation provided incentive funding for a wide range of interest groups—farmers, ranchers, chambers of commerce, municipalities, state and federal agencies, developers, outdoor enthusiasts, and environmental organizations—to collaborate on competitive proposals for federal matching grants. President Clinton claimed that his "lands legacy initiative" represented "the single largest annual investment in protecting our green and open spaces since Theodore Roosevelt set our nation on the path of conservation nearly a century ago."[65]

The opportunity to gain federal funding for the purchase of valuable lands or easements prompted Governor Hodges to create South Carolina's own Land Legacy Initiative. Chaired by Hugh Lane Jr. of Charleston, it represented a cooperative effort involving business and community leaders as well as various organizations across the state. In its final report the Land Legacy Initiative promoted efforts to preserve South Carolina's historic "quality of life" by creating more greenways, open space, and parks, wildlife habitats, natural areas, historical sites, sites of unique ecological significance, forestlands, farmlands, and watersheds.[66]

The Land Legacy Initiative was an essential catalyst for the passage of the land bank program. It helped convince a bipartisan coalition of political leaders, chambers of commerce and business trade associations, outdoor recreation advocacy groups, and environmental organizations to support landmark legislation to create an annual funding stream for the state to preserve important land parcels, either through purchase or the negotiation of conservation easements. Although one state representative dismissed the bill proposing the creation of the South Carolina Conservation Bank as "the devil's work," the legislation in fact garnered "unprecedented support" from both property-rights advocacy groups and environmental organizations, chambers of commerce, the state tourism council, the realtors' association, the Farm Bureau, and the League of Women Voters. The Conservation Bank Act was worded so as to ensure that property could only be bought with the consent of owners rather than "taken" by the state. It also was phrased so as to encourage the leveraging of state monies through partnerships with private and federal dollars. Campsen sponsored the legislation, arguing that, as an ardent Christian, he felt a moral obligation to be a good steward of the state's natural resources. In addition, the state land bank was needed because conservation easements were mainly attractive to wealthy landowners who could benefit from tax credits. "But for the guy who's land rich but cash poor, who doesn't have much income, a tax credit or a tax deduction doesn't do a whole lot for him," Campsen explained. The Conservation Bank bill "was really about, to a large extent, allowing the land rich but cash poor person to get into the conservation game."[67]

The debate over the bill in the General Assembly was spirited. Campsen recalled being called "a socialist" by one colleague. The irony of such name-calling bemused him. "I am one of the most conservative members in the General Assembly, and I am one of the most well-versed in free market economics. . . . But

I was actually called that because . . . in some corners of the General Assembly, and among the general public, there's a reflexive . . . reaction. If it's about the environment, [conservatives oppose it] . . . because it involves big government and big regulation, and it is depriving people of property rights. Or if the Sierra Club is for it, it can't be good, and [therefore] I'm going to be against it."[68]

Yet Campsen persevered. He told his fellow legislators that the need for the Conservation Bank was urgent and compelling. "Unless we do something at this juncture, the quality of life that makes us so attractive in the first place is in grave jeopardy." The lieutenant governor, Republican Bob Peeler, agreed. "This is our opportunity. We must seize it." With the help of the Land Legacy Initiative task force members and many others, Campsen gained legislative approval of the bill on April 18, 2002. "This is great news for our state," said Governor Hodges. "The active coalition of many groups of businesses, conservationists, environmentalists, state agencies and the bipartisan efforts of our legislature have culminated in a law that will add a great deal to our quality of life." Similarly Senator John Drummond of Greenwood, the state's longest-serving legislator, remarked that the Conservation Bank Act in the end garnered more support than any other legislation he had encountered in thirty-seven years. "Passage of the bill was the result of a cooperative, nonpartisan effort by lawmakers from across the state who are concerned with protecting the natural and cultural landscape of South Carolina, while ensuring future economic growth in the process."[69]

Hodges, Campsen, and others had argued that the Conservation Bank would save the state's most ecologically sensitive areas by encouraging "cooperation and innovative partnerships among landowners, state agencies, municipalities, and non-profit organizations to work together." The creation of the bank reflected still another instance of the state's environmental organizations collaborating effectively for a common cause. "This is the most important piece of environmental legislation passed in South Carolina," said state Sierra Club director Dell Isham.[70]

Since the Conservation Bank was first funded in 2004, it has received an average of about fifteen million dollars a year that has helped preserve almost two hundred thousand acres across the state. The appointment of Charles Lane as the first chair of the Conservation Bank board testified to the political influence of the lowcountry conservation culture. In 2006 Governor Mark Sanford allocated twenty million dollars from the executive budget to supplement the Conservation Bank fund. His motive was to accelerate the efforts across the state to combat the negative effects of sprawl by using a "market-based incentive for private land conservation" (through the state's purchase of key parcels from individual property owners). "Preserving the way South Carolina looks and feels," he explained, "is key to our quality of life, which is an important competitive advantage for our state. With the growth we're expecting to see in our state over the next ten years, now is the time to make sure our natural resources are protected going forward." He noted with pride that his Republican administration "has already set aside more land than any other in South Carolina history."[71]

The passage of the South Carolina Conservation Bank Act was a major turning point in the evolution of the conservation culture. It not only accelerated the land-based preservation strategy in the lowcountry; it also stimulated similar programs at the local level. Both Charleston and Beaufort Counties have created their own funding mechanisms for land acquisition and conservation. In Beaufort County voters decided in 2000 to support a forty-million-dollar bond issuance that established the Rural and Critical Lands Program. The new program was the first in the state focused on purchasing green space as a means of improving a county's quality of life. Land purchases are evaluated by an eleven-member board made up of citizens appointed by the county council. From 2000 to 2003 the program used the forty million dollars to acquire 120 acres of historic properties, more than 9,000 acres in preserves, and more than 600 acres in conservation easements. These purchases included farmland, coastal forests, freshwater wetlands, ancient Indian villages, historic forts and plantations, and beach frontage on St. Helena Island. The program's popularity led voters to approve an additional fifty million dollars for continued conservation purchases.[72]

In November 2004 Charleston County voters approved a new one-half-cent transportation sales tax to fund various infrastructure projects (roads, bridges, drainage) as well as "greenbelt" land purchases. Seventy percent of the Charleston County Greenbelt Bank funds target strategic rural lands; the rest are available for the acquisition of urban parks. To qualify for funding, projects proposed by conservation organizations and land trusts must "promote rural land conservation, wetlands protection, historic and cultural preservation, parkland acquisition, greenway and trail acquisition, and waterway access acquisition." The Charleston County Greenbelt Plan won the 2006 Outstanding Planning Award from the South Carolina chapter of the American Planning Association. The Greenbelt Plan has become one of the most progressive municipal efforts to preserve rural land, acquire parks, and maintain green spaces. Louise Maybank, chair of the program's advisory board, said it provides a bold vision for the next twenty-five years to conserve and protect the lowcountry way of life. "It is an exemplary result of the citizens and the government working together," Maybank observed. The land acquisition initiatives have been popular. In 2010 the editors of the *Charleston Post and Courier* issued a glowing assessment of the greenbelt programs in Charleston and Beaufort Counties: "The green-space programs in Charleston, Beaufort, and Dorchester counties have successfully concentrated on preserving rural land, forests and wildlife habitat that include scenic vistas. They have been able to leverage major contributions to their programs from other public and private sources."[73]

The willingness of voters to use tax monies for such government-sponsored land acquisitions illustrates how the conservation culture had penetrated public awareness and garnered widespread political support. The South Carolina Conservation Bank had the potential to play a transformational role in the effort to protect and preserve lands with great ecological value. "In the mid-1980s," Dana

Beach noted, "it began to fall in place that this type of government-financed conservation was scalable; the alternative was Florida, where land is protected by fee and market values."[74]

The passage of the South Carolina Conservation Bank Act displayed how the culture of conservation's emphasis on land had blossomed into an array of overlapping acquisition and preservation efforts: private, public, and private-public partnerships. The results were both tangible and intangible: more land preserved as well as rising levels of public awareness. The Conservation Bank accelerated the growth of a culture of conservation in the lowcountry. In its first year of operation "it has already made a tremendous difference in the lowcountry," said Will Haynie, executive director of the Lowcountry Open Land Trust in 2005. "It has really raised awareness of the importance of conservation in South Carolina." That same year a journalist writing in the *Charleston Post and Courier* encouraged readers to notice that the lowcountry was changing—for the better. Because of the region's growing conservation culture, residents could now enjoy mile after mile of marsh and tidal rivers, pineland and beach, the remote barrier islands of Cape Romain and the Francis Marion National Forest, down to the vast estuaries of the ACE Basin. "Maybe no other East Coast city is fringed with as much public or privately conserved land as Charleston." In applauding the conservation culture's emphasis on land preservation, the author credited the remarkable effectiveness of numerous public/private partnerships in creating an interconnected swath of valuable land trusts, preserves, refuges, and easements. "The private-public, hand-in-hand weave that kept it together is all but unique to the lowcountry. It might be the distinctive feature of the place in the future." For his part, Dana Beach highlighted the success of the lowcountry's emphasis on public-private land protection partnerships compared to other efforts across the nation. "It's unique. There's only a couple of places like it—beautiful, functioning, regional community with a protected landscape. We are on the right track. We have made tremendous progress." Since 1989 the land-centered, partnership-based culture of conservation has blossomed. Protecting the environment and preserving the coastal region's cultural heritage is no longer a secondary concern. As the *Charleston Post and Courier* declared in 1998, the lowcountry's "grass-roots conservation work has far surpassed that of other states." The Conservation Land Bank was the linchpin of such success.[75]

FIVE

Growing by Choice:
Community Planning

The tiny hamlet of Awendaw, northeast of Mount Pleasant in Charleston County, was devastated by Hurricane Hugo in 1989. No sooner had the storm moved north than I traveled to help friends who had lost their home. What I found on arrival was heart-wrenching. The storm-ravaged area that included pockets of extreme poverty was a tragic landscape. Public services were minimal or non-existent. Yet the mortal immediacy of the situation helped the distraught community band together to bridge traditional racial and class differences. Everyone joined together to help those whose lives had been shattered.

Seventeen years later, in 2006, another storm, this time over growth, had a different effect on Awendaw. It fragmented rather than unified the community. That year, Lewis C. White, a local real estate agent, announced his intention to sell a 324-acre parcel he owned near Awendaw. The purchaser, Watertree Properties based in North Carolina, planned to pay seventeen million dollars for the land and construct three to four hundred houses on the site. The upscale homes would cost between four hundred thousand and one million dollars. The gated community would double the population of the predominantly African American rural town and transform its racial makeup. Proponents of the project claimed that the "environmentally friendly" development would include clustered housing, nature preserves, and open spaces. It would also bring desperately needed property tax revenues and infrastructure to the poor community, which still depended on wells for its water and septic tanks for its sewage treatment. Opponents countered that the development would destroy one of the most ecologically important areas in the lowcountry. "I think it's horrible," exclaimed one resident. "I think it's totally out of character with what the majority of residents want. It just makes no sense for Awendaw."[1]

Had the project in Awendaw been proposed twenty years earlier, it probably would have been approved with little notice. In 2006, however, several factors transformed the proposed development of the "White Tract" into a prolonged, complicated controversy involving racial and class overtones, tensions between newcomers and longtime residents, and charges of croneyism. First, the White Tract, nestled between the Francis Marion National Forest and the Cape Romaine National Wildlife Refuge and running along the Intracoastal Waterway, was both ecologically sensitive and geographically strategic, having received designation as a Class I wilderness, one of only 158 places in the nation to receive such distinction.[2]

Second, the lowcountry's conservation coalition mobilized its considerable forces to oppose the project. "This can't happen," declared John Brubaker, a past president of the South Carolina Native Plant Society who lived near the White Tract. "The conservation community is prepared to do everything and anything that it can to ensure that it does not happen." Because no sewer lines connected the proposed development to Awendaw, septic tanks would have to be used to handle wastewater. The threat that sewerage seeping from the subdivision would despoil sensitive waterways as well as shorebird habitat and nesting territory for loggerhead turtles spurred the involvement of environmental organizations. "It's just absolutely the wrong place [for a development]," stressed Dana Beach of the Coastal Conservation League. "The property has extensive wetlands. It's one of the most globally important ecological areas in the east. For that reason alone, the town ought to turn it down."[3]

A third factor complicating approval of the proposed development was that the property owner, Lewis C. White, a lifelong resident, chaired the town's planning commission. People opposed to the development questioned whether the town council could make an objective decision about a project spearheaded by such a prominent local figure. That the planning commission and the mayor publicly endorsed the project only fueled suspicions of a "good-old-boy" network controlling the approvals process. For his part White dismissed critics of the project as "not-in-my-backyard" new residents who opposed any additional growth in the area. "They come to Awendaw, buy land, build a home and don't want anyone else to do the same," he charged.[4]

A fourth factor affecting the fate of the White Tract was perhaps the most crucial: in the mid-1990s the South Carolina General Assembly had mandated that all communities with planning commissions must develop comprehensive long-range land-use plans to manage growth more effectively. The proposed development of the White Tract therefore had to satisfy the requirements of the Town of Awendaw's 1999 comprehensive plan, updated in 2004, which included restrictive new zoning classifications designed to regulate growth so as to maintain the town's rural character. Those zoning rules would have to be changed in order for the development to go forward. Specifically the developer requested that the town change the zoning designation of the White Tract from "agricultural" to a "planned development."

The rezoning request divided the town's residents. The planning commission (White recused himself from the vote) recommended that the town council approve the rezoning request. At a council meeting in December 2006, Sam Robinson, a council member who led the fight against the White Tract by forming the Awendaw Community Action Group, urged the mayor and council members to look again at the comprehensive land-use plan they had approved in

1999. Its preamble stated that the mission of the plan was to manage growth to ensure the preservation of the town's rural character. "Mr. Mayor and Council," Robinson added, "what you are proposing relative to the rezoning of the White Tract will . . . trample upon that statement. It would not, sir, preserve Awendaw's rural characteristic; it is not, sir, managed growth." Robinson argued that approving the controversial development would violate the comprehensive plan's emphasis on "rural and environmental preservation and affordable housing." In the end the town council narrowly approved the rezoning request, but the fuss and furor eventually led the developer to abandon the project. The dispute over the White Tract transformed the town's political dynamics. In 2009 Robinson defeated the longtime mayor, William Alston, who had endorsed the development of the White Tract.[5]

Land-use Planning in the Lowcountry

The fractious dispute in Awendaw over the White Tract revealed one of the most tangible accomplishments of the conservation culture in the lowcountry since Hurricane Hugo: the transformation of land-use policies and practices. Building codes, zoning ordinances, and historical preservation restrictions are among the most powerful means of conserving the environment and preserving a region's cultural heritage. Until the late 1980s the lowcountry's traditional land-use governance system remained in thrall of car-driven growth models and decisions. The decades-old framework for its land-use ordinances and building codes favored low-density, spread-out development and rigidly separated residential, retail, and commercial areas, thereby requiring daily vehicular use. The long-standing "single-use" zoning ordinances favored suburban expansion through a concentric pattern of car-dependent subdivisions. Codes encouraged large single-family homes with deep setbacks on large lots with manicured lawns served by generic shopping centers, strip malls, chain restaurants, and convenience stores. As the lowcountry developer Vince Graham asserted, the traditional land-use protocols used by state and local governments were designed to "enable and even encourage sprawl."[6]

Such conventional "sprawl-oriented" land-use planning hindered alternative efforts to promote mixed-use communities in which homes, schools, shops, stores, and offices would be commingled to reduce dependency of the automobile. Sprawl zoning also overstretched municipal budgets by requiring expensive infrastructure: more roads, utilities, sidewalks, and police and fire protection. The conventional building codes and zoning ordinances encouraged suburbia to gobble up farmland, open space, wetlands, and woods; displace wildlife; threaten water supply; and compromise air quality. In sum, sprawl was the foundational premise of conventional lowcountry land-use planning and zoning codes, and the resulting impact on the environment and the quality of life was unsustainable.

The deeply entrenched system of suburban-centered land-use planning and building ordinances was stubbornly resistant to change. The progrowth regime—

In the Town of McClellanville a tire swing suspended from an
old oak and an aging dock with views of new construction.
Photographs by Angela C. Halfacre.

planners, developers, raltors, and elected officials—had come to depend on it.
Sprawl had been so dominant for so long that it was the only approach that home
buyers, developers, builders, elected officials, and municipal planners knew.
Inertia and special interests prevailed. Growth of virtually any sort was deemed
good for counties and municipalities, and, because land was relatively cheap in
the decades after World War II, real estate development had become synonymous
with highly inefficient use of land and natural resources. Zoning boards and
county and city officials often practiced a culture of concession to developers,
contractors, and realtors. Through apathy or ignorance the voting public abdi-
cated its role in land-use policy-making to developers, business leaders, and realtors for whom profit was the determining, if not sole, motive. Deals were often

made with a handshake and behind closed doors, and bulldozers were often at work before area residents knew about a new project in their neighborhood.

No more. During the 1990s and since, lowcountry developers, professional planners, elected officials, and residents have been rethinking how they build on the land, in part because of maddening traffic congestion, air and water pollution, and soaring infrastructure expenses, in part because of a growing fear that the coastal region was losing its distinctive quality of life. A conservation ethic and innovative approaches to growth management and real estate development have penetrated the permitting process and the political arena as well as the culture of land-use planning, neighborhood design, and residential and commercial construction. As a result the concept of sustainable development has moved from the periphery to the mainstream of lowcountry growth-management strategies.

The staff members of conservation organizations interviewed for this book repeatedly complained about the state's history of short-sighted land-planning policies and outdated local zoning codes. For example, one Lowcountry Open Land Trust executive argued that "everything about our zoning, our roads, our utilities—the way new development is funded, the way it's planned—means that the only thing we can do is convert land [into a built environment]." It was not until the end of the twentieth century, in the aftermath of Hurricaine Hugo, that lowcountry counties and municipalities adopted a more flexible and sustainable system of building codes, zoning ordinances, and land-use guidelines. "Green" conservation principles and environmental priorities, to one degree or another, have been integrated into the local ordinances and regulations governing residential and commercial development.[7]

By the end of the twentieth century, lowcountry land-use and development policies were no longer uncontested and unregulated. Smart-growth control measures, when enforced, began to have a tangible effect in shaping real estate development. Buoyed by changes in land-use planning philosophy and bolstered by new zoning codes and project approval processes, conservation organizations have developed an effective strategy. They scrutinize every major construction or road-building project, in some cases entangling developers in a web of costly and time-consuming legal maneuvers and lawsuits. Developers must now engage in a transparent, convoluted process of reviews, hearings, and approvals before a new project can begin. As the town manager of Awendaw said in 2006, developers no longer can "receive a rubber-stamp deal. Staff will make sure that things are done right." In 1998 James J. Chaffin Jr., one of the lowcountry's leading practitioners of sustainable development, noted that real estate developers were now enmeshed "in a never-ending paradox of moral complexity, balancing the competing imperatives of ecological sensitivity and economic sensibility."[8]

A related sign of the culture of conservation's vitality is its growing diversity—and, ironically, its own internal cleavages. At times particular development projects have pitted the various elements of the "slow," "smart," or "anti-"growth coalitions against each other. Conflicts between groups trying to preserve the

Litchfield Beach marsh-side docks. Photograph by Angela C. Halfacre.

lowcountry environment and its cherished way of life have demonstrated how diverse—and at times fractious—the conservation community has become. How best to manage growth and preserve the environment often involves subjective values and opinions, and well-intentioned people and organizations at times disagree fervently on the best practices related to growth management and environmental protection. Sean Blacklocke, an environmental consultant asked to assess the comprehensive land-use planning dynamics in South Carolina counties and municipalities, acknowledged in 1999 that "it's all just been a clash of value judgments, as best I can tell."[9]

Parochial Planning

A vocal—and often angry and chaotic—element of any culture of conservation is NIMBYISM (Not in My Backyard). Residents often adopt a no-growth stance when it comes to proposed new construction near their neighborhood. While it is understandable that property owners want to preserve and protect the quality of life they originally invested in, NIMBYISM by its very nature is often passionately insular: reactive, defensive, parochial, and shortsighted. Just saying no is a questionable basis for land-use policy in fast growing communities. The power to stop growth has often clashed with efforts to promote smart growth. Whatever its tone or method, NIMBYISM usually has the effect of slowing development or deterring it altogether—even projects that are designed to be environmentally friendly.[10]

Until the 1990s city and county councils as well as planning commissions across the lowcountry rarely assessed the long-term impact of new development projects on the environment—or on municipal budgets. Even rarer were instances of the various lowcountry counties and municipalities coordinating their planning efforts with one another so as to minimize environmental damage and avoid duplicating infrastructure expenses. As a Lowcountry Open Land Trust staff member asserted, "we absolutely cannot have five, six, or seven jurisdictions in the tri-county [Charleston] area dispensing [land-use] permits. They're going to fight each other. They're going to be at odds. Every politician wants to preserve [and grow] his little kingdom."[11]

Such fragmented behavior among municipal planners and elected officials resulted from a variety of factors: stereotypical governmental bureaucracy, inertia, and competitiveness among counties and cities; understaffed (or nonexistent) municipal land-planning departments; the disproportionate political influence of developers and realtors; and the unwarranted assumption that growth of any type was inherently good and would always generate increases in net revenue for local governments.

Over time the absence of ecosystem management and conservation science principles in lowcountry land-use protocols created significant problems. In particular municipal planners seemed unaware of the crucial role played by preserved open space in fostering healthy wildlife habitats, ensuring water quality, and enhancing property values. Conservation scientists also highlighted the lack of regional (multicounty) environmental-impact assessments. Without such data state and local agencies—as well as nonprofit environmental organizations—lacked the information needed to engage in the meaningful management of natural resources. At the same time, and for much the same reason, gaps occurred in the efforts to preserve several native species and ecosystems. During the 1990s and since, however, scientists have recommended better ways to protect such species and systems in lands designated for conservation (private and public), and both municipal planners and elected officials have come to acknowledge—to one degree or another—the significance of environmental issues and priorities.

Comprehensive Land-use Plans

The most substantive change to the planning culture in South Carolina occurred in the 1990s when the General Assembly, after years of allowing essentially unrestricted and ill-coordinated development across the state, declared that every community with a planning commission must engage in strategic, long-range land-use planning. Such an initiative was long overdue. In 1993 forty civic, political, environmental, and business leaders from across the state had attended a forum in Columbia focused on finding better ways to manage growth so as to enhance the long-term quality of life. At that time South Carolina was one of only two states along the East Coast without a coordinated growth-management office, agency, or task force. "Unplanned growth is wasteful and costly, and the product is not of quality," Mayor Joe Riley of Charleston told the participants. "Growth at any cost is not a sound public policy. It wastes money, it wastes resources." Conversely, "wise planning, high-quality growth planning, ends up producing an economic development product that is unparalleled." Riley pointed out that the greater Charleston metropolitan area was one of the fastest growing regions in the nation, yet it contained twenty-eight separate county and town/city governments with a tradition of making uncoordinated decisions about the nature, location, and timing of new roads and development projects. Such a piecemeal approach to metropolitan planning had resulted in unnecessary duplication of infrastructure projects and chaotic sprawl. Riley and the other forum participants resolved to convince the state legislature to address the need for growth management through systematic planning.[12]

The lobbying efforts culminated in the Local Government Comprehensive Planning Enabling Act of 1994. The pathbreaking state legislation required every local government that engaged in zoning to create—within five years—comprehensive long-range plans to manage growth more wisely and in the process "protect, restore, or enhance" each community's natural and cultural resources. Public hearings had to be held before any plan could be officially approved. Once approved, the comprehensive plans must be updated every five years and redone every ten years. Although the enabling legislation required municipalities to create such plans, it did not require that the plans be submitted to any state agency for review and approval.[13]

The comprehensive land-use plans mandated by the 1994 legislation were required to address seven basic elements: land use, population projections and dynamics, economic conditions, housing, community facilities, cultural resources, and natural resources ("coastal resources, slope characteristics, prime agricultural and forest land, plant and animal habitats, parks and recreation areas, scenic views and sites, wetlands, and soil types"). The law also stated that each community's comprehensive plan must include a future land-use map showing areas that should absorb most of the new growth and places that should remain rural.[14]

For many counties and municipalities the 1994 legislation triggered their first effort at comprehensive community planning. As recently as 1990, for example, Beaufort County had no formal land-use planning process nor any professional planning staff members dedicated to land-use issues. The county's historic poverty prompted most of its elected officials over the years to pursue growth for growth's sake in order to raise tax revenues. "The temperament and mentality for generations," remembered the county planning director Tony Criscitiello in 2007, "was we want growth, and we want it no matter what."[15]

The requirement to create a comprehensive land-use plan provided the impetus for many counties and municipalities to include natural resources as an explicit priority of their planning efforts. The comprehensive planning process has also required planners, mayors, and council members to involve community stakeholders in a grassroots process intended to better regulate—and mitigate—the effects of sprawling growth.[16]

Such intensive, professional, transparent planning was the single most important step in the emerging efforts to better manage growth at the end of the twentieth century. Suddenly with the passage of a state law, the conservation culture in the lowcountry had its most effective weapon—in theory, at least. But comprehensive land-use planning—especially in the lowcountry—was—and remains—controversial, contentious, and imperfect.[17]

Beaufort County, the state's fastest growing county, was the first to complete a comprehensive plan and officially approve it, in December 1997. The plan encouraged "infill" development in areas that already had water and sewer service and a network of roads. Charleston County and most of the other lowcountry counties and municipalities followed suit in 1999. As the communities completed their new development plans and land-use policies, however, flaws emerged in the process. It was one thing to produce a comprehensive plan and quite another to enforce it. In Beaufort County, for example, the pace of growth was so furious that it overwhelmed the county and municipal government staff members responsible for overseeing the comprehensive plan. In addition, developers who chafed at the county's strict new zoning restrictions often circumvented them by convincing the incorporated towns of Beaufort and Bluffton to annex their new developments so as to avoid county mandates.

In 2001 several dozen concerned Beaufort County residents submitted a manifesto to the *Beaufort Gazette* titled "A County in Crisis." They declared that the county's traditional quality of life was "in steady decline" because government agencies, zoning boards, and building inspectors had not adequately addressed the challenges of sprawl. "Explosive, unsustainable growth must be controlled," yet the county had not allocated the resources needed to manage the situation. Without "a sufficient number of planners and inspectors on staff, neither the county nor the municipalities of Beaufort, Bluffton, and Port Royal can handle the development already completed and certainly not that coming in the future." Marvin Dukes, vice-chair of the Beaufort County Council, declared that the county's comprehensive plan and its companion zoning and development ordinance were well-intentioned initiatives, but in terms of managing growth they were an example of "too little, too late."[18]

Still another weakness of the comprehensive plans was their parochialism. Adjoining communities rarely consulted one another about overlapping issues and projects. Too often a particular community's long-range plan for new roads, public schools, and water and sewer lines was not coordinated with the plans of neighboring communities. The result was chaotic and wasteful, as adjoining communities failed to recognize that problems such as waterway pollution and traffic congestion "do not recognize county and municipal boundaries." DeWayne Anderson, a planning consultant, explained that the "idea of controlling growth with a [single] county or city plan is a myth. Planning has to be done at the regional level. If people from Allendale are commuting to Hilton Head Island to work, then both counties need to be part of the planning process if governments want to control growth."[19]

To address the lack of regional coordination in land-use planning a coalition of groups—the Coastal Conservation League, the South Carolina Realtors Association, the Municipal Association of South Carolina, the South Carolina Association of Counties, the South Carolina Home Builders Association, and the Governor's Quality of Life Task Force—convinced the General Assembly to improve the original legislation. Thanks to their efforts, in May 2007 Governor Mark Sanford signed the Priority Investment Act. It amended the 1994 Local Government Comprehensive Planning Enabling Act so as to require regional coordination among "adjacent and relevant jurisdictions and agencies" in order to reduce haphazard development and sprawl.[20]

Planning in Charleston County

The process that Charleston County used to develop its first comprehensive plan is instructive. In late 1996 the Charleston County Council appointed twenty-five volunteers to lead the visioning and planning effort. The members of the new Joint Planning Policy Committee were asked to address several key issues: where should growth occur and where should it be excluded? What should growth look like? How should economic development, population growth, and environmental stewardship be balanced? How many tourists could the lowcountry host annually without compromising the region's quality of life and environmental resources? What should the zoning density be for undeveloped farmlands? Such contentious, complicated issues were challenging enough. Adding to the committee's challenges were concerns about its composition. The all-white county council included only one African American and two women among the twenty-five appointees to the joint planning committee. When criticized for the committee's lack of diversity, the chair of the county council explained on December 2, 2011, that he and others had sought to appoint planners, developers, and property owners to the committee, and there were very few African Americans or women in any of these groups.[21]

During 1997 the Joint Planning Committee hosted several public meetings at which residents were invited to share their views and priorities related to growth. Those who spoke expressed a desire to preserve the area's heritage, protect its waterways and farmlands, and find alternatives to sprawl. Thereafter the comprehensive planning process centered on the key question that had long been facing the lowcountry: how could the comprehensive plan help protect and preserve the region's natural resources and distinct way of life while providing for orderly growth and economic development? In January 1999 the Joint Planning Committee shared the first draft of the comprehensive plan with the public. The plan's preface emphasized the broad consensus that the "sprawling nature" of modern development in the lowcountry must be addressed boldly and creatively. In doing so, the plan emphasized, "a balance must be maintained between fostering ["quality"] growth and development and preserving our natural and cultural resources."[22]

The plan itself highlighted new approaches to control sprawl and preserve farmland, including the creation of an innovative Urban Growth Boundary (UGB), a distinct dividing line between rural and urban/suburban areas intended to promote infill redevelopment of already built-up areas and thereby slow the rate of new sprawl. In essence the UGB created a greenbelt outside urban areas made up of agricultural land or open space. Since 1999 the county's UGB has been incorporated into other area plans, including that of the City of Charleston.

The Charleston County planners decided that the most effective way to impede sprawl was to use zoning restrictions to reduce the density (the number of dwelling units that can be built on a particular parcel) of new residential developments in unincorporated rural areas. New homes in rural areas would have to be placed on large lots having a minimum of seven to fifteen acres, thereby precluding any conventional suburban tract development. At public hearings on the draft plan officials from Charleston and Mount Pleasant, representatives of environmental and preservation groups, and residents of several sea islands spoke in favor of the plan's restrictions on growth and urged the council to resist pressure from developers and realtors to dilute the proposals.

By March 1999, however, the Joint Planning Committee was being threatened with lawsuits. Some farmers who had been counting on selling some or all of their property to developers feared that they would lose money if the proposed restrictions on rural development were approved. Committee members responded that they were doing their best to balance the rights of property owners with the widespread desire to preserve the county's rural areas. An example of such balancing efforts was a provision in the draft plan for "clustered" development. It allowed a developer to cluster homes together in a new subdivision if a majority of the parcel's acres were designated for permanent conservation.[23]

On April 20, 1999, after two years of intensive discussion, debate, compromise, and consensus, the County of Charleston Comprehensive Plan was unanimously approved by the county council. "There's some shortcomings in all of it, but looking at the big picture, it was the best overall plan," said council chair Barrett Lawrimore, who was among many who had raised questions about the plan's impact on property owners. Two years later, in 2001, the county enacted the detailed Zoning and Land Development Regulations necessary to implement the comprehensive plan.[24]

Charleston County's first comprehensive plan pleased the antisprawl forces by including some of the most restrictive land-use policies in the state. But it generated a backlash among those opposed to growth controls. No sooner was the comprehensive plan approved by the county council than opponents began mobilizing to stop its implementation. Charlestonian John Templeton, president of Special Properties, a rural land brokerage company, founded the South Carolina Landowners Association (SCLA) to oppose the new zoning ordinances intended to restrict rural development. Within a few years the SCLA claimed to have attracted more than five thousand members representing 1.5 million acres of property. "Many people who live in the country are land-rich, not cash-rich," Templeton noted. "There are numerous start-up businesses that depend on land as their equity line [of credit]. The county has noble goals, but they are eliminating people's property rights." He predicted that the restrictive new zoning ordinances for rural areas would allow only wealthy migrants to build homes in the countryside. Tougher land-use regulations "drive up the price of property so that only out-of-towners can afford to purchase land" in coastal rural areas.[25]

Planning in Mount Pleasant

The disputes generated by comprehensive land-use planning were especially contentious in the burgeoning suburban community of Mount Pleasant, just across the Cooper River from Charleston. During the 1990s it was the coastal region's fastest growing community, welcoming seven new residents each day for an annualized growth rate of 11 percent. Such rapid growth was expensive—and unsustainable. In 1998, after a year of study and numerous public forums, the group orchestrating the town's comprehensive plan proposed an array of stringent measures intended to cut in half the projected population growth rate of 6 percent a year. They imposed impact fees (fees charged to cover the financial impact of the development on schools, roads, water resources, and so forth) on the developers and residents of new communities, and they restricted the annual rate of building permits issued by the town. The result was the strictest comprehensive plan in the state.

One of the primary goals of Mount Pleasant's comprehensive plan was to encourage infill development in ways that maintained the community's rural heritage and conserved green space on the town's periphery. To do so planners proposed their own Urban Growth Boundary to discourage high-density development in areas lacking adequate infrastructure and to create a rural transition zone between the town's suburbs and the rural countryside north of town. Like the UGB in the Charleston county plan, the boundary was intended to channel growth and slow sprawl. Development would be allowed within the line on vacant properties in already built-up areas and where public infrastructure was already in place. Outside the UGB rural development would be limited to conservation projects, green space, and low-density residential projects (one house per three acres). If a developer, however, proposed constructing a compact planned community according to "conservation subdivision" or "traditional neighborhood design" principles, the density could be much higher.[26]

The proposed Mount Pleasant UGB provoked fierce opposition. A Real Estate Issues Council formed by the Charleston Trident Home Builders Association published a letter calling the boundary line an "arbitrary" effort "to force growth patterns." To the home builders the boundary line represented a governmental effort "to dictate consumer buying habits within the real estate industry. This approach discards the principle of free market competition upon which our economy is based." While the boundary line was intended to be a "greenbelt," it was "really a tool to stop outward growth and intensify it inward." Despite such complaints, the town council in 1999 approved the UGB and other elements of the land-use portion of the comprehensive plan. Within a year, however, the town council had decided that it needed even more stringent methods to control growth, including capping the number of annual building permits the city would issue.[27]

Osprey Point: A Case Study of Land-use Planning to Shape Growth

The role and nature of conservation-oriented communities are determined by the guidelines and ordinances contained in the comprehensive municipal and county land-use plans developed in the lowcountry since the mid-1990s. The regulatory scrutiny given to proposed new subdivisions or mixed-use communities is a direct outgrowth of the comprehensive planning process and the emergence of the culture of conservation in the region. A good example of the changing dynamics of growth and conservation in the lowcountry is the way in which Beaufort County planners and elected officials handled a proposed new development called Osprey Point.

In 2007 Lowcountry Partners, a real estate development company, sought to construct Osprey Point, a conventional subdivision on a 119-acre parcel near the headwaters of the Okatie River northwest of Bluffton. To do so two of its executives asked the Beaufort County Planning Department to rezone the parcel to increase the housing density nearly 4.5 times as much as allowed by the county's comprehensive plan. They wanted to build 138 homes on the site. Members of the county's professional planning staff balked, however. In their view the proposed neighborhood was a throwback to the days of cookie-cutter, bulldoze-and-build suburban subdivisions; it violated the premises and spirit of the comprehensive plan and the county's effort to ensure smart growth. They worried about its impact on schools, traffic, and the environment. To them Osprey Point was simply "more of the same" old-style development that had created so many environmental problems in the lowcountry. Their memo to the planning commission was blunt: "Such a development is unsustainable and simply adds to the problem of urban sprawl."[28]

Instead of simply denying the rezoning request, however, the small planning staff proposed a better idea. Just a few months before the Osprey Point rezoning request was filed, a similar proposal had been submitted by developers for a new subdivision called Okatie Marsh. It would be adjacent to Osprey Point, and the two neighborhoods would share an entrance. The rezoning request for Okatie Marsh called for nine times the allowed density. County planners fastened on a creative alternative that drew upon the overlapping emphases of smart growth, new urbanism, and conservation subdivisions. They urged the two developers to combine their properties with the rest of the undeveloped property in the area and construct a multiuse village that would be largely self-sustaining and provide a healthy mixture of housing types and prices, including apartments and condominiums. "What we're trying to avoid here is 'placeless' sprawl," explained Tony Criscitiello, the county's planning director. "This is an opportunity to create a place with some identity that 50 years from now we can say: 'Hey we did it right.'"[29]

The developers first had to agree to the suggested transformation of their properties. For months they wrestled with county planners over how best to pay for the impact of the development on the area's already overcrowded schools, roads, and parks. By January 2008 the discussions had progressed to include a third complementary development: a continuing care retirement community called River Oaks. All three contiguous neighborhoods—Osprey Point, Okatie Marsh, and River Oaks—would be combined to create an integrated, walkable smart-growth community called Okatie Village. It would include 1,252 homes on 284 acres. The architect who developed the site plan said that residents would have the option to work, shop, and play within their community. Such a neo-traditional neighborhood development would save the county money by pulling drivers off heavily traveled highways. He expressed the hope that Okatie Village would become a model for the county's efforts to absorb a rising tide of new residents. "You're not going to stop growth," he asserted. "Either manage it, or it runs you over."[30]

Okatie Village was explicitly designed to "contain sprawl." It would include retail and professional offices, parks, lakes, ponds, and interconnecting bicycling and walking trails. There would be no golf course and no security gates. In its efforts to reduce automobile dependency, the plan included provisions for future public transit stops. Specimen trees on the site would be protected, and an ongoing environmental education program for residents would be created. As the developer of Osprey Point predicted, "residents who are aware of the needs of the environment and are properly educated will be the best protection for the Okatie River."[31]

As the developers of Okatie Village navigated the complicated process of gaining required approvals from the planning board, residents of a neighborhood near the proposed development mobilized in opposition. Conventional NIMBY arguments held sway, as they imagined the pollution and congestion resulting from Okatie Village corrupting their "quiet" and "serene" subdivision. At the same time, members of the planning commission kept asking the developers for more concessions to improve the project, such as an explicit commitment to affordable housing, and more information about Okatie Village's probable impact on roads, schools, parks, libraries, and police and fire protection. "When you are getting into a project of this magnitude, I think you need to look at it more closely," said planning commission member Mary LeGree. Others insisted that the developers put in writing all of their promises. Wendy Zara, a member of the Steering Committee of the Coalition for Smart Growth, expressed general support for Okatie Village, but she too asked for more detailed commitments from the developers. The developers, she believed, had not adequately explained how they planned to incorporate "affordable" housing in the project, nor had they specified the amount of impact fees they would provide to cover school and road improvements. She asked the commission to put the project on hold until all relevant questions are answered. "If we don't know some of these details now," she warned, "smart growth can turn into dumb growth pretty quickly."[32]

Lowcountry conservation organizations agreed that the proposed Okatie Village development needed to be managed wisely. At the public hearing before the planning commission, Reed Armstrong of the Coastal Conservation League applauded the developers for aligning their plans with the premises of smart growth. They "seem to meet the land use and natural assets goals with design features such as mixed-use development, interconnectivity, limited access points, walkability, generous open space and wetland protection, parklands, recreational facilities, storm-water management, and river buffers that exceed County standards." But Armstrong cautioned that the proposals did not include adequate information related to the county's projections for growth capacity. More data was needed before approval should be given.[33]

In March 2008 the Beaufort County Planning Commission recommended that the county council turn down the rezoning request for Okatie Village. Although the developers had pledged to pay impact fees, including six thousand dollars per home for the support of public schools, the commissioners remained concerned about public monies that would be spent on road widening projects and new schools. By June, however, the planning commission reversed its vote, explaining that more concessions by the developers had resolved their doubts. In October 2008 Beaufort County Council finally approved the Okatie Village project. The tortuous, prolonged negotiations had resulted in the developers pledging to pay $10.7 million to the county for school subsidies and road construction. They also agreed to set aside thirty-two homes and thirty-four apartments at federal "affordable" housing rates. And they mollified many of the neighboring residents by promising to extend water and sewer lines to the existing subdivision adjacent to Okatie Village. Finally the developers accommodated environmental concerns by promising to adhere to stringent storm-water runoff standards, including monitoring runoff during and after construction.[34]

The process by which Okatie Village was conceived, proposed, revised, and approved testifies to the deepening significance of both comprehensive land-use planning and the culture of conservation in the lowcountry. Citizens, professional planners, elected officials, environmental organizations, and the media— all displayed an aroused interest in the environmental impact of development and the imperatives of smart growth. By taking their due diligence responsibilities seriously, those involved in the process of assessing the rezoning request provided both systematic oversight and creative input. As a result of the issues raised and questions asked, the developers had to hire additional land planners, engineers, and environmental consultants to fulfill the project's responsibility to protect wetlands. They also were prompted to consult with the U. S. Army Corps of Engineers, the South Carolina Department of Health and Environmental Control and its Office of Ocean and Coastal Resource Management, the local fire department, school district, and many other government agencies. County planning director Tony Criscitiello noted that his goal throughout the Okatie Village planning process was to ensure smart growth by substituting "a cohesive and integrated community" plan for the "piecemeal and disjointed development" that was initially envisioned.[35]

An interested observer of the protracted process by which Okatie Village was conceived, modified, and eventually approved was Charlie B. Fraser, a Hilton Head realtor and the nephew of Charles E. Fraser, the fabled developer of Sea Pines Plantation. To him the example of Okatie Village revealed "that our local government is looking out for us. We cannot buy up all of the undeveloped land in Beaufort County, so we need to make sure what is developed is done in an environmentally sensitive way with the least amount impact on the environment. Less density, more runoff retention, natural filtration in the runoff ponds. . . . Do not allow clear cutting, require that lots keep the trees that are currently on the property, and do your best to build to [the natural features of the] lot." Realtor Fraser spoke for the lowcountry's culture of conservation when he urged the citizenry "to make sure our local governments are doing the oversight work necessary to make sure the developments are being built correctly. Be a good neighbor and keep your eyes on what is going on." Okatie Village has since become one of the greenest of the planned conservation communities in the lowcountry.[36]

Taking the Long View: Sustainable Planning

The example of Okatie Village illustrated that managing growth so as to protect the environment and the lowcountry's cultural heritage is a delicate process of balancing community priorities and private property rights. Yet by the start of the twenty-first century, public attitudes were shifting dramatically in favor of controlling growth. In 2000 the University of South Carolina conducted a statewide survey focused on land-use planning. The results were surprising. More than 70 percent of the respondents favored tougher growth controls, including required local land-use plans and creating construction-free zones, or greenbelts, around towns and cities. More than half of those who supported growth controls said they would pay higher taxes to purchase property for greenbelts. Some 60 percent of the participants said they would pay more taxes to enable state and local governments to buy sensitive environmental areas. "To be honest, we didn't think people would care that much about this issue," admitted researcher Robert Oldendick, director of the university's Survey Research Laboratory. "But it's clear that this is a very important issue at the local level." The survey revealed that white respondents displayed greater support for controlling how and where growth would occur. Sam Passmore, a staff member of the Coastal Conservation League, commented that the survey results aligned with South Carolinians' historical respect for nature and desire for a high quality of life. "The over-arching observation is that the public wants to see economic growth, but it also wants more intense management," Passmore said. "The good news is that is not an either/or proposition."[37]

By the start of the twenty-first century, the balancing act between growth and the environment was becoming more effective. It was not yet perfect, nor uniformly practiced, but comprehensive land-use planning and the growing number of new conservation-oriented communities testified to changing public attitudes in the lowcountry. As Mayor Riley emphasized in 2005, without new growth "being well planned, you . . . create a development that is not sustainable."[38]

SIX

Conservation Communities

Summertime barbecues and picnics are commonplace across the United States, but few of them serve alligator meat. Even less common is a gathering to celebrate the capture of a rogue alligator found in a residential neighborhood. During the summer of 2007 I'On, a new-urbanist community in Mount Pleasant, hosted such a celebration (at the time I owned a house in I'On). The home owners' association newsletter reported: "Some great news! Last Tuesday, our 8–1/2' Eastlake visitor [an alligator] was finally captured and removed in handcuffs. To celebrate, your trusty Board has organized 'Gator Night at the Creek Club' to educate everyone on how to live safely and in harmony with alligators: some tips, some tricks, some do's and some don'ts." The event-planning committee wanted the evening to be "a family affair, so we'll begin with a Potluck Dinner before the one-hour presentation by South Carolina's foremost alligator expert, Ron Russell. We'll also have a 'live' 3-foot alligator for the kids and brave grownups to play with. . . . We'll also throw in some Bar-B-Q Alligator for everyone to enjoy as well as a terrific presentation."[1]

Gator Night at the Creek Club was intended to be both fun-loving and educational. It was well attended by residents and children who wanted to learn more about alligators and their habitats. The environmental emphases of the widely acclaimed I'On development provide a prime example of the numerous conservation-oriented communities that have emerged in the lowcountry since the 1980s. While golf courses, tennis courts, and country clubs retain their popularity, the ultimate residential amenity in the lowcountry is access to the natural landscape and its wild creatures.[2]

The growing interest among home buyers in environmental amenities reflects a national trend. In 2006 a home owner's survey conducted by the National Association of Home Builders found that baby boomers (people born during the 1940s and 1950s) choosing a home prized green space. More than 25 percent of respondents aged fifty-five and older said they wanted to buy real estate directly on, or with a view of, a lake, river, pond, or ocean. More than 27 percent wanted to see green space out of their windows, while nearly 12 percent reported that they would like to buy real estate "surrounded" by green space. Twenty-seven percent of respondents wanted to be able to walk to bicycling or hiking trails from their homes.[3]

Conservation-oriented communities in the lowcountry cater to such evolving interests. They are distinguished from conventional subdivisions by the explicit attention given to landscape conservation in their planning, marketing, design, construction practices, and governance protocols. There is no single template or model for such communities or subdivisions. Rather they represent a wide spectrum of strategies and elements associated with the various antisprawl philosophies represented by the three most prominent national developmental models: smart growth, new urbanism, and conservation subdivisions. What they share are the same basic priorities—the preservation of open space and minimal disturbance to the natural environment through their initial design as well as the creation of environmentally sensitive governance covenants and conservation easements.[4]

Developmental Models for Conserving Land and Natural Resources

The process by which lowcountry communities have been developing comprehensive land-use plans has necessarily involved philosophical discussions about the best ways to preserve the lowcountry quality of life and the coastal region's environmental amenities. Many theories and perspectives have guided the efforts to manage growth more wisely, some of which at times have been at odds with others. The most prominent alternative developmental models have been drawn from three overlapping national movements to promote ecological health and community welfare by combating negative aspects of sprawl: smart growth, new urbanism, and conservation subdivisions. Taken together they have created a new paradigm for land-use policies and growth management strategies.

Smart Growth

Smart growth is a national movement that emerged in the 1970s as the first systematic alternative to urban decay and suburban sprawl. It does not advocate no-growth or even slow growth. Proponents of smart growth acknowledge the benefits that derive from new development: jobs, tax revenues, and amenities. But they want to garner such benefits without degrading the environment, raising local taxes, worsening school overcrowding and traffic congestion, or busting municipal budgets. Smart growth involves investing time, creativity, and resources in restoring community and vitality to existing urban areas and older suburbs so as to reduce growth pressures on outlying areas, open space, and farmlands.

Such an emphasis on so-called infill development was designed to place more new homes and businesses into already developed areas, typically in the heart of a town or city. Infill neighborhoods would reduce traffic and infrastructure expenses—and promote a more active sense of community. "Live near where you work, work where you live," explained Christiane Farrell, the head of the

Mount Pleasant Planning and Engineering Division. If development on new property is unavoidable, smart growth promotes more compact, town-centered and pedestrian-oriented planned communities that include a robust mix of housing, commercial, and retail uses. It also preserves open space and ecological resources while encouraging widespread use of mass transit systems.[5]

Smart growth views residential development from an ecological as well as an economic perspective. It seeks to change zoning laws and public attitudes so as to reduce the impact of residential and commercial growth on the environment while minimizing infrastructure costs—both to developers and to municipalities. Smart-growth ideas are evident at Dewees Island, an ecological community northeast of Charleston that opened in 1997. The island's site development and infrastructure expenses were 60 percent lower than average because it employed impervious roadway surfaces (aggregate and sand) and disdained conventional landscaping in favor of native plants and natural vegetation. "When you don't have . . . manicured landscapes and paved roads, you end up with enormous reductions in infrastructure costs," explained John Knott, the chief executive of Island Preservation Partnership, the "green" island's developer.[6]

Perhaps the most distinguishing aspect of the campaign for smart growth is its emphasis on comprehensive land-use planning. Advocates of smart growth urge communities to "grow by choice rather than by chance" and to consider the long-range and indirect implications of growth. In practice this means placing as much new development as possible in old (already developed) areas—areas that have the infrastructure (roads, water and sewer water lines, and utilities) to support new growth.

Smart Growth America, a coalition of national, state, and local organizations working to improve the quality, consistency, and coordination of land-use planning, succinctly described their mission:

> We believe that the American people deserve healthy cities, towns and suburbs; homes that are both affordable and close to jobs and activities; fewer hours in traffic and more opportunities to enjoy recreation and natural areas; air and water of the highest quality; and a landscape our children can be proud to inherit. We believe that ordinary citizens deserve a much greater say, and better options, in choosing their communities' future. To that end, our members work with citizens across the country to preserve our built and natural heritage, promote fairness for people of all backgrounds, fight for high-quality neighborhoods, expand choices in housing and transportation and improve poorly conceived development projects.[7]

Those promoting smart growth challenge local planners, elected officials, and developers to avoid the negative effects of sprawl by changing the policies and practices associated with land development: providing incentives as well as disincentives to developers, and changing the way that states and localities fund the infrastructure associated with development. They call for compact neighborhoods with higher densities, smaller lots and houses, grid-connected neighborhood streets rather than culs-de-sac, and richer civic cultures; creating (or restoring) a collective sense of community and pride of place; a wider range of transportation, employment, and housing choices; preserving and enhancing a site's natural and cultural resources; and promoting public health through walking, outdoor recreation, and pollution-free communities. Developers applying smart-growth principles incorporate substantial open areas, or commons, into their site plans, and they seek to protect and preserve a site's sensitive ecological areas.[8]

South Carolina was late in embracing smart-growth ideals. In 1999, however, state senator Phil Leventis, a Democrat from Sumter who was then serving as chair of the Senate Agriculture and Natural Resources Committee, appointed an ad hoc Committee on Urban Growth that introduced smart-growth legislation to curtail unplanned growth. Leventis and his supporters noted that South Carolina had traditionally been one of the worst states in protecting open space from development. The state's history of weak local governments and even weaker regional cooperation among cities and counties had compromised effective land-use planning for decades, Leventis believed. If South Carolina's counties and cities were ever to grow in an orderly, manageable, smart way, they must control urban sprawl. To do so, he argued, they must do a better job of land-use planning—together. The costly result of South Carolina's being among the top five states in encouraging sprawl, he said, "is isolated subdivisions, each of which demands separate roads, sewer, water and other services for small sites that do not pay for the expenditures." His proposed bill provided state financial support for communities (voluntarily) to improve the quality of their comprehensive long-range land-use planning efforts. It also would have created a state office in Columbia to collect and analyze the plans from throughout the state so as to encourage the adoption of best practices and more regional collaboration.[9]

The smart-growth bill proposed by Senator Leventis coincided with a bipartisan proposal by Representative Chip Campsen, a Charleston Republican, and Democratic Governor Jim Hodges to allocate five million dollars annually for an Open Space Matching Grant Program (later renamed the State Conservation Bank) to help local governments purchase and preserve green space across the state. Both proposals were the subject of lively discussion at the state's first Governor's Summit on Growth, held in Greenville in March 2000. Convened by Governor Hodges, the three-day conference attracted four hundred participants. It was the first time that the state's political, business, conservation, and land development leaders had met to discuss how to rein in the state's runaway growth. No decisions were made, but there was consensus among the diverse participants that South Carolina was going to continue to experience rapid population growth and land development. Therefore local and state government officials needed to become more intentional and "smart" about where and how growth should occur. The group also agreed that protecting green space or open space is good both for the environment and for property values. And they acknowledged that residential development in general should become more compact and less sprawling.[10]

As Senator Leventis's smart-growth proposal worked its way through various legislative committees in the General Assembly, the editors of the *Spartanburg Herald-Journal* emphasized that even such a modest effort at promoting "voluntary" statewide planning would face massive resistance in conservative South Carolina. Legislators "shouldn't pretend that successfully pursuing smart growth will be an easy and harmonious process. It won't."[11]

To help build support for the bill a delegation of lowcountry elected officials, business leaders, and conservationists traveled to Columbia to urge lawmakers to encourage more coordinated land-use planning. "The [lowcountry] region is governed by an inconsistent patchwork of regulations," said Sam Passmore, then a staff member with the Coastal Conservation League. While acknowledging that zoning should remain a local responsibility, the lowcountry delegation encouraged a larger role for the state in real estate development because it often provided roads, social services, and environmental regulation for such projects. To illustrate the urgency of the problem in the lowcountry, Ted Power, a Mount Pleasant Town Council member, shared with the lawmakers the extreme measure his fast-growing community had taken to slow down sprawl: implementing a six-month moratorium on new residential projects.[12]

Critics of Leventis's smart-growth proposal raised legitimate questions about volatile issues associated with government efforts to manage growth. Private property rights were threatened—as well as a suburban way of life that had governed the United States since the end of World War II. "I'm fed up with land-use planning," said John Templeton of Charleston. "Why do we need to create another level of government? We're just going to spend more taxpayer dollars for regulation we don't need." Business lobbyists and conventional developers warned lawmakers to avoid any statewide initiatives related to growth management and land-use restrictions. Opponents claimed that smart-growth ideas violated private property rights and would undermine economic growth. Although state lawmakers approved the South Carolina Conservation Incentives Act in 2000 that provided tax benefits to property owners who permanently preserved land with easements, the proposed smart-growth legislation, as well as the governor's effort to create a state-funded conservation land bank, were both voted down. "They acted as if we were communists out to take everything they had," Leventis said of the opponents of his modest proposals promoting comprehensive land-use planning. Those opponents included the Chamber of Commerce, the Home Builders Association, the Realtors' Association, the Manufacturers' Association, and other prodevelopment interests. Leventis dubbed them the "property rights crowd." In his view his critics "call it property rights, but what they mean is the right to develop everything in the state."[13]

One of the outspoken critics of smart-growth land-use planning and zoning restrictions was John Cone of the South Carolina Home Builders Association. He opposed the legislature's creating an entity to tell counties and cities how best to engage in land-use planning and zoning. The right of people to do what they wanted with their property, he implied, was sacrosanct. Other opponents stressed that smart growth was not so smart. "You've heard that growth [sprawl] is getting a bad name," said Nick Kremydas, general counsel for the South Carolina Realtors Association. "We thrive and live on growth." He warned that legislative efforts to promote smart growth would hurt economic development in communities that desperately needed jobs. He added that decisions about land use were best made at the local level; lawmakers should not copy smart-growth best practices from other states. "We have to look for a South Carolina answer to a South Carolina problem," Kremydas stressed.[14]

Yet despite the defeat of the proposed legislation, the notion of pursuing smart-growth land-development strategies gathered momentum in the lowcountry with each passing year. Conservationists repeatedly demonstrated that they could protect private property rights while promoting land preservation. In October 2001 the City of Charleston cosponsored a two-day conference of business and political leaders focused on managing growth, curbing sprawl, and revitalizing urban life in the lowcountry. Speakers highlighted the need for saving green space, remediating environmental pollution, expanding public transportation, and providing more affordable housing.[15]

That same year a similarly diverse group of public officials, real estate developers, planners, and environmentalists formed the South Carolina Smart Growth Initiative. Jim Chaffin, the developer of Spring Island, cochaired the initiative along with Charleston's Mayor Riley. Chaffin told a Charleston symposium in 2002 that the state must find ways to accommodate the continuing influx of new residents while balancing "economic vitality, environmental sensitivity, and community livability." He added that wisely managing growth required fresh ideas. "None of us are here with a handful of instant solutions. There is no one-size-fits-all answer."[16]

The Charleston symposium—and the Smart Growth Initiative—were sponsored by the Washington, D.C.–based Urban Land Institute and the University of South Carolina's Center for Real Estate. Their purpose was to evaluate growth trends across the state and promote smart-growth alternatives. J. Terrence Farris, the director of Clemson University's Center for Real Estate Development, predicted that 90 percent of the state's residential growth in the next quarter century would be in the suburbs. "The American paradox," he observed, is that "we hate density and we hate sprawl," but "it's kind of hard to hate both." He pointed out that "people want a single-family house, they want a [large] lot, they want reasonable prices in the suburbs," but he urged planners to encourage urban redevelopment (infill) whenever possible rather than encouraging more sprawling suburbs on diminishing farmlands. Richard M. Rosan, president of the Urban Land Institute, said that the lowcountry needed to revise its notion of residential density. He preferred development "that is more clustered and less sprawling."

Higher-density neighborhoods—if done right—could generate increased jobs and tax revenues, expanded affordable housing options, additional recreational amenities, and the revitalization of blighted areas.[17]

During 2002, Chaffin, Riley, and the three dozen members of the Smart Growth Initiative convened nine public forums across the state that led to the publication in 2004 of a comprehensive white paper titled "Growing by Choice or Chance: State Strategies for Quality Growth in South Carolina." It encouraged South Carolinians to embrace smart-growth ideas and foster a "sustainable land ethic" over the next twenty-five years, during which the state would add a million more residents. "South Carolina is at a crossroads," Riley said. "We are growing at the fastest pace the state has ever grown in its history." The state, said the report, had developed a strong economy, robust entrepreneurial spirit, and thriving tourism industry. At the same time South Carolina "also has a long history in both the public and private sectors of national leadership in historic preservation and land conservation. This conservation ethic is a fundamental cultural value of its citizens and will continue to shape the built and natural environment of the state as growth and development occur."[18]

So how was cascading growth to be transformed into smart growth? Although sprawl had shaped the state's development since 1945, Chaffin noted, it was "not too late to change the way growth occurs." Smart growth would balance "economics, livability and the environment," he added. "The idea is not to stop growth, but to make sure that it does not ruin the things that make the state appealing. Property rights have to be respected," but there are better ways to promote planned growth. "Growing by Choice or Chance" listed ten strategic principles to ensure sustainable growth across the state, including preserving the state's "quality of life; revitalizing existing communities; preserving open space, natural resources, and the environment; balancing private property rights with community values; fostering greater collaboration and coordination among local and state government agencies; and promoting more compact, mixed-use development, where housing, shopping, parks, schools, and workplaces would be built in close proximity to one another so as to reduce the overall footprint of a development and encourage walking rather than driving. Mayor Riley said that Daniel Island in Charleston, a new multiuse community, represented a good example of the kind of sustainable, conservation-oriented development that the Smart Growth Initiative envisioned. In a similar vein Eric Meyer of the Coastal Conservation League declared that the time was ripe for the lowcountry to confront in a holistic way the challenges of population growth and land-use policies. The region was "at a tipping point for smart growth," he said.[19]

"Growing by Choice or Chance" acknowledged that it would not be easy to slow sprawl in a state long known for its feisty protection of private property rights and skepticism toward government planning and regulation. "Yet with strong state leadership, it is possible to overcome many of these barriers." Outspoken fiscal conservative Mark Sanford assumed the governor's office in early

2003, and he surprised many observers by promoting smart-growth principles. Instead of the term *smart growth*, Sanford preferred phrases such as "coherent growth" or "sustainable growth," but his initiatives promoted the same ideas intended to deter sprawl. In one of his first acts as governor he appointed in December 2002 a twenty-nine-member statewide Quality of Life Task Force, headed by lowcountry conservationist Elizabeth Hagood. The task force's mission was "to protect the land and water resources of South Carolina in balance with economic growth by emphasizing: education, incentives over regulation, market principles, and respect for private property rights." The resulting report included some sixty recommendations intended better to balance the preservation of the environment with economic development. In 2007 Sanford told the South Carolina Republican Convention that aligning "the state's infrastructure construction policy with existing patterns of growth" was smarter than adding new roads to serve new neighborhoods in sparsely populated areas. To curtail new sprawl and ease congestion in already developed areas, Sanford urged that state infrastructure monies should be allocated based on a "merit-based system," not a "good-old-boy" arrangement, which traditionally assigned priorities to projects on an idiosyncratic basis, such as the location of a powerful lawmaker's "favorite fishing hole."[20]

In his annual State of the State address in January 2008, Sanford announced the creation of a Land Use Planning Task Force to bring greater coherence to efforts across the state to slow the growth of sprawl. He had become increasingly concerned that South Carolina was losing the distinctive quality of life afforded by its "scenic beauty." If we lose it, he predicted, "we will lose a big part of what makes this state so special—and a big part of what drives our economic engine." He emphasized that "we need to also look at more options in the way our state grows and develops." To that end he appointed the Land Use Planning Task Force "to look at the root causes of congestion, a full menu of options to better roads in our state, and the way that our towns grow and connect. I think there are some great new market-based ideas in impacting congestion and transportation and growth that are worthy of a careful study and policy implementation."[21]

Others echoed Sanford's efforts to use more coordinated land-use planning to promote smart growth. By 2009 the four-thousand-member Charleston Trident Association of Realtors (CTAR), which previously had balked at endorsing statewide or regional growth management proposals, officially began promoting smart-growth principles. "No longer should traffic congestion and sprawl that harm our environment and deteriorating school systems be the norm," commented the CTAR legislative chair Herb Koger. CTAR launched an informational website called Preserve Our Lowcountry, which declared: "We need to protect our quality of life and focus our efforts on reducing road congestion, creating better paying jobs, improving the quality of our schools, ensuring that our residents have affordable places to call home and the preservation of our pristine environment."[22]

The New Urbanism

Among the new market-based smart-growth ideas that Governor Sanford found attractive was what had come to be called the new urbanism, a neo-traditional planning and architectural concept that emerged in the late 1980s. Where smart-growth advocates concentrated on regional growth management and broad land-planning issues, principles, and ordinances, visionary planners and progressive architects focused on the ways that innovative spatial arrangements could foster community. New urbanism, a term often used interchangeably with the labels *neo-traditional design* and *traditional neighborhood development*, embraces carefully designed and aesthetically rigorous mixed-use planned communities that are neither cities nor suburbs but instead are hybrids of old-fashioned practices and sophisticated new designs. In the lowcountry, examples of new-urbanist communities included I'On in Mount Pleasant and Habersham near Beaufort, both built in the late 1990s.

The leading evangelist for new urbanism is Andres Duany, a provocative, flamboyant, brashly self-assured Cuban American community planner based in Miami who in the 1980s designed the celebrated—and controversial—planned communities, Seaside, Florida, and Kentlands, Maryland. Duany wanted "to make places that are so wonderful, people will never want to leave. They will never think of living anyplace else." He dismissed the conventional suburb as being "less a community than an agglomeration of houses, shops, and offices connected to one another by cars." Duany and other zealous new urbanists insisted that many American villages and towns before the advent of the automobile had it right: they were designed on a pedestrian scale and centered on compact, convenient, high-density self-sustaining neighborhoods where residents worked, shopped, worshiped, attended school, and played—all within walking distance of their single- and multifamily homes.[23]

In 1993 Peter Katz, a San Francisco design consultant, founded the Congress for the New Urbanism, a coalition of reformist architects, builders, developers, landscape architects, engineers, planners, realtors, and supporters committed to restoring the nation's public culture and human-scale communities by designing neo-traditional projects. Katz explained that they were determined to address the problems of suburban sprawl: "We've been building great houses but lousy communities. The problem isn't growth but the model we're using. The suburban pattern of the past 40 years is unsustainable." He insisted that the new urbanism is much more than a stylized design ethic: "It's about how buildings relate to each other and what kind of public space they create."[24]

Katz and his allies outlined their beliefs in *The Charter for New Urbanism*. It listed the fundamental tenets of the new approach to community design: "Neighborhoods should be diverse in use and population; communities should be designed for the pedestrian and transit as well as the car; cities and towns should be shaped by physically defined and universally accessible public spaces and community institutions; urban places should be framed by architecture and land-scape design that celebrate local history, climate, ecology, and building practice." In promoting earth-friendly architecture, energy efficiency, historic preservation, and accessibility, new-urbanist designers work in tandem with smart-growth principles. They strive to use less land, reduce automobile use, nurture a "neigh-borly" sense of place and community, and minimize environmental damage. There are now hundreds of new-urbanist communities across the nation.[25]

New urbanists focus on creating interactive neighborhood communities rather than constructing sprawling subdivisions. Genuine neighborhoods, they believe, should be much more than a collection of separated houses; they should be integrated, self-contained communities that foster neighborly interaction. As the developer of a new-urbanist community in North Carolina explained in 1999, "I've had to relearn everything we've forgotten since World War II. But I do want to start building communities for people instead of for cars." New-urbanist designers place houses (with inviting front porches and garages hidden along alleys in the rear) near sidewalks at the front of small lots and clustered around public spaces that include parks and playgrounds, as well as civic, retail, office, and commercial facilities. The aim of such neo-traditional communities "is to reduce the need for constant car trips, wasteful land use, ugly strip malls, and the bland homogeneity of ranch houses and office compounds that produce sub-urban blight." Intentionally narrow tree-lined streets slow traffic and encourage walking, biking, and social engagement. Ward Reynolds, an environmental plan-ner living in I'On, said that neo-traditional neighborhood developments could help reduce sprawl. "By developing at higher densities with smaller lots," he ex-plained, "you can fit more people into the neighborhood," thereby reducing the need for further intrusion into farmlands and forests on the suburban fringe.[26]

New urbanism in practice, however, has often fallen short of its ideals. Crit-ics have highlighted its nostalgia, spotty marketing appeal, design failures, unin-tentional environmental consequences, and lack of social and racial diversity in its model communities, many of which are so meticulously planned that they seem artificial and antiseptic. The small house lots in new-urbanist villages often come at lofty prices. And residents have to be willing to surrender some of the individual freedoms enjoyed in conventional suburban subdivisions (no picture windows, no chain-link fences, no raised ranch houses).[27]

While new-urbanist communities tout their eco-friendly features, they have not always promoted energy and water efficiency, sustainable construction mate-rials and practices, or landscaping with only native plants. Several studies have documented the ways in which new-urbanist communities have failed to create the desired social diversity. Home owners in new-urbanist communities have tended to be exclusively upper-class white people. Such unintended elitism flies in the face of new urbanism's emphasis on racial, ethnic, and socioeconomic diversity. As Duany has repeatedly stressed, new urbanism seeks to celebrate the variety and complexity of human society. His goal in designing communities is to avoid "monoculture." Yet too many of the first-generation new-urbanist communities were homogeneous, theme-park-like enclaves for rich white residents. An extensive study of Celebration, the new-urbanist community near Orlando built by the Disney Company, found that many residents regretted that their stylized and highly regulated Disney village lacked a felt sense of community or even reality. Living there seemed artificial, almost like living in one of the faux communities at the nearby Disney World theme park. According to one resident, Celebration felt more like a "hierarchical corporation rather than an American community."[28]

Only recently have scholars begun to assess the actual results of new-urbanist communities. Their questions are often equally relevant to smart-growth projects. Do pedestrian-friendly communities in fact reduce automobile use? The early evidence reveals that vehicular trips are not reduced as much by new-urbanist design principles as they are by smart-growth regional land-use planning. Attractive human-scale streetscapes are not in and of themselves sufficient to get people out of their cars. Few of the new-urbanist communities in the South have found ways to create mass-transit options for their residents. In many respects the logic of new urbanism makes public transportation a requirement, not a possible option in the distant future. As one critic pointed out, "how does a neo-traditional subdivision sitting off a standard suburban highway end up as anything but a conventional suburb?"[29]

Can new-urbanist villages and towns truly enhance the residents' sense of community? Sociologist David Brain argues that new-urbanist architects and developers are better at promoting "civility" within their neo-traditional villages than at generating a deeper "sense of community." There is little tangible evidence that the sense of community is qualitatively better in new-urbanist communities than in conventional subdivisions. Do new-urbanist communities display a more sensitive ecological consciousness? Initial studies suggest that smart growth's emphasis on regional ecosystem planning is more beneficial to the environment than new urbanism's neighborhood-based efforts.[30]

Whatever the actual effects of new-urbanist communities, the ideas undergirding them struck a resonant chord with many people in the lowcountry. In 2007 Governor Sanford convened a state conference on land-use planning moderated by Andres Duany. South Carolina, Sanford observed while introducing Duany, had reached a "tipping point in wrestling with rapid growth." He was increasingly worried about "profound quality of life issues" caused by sprawl. He urged developers, planners, and environmentalists to find new "constructive ideas" designed to better balance growth and conservation. Although few Republican state executives across the nation had made land-use planning a priority, the libertarian-leaning governor was willing to promote smart-growth ideas and new-urbanist models to curb sprawl and improve air and water quality, starting with the Priority Investment Act, which required adjoining cities and counties to coordinate their comprehensive land-use plans. Dana Beach also attended the conference. He noted that, while "there is some dissonance" between conservatives and conservationists, "what is driving the governor on this is a moral commitment to preserving the landscape."[31]

Conservation Subdivisions

In the 1990s an important variation on the overlapping goals of smart growth and new urbanism surged into prominence when Randall Arendt, an award-winning conservation planner and site designer based in Rhode Island, began championing the concept of conservation subdivisions, also called open-space developments. Like the smart-growth and new-urbanist movements, conservation subdivisions promote compact neighborhoods and clustered development as a means of alleviating the cancerous growth of sprawl and its damaging effects on the environment. In fact, the three approaches to environmentally sensitive design have many overlapping principles. Conservation subdivision design primarily differs from smart growth and new urbanism in making the preservation of the largest amount possible of open or natural spaces (and their resident biodiversity) the primary focus of planned communities.[32]

In a series of influential books, articles, lectures, interviews, and workshops, Arendt acknowledged that growth is inevitable, but he insisted that planners and designers should be much more intentional, comprehensive, and farsighted in deciding how best to manage growth so as to preserve a community's natural resources, cultural and historic heritage, and quality of life. He also believed that the United States could house growing numbers of people *and* preserve the environment. To do so, however, developers must break out of the conventional cookie-cutter suburban mold of dividing all available land into lots and streets and then building the maximum number of large look-a-like houses. Why? Shortsighted, sprawling development, Arendt documented, consumes land and natural resources at an unsustainable rate.[33]

Unlike conventional "wall-to-wall" suburban developments with little or no open space, Arendt's concept of conservation subdivisions focused first on the land itself. The crucial step in the design of new neighborhoods or integrated mixed-use developments, he argued, should be an audit of the site's natural areas and historic features. Planners should "outline the open space first" and then "let its size and location become the central organizing element driving the rest of the design." By open space he meant not just wetlands and ravines that could not be developed anyway, but meaningful open space such as woodlands, meadows, and fields, productive farmland, significant wildlife corridors and habitat areas, historic and culturally important sites, and scenic viewsheds as well. Such environmental amenities should be "greenlined"—permanently protected through conservation easements or deed restrictions embedded in the title of each lot sold and in the community association governance documents. Only then should house sites be identified and clustered so as to reduce their footprint and to take maximum advantage of the natural areas, to form neighborhood squares, common spaces, recreational fields, and woodland preserves. Laying out the streets and trails should come third, followed by the fourth, and last, step: drawing the lot lines. Once built out, such conservation subdivisions would, Arendt contended, preserve at least half of the development's buildable land. And such environmental priorities would be sustained through the ongoing governance protocols of the community associations.[34]

The strategy of first preserving a site's most valuable open space while increasing the housing density has proven to be both popular and successful in low-country conservation communities. At Dewees Island, for example, 784 out of the total of 1,200 available acres, including a 200-acre tidal lake, were set aside as a perpetual wildlife refuge; houses could not be built on the shoreline, gasoline-fueled cars were prohibited, and the footprint of houses and driveways must be less than 7,500 square feet. At Spring Island (1992), southwest of Beaufort, 1,000 acres, one-third of the island, were permanently designated a nature preserve.

While Dewees and Spring Islands were intentionally created as low-density developments because they were fragile island ecosystems, Arendt championed high-density, clustered housing in environmental communities. He marshaled considerable data to support his contention that such conservation-centered subdivisions can include the same number of houses as a conventional subdivision on the same site ("density-neutral") and be even more profitable. True, the lots and homes would be smaller, but the sense of community and of its quality of life would be enriched because of the large common areas and open spaces. Conservation subdivisions, Arendt demonstrated with concrete examples of actual communities, "offer distinct and measurable economic advantages over conventional layouts." They lower engineering and construction costs by reducing site preparation and infrastructure expenses. By preserving natural areas and clustering homes on smaller lots, the contractor has to remove fewer trees, grade less land, pave fewer streets, and install less water and sewer piping. And the home values in conservation subdivisions appreciate faster than those of houses in neighboring conventional subdivisions. The conserved "green" areas enhance a development's marketing and sales advantages by enhancing its aesthetic impact and its philosophical appeal. Conservation subdivisions, Arendt revealed through his own actual design projects, can also include affordable housing on a variety of lot sizes in response to market demand. This allows for a more diversified housing stock to meet the needs of an increasingly diverse and multicultural society. Conservation subdivisions are said to be "twice green" in that they conserve the environment while generating profits for their developers and property owners.[35]

Arendt has been as passionate about needed zoning changes as he is about the actual design process. While many towns, cities, and counties have comprehensive long-range land-use plans that often include admirable environmental sensitivity and explicit conservation goals, their construction ordinances are frequently outdated and ineffective; they actually work at cross-purposes with their comprehensive long-range plans. Most large-lot acreage zoning ordinances were designed simply to encourage growth by enabling the "orderly conversion of natural lands into developed properties." Such traditional zoning codes impede efforts to promote smart growth. They encourage low-density, land-intensive development by requiring large minimum lot sizes, wide streets, deep setbacks, and excessive parking. By contrast conservation-oriented zoning emphasizes flexibility, allowing both greater unit density in exchange for greater preserved acreage and the integration of retail and commercial activities within residential neighborhoods.

Arendt laments the contrast between the environmental concerns expressed in comprehensive community plans and their conventional zoning ordinances, which almost force developers and builders to create stereotypically sterile and generic subdivisions. "I am outraged by this absurd situation," he said in 2006. "The towns say: 'We'd like to have farmland, wildlife habitat, woodlands, scenic views, rural character,' and then they adopt crazy ordinances that wipe it all away—that's what outrages me."[36]

Sustainable Communities in the Lowcountry

The overlapping premises and practices associated with smart growth, new urbanism, and conservation subdivisions focus on a single concept—sustainable growth—that is taking root among lowcountry planners, developers, builders, and home owners. In 2003 the *Charleston Post and Courier* reported that antisprawl communities "are gaining popularity around the country among property owners, land planners and environmental groups." Edward T. McMahon, then the vice president of the Conservation Fund, an Arlington, Virginia, land preservation group, explained that a "growing number of savvy developers are saying, 'Gee, maybe we can build a golf course development without the golf course.'" There is no precise number of conservation-oriented communities, but county and city land-use planners, developers, staff members of environmental organizations, realtors, and elected officials readily acknowledge their growing popularity and influence. The lowcountry has more conservation-oriented subdivisions than any other region of the state.[37]

Over the past forty years or so, a phalanx of antisprawl planners, developers, designers, realtors, and elected officials has been promoting the construction of more sustainable and more "livable" communities. Sustainable development/ design involves the intentional balancing of social and environmental priorities with financial considerations (profits) in projects of every scale and type. "Sustainable design," wrote Philadelphia-based landscape architect Carol Franklin in 1993, "is not a reworking of conventional approaches and technologies, but a fundamental change in thinking and in ways of operating."[38]

The antisprawl planning and design movement is designated by many terms: *sustainable development, slow growth, wise growth, smart growth, quality growth, new urbanism, green building, traditional neighborhood development, healthy neighborhoods, organic development, open space development,* and *conservation subdivisions.* What all of these different terms share is the premise that conventional suburban sprawl is unsustainable; it must be discarded in favor of more compact, pedestrian-friendly neighborhoods with narrow tree-lined streets, clustered smaller energy-efficient homes on smaller lots designed to promote community interaction and reduce infrastructure costs, and permanently preserved open spaces, ecologically sensitive areas, and historical sites. Conservation-oriented developments, to one degree or another, try to minimize their ecological damage on and off site while explicitly seeking to protect (and nurture) a cluster of possible environmental values: biodiversity, working farms and ranch lands, scenic landscapes, wetlands, and outdoor recreation opportunities.[39]

Such environmentally responsible planning, design, and construction offers many potential benefits to property owners, developers, and the community. Green development can lower infrastructure expenses, reduce the operating costs of structures and their landscaping maintenance, appreciate in value faster, and minimize environmental impact. Conservation-oriented residential neighborhoods and planned communities began appearing in significant numbers in the lowcountry during the 1980s, and they have grown in popularity with each passing decade.[40]

Home Owners' Associations

A sustainable society requires not only effective planning and regulatory enforcement. It also requires a citizenry willing to exercise grassroots governance. In *The Good Society* (1991) Robert N. Bellah and other social scientists argued that the concept of subsidiarity is an essential element of a "good society." Subsidiarity, they wrote, "implies that high-level associations such as the state should never replace what lower-level associations can do effectively."[41]

Home owners' associations are an example of such subsidiarity. Residential governance is an essential feature of conservation-oriented communities. It is grassroots democracy at work. Community or home owners' associations are private not-for-profit corporations founded by the developer and financed by annual assessments or monthly regime fees. Such associations are run by boards elected by home owners, boards that collect the monthly dues (or regime fees) from residents. The associations are governed by the home owner agreement. Such associations originally emerged out of dissatisfaction with the public services provided to/for residential neighborhoods by local governments, such as security and water and sewage. In 1970, about 1 percent of Americans belonged to private community or home owners' associations. By 2010 membership had grown to more than 20 percent nationwide. The explosive growth of home owners' associations in the lowcountry has often reinforced the culture of conservation by assigning the responsibility to protect the community's environment to the residents themselves. The regulatory powers wielded by such private governments often exceed those of local governments. In addition to providing services—security, landscaping, outdoor lighting, water and sewage, storm-water management, and the maintenance of common areas and outdoor recreation facilities—lowcountry home owners' associations have also assumed responsibility for conservation-related activities and areas, such as ponds, lakes, and wetlands. On Kiawah Island, for example, the community association oversees 330 acres of ponds and 46 miles of pond shoreline. The legally binding conditions, covenants, and restrictions that accompany conservation-oriented subdivisions are intended to maintain the character of the community and thereby protect property values.[42]

Not all community associations, however, are effective managers of common areas and other services. Home owners' associations face the same challenges as local governments in their maintenance of common property and their enforcement of community regulations. Participation in decision making and management is voluntary, not required. Not surprisingly some residents are apathetic. In one gated community, for example, most residents were not even aware of their governance responsibilities when they purchased their property. Environmental management can also be complex. Many—often most—property owners lack the knowledge or skills to manage the natural amenities in their community. Another challenge is motivation. Many property owners are more concerned with aesthetics and recreational use of common areas than with ecological integrity or ongoing natural resource management. To the extent that community associations develop particular responses to environmental issues, the responses are usually conditioned by the environmental perceptions of the property owners, shaped by the economic and ecological forces operative in the common natural areas, and influenced by the prevailing ideas related to environmental management practices. From this perspective conservation-oriented residential projects and their community associations offer a window into the ways in which conservation as a social process is both literally and figuratively constructed.[43]

Shifting Attitudes toward Development

Like the simultaneous efforts in the lowcountry to create more conservation land trusts and easements, many conservation-oriented neighborhoods and planned communities have benefited from the resources available through the region's network of environmental organizations, government agencies, and local planners. A good example is the Sewee Preserve, a five-hundred-acre conservation-oriented gated community overlooking the Intracoastal Waterway and Capers Island between Mount Pleasant and Awendaw, northeast of Charleston. The developer, Dennis Avery, recalled that he had initially viewed the development "from a more conventional perspective" that would have crammed from three hundred to four hundred homes on the parcel. But he had an epiphany that changed his mind. "All of a sudden," Avery remembered, "we were in a reverse thinking mode: How little land can we use?" The site overlooking the marsh adjacent to Whiteside Creek was so breathtakingly beautiful that he decided to build only thirty high-end homes on ninety of the site's five hundred acres. The other 410 acres would be preserved. His new objective, along with that of his partner William "Pug" Dudley, was to create a residential preserve with hundreds of acres of green space immune from future development. "The goal of preserving this special tract of land is to demonstrate that it is possible to balance ecology and economy," Avery declared. "By offering super low-density housing, we are able to protect the lowcountry's natural heritage." He decided "to preserve the land and its pristine environs in a way that was economically viable by following the principles of conservation development."[44]

Avery's epiphany was in part the result of his meeting with attorney Edwin Cooper, a private conservation-easement consultant who later became the director of Ducks Unlimited in the lowcountry. Cooper explained to Avery and his partner that they could set aside the 410 acres to be permanently preserved under the supervision of Wetlands America Trust—a move that would yield them generous federal tax deductions—and lay out about thirty home sites on the remaining ninety acres along the saltwater marsh. "Logic will tell you that people want the vistas on the water," Avery said. The developers demonstrated their heightened environmental consciousness when they decided to build a complete water and sewer system for the preserve rather than rely on individual wells and septic tanks. They also added a horse paddock and seven miles of equestrian trails, and a fifty-acre freshwater lake with a lodge and boathouse. And they formed a partnership with the South Carolina Center for Birds of Prey to use Sewee Preserve as a haven for injured birds of prey: hawks, owls, eagles, osprey, and other raptors. The property owners become honorary members of the rehabilitation and education center. Their goal is "to preserve, protect and respect all the wildlife that calls Sewee Preserve home."[45]

Traditional low-density suburban development is expensive, since the infrastructure expenses must be allocated to a small number of lots. By contrast, clustering the home sites according to new-urbanist principles increases density and reduces infrastructure costs. "Putting pipes in the ground is very expensive," Avery said. It was the federal tax incentive for creating the conservation easement that convinced the developers to shift their thinking to a low-density concept that would preserve green space and stem suburban sprawl. "Without those incentives, old development habits will be hard to break," he predicted. Avery benefited from the expertise of various environmental activists and organizations in fastening on the eventual conservation-oriented design of Sewee Preserve. He confessed that his own outlook about development had been transformed by the experience. The Sewee Preserve was "the most rewarding" project he had ever undertaken. "Having done it, I've seen the impact in terms of environmental quality, and I've also seen how economically viable it is," he concluded.[46]

Low-density conservation developments such as Sewee Preserve minimize the impact of residential development on particular parcels. But do they address the larger issue of helping to slow cascading regional growth? Some environmentalists were skeptical of the Sewee Preserve's low-density gated-community model of a few dozen multimillion-dollar homes on lots that sold for $650,000. After Avery wrote an op-ed column about the virtues of Sewee Preserve in Columbia's *State* newspaper, Will Haltiwanger, an avid cyclist, wrote a letter to the editor asking readers to reconsider the numbers that Avery touted. The five hundred acres making up Sewee Preserve were originally zoned for four hundred homes, yet Avery had decided to build only thirty. So the other 370 homes would have to be constructed somewhere farther away from rapidly growing Mount Pleasant, necessitating the expense of extending utilities—water, sewer and roads, police, and fire protection—to serve them. More land "would have to be dedicated to rights-of-way, and everyone would pay higher taxes to the very government that is providing incentives to Mr. Avery to build low-density housing." In Halti-wanger's view, "the overall impact [of Sewee Preserve] on the environment may well be greater. If every developer used this approach, it would require almost 6,700 acres to provide housing for the four hundred homes that could have been placed on 500. This low density forces people to drive to schools and businesses rather than encouraging walking and cycling. This means more school buses and cars on the road, more accidents, more pollution and more obesity."[47]

Haltiwanger's letter provided an excellent example of the internal debate emerging within the culture of conservation about the best approaches to residential development in the lowcountry. In general, low-density large-lot development is not the best way to preserve farmland or protect wildlife habitat because it can exacerbate sprawl. But there are exceptions to that general rule. Conservationists in favor of Sewee Preserve argued that such a low-density development was appropriate because the site was so ecologically significant (it adjoins the Francis Marion National Forest). They also pointed out that the likely alternative to Sewee Preserve would be a conventional sprawling suburban subdivision with a strip mall. As Michelle Sinkler, then a land-use specialist with the Coastal Conservation League, observed, "if nothing were done, what we were going to see was the trend of stripped-out, commercial big-box development with pods of single-family residences behind it continue to march north on Highway 17."[48]

Marketing the Environment

A tangible sign of the growing culture of conservation in the lowcountry is the willingness of people to purchase property in so-called green subdivisions. Conservation-oriented communities such as the Sewee Preserve are indeed profitable. One reason they have had such robust returns on investment is that their distinctive environmental features have garnered extensive media exposure that has enabled them to reduce their own expenditures on marketing and advertising. John Knott, the developer of Dewees Island, estimated that the conservation amenities he incorporated into the community generated five-million-dollars' worth of free media coverage during its start-up phase. Journalists were intrigued by the bridgeless island development's nature-centered emphasis and absence of cars. The money that was spent on marketing the exclusive eco-community targeted the growing number of prospective buyers who were conservationists, people who were not primarily interested in golf or tennis or country-club networking. Dewees Island eventually fastened on a marketing message that highlighted its green philosophy: "Dewees Island—a private, oceanfront retreat dedicated to environmental preservation." Residents must use boats to access the mainland. However, few of the property owners are year-round residents.

Lowcountry conservation communities have displayed marketing messages in numerous billboards along the region's major thoroughfares. Many promote new homes in "special places." All showcase the aesthetic and communitarian appeal of the coastal region's distinctive environment. A billboard on Interstate 26, the main artery into downtown Charleston, invites people to visit the planned multi-use community Daniel Island, "A Town, An Island, A Way of Life," or to enjoy "naturally unexpected living" at Taylor Plantation on the Ashley River.

Similarly the occupants of vehicles heading south on SC 170 outside of Beaufort during the early twenty-first century saw a billboard promoting Callawassie Island, a gated golf-centered conservation community. The billboard showed the large forested island fringed by marsh. Its caption proclaimed its essence: "splendid seclusion." A website touting the island resort explained that Callawassie is a "member-owned community set on a spectacularly natural sea island with ancient oaks, fertile salt marshes, and inspirational vistas." The promotional descriptions showcased the plants, birds, ecological habitats, and the powerful "sense of place" resident at Callawassie.[49]

The billboards promoting conservation communities have been part of a much larger marketing campaign that includes glossy brochures found in real estate offices and visitors' centers, as well as dazzling websites that allow those far away to take virtual visits to these beguiling places. Such promotional efforts are intended to blur the distinction between actual, authentic experience with the natural environment and a superficial imagining of the environmental elements in the community. The actual texture, complexities, subtleties, and nuances of the lowcountry landscape are lost in translation. The Sewee Preserve's website, for example, opens with a dramatic scene of a diving osprey snatching a fish in its talons while songbirds chirp in the background. Home buyers are invited to join a unique community

Sewee Preserve site plan. Courtesy of Dennis Avery.

"dedicated to the preservation of the lowcountry environment and lifestyle." The website stresses the "environmentally sensitive construction [practices] and use of indigenous landscaping" at Sewee Preserve.[50]

The website for the Palmetto Bluff gated community near Beaufort opens not with a nature scene but with an element of the region's folk cultural heritage: the sight and sounds of an African American gospel choir. The slide show celebrates the development's environmental distinctiveness: "where islands in the stream give way to sound and sea," "where one can take the road less traveled," "where 'dining out' takes on a whole new meaning," and "where daily life is fed by flowing rivers." Each slide-show image reinforces the environmental priorities of Palmetto Bluff: an aerial photo of islands nestled in a coastal river; a father sitting under a live oak with his daughter on his shoulders and his son at his side; the imprint of vehicle tracks through an overgrown meadow fading into the distance; a family seated at a cloth-draped picnic table shaded by majestic hardwoods; and moss-draped oaks standing like sentinels guarding the marshy edge of a river channel. Whereas Sewee Preserve distinguishes between nature and culture in its marketing of lowcountry ecology, Palmetto Bluff portrays nature as providing the integrating nexus where family, food, outdoor recreation, and place converge to form community. The former invites potential buyers to consume nature in its wildest forms, while the latter suggests a natural environment that nurtures spirit, family, and community.[51]

Yet the differences between the Sewee Preserve and Palmetto Bluff are more subtle than significant. The role of land use and commons areas within the two communities is still evolving. Commons areas include open spaces such as preserves, agricultural areas, golf courses, trails, and recreational fields accessible to community association members. For example, Sewee Preserve's website stresses the role of community gardening in the development, asking "when's the last time you held a summer tomato still warm from the vine?" The website pictures a small farm within the development, where property owners are encouraged "to pick freshly-grown vegetables like sweet corn, potatoes, squash, beans, tomatoes and more," thereby preserving the traditional agricultural uses of the property. Likewise, a virtual tour of Palmetto Bluff's conserved acreage reveals the diversity of habitats and species found in the community. In addition, the marketing material reminds prospective buyers of their responsibility to be good stewards of the land for future generations.

Ironies abound within the growing number of conservation-oriented communities in the lowcountry. While all such developments tout their commitment to environmental stewardship, many of them also are centered on golf courses, which often degrade a site's ecology and habitats. Golf has long been associated with the South Carolina lowcountry. The region has become widely known as the nation's "golf mecca," and the golfing culture dominates many of the conservation-themed residential developments. Yet the marketing materials produced by many of the newest communities reveal how prospective property owners are being conditioned (or reinforced) to think differently about the natural environment. When compared to conventional ways of thinking about and marketing suburbia and exurbia, the promotional strategies of the Sewee Preserve, Palmetto Bluff, and other similar developments suggest very different commitments to residential space and its natural environs. John Reed, a prominent developer of golf resorts near Hilton Head, acknowledged that he had changed his focus to accommodate the emergence of the conservation culture in the lowcountry. "We've been successful," he explained in 2002, "because we're not just selling golf, but community, too. As a country, we're getting back to the basics in life—back to family, back to nature, back to the Lord. We try to encourage this by utilizing traditional architecture, incorporating gathering spots into our communities."[52]

A Survey of Lowcountry Residential Developments

The promotional messaging developed by the Sewee Preserve and Palmetto Bluff communities is representative of a larger sampling of thirty-five other lowcountry residential subdivisions and communities undertaken in 2006 and 2007. These thirty-seven communities were identified through interviews with real estate agents and planners to ensure that a wide range of subdivisions was included in the survey. Fifteen of the subdivisions were created prior to 1990, and the remaining twenty-two were constructed in 1990 or after. The table below lists the selected subdivisions, dividing them into three geographical clusters: Horry and Georgetown Counties (HG), Berkeley, Charleston, and Dorchester Counties (BCD), and Beaufort, Colleton, and Jasper Counties (BCJ).

Two-thirds of the thirty-seven subdivisions can be classified as conservation-oriented communities. More than half of the communities' marketing materials showcased environmental amenities and common areas. They highlighted the abundance of opportunities for outdoor recreational activities: access to waterways, boat docks, swimming pools, tennis courts, hunting, fishing, birding, and walking and cycling trails. The most common natural amenities were ponds (74 percent), flower gardens (68 percent), open spaces (60 percent), and woodlands (54 percent). Many of the thirty-seven subdivisions incorporated ecological conservation areas in their master plans, explained how such green spaces were managed, and outlined the rules that govern human interactions with these ecological spaces. More than half (eighteen of thirty-seven) of the subdivisions devoted at least 40 percent of their land to open space.[53]

Some of the selected subdivisions focused on ecological education and initiatives while others emphasized landscaping aesthetics. A few were pioneers, embracing environmental concerns long before a widespread culture of conservation had emerged. For example, Sea Pines Plantation (now Sea Pines Resort) on Hilton Head opened in 1956, and Kiawah Island and Seabrook Island (southwest of Charleston) were completed in 1972 and 1974 respectively. The much-trumpeted success of these environmentally sensitive island golf resorts, coupled with the emergence of the conservation culture in the lowcountry, encouraged

Lowcountry Sample: Subdivision Parameters

Site Name	Built	Gated	Acres	Detached Housing Units	Attached Housing Units	Mean lot size, acres
Briarcliffe Acres	1950	No	335	243	0	1
Ricefields	1991	No	130	262	0	1
Hagley Estates	1965	No	869	854	0	1
Tidewater Plantation	1990	Yes	563	655	444	0
Belle Island Yacht Club	1974	Yes	412	127	N/A	1
Carolina Yacht Landing	1996	Yes	50	0	283	N/A
Debordieu Colony	1970	Yes	2119	1250	N/A	.25–5
Litchfield Beaches	1967	No	253	750	N/A	0
The Reserve at Walkers Woods	2006	No	52	97	0	0
Waterford Plantation	1996	No	257	526	0	0
Dewees Island	1991	No	1383	150	0	2
Sewee Preserve	2001	Yes	510	30	0	3
Village Green	1992	No	187	658	0	0
Crowfield Plantation	1981	No	2423	>2,000	N/A	0
Ivy Hall	1994	No	74	252	0	0
Hobcaw Point	1953	No	256	378	6	1
King's Grant	1970	No	177	437	0	0
Greenhill	1870	No	56	193	4	0
Pepper Plantation	1992	Yes	372	31	0	3
Selkirk Plantation	1997	No	892	29	0	3–130
Raven's Bluff	1993	No	155	21	0	2 to 10
Daniel Island	1996	No	4000	1120	825	0
Kiawah Island	1974	Yes	16776	3300	1200	.1–2
Seabrook Island	1972	Yes	4402	1970	571	0
I'On	1998	No	393	762	0	0
Callawassie Island	1985	Yes	806	724	0	1
Spring Island	1990	Yes	2796	420	0	.25–2
Palmetto Bluff	2000	Yes	18000	2920	N/A	.1–30
Oldfield	2000	Yes	921	550	0	1
Belfair	1995	Yes	1055	750	0	1
Sun City Hilton Head	1994	Yes	5377	7-10,000	N/A	0
Habersham	1999	No	221	650	52	0
Islands of Beaufort	1998	Yes	100	187	0	1
Palmetto Dunes	1967	Yes	1642	2200	1241	0
Wright's Point Plantation	2000	No	53	65	0	0
Newpoint	1992	No	44	127	0	1
Sea Pines Plantation	1956	Yes	3603	>2,000	N/A	0

the construction of numerous conservation subdivisions and new-urbanist developments in the 1980s and since.

Several conservation-oriented communities embodied many or all of the attributes associated with smart-growth concepts, new-urbanist ideas, and conservation subdivisions. For example, Spring Island near Beaufort (1990), Oldfield near Bluffton (2000), Dewees Island near Isle of Palms (1991), and Sewee Preserve (2001) included all of Randall Arendt's essential criteria for conservation subdivisions. Each community boasted a plethora of open spaces, including protected forests, wetlands, and fields. The homes were also clustered to reduce their footprint. And the developers and managers of the communities actively nurtured the property's ecological integrity (biodiversity, habitat protection, natural resource conservation).

Other lowcountry communities incorporated Arendt's required percentage of open space, but they lack ongoing ecological management protocols and resources. In most cases these communities emphasized the recreational value of their natural areas rather than their ecological integrity. Examples of such developments include Sea Pines Plantation (1956) and Palmetto Dunes (1967) on Hilton Head Island, Belfair Plantation near Bluffton (1995), Belle Isle Yacht Club near Georgetown (1974), Debordieu Colony near Pawleys Island (1970), and the Reserve at Walkers Woods near Myrtle Beach (2006).[54]

Subdivisions that contained many conservation-oriented elements included Palmetto Bluff (2000) and Callawassie Island (1985) near Beaufort, Pepper Plantation near Awendaw (1992), and Selkirk Plantation on Wadmalaw Island (1997). Palmetto Bluff, for example, hosted a working forest, Callawassie Island organized its own home owners' ecology committee, Pepper Plantation was designed as an "equestrian retreat," and Selkirk Plantation donated a significant conservation easement to the Lowcountry Open Land Trust.[55]

When viewed collectively the various conservation-oriented communities in the lowcountry helped reduce the damage inflicted by sprawl on the environment. The reverence for the coastal landscape was the animating impulse most often cited, along with continued strengthening of an environmental consciousness nationwide. Nature sells in the lowcountry. Subdivisions with views of water features, marshlands, or woodlands and governed by strict conservation guidelines were and are much preferred over conventional tract neighborhoods. Residents with the highest degree of neighborhood satisfaction tended to be those with the greatest access to natural areas and community gardens within their subdivision. But it is not just an appreciation for nature that has fostered open-space development. By setting aside land for commons areas, nature preserves, and wildlife refuges, builders satisfied local code requirements and sometimes garnered significant tax incentives. Developers also marketed such conservation-oriented properties to retirees and people seeking a second home who are attracted by a connection to nature but desire the amenities of a first-class resort.[56]

Numerous scholarly studies have shown that the quality of a community's physical surroundings greatly influences well-being and one's sense of place and quality of life. It is in this context that the growing popularity of conservation-oriented communities has both reflected and reinforced the broader culture of conservation in the lowcountry. Residents with a strong pride of place are more engaged: they try to ensure that their community (and neighborhood) values protect the natural environment. In turn, environmentally sensitive developments help incubate and manifest a culture of conservation.[57]

Conservation-oriented subdivisions (or entire multiuse communities such as Charleston's Daniel Island) have many different forms. Some prize low-density development in order to preserve fragile ecologies while others feature high density to minimize the footprint of the built environment and preserve open space. Conservation-oriented residential communities also differ in their emphasis on protecting the environment—at every phase of development: site planning, home design, construction practices and materials, environmental and wildlife management protocols, and home owner governance, education, and stewardship.

Amid South Carolina's unrelenting coastal development, stern questions arise. Should barrier islands be developed at all? Are golf courses and tennis courts inherently antithetical to a conservation ethic? Is building a social environment or sense of community in a new subdivision as important as preserving the natural environment? That these questions and others have been addressed in diverse ways helps reveal how complicated it is to manage growth with the environment in mind. It is indeed a delicate balancing act.[58]

SEVEN

Sustainable Subdivisions,
Conservation Communities

"Nature is Kiawah Island's most enduring asset and serves as the defining element of life on Kiawah," declared Charles P. "Buddy" Darby III, the president and chief executive officer of Kiawah Development Partners, in 2004. In trying to create a better balance between the ill effects of development and the integrity of the environment, self-styled "progressive" developers have sought to work more in harmony with the landscape and the conservation community. Kiawah Island and other such "green" enclaves of wealth and leisure are meticulously planned and highly regulated places of privilege. They also are nature-friendly. They feature protected commons areas and conservation easements, nature preserves, freshwater ponds, protective covenants, and low densities—as well as very high prices. Such conservation-centered communities are not cheap; they are havens for the affluent.[1]

Palmetto Bluff, for example, is a massive new planned community on twenty thousand picturesque acres (roughly the size of Manhattan Island) along the May, New, and Cooper Rivers in Beaufort County, near Bluffton and Hilton Head. The community includes an award-winning golf course, riverfront retail village, luxurious spa, and as many as five thousand home sites priced from $300,000 to $3.9 million. Yet the developers, Crescent Resources, LLC, highlight their environmental priorities in showcasing the new community. They want to create a "place," not a "project." Palmetto Bluff's "guiding principle is to preserve and protect one of America's most unique and treasured landscapes while creating an exceptional human community within it." The developers claim that "the intrinsic value of this place lies" not in its profitability but "in its beauty, vastness and richness." Their decisions, they promise, will always be guided by a commitment to protect "the land, the wetlands, the diverse maritime forest and the miles of marsh and river edge that define this remarkable property."[2]

Too good to be true? Perhaps. Scholars have yet to analyze the overall effectiveness of such conservation-based communities in fulfilling their promises to minimize their environmental impact. Several key issues help gauge the success and authenticity of conservation-based communities. Do the common areas and open spaces in such developments help conserve crucial ecosystems, such as wetlands and longleaf pine forests? Or are the common areas valued more for their aesthetic and marketing benefits? So-called greenwashing is common among many communities claiming to be conservation-oriented. As a major developer of such subdivisions admitted, "create a conservation area and you create [monetary] value." Do conservation communities seek to educate their property owners about the premises and practices of environmental sustainability? How do the community's covenants address issues related to environmental conservation and cultural preservation?[3]

Generalizations about planned conservation communities rarely do justice to their diversity or their texture. Three quite different lowcountry coastal developments—Sea Pines Plantation on Hilton Head Island, Spring Island near Beaufort, and I'On in Mount Pleasant, across the Cooper River from Charleston, deserve closer examination because they reveal the evolution, complexity, and variety of planned conservation communities. They also reveal how different self-styled environmentally conscious developers display quite different notions of conservation. Finally they show how interest in environmental amenities and their ongoing management has increased over time with the maturation of the region's culture of conservation.

Sea Pines Plantation: Aesthetic Coastal Development

The first explicitly environmentally oriented residential development in the low-country was built on Hilton Head Island, thirty-five-miles north of Savannah, Georgia, and a hundred miles southwest of Charleston. Charles Elbert Fraser, a Hinesville, Georgia, native and Yale Law School graduate interested in architecture and planning, was in the vanguard of what would become a new generation of developers focused on transforming the lowcountry coast into affluent golf-centered resorts. In 1956, fresh out of law school and following a stint in the U.S. Air Force, he began envisioning the transformation of five thousand unspoiled acres on the southwestern end of Hilton Head Island into an exclusive, meticulously planned gated resort enclave called Sea Pines Plantation that would blend seamlessly into the island's beaches, marshes, and live oak forests.

Hilton Head derives its name from William Hilton, an English sea captain who explored the island in 1663, claimed it for the British crown, and assigned it his name. During the eighteenth and early nineteenth centuries, Hilton Head emerged as a profitable source of indigo, rice, and sea-island cotton. Some two dozen plantations dotted the island. But the slave-based plantation system came to an abrupt end early during the Civil War when a fleet of Union ships anchored offshore and twelve thousand Federal soldiers took control of the island. The white planters fled to the mainland, and their lands were confiscated. For the enslaved islanders "the day of victory for the Union was a day of freedom." Freed slaves were able to acquire small parcels during and after the war, mostly on the northern end of the island where a small settlement called Mitchelville was established. When a boll weevil infestation destroyed the cotton crop, island black residents eked out a living by growing corn and vegetables and harvesting oysters.[4]

During the early twentieth century sports enthusiasts from the Carolinas discovered Hilton Head Island, where they established exclusive hunting clubs. At the same time wealthy northern investors bought large parcels of timberland for a pittance. By 1950, when the newly created Hilton Island Company acquired nineteen thousand of the mosquito-infested barrier island's twenty-five thousand acres, there were only fifteen hundred black and twenty-five white residents making up one of the poorest and most isolated island communities in one of the state's poorest counties (Beaufort). There was no bridge to the mainland, no electricity, no telephones, and only ten houses had indoor plumbing. Yet the black community had built one-room schoolhouses, family-owned groceries, praise houses and churches. They used small wooden boats to get to the mainland. The bridgeless island was so isolated that residents were not required to have driver's licenses or license plates. Most of the African Americans used mule-drawn wagons to traverse the island.

In 1951 the Hilton Head Company set up tree-cutting operations and sawmills on the island. Within a year millions of feet of lumber—mostly virgin longleaf pine—had been processed and shipped. The company's directors then began preparing the island for development as a resort. Electricity was provided in 1951. Two years later the South Carolina Highway Department launched a ferry service to the island, using a barge that could accommodate five cars a trip. But what the developers most needed was a two-lane vehicular bridge. When the state balked at the expense of a bridge, the Hilton Head Company formed the Hilton Head Toll Bridge Authority and financed the construction themselves. The bridge opened in May 1956, and during its first year more than two hundred thousand people visited the island.

By 1957 all of the ingredients were in place for Hilton Head to be developed intensively. In June, Charles Fraser created the Sea Pines Plantation Company. At that time residential and commercial development on the Atlantic coast usually followed the model prevalent in Florida and at Myrtle Beach: bulldozing the dunes, destroying marshlands, filling in the wetlands, and clearing the coastal forests so as to allow for the maximum number of beachfront cottages and high-rise beachfront condominiums and hotels. Profit trumped environmental concerns, and there was minimal governmental regulation of coastal construction.

Fraser, however, shifted the priorities. Since first visiting the island in 1950 he had envisioned something different at Hilton Head. The isolated island was "just too attractive to let it go the way of all typical United States beach developments, which have a way of becoming a hodgepodge of conflicting uses, a joy and delight to all maniac builders and hot dog stand operators, but a nightmare to anyone with reasonable aesthetic standards."[5]

Fraser resolved to break out of the traditional coastal development mold: he wanted to create a unique, environmentally sensitive and tightly controlled private resort community nestled into its island landscape. He was only in his early twenties when he decided to create Sea Pines Plantation, but several factors made

Charles E. Fraser at Sea Pines.
Courtesy of Sea Pines.

up for his youth and inexperience. First, he gained access to the land on generous financial terms from his timber baron father, Joseph B. Fraser Sr., a retired
army general who had been the commander of the South Carolina National
Guard. The elder Fraser was the controlling partner in the group that had formed
the Hilton Head Company in 1949. Second, Charles Fraser was a precocious
visionary and an unbridled optimist, a brilliant, courageous, brashly self-assured,
and at times egotistical young man with a determined passion to create the first
conservation-oriented resort community on the East Coast. His dogmatic ideals,
combative personality, and "wild visions" created a rift among the Hilton Head
Island Company partners, most of whom were wary of the young man's uncon-
ventional notions. Even Fraser's father found his ideas and forthrightness "some-
what startling," but he supported him nevertheless.[6]

Charles Fraser was convinced that undiscovered Hilton Head Island would
not attract high-income residents unless "the continued maintenance of the natural beauty of the surrounding areas is assured." To implement his unconven-
tional vision of an island paradise, he hired the nation's best land planner, Hideo
Sasaki, based in Boston. Fraser then developed a list of priorities for his Sea Pines
Company. "Making a profit" was listed number four. Ahead of it were "achieving
high standards of ecological and community planning," creating environments
for the "rejuvenation and recreation" of "creative and responsible" people, and
helping Sea Pines associates to find "personal growth and fulfillment."[7]

To ensure the success of such priorities Fraser assumed almost dictatorial
powers. He used his absolute control over Sea Pines to demand that the site planners do everything possible to protect the natural features of the island. Houses
would be carefully sited to blend in with the natural environment. The resort's

lushly landscaped parkways would not be linear but instead would meander their way around majestic trees and picturesque water features. Fraser required that he personally approve which trees could be removed, and he fined builders and contractors one thousand dollars for each tree illegally destroyed. Stories about his love for noble trees have become legendary. While laying out the site for the Harbour Town yacht basin, he spied a magisterial moss-draped live oak and declared that the site plan must be redrawn in order to save the noble tree. The stately oak, he vowed, would come down "over his dead body." As it turned out, the tree outlived Fraser, who dubbed it the Liberty Oak and was buried under it in 2002 after being killed in a boating accident in the Caribbean.

Fraser also exercised strict control over the siting, design, materials, and colors of individual homes. One of his most effective requirements was to deter beachfront building by insisting that the main arterial road—Sea Pines Drive—be situated well back from the ocean dunes and that walkways be used to connect residents and visitors to the beach. Fraser told the select group of architects invited to design homes at Sea Pines that they must carefully adapt buildings to their particular sites—and that they must protect the trees and their canopies in the process. He also required that houses blend in with the texture and colors of the island. They must be cladded with natural materials—cedar, cypress, and redwood—and only earth-toned stains and paints were allowed. The houses at Sea Pines would have large windows and skylights to let nature in and provide views of the ocean, marshes, rivers, creeks, and golf courses.[8]

When judged by later standards, Fraser's concept of environmental preservation had its limitations—and its critics. Although he built bicycle paths to reduce automobile use and set aside 1,400 acres for parks and "managed" nature preserves, his primary interest in the environment was aesthetic rather than ecological. He loved the island's natural look, but he did not fully appreciate complex concepts such as habitat integrity or biodiversity. Several of his natural "preserves" were in fact poorly preserved. They ended up hosting the island's debris yard, water and sewage treatment facilities, an incinerator, and a shooting range. Likewise, Fraser's focus on environmental aesthetics depended on strong, consistent enforcement of the community's covenants, restrictions, and maintenance protocols. As long as he exercised his dictatorial grip on the gated community, such environmental controls were consistently maintained. After he sold Sea Pines in 1983, however, his successors were not nearly as vigilant or as virtuous when it came to environmental conservation.[9]

Fraser failed to appreciate the pressures that chockablock golf-course subdivisions would exert on the island's public services, especially its water supply. He genuinely "cared about the environment," as one scholar has written, but he "was a developer rather than a preservationist. . . . Nature was an essential part of what he was selling, and he sought to use Hilton Head's striking beauty as a backdrop for his Sea Pines." At Sea Pines Fraser bet on a bold new concept: that protecting the majestic natural beauty of Hilton Head would attract more affluent buyers and enable him to charge higher prices and generate high revenues. He was right.[10]

To ensure that Sea Pines would remain a conservation-oriented community, Fraser created a forty-page list of deed-restrictive covenants and architectural standards that governed everything from paint colors to mailbox placement to street and retail signage to the species of plants that could be used for landscaping. The covenants stipulated that Fraser reserved the right to reject any building specification for whatever reason he chose. Only such legal covenants and his version of benevolent dictatorship, he believed, could provide "permanent protection against blighted neighborhoods, encroaching commercial establishments, overcrowding, intermixing of public and residential areas, unsightly buildings and other conditions which plague older beach areas."[11]

Fraser's risky vision worked better than he had dreamed possible. In its first twenty-five years, the Sea Pines Company built more than three thousand homes, four golf courses, seventy tennis courts, riding stables, two marinas, several playgrounds and swimming pools, fifteen miles of bike and jogging trails, and walking trails and fishing ponds throughout the six-hundred-acre Sea Pines Forest Preserve. By the early 1960s Fraser's dream was flourishing. Within thirty years after Sea Pines sold its first lot, Hilton Head Island had more than twenty-thousand residents and was attracting more than a million visitors a year. Those numbers have since more than doubled.[12]

Fraser experienced the paradox of successful real estate development: too much of a good thing erodes its goodness. Much of what was originally attractive about Sea Pines and Hilton Head Island disappeared as growth mushroomed. Fraser could not exercise the same control over the island's other developers and building contractors as he did over the residents of Sea Pines. Many of them lacked Fraser's love of the island and his aesthetic priorities. As the Charleston architect Chris Schmitt said, "people looked at Sea Pines from a distance and said, 'I'm going to copy that.' But they never understood Fraser's real concepts, and they just ended up building hollow imitations."[13]

The developers of Palmetto Dunes Plantation, for example, were not content to integrate their new community into the natural environment. They decided to transform the landscape, draining and dredging a ten-mile network of wetlands to create golf courses, canals, lagoons, ponds, lakes, high-density condominiums, a shopping center, office parks, and a hotel. Other developers were blinded by the opportunity of high profits; they lacked Fraser's aesthetic standards and environmental concerns. Arthur Schultz, the president of Carolina Bay Company, which shoehorned 350 condominiums onto a few acres on the northern end of the island, dismissed Fraser's philosophy of conservation-oriented development. "This is not Hilton Head anymore—it's not a pristine place where you're going to see sea gulls flying. It's essentially cast to be a high-rise condominium place." Many of the new plantations and subdivisions, according to the historian of Hilton Head Island, "were badly designed and poorly sited, testaments to greed and bad taste; and more would come as growth spread to land beyond the control of Sea Pines and the Hilton Head Company."[14]

Conservation is a field of endeavor stippled with irony. Few efforts to preserve environments are completely successful. Every conservation tool has its limitations. And even the most well-intentioned conservation efforts can create unintended consequences. Certainly that has been the case at Hilton Head. The very success of Fraser's environmental emphasis at Sea Pines "opened the flood gates for growth of all sorts." The runaway scale and pace of Hilton's Head growth outstripped the efforts of Fraser and others at comprehensive planning. The island's population doubled during the 1960s, quadrupled during the 1970s, and doubled again during the 1980s. The number of tourist visitors grew at an even faster rate. More residents and tourists, of course, brought more businesses. Hilton Head Island became a resort growth machine fed by an unending stream of retirees, golfers, and vacationers. Most of the businesses, from golf shops to realtors to grocery stores, depended on constantly rising numbers of people. Traffic skyrocketed on the island's only main road with the introduction of condominiums and time-share vacation rentals. Tens of thousands of annual vacationers soon soared into a million, then two-and-a-half million. Sea Pines Plantation was eventually surrounded by more than a dozen major developments ("plantations"). Congestion—both automotive and human—eroded much of the island's serenity and ecology. In the 1980s and after, wealthy newcomers to the island built huge cookie-cutter "McMansions'" that defied "the quiet blending with nature that is supposed to be the community's guiding principle."[15]

In 1966 concerned residents of plantations across the island, many of whom were retired executives or military officers with time to spare, formed the Hilton Head Island Community Association to control growth and "retain the natural beauty of the appealing environment which has attracted many newcomers." But the association lacked the resources and clout necessary to be a significant factor in regulating growth. By the early 1970s tensions between Sea Pines property owners and Fraser over the pace and scope of continuing development boiled over. Home owners grew frustrated by constant construction-related disruptions, dismayed by the threat of overbuilding, and exasperated by the annual invasion of tourists. Some full-time residents of the island were only half joking when they suggested removing the bridge to the mainland so as to preserve their sanctuary. As one of them said in 1973, "the chief threat to this island, most residents now agree, is 'people pollution' and the inevitable defacement of landscape and lifestyle that go along inexorably with unregulated growth." Fraser admitted that Hilton Head was growing too fast. In 1971 he acknowledged that "there has been too much building at one time within Sea Pines Plantation, and we hope that we can bring the pace of construction and the volume of construction to a more orderly level."[16]

Not all Sea Pines residents were persuaded by his pledge, however. Two years later, in 1973, they formed the Association of Sea Pines Plantation Property

Owners in an effort to force Fraser to reduce the number of planned dwelling units, both houses and condominiums. Members of the association thereafter sat on the plantation's architectural review board and took responsibility for maintaining all open spaces. Similar property-owner takeovers occurred at the other Hilton Head plantations. By 1991 Fraser was so disheartened by the frenzied development on the island that he called for a moratorium on further growth. "If I could freeze Hilton Head today, it would be an extraordinary island," he said. Fraser, who sold Sea Pines in the fall of 1982, admitted that the explosive development of golf resort communities in the lowcountry was outpacing the region's resources, especially the water supply, and thereby threatening the quality of the environment. The fragmented process of separately developing a dozen individual plantations and adding more golf courses negated efforts at comprehensive island-wise planning. "Nobody looked at the island as a whole," noted Dana Beach of the Coastal Conservation League. "There was less open space as more money was to be made. The only open spaces left on some plantations are golf courses, and that's no refuge for wildlife. The orientation for golf went too far." By 1991 there were two dozen golf courses on the island and more under construction.[17]

From the start of its development as a resort community, Hilton Head was peculiar in that the island was unincorporated and therefore largely "governed" by the private developers who owned the gated plantations making up most of the island's acreage. With no public zoning codes or municipal land-use policies, the developers were free to follow their own guidelines in the pursuit of profits. For a while Fraser's conservation-oriented values held sway among his counterparts. But one-quarter of the island was outside the boundaries of the plantations. This undeveloped land, much of it "heirs' property" owned by the island's African American community, had neither public nor private land-use protocols. Over time, as owners sold their land to a new generation of developers, chaos ensued. High-rise condominiums were built next to single-family homes, density thresholds were ignored, sewage and water treatment systems were substandard, and trees were cavalierly removed and wetlands filled in. By 1985 almost half of Hilton Head's residents lived outside the regulated planned communities.

The shoddy practices of developers and contractors outraged many plantation residents who had been initially attracted by the island's environmental ethic. Beginning in the 1970s, year-round residents began to explore the idea of incorporating the island as the best way to regulate uncontrolled development. Most of the African American property owners opposed the idea, however. The lives of Hilton Head's black residents had been turned topsy-turvy by the development of Sea Pines and the other upscale resorts on the island. African Americans had owned about 20 percent of the island in 1957, but they had been allowed to traverse the entire island at their will, hunting and fishing on lands that belonged to affluent absentee white property owners. But the development of resort plantations saw the erection of gates and fences, barricading the island's black communities from their historic hunting and fishing venues as well as their family cemeteries. Except for electricity, utility services were provided only in the resort plantations, not within the historic African American, or Gullah, communities. What was once a black majority population on the island became a declining minority with the influx of white residents after 1957. True, the resorts also brought needed infrastructure—physicians, a hospital, public services (including electricity), and jobs (mostly minimum wage) at the resorts. Rapid development, however, also brought higher taxes and a higher cost of living.[18]

By the 1970s proposals for the incorporation of the island into a township raised the potential of added burdens on the island's black community. Municipal land-use restrictions, building codes, zoning ordinances, growth caps, and density controls, they believed, would drive them from their property, impede their selling land to developers, and lower the dollar value of their property. African Americans denounced what they called the "zoning slavery" that would accompany incorporation. Government regulations would benefit the "rich residents of the island at the expense of poor blacks" and subject them to higher taxes. White people would impose strict environmental codes that would transform the black way of life. "I can just see one of the first city ordinances outlawing trailers [mobile homes]," predicted one African American islander. "Most blacks can't afford new homes. They live in trailers." African Americans were also a diminishing minority on the island. They understandably worried that the growing majority of affluent white people (87 percent of residents in 1980) would dominate the political dynamics of an incorporated Hilton Head.[19]

Such concerns did not sway white voters, however. The affluent white majority living on Hilton Head, preoccupied with finding new ways to control rampaging growth and the clear-cutting of lots, voted on May 10, 1983, to create the Town of Hilton Head. Those living in Sea Pines and other plantations overwhelmingly supported incorporation while the black community overwhelmingly voted against the idea. Majority rule now took control of the island's fate, and the struggling black community felt increasingly marginalized. "There is bitterness here that may not be articulated," said community activist Roger Pinckney, "but it is certainly felt."[20]

The town government was created for one explicit purpose: to regulate the growth on the island outside of the plantations, which mostly meant apartment complexes, shopping centers, and commercial buildings. Voters expected the new town officials to mimic what Fraser had done at Sea Pines and create land-use plans and zoning restrictions to preserve the island's natural beauty and environmental quality. The new town government did create some restrictions. No billboards or neon signs were allowed. Commercial and retail buildings could not be generic; they had to be designed to blend into the island's architectural motifs and natural setting. Perhaps the most distinctive regulatory effort of the new town government was the creation of one of the most comprehensive and restrictive tree ordinances in the nation.[21]

But it was unrealistic to expect the infant town council to achieve the same degree of growth management and conservation practices that Sea Pines Plantation had enacted. Virtually no community in the nation had land-use and design protocols as strict as those developed by Fraser for Sea Pines Plantation, and the new town council had no jurisdiction over the plantations. Moreover, by 1983 the pace of growth on the island had developed a momentum of its own. Hilton Head was no longer an "unspoiled little Eden," as *Time* magazine had described it in 1970. It had become the richest community in the state. The rapidly growing population on the island had also developed diverse views about growth and conservation. Neither Fraser's benevolent dictatorship nor the restrictive covenants used by the plantations to enforce uniformity and protect the island's natural beauty were available to the town council. The African American community continued to oppose restrictions on growth and supported developers in the hopes of creating more jobs and increasing their land values. The new town government was in a classic no-win situation. Critics pilloried the elected officials for failing to control runaway growth. Petitions emerged demanding a moratorium on new development.[22]

The primary result of such turmoil was the creation in 1985 of the town's first comprehensive land-use plan. The 252-page document included some of the most creative approaches to growth management in the United States, establishing strict standards for building and landscaping design as well as signage. The centerpiece of the plan focused on using traffic capacity as the means of restricting commercial and residential development. But its enforcement mechanisms were weak because town officials worried about possible challenges. As a result the comprehensive growth management plan, lamented a resident in 1991, had "lost its soul." In the end, as Charles Fraser's brother Joseph observed, the efforts at growth management and environmental conservation implemented by "responsible developers" were "more effective and more predictable than regulation subject to public pressure and changing interests."[23]

The development of Sea Pines Plantation at Hilton Head as a conservation-oriented community provided a powerful model in several ways. Charles Fraser demonstrated that an island resort could focus on the preservation of nature and the blending of structures with the environment—and still be profitable. In 1958 a beachfront lot in Sea Pines Plantation sold for $5,350; today such lots would sell for $2.5 to $7.5 million. The phenomenal profitability of Sea Pines catapulted Fraser into the front rank of resort developers. He went on to help design Amelia Island in north Florida and Kiawah Island south of Charleston. Fraser's charisma helped him attract to his staff a corps of precociously talented young planners and designers such as James Chaffin and James W. Light, as well as an informal protégé, Vincent Graham, all of whom would sustain and improve upon Fraser's concept of conservation-oriented communities in developing their own projects in the lowcountry. Sea Pines Plantation "became the role model for coastal developments," remembered Chris Schmitt. "The people Fraser put together as a team have been a major influence on resort development around the country."[24]

Efforts to conserve the environment often generate powerful ironies and make for strange bedfellows. Charles Fraser's genius for promotion and design did more than sell lots and generate profits. It also nurtured a pride of place and a culture of conservation among residents. For all of the infighting and tensions related to growth on Hilton Head Island, the Sea Pines property owners and Fraser shared a fierce determination to fend off threats from the mainland.

The determination of residents to protect Hilton Head's environment from outside forces was powerfully displayed in the fall of 1969, when BASF, a giant German-owned chemical company, announced plans to construct a massive dye-stuff and petrochemical plant on an 1,800-acre site at Victoria Bluff (now Colleton River Plantation) in Beaufort County, three miles from Hilton Head Island. The site sat astride the estuary of Port Royal Sound, into which the plant would daily discharge 2.5 million gallons of treated waste. It would be the third largest industrial plant in the state. State political and business leaders, including the governor, wholeheartedly endorsed the project and provided enticing real estate and tax incentives to BASF. Canals would be built from the Savannah River to provide the massive volumes of water needed by the plant, and the state would construct a deep-water port and dredge ten miles of shipping channels in Port Royal Sound to enable two-hundred-foot-long tankers to load forty thousand barrels of naphtha (a petroleum distillate) a day. Roads and a railroad spur would also be built. Beaufort County officials were ecstatic about the proposed plant. As a political official said, "what BASF will mean ultimately is that we won't be a sleepy village any longer, with a lot of open spaces and untromped-on places. This just has to be. Change is inevitable, you know."[25]

The announcement of the massive petrochemical plant set off a firestorm of opposition on Hilton Head. "I've never seen a chemical plant that didn't pollute," declared Fraser. Within days of the press conference announcing plans for the BASF plant, an unlikely coalition of conservationists, affluent Hilton Head property owners, and black fishermen and their families sprang into action. Orion Hack, whose family, along with Joseph and Charles Fraser, were the original owners and developers of Hilton Head Island, welcomed scores of idealistic long-haired young activists from around the country who converged on Beaufort to protest the plant's construction. "If the kids go out and lie down in front of the bulldozers, I hope no one gets hurt. But I'll be on their side. I'm a radical when it comes to conservation."[26]

Initially the German executive appointed to manage the plant, Herbert Ende, scoffed at the protesters. He told a young attorney representing the plant's opponents that "we are a two-billion-dollar organization. We can flush all of you down the drain. We can wipe you out." But the protesters persisted, demonstrating daily for weeks at the plant site and at the company's suite of Hilton Head offices. The Hilton Head Island Community Association forged an alliance with the

Audubon Society, Friends of the Earth, and prominent developers. Jimmy Chandler, the crusading environmental attorney from Pawleys Island who founded the South Carolina Environmental Law Project, coordinated the effort that eventually convinced BASF to nix the proposed plant. It was the first major example in the lowcountry of environmental concerns trumping economic development, and it set a visible precedent for the emergent culture of conservation in the lowcountry. Soon thereafter the Hilton Head Island Community Association and other concerned citizens fended off efforts to construct offshore drilling platforms and a ten-story liquefied natural gas terminal near Victoria Bluff.[27]

Perhaps the most tangible illustration of the island community's burgeoning culture of conservation was in 2004, when the Town of Hilton Head officially resolved in its comprehensive plan to do more "to protect the natural resources of the Island" in order to "maintain the environment and quality of life" in the face of "continuing development." The "protection of natural resources" needed to become "a top priority" within the community. Since then Hilton Head has created a program that uses property transaction fees to purchase land for parks and open spaces. Town Manager Steven Riley attributed the island's growing environmental awareness to Fraser's original vision for Sea Pines Plantation. He "really did set the standard for a lot of what is considered progressive development these days." Was he "an environmentalist to the core? Not really. But he knew if he mowed down all the oak trees and Spanish moss, it would be just another place."[28]

Spring Island: Intentional Underdevelopment

The legacy of Charles Fraser's "wise growth" approach to resort development extended far beyond Hilton Head. Among his most talented associates at the Sea Island Company were two young men, James Chaffin Jr. and James Light, who also helped Fraser design Amelia Island and Kiawah Island. During his nine years with the Sea Pines Company, Chaffin began in sales and quickly became senior vice president of sales and marketing. Light had a similarly meteoric career. He spearheaded the planning and execution for the development of Harbour Town at Sea Pines Plantation, the most ambitious private harbor development on the East Coast, and he was named president of Sea Pines Company at age thirty-one.

In 1978 Chaffin and Light formed their own sustainable-development design firm, called Chaffin/Light Associates. The new company's goal embodied what they learned from Fraser: to develop high-quality conservation communities that respected the land. They were convinced that more and more Americans, especially baby boomers with high net worth, were attracted to conservation-oriented communities. In fact, their survey research showed that a growing number of highest-income Americans were becoming more "principle-driven" and less "status-driven" in their choice of homes and communities. To attract such residents Chaffin and Light envisioned exclusive low-density communities that would leave the land, air and water virtually unchanged, yet in the process would enrich the lives of residents.[29]

Spring Island, situated between the Colleton and Chechessee Rivers thirteen miles southwest of Beaufort and twelve miles northwest of Hilton Head, focuses on environmental preservation through low-density development. The three-thousand-acre island, festooned with moss-draped live oaks and picturesque salt-water and freshwater ponds, has long exercised an intoxicating effect on visitors. "When I [first] came to this island [on Thanksgiving Day 1988]," said Chaffin, "I knew I had to find a way to spend the rest of my life here." He and his wife were struck by the "mystical quality of the place." Spring Island is home to some of the most unusual wildlife and natural archaeological features in the low-country. A five-hundred-acre live oak forest is one of the largest on the eastern seaboard. Original island structures include examples of the pre–Civil War use of tabby, a cementlike mixture of lime, oyster shells, sand, and water, as a con-struction material. Spring Island also hosts huge populations of migratory wad-ing birds, several endangered species such as the bald eagle, roseate spoonbill, and wood stork, and many rare wildflowers and plants.[30]

Spring Island is also an important piece of a larger ecological area. It is sur-rounded on three sides by state and federally protected natural areas. The Daws Island Heritage Preserve, a state-owned conservation area managed by the South Carolina Department of Natural Resources (SCDNR), lies across the Port Royal Sound to the east. The 1,111-acre Victoria Bluff Heritage Preserve, also managed by SCDNR, lies to the south. Archeologically rich Pinckney Island National Wild-life Refuge is nearby. Ducks Unlimited holds a 286-acre conservation easement on Oak Forest plantation.[31]

Since 1706 only four multigenerational families had owned Spring Island. After the Civil War, with the decline of the lowcountry plantations, the owners had preserved the land in its natural state so as to enhance the environment for outdoor recreation: hunting, fishing, birding, and hiking. Chaffin had similar goals for the island, which he and other investors purchased for seventeen mil-lion dollars in 1989. He initially offered to sell the island to the state for the same price he paid for it, urging the state to convert it into a park. But government offi-cials claimed they did not have seventeen million dollars to allocate for such a project. Chaffin and Light then set about creating a distinctive environmental resort community that would preserve a sensitive island habitat through inten-tional underdevelopment.

To stimulate their visioning they invited eight prominent resort developers to visit the island and recommend strategies. Their composite recommendation was dishearteningly conventional: to construct at least three thousand homes and three golf courses. Chaffin and Light were chagrined. They wanted Spring Island to be a unique nature-first resort, not another golf-centered island community. So they ignored the recommendations and drastically reduced the approved zoning density from 5,500 to 500 high-end home sites (later reduced to 410), ensuring

Tabby ruins of a mansion on the Old Tabby Links golf course, Spring Island, above, and Spring Island house, below. Courtesy of David Soliday.

that Spring Island would have one of the lowest densities of any community on the Carolina coast. In 1992, for example, Hilton Head Island had 15,000 housing units on 23,000 acres; Kiawah Island had 2,000 units on 10,000 acres; and Seabrook Island had 1,700 units on 3,000 acres. (Their densities have since increased.)

Chaffin and Light broke new ground not only by such dramatic downsizing; they also decided to build only one golf course, using for its site cornfields that previous owners had planted to enrich sport hunting by attracting quail, ducks, and game animals. True, a golf course contradicted the environmental premises of the development, but they saw it as a necessary marketing "safety valve" to cushion the financial risk they and their investors were assuming. "At this point in our careers," Chaffin explained in 1992, "we risk not only money but also reputation. If you get too far out in front, you get arrows in your back." Chaffin later said that if Spring Island were developed today it would not need the golf course because the culture of conservation had become strong enough to support such environmental developments.[32]

To help crystallize their vision of Spring Island, Chaffin and Light assembled a team of diverse land-management experts—a biologist, naturalist, plantation manager, forester, ornithologist, and an environmental scientist—to inventory and assess the island's flora and fauna and then develop a plan to preserve and nurture the critical wildlife habitat, wetlands, vegetation areas. As Chaffin explained, developers need to exercise "humility regarding the importance of a property's natural amenities. We often believe that we can 'improve' the value of property, or enhance the customer experience through man-made facilities. I believe that the first goal should be the thorough assessment of, and the protection and enhancement of, a property's natural features." The multidisciplinary team of experts developed detailed recommendations for maintaining Spring Island's natural amenities and protecting its ecological aesthetics: prescribed burnings, active tree, pond, and wildlife management programs, and natural succession areas. To ensure that conservation would remain the focus of the Spring Island development, Chaffin and Light deed-restricted the low-density project (earmarking nearly one-third of the total acreage as a nature preserve) and formed an environmental trust to preserve in perpetuity the land (live oak forests, marshlands, ponds, and wildlife habitats) and its historic features. "Providing the opportunity for personal connection with the natural environment," Chaffin stressed, "offers more personal nourishment and spiritual fulfillment than any of our 'developer' amenities. What greater product can we offer our customers [than unspoiled natural beauty]?"[33]

Chaffin's wife Betsy, a photographer and conservationist, suggested the formation of the nonprofit land trust in 1990 as a means of constructing a "firewall" to prevent future development. "The Spring Island Trust is an innovative model which brings the ideals of the developer and the environmentalist into a successful working relationship," she explained. "We envisioned Spring Island becoming sort of a private park; that through careful application of land steward-ship techniques, we could preserve for future generations everything that is rare and special about this place while still creating a community in the truest sense. The trust provides our assurance that this will take place."[34]

The Spring Island Trust has three major functions. It manages the island's rookery ponds, forest sanctuaries, open spaces, and nature trails; it provides ex-tensive environmental programs for members, guests, and visiting students; and it oversees the ongoing resort management plans intended to protect the island's ecological integrity and cultural heritage. The trust also fosters environmental and historical research by inviting scientists, historians, and artists to the island for consultation, study, instruction, and inspiration. "It's clear that government and nonprofits cannot by themselves conserve and manage all the open space they would like to preserve," said Chaffin, who lives on the island. "If we can do more private-public partnerships where homeowners begin to feel they are the stewards of their environments, then there might be a formula here to conserve more land."[35]

Chaffin/Light initially decided to fund the ongoing maintenance of Spring Island's 1,300-acre preserve through a unique form of real estate transfer fees: annual home owners' assessments, a 1.5 percent tax on property sales, and a 1 percent tax on re-sales. The money also helps pay for a private nature center, the Lowcountry Institute, with four full-time staff naturalists who provide environ-mental education programs for residents and visitors. To ensure that the property owners embrace the island's culture of conservation, they are required to attend a three-day workshop conducted by a staff naturalist to learn about the ecologi-cal dynamics of their lot before construction. The island's governing documents emphasize that every lot is part of a fragile habitat supporting the coastal region's rich biodiversity. Each property owner is expected to preserve and nurture the island's natural environment and its creatures.

From its inception Spring Island has sought to minimize the environmental impact of its neighborhoods. "Our philosophy was to create a community within the park, not a park within a community," explained Chaffin. As was true at Sea Pines, all house and landscaping plans must pass the scrutiny of the island's archi-tectural and habitat review boards. No house can be larger than 4,500 square feet, and all homes must be placed at least 150 feet away from roads or water. Houses must be energy efficient and use materials that both blend into the natural land-scape and come from sustainable sources. During the original site preparation for the development, mature trees were transplanted rather than destroyed. There are no paved roads on Spring Island. Each house must also maintain a fifty-foot "curtain" of natural vegetation. The green curtain provides vital habitat for ani-mals while maintaining the visual illusion of a wilderness. The required vegeta-tion curtain is also intended to impede the human appetite for conspicuous display. "Glitzier is not nicer, bigger is not better" in Chaffin's view of sustainable development. "When the houses are hidden, people feel less of a need to show off," he explained.[36]

Chaffin and Light's gamble in creating an environmental preserve at Spring Island paid off. During the 1990s Spring Island attracted affluent property owners: physicians, attorneys, corporate executives, entrepreneurs, financiers, and retired military officers. They came from across the nation, mostly from the Northeast. Chaffin reported that a "third of them are interested in hunting, a third in golf, and a third just want to be there." Spring Island's unique environmental amenities and strict conservation covenants did not deter buyers; in fact, the uniqueness of the eco-community enabled the developers to charge high prices for lots sized between three-quarters of an acre to ten acres. The first phase lots sold for an average of three hundred thousand dollars, higher at the time than any other island resort in the lowcountry, including Hilton Head and Kiawah. And the home prices range from one million to four million dollars. Joe Williams, a former chairman of the Nature Conservancy's board of governors, moved to Spring Island from San Francisco. "I was attracted to the extraordinary natural beauty of this place along with the Chaffins' commitment to ensure that the island's natural resources were preserved," he explained. Several developers from across the United States have since mimicked the environmental emphases of Spring Island. "I feel like my idea has had an impact," said Betsy Chaffin. Her husband added: "Look at the sprawl in Atlanta. We can argue all we want about growth, but growth is inevitable." Managing growth so as to preserve environmental quality, he emphasized, remained the greatest challenge for developers and land planners. "How are we going to balance economic viability, environmental sensitivity, and community livability?" His answer to the sustainability question was simple: Spring Island.[37]

However well designed or regulated, conservation developments ultimately depend upon the residents themselves to sustain the community's ecological premises. At Spring Island environmental stewardship is engrained in the island's civic culture. The official mission of Spring Island residents "is to preserve the natural surroundings that we have inherited so that we might take pleasure in the peaceful enjoyment of its marshes, forests and fields. . . . Everything that is natural and beautiful about the island will be maintained, and human presence will always be subtle and unassuming." The people who have purchased lots or homes at Spring Island are presumed to have embraced its culture of conservation. Resident Jim Kothe, who moved to Spring Island from Charlotte, North Carolina, noted that "our first commitment as a community is to the preservation and enjoyment of our habitat. Now that's unique, and, it isn't for everyone, which frankly, we like because it means that those who do become owners/members have bought into this shared vision." Another Spring Island resident highlighted the community's environmental philanthropy as well as its stewardship: "Most of the people who live on the Island are very active in conservation matters with their pocketbooks as well as their voices. So you will find in the roster of any of the local or national conservation organizations [that] Spring Island is very well represented [by] donors. That's very crass, but that's a contribution and it's a big one." Another resident emphasized that Spring Island has become "a real community. It's not a resort. It's not a golf community. It's a real community, in a beautiful place, and the community cares about this beautiful place."[38]

In 2000 Chaffin and Light turned the governance of Spring Island over to the Spring Island Property Owners Association (SIPOA). The Spring Island Trust Board and the SIPOA Board work in partnership to ensure that the development is maintained as a residential community within a nature preserve. SIPOA created a Habitat Review Board to oversee land-management issues in compliance with the Spring Island Habitat Review Guidelines. SIPOA also includes an environmental stewardship committee. To qualify as a committee member, a resident must learn about the island's biodiversity inventory and monitoring measures, the significance of rare plants and specimen trees, the scope of preservation efforts, and the rationale for maintaining habitat acreage sufficient to support specific animal species of concern. Potential committee members can meet such requirements either by achieving master naturalist status or through practical demonstration of their expertise.

In 2000 the Urban Land Institute presented its Award for Excellence to Spring Island. The citation described the conservation resort as "a purist's recreational community that focuses on protecting its environmental heritage. Its no- and low-impact land and habitat management philosophy emphasizes economic viability, community livability, and environmental sensitivity in preserving an authentic piece of South Carolina's lowcountry for future generations." Spring Island's residents take great pride in such awards and in their own ecological sensitivities. Yet there are understandable differences of opinion about what it means in practice to live on an island that defines itself as an environmental preserve. For example, residents acknowledge that "different people have different ideas as to just exactly what the flora and fauna should look like." One resident expressed concern about the oversight of the island: "I think the current political situation on the Island is one that tends to micromanage and not let the Island take care of itself, and I think that's dangerous. They've got to let the committee system work, and they are not doing it the way it has been done for the past twelve years." At the same time a resident interviewed for this book suggested that the island's educational outreach efforts may temper these issues. "There's a lot of emphasis, too, on having us understand [the complexities of ecological dynamics]. . . . I have complete faith in this: . . . the people managing the land." Perhaps the greatest testimonial to the success of Spring Island came from Charles Gatch, a veteran staff member of the Beaufort County planning office who had frequently hunted on undeveloped Spring Island as a child. He commented that Chaffin and Light had exceeded all expectations with their environmental preserve "given that the island eventually would be developed [by someone]."[39]

In sum most Spring Island residents are satisfied with the ecological resort's efforts to ensure that its conservation ethic is genuine. They believe that the local governing bodies in Beaufort County are getting even better at addressing environmental management issues. And they are convinced that the community's emphatic culture of conservation enhances the economic value of their investment in its real estate. They wish such values and practices were more common across the entire lowcountry region—and beyond. But Spring Island is not a scalable model for conservation communities. Only the wealthiest Americans can afford to live in such a well-planned coastal community. And there are not enough barrier islands to go around.

I'On: A New-urbanist Development

In 1992 Dana Beach told the *New York Times* that Spring Island "represents a marked improvement over some of the other developments on South Carolina islands. There are abysmally few examples of good [environmentally sensitive] developments along the coast." Yet some developers thought that Spring Island could have been improved. In August 1989, just a few weeks before Hurricane Hugo devastated the Lowcountry, Vincent G. "Vince" Graham, a bright young staff member at Chaffin/Light Associates, sent a detailed memorandum to his two bosses. Titled "Thoughts on Spring Island Master Plan," it acknowledged that the island was a "rare jewel" that provided a unique development opportunity, but it should also carry with it "a tremendous obligation to do the island justice by creating something truly different." He then asked Chaffin and Light what they thought the marketing focus of Spring Island should be. Exclusivity was an obvious selling point, he surmised, with only four hundred homes on three thousand acres. But was such a low-density resort the wisest use of the land? Did they really want Spring Island to nurture in its residents a "plantation mentality" whereby large houses were built on multiacre parcels out of sight of their neighbors? Look at the historic districts of Beaufort, Charleston, and Savannah, Graham advised. They are densely populated, pedestrian-friendly neighborhoods that exude a graciousness and charm "that to me are as much a part of the Low Country atmosphere as the marsh, live oaks, and palmettos. Could Spring Island be more than a nature preserve and golf/tennis/equestrian resort for a small, isolated number of millionaires?"[40]

Graham then asked Chaffin and Light to consider dedicating some of Spring Island to neo-traditional, or new-urbanist, neighborhoods. "I think the best thing to do (and what people would want)," Graham wrote, "is to make the lots much smaller and preserve the balance of the island as plantation." By reducing the lot sizes and making the neighborhoods more compact, by designing smaller, yet meticulously detailed houses with inviting verandas and front porches, and by providing tasteful retail areas within walking distance of residences, they could create "an original community rather than simply subdivide the island" into a nature preserve for a relatively few wealthy—and well-intentioned—residents.[41]

For all of his passion and conviction, Graham failed to convince Chaffin and Light that his new-urbanist concepts made sense for Spring Island, but he did not abandon his communitarian notion of conservation development. Instead he decided to transform his ideas into reality by designing his own neo-traditional lowcountry communities. Graham is an ardent proponent of new urbanism. Born in 1964 and raised in suburban Atlanta, the son of a real estate developer, he spent family vacations in the lowcountry. After graduating from the University of Virginia in 1986, he returned to Atlanta and began a career as a banker. Within a few years, however, he had grown disenchanted with the financial-services industry and disillusioned with Atlanta's unrelenting sprawl—"where you have to drive everywhere and are a slave to your car." He relocated to Beaufort in 1989 and began working as a project manager for the new Spring Island conservation community.[42]

While working at Spring Island and living in the historic district of Beaufort, Graham restored a dilapidated ninety-nine-year-old house where he lived. In the process he became smitten with the coastal town's grace and beauty. He "got to know everybody in the neighborhood. It was the real South. It was the South I wanted to live in." The social cohesion of the town's historic district inspired him, and he began imagining a planned neo-traditional development that would mimic Beaufort's virtues. He also visited Charleston and Savannah to study their historic districts and to understand better the success of their revitalized downtown areas.[43]

Graham also read widely in an effort to develop his own philosophy of community design. Jane Jacobs's classic analysis of the disintegration of modern urban life, *The Death and Life of Great American Cities* (1961), had a profound effect on him. Jacobs, a self-taught urban activist, argued that the massive urban renewal efforts in the 1950s were abysmal failures because they focused on bulldozing slums and replacing them with massive high-rise housing that fostered isolation, insecurity, and crime. Their emphasis instead should have been on promoting dense multiuse neighborhoods remarkable for their diversity, energy, community spirit, and public spaces. Neighborhoods, Jacobs argued, should be dynamic organisms rather than sterile inner-city breeding grounds for alienation and crime. Too many cities had allowed their civic cultures to disintegrate because urban planners tried to impose order and structure on neighborhoods rather than allowing the natural culture of neighborhoods to flourish. Planners needed to become intentional about creating interactive public spaces. And they needed to restore the delicate balance among "physical-economic-ethical processes." That is what would enable modern cities to thrive. As Jacobs declared, "streets and their sidewalks, the main public places of a city, are its most vital organs. Think of a city and what comes to mind? Its streets. If a city's streets look interesting, the city looks interesting; if they look dull, the city looks dull."[44]

Graham was enthralled with Jacobs's description of thriving traditional neighborhoods centered on a pedestrian-friendly street culture. In fact, he named one of the streets in l'On in honor of Jacobs. "In building l'On," he recalled, "we created a design code that set forth a small set of simple rules for proportion, scale, materials and building orientation to the public realm. This code serves as the neighborhood's 'DNA.' We then strove to encourage conditions that would enable a sense of community to grow." Like Jacobs, Graham believes that neighborhoods are not static; they change as people change—and that is good. "The l'On we know today will be remarkably different 10, 20 and 50 years from now," he predicted. "It is my hope that its future residents will appreciate the spontaneous change that Jane Jacobs advocated and that will enable our neighborhood organism to continuously improve and flourish."[45]

While the ideas and ideals of Jacobs were shaping Graham's understanding of a vibrant neighborhood's civic culture, Hilton Head's Charles Fraser was instrumental in revealing to Graham the importance of environmental aesthetics and amenities in enriching a lowcountry community's quality of life. Graham met Fraser in 1989. Over the next two years the celebrated developer of Sea Pines Plantation became a mentor to the younger man. His "strong appreciation for the land" was "a great inspiration for me," Graham recalled. He credited much of his own "sense of stewardship and love of the land" to his relationship with Fraser as well as his frequent trips to the lowcountry as a youth.[46]

By 1990 Graham had decided that he was ready to design his own distinctive conservation development. Unlike Fraser and Chaffin, however, he was most interested in the social and civic dimensions of a community. He wanted "to build . . . dense urban places rather than blend [homes and neighborhoods] into the countryside." He had come to view the subdued "housing style on Hilton Head, with the natural colors that blend in . . . as apologetic architecture. Somehow in peoples' psyche, that's like apologizing for humans, for being around, but humans are part of the natural ecology too." To create his ideal of a "human-centered" conservation-oriented community, he found a fifty-four-acre site on Lady's Island, across the river from historic Beaufort, and he quit his job with Spring Island to begin formulating plans for a traditional walking neighborhood called Newpoint.[47]

Completed in 1991, Newpoint represented Graham's effort (along with partner Bob Turner) to replicate many of the virtues he saw in old Beaufort—compact housing (126 single-family homes), a pedestrian scale, and a vibrant social and civic life. Its meticulously designed plan promoted biking and walking, preserved and buffered the small wetlands on the site, left the waterfront property undeveloped, and saved many of the live oaks. To foster community interaction Newpoint's neighborhood design standards required quarter-acre lots (the smallest allowed by the local zoning ordinance), narrow tree-lined streets, and houses built within twelve to eighteen feet of the front property line. Front porches designed "for use rather than looks" must be at least seven feet deep, and the ground floor must be elevated at least three feet above ground. Garages had to be placed behind houses along rear alleys. Meaningful open spaces were scattered throughout the development, and a large public park was created on the bluff overlooking the estuary. Newpoint was an immediate success. Stories about it appeared in the *Wall Street Journal* and *Southern Living* magazine. And it garnered awards from The South Carolina Department of Natural Resources and the American Institute of Architects.[48]

Four years later, in 1995, Graham (with the backing of his father and brother) applied new-urbanist principles on a much larger scale when he began developing the neo-traditional community called I'On. He named it in honor of Jacob Bond I'On (1782–1859), a nineteenth-century planter who distinguished himself as an army officer during the War of 1812 and then served as mayor of Sullivan's Island and as president of the South Carolina Senate. I'On, "a true Carolina gentleman," was buried alongside his wife in the family cemetery on the 243-acre infill parcel called the Jordan Tract that Graham and his partners purchased in Mount Pleasant.

Working with Miami-based Andres Duany, Graham tried to build at I'On a "sustainable human-scale multiuse village" that would feature high-density yet "neighborhood-friendly" residential areas by clustering home sites on tree-lined streets with contiguous retail and office space. As at Newpoint, detailed architectural standards would ensure compatibility with the community's design philosophy. But I'On would be more than a neighborhood; it would be a diverse mixed-use community. Graham's original concept for I'On called for almost ten times as many residences (1,250) as Newpoint had, on only five times as many acres (243). In addition, I'On would include retail and office spaces, two churches, playgrounds, and a Montessori school.

Graham, a self-described maverick who bristles at conventional thinking, was convinced that I'On would align perfectly with the Town of Mount Pleasant's recently crafted "smart-growth-oriented" long-range plan. In 1992 the town council had unanimously adopted a Master Plan that embraced Traditional Neighborhood Design (TND) principles. Two years later the town council unanimously approved its Comprehensive Land-Use Plan which also promoted compact neo-traditional neighborhoods. Despite such policy recommendations, however, the town council had not modified its zoning ordinances to support such progressive planning concepts. When Graham began developing the design for I'On, the Jordan Tract was zoned "R-1," which meant that house lots must be a minimum of ten thousand square feet with the accompanying requirements of conventional developments (minimum lot widths, setbacks, and so on). To enable the dense clustering of houses associated with new-urbanist principles, Graham had to request a zoning waiver. "I still am naïve," Graham reflected in 2010, "but I was really naïve then, politically. We had read the town's Master Plan document and thought, wow, we share the same kind of ideas about development. We'll hire the best planners in the country and get 'em here, and give 'em just what they [the town planners] want." What Graham failed to realize was that "any rezoning involves a political campaign."[49]

In late April and early May 1995 Graham hired Duany and a dozen other designers and engineers to conduct an intensive public charette, a free-flowing group design workshop—with public input—that produced a site plan and neighborhood drawings for I'On in a week rather than the typical six months. The creative exercise also included visits to Savannah, Beaufort, Charleston, and Mount Pleasant as well as conversations with elected officials, town planners, traffic consultants, and private citizens. On May 3 Duany presented the results of the charette at a Mount Pleasant Town Hall meeting overflowing with area residents, environmentalists, developers, contractors, realtors, and town officials. The initial plan for I'On called for 800 single-family lots, 440 multifamily units, 90,000 square feet of commercial space, professional offices, and civic facilities. The development would include playgrounds, parks, lakes, and three dispersed neighborhood retail centers located so that any resident could access them with no more than a five-minute walk.[50]

To construct I'On, however, Graham needed to get the development rezoned from "residential" to "planned unit development." And that meant public hearings—where outraged residents living in nearby neighborhoods let Graham know that they thought I'On was an awful idea. The intensity of the criticism surprised Graham. He felt ambushed. "None of us were expecting this buzz-saw of opposition," he recalled. His "progressive" plan had become a lightning rod for a much broader issue: the clash between high-density smart-growth principles and conventional low-density suburban sprawl. While many neighboring residents embraced the premises and protocols for such a new-urbanist community, others resented Duany's self-righteous, condescending dismissal of conventional suburban subdivisions. Critics also balked at the higher density philosophy at the heart of I'On and the new urbanism. They feared that such a concentration of new residents would exacerbate rather than relieve traffic congestion, further tax already overcrowded schools, and lower property values. They also claimed that I'On's intentionally narrow streets, designed to foster community interaction, would inhibit fire trucks and other emergency vehicles. An innovative new high-density community nearby was "a very emotional thing to people," Graham remembered. They had developed a "mindset that when we were going to change from the sacred R1 zoning, that they were being wronged. . . . So it became very emotional and that was hard to deal with." Graham came to realize that "any form of innovation involves subverting the status quo. And the status quo . . . doesn't want to be subverted."[51]

Opponents of I'On formed the Mathis Ferry Preservation Association and launched a petition drive that gathered more than two thousand signatures. "We're not going to change [our] opposition to the I'On project," said a spokesman for the critics. Their differences with Graham's new-urbanist vision were "irreconcilable."[52]

Both sides claimed to be preservationists. Those opposed to I'On were seeking to preserve the quality of life afforded by their conventional subdivisions. To the "no-growth" neighbors, even the most progressive forms of smart growth meant more congestion. More houses meant more cars, more children enrolling at already crowded schools, and, in the long run, higher taxes. Because their neighborhoods were zoned R-1 for large single-family homes on large lots, they argued, all new communities in the area should be R-1 as well. Such no-growth NIMBYISM dismayed one resident who observed that Mount Pleasant's master plan was intended to slow suburban sprawl, and the proposed I'On project "agrees with the [town] master plan to the letter." By adopting such a smart-growth master plan the Town of Mount Pleasant had invited innovative developers such as Graham and his father "to come to our community. They are offering the kind of leadership required to preserve the high quality of life in Mount Pleasant. We should allow the Grahams to do what we invited them here to do."[53]

The strident opposition forced the I'On team to spend several months revising the proposed plan and reducing its density. They also solicited significant support among environmental organizations and many residents who were excited by the new approach to suburban development. And they gained approval from the Mount Pleasant planning board. Yet in December 1995 the town council voted five to four against approving I'On. Graham refused to give up, however. "We aren't going to go away," he pledged. Throughout 1996 he continued to shrink the plan for I'On. Streets were redesigned, and the proposed commercial space was cut by two-thirds. All of the planned apartments were eliminated, much to Graham's chagrin, for the multifamily component of the project was intended to ensure a healthy mix of income levels among residents. In January 1997 the Mount Planning Board of Planning and Zoning approved by a seven to one vote Graham's request to rezone the property from R-1 to PD, or planned development. The following month, with the Coastal Conservation League's explicit support of I'On, the town council reversed its earlier opposition and approved the rezoning request.[54]

But the most controversial proposed development in lowcountry history was not yet a reality. I'On's no-growth opponents started a new petition drive, this time to force a town-wide public referendum on the issue. By June 1997, as site work began at I'On, they had amassed 4,500 signatures, 800 more than the required 15 percent of registered voters. Meanwhile Graham moved ahead with the first phase of the development. In July he convinced a circuit judge to issue a temporary restraining order preventing the Town of Mount Pleasant from proceeding with the referendum until the court assessed the validity of the petition effort. The following month, however, the town council voted unanimously to hold the referendum in November. Graham then filed an appeal of the council's decision. In October 1997 the court ruled that a municipality could not hold a referendum on zoning issues. The town council accepted the judge's decision, but the opponents of I'On filed an appeal. In January 2000 the South Carolina Supreme Court unanimously affirmed the lower-court decision. As the legal battle worked its way through the court system, the political fallout associated with

Community square in I'On. Courtesy of I'On Company.

By West Lake at I'On. Photograph by Angela C. Halfacre.

the I'On controversy continued. Over the next two town council elections, five of the six council members who supported the I'On rezoning proposal were defeated for reelection, and the sixth supporter chose not to run again.

For all of its controversial beginnings I'On has since become a much-celebrated success—on a local as well as national level. Its lot and house prices rose substantially after the first neighborhood was built, and I'On's property values have consistently outperformed the market in the greater Charleston area. Lots in I'On range in size from one-twentieth to one-half acre, and the architecturally diverse homes have ranged in price from $160,000 to $1,700,000. The architectural requirements, embodied in a nine-page document called the I'On Code, were the strictest in the lowcountry.

I'On's emphasis on high-quality architectural and aesthetic details, environmental protection, and community vitality drew widespread praise—even from its original critics. "Looking around the new neighborhood," wrote a journalist in 1999, "it's hard to understand what all the fuss was about a few years ago when Mount Pleasant officials were debating how densely I'On could be developed." Steve Brock, a resident of a neighboring subdivision who was one of the most vocal opponents of I'On's rezoning request during the mid-1990s, has since offered Graham "a peace pipe" and admitted that I'On is beautiful, "its style is enviable," and its amenities enticing.[55]

I'On has become a national model for new-urbanist design. It has been featured in *National Geographic, Southern Living* magazine, and other national publications, and it has garnered many high-profile awards. In 2000 *Professional Builder* magazine named it a "best community." Three years later the Congress for the New Urbanism presented its Charter Award to Graham for outstanding urban design. The following year, in 2004, the neo-traditional community was voted "best smart growth community in the nation" by the National Association of Home Builders. The South Carolina Chapter of the American Society of Landscape Architects (SCASLA) has also honored Graham with the first Charles E. Fraser Award. It honors people who distinguish themselves in the careful planning and artful design of cultural and natural environments. The organization specifically recognized Graham's ecologically sound smart-growth developments that nurture relationships between the public and private realms to create places with social and economic value. SCASLA trustee David Lycke and member Bill Eubanks, who jointly nominated Graham, said the developer of I'On shared ideals similar to those of Charles Fraser in promoting smart growth."[Vince] is doing what Charles would be doing today if he were still here," noted Edward Pinckney of the Florida ASLA, who was on the jury that selected Graham as the award recipient.[56]

The I'On community is not all that Graham had envisioned, since he had to eliminate the diversifying element of affordable housing, substantially reduce the residential density and retail space, and eliminate connector roads into neighboring subdivisions. In the end the housing density of I'On is only slightly higher

I'On, aerial view.
Courtesy of
I'On Company.

than a conventional subdivision. While the spatial scale of the community enables residents to walk to neighborhood shops and stores, people living in I'On lack public transit options. The density in I'On would need to be three to five times higher to provide enough volume to support mass transit. The residents remain dependent on their automobiles to get to work and go to school because I'On is a new-urbanist island surrounded by conventional suburban infrastructure.[57]

For all of its limitations, however, I'On has demonstrated that people in the lowcountry will support the communitarian premises of neo-traditional neighborhood development. Like Andres Duany, Graham insisted that fostering a shared sense of community is the most important element of neighborhood planning and sustainable development. So he focused his attention on creating enticing public spaces in I'On—pedestrian-friendly streetscapes, alleyways, courtyards, parks, and playgrounds—that promote social interaction and enhance the residents' sense of place and community. As Graham explained, "We always talk about how it takes a village to accomplish this or that." But instead of just building houses, "you create within the village a vast public realm, places that we share." Building a sense of community is a voluntary process; it cannot be forced upon people. In I'On's neighborhoods, the residents create the sense of community, but the design aesthetics encourage and facilitate shared social and civic life to a much greater extent than what is found in most subdivisions. "I know more of my neighbors here than anywhere I've lived," said Anne Kendrick, one of the community's first-phase residents. Kendrick, who has two young children, said the neighborhood felt and looked inviting. "It's great because there are parks everywhere," she said.[58]

Development as a Means of Conservation

The three case studies—Hilton Head, Spring Island, and I'On—demonstrate the variety of conservation-oriented communities and reveal their philosophical differences. While the environmental awareness that Charles Fraser displayed at Sea Pines Plantation in the 1950s was ahead of its time, its time has come—and gone.

In fact, Fraser's pathbreaking efforts at green development now seem timid and outdated to advocates of smart growth and new urbanism. Critics have highlighted how Hilton Head today is vastly different from the Sea Pines ideal that Fraser championed. Andres Duany, for example, said in 2000 that Hilton Head "is a good-looking place. They saved all the oaks. And it has certain ecological pretensions. But the fact is that it's a little Los Angeles." For all of its much-trumpeted bicycle paths, the overcrowded island resort is even more dependent upon automobile use. The maddening traffic on the overdeveloped island "is all that people talk about."[59]

The effort to use innovative approaches to coastal development as a means of protecting more open space, enhancing community, and improving the quality of fragile ecosystems has strengthened the reach and appeal of the lowcountry culture of conservation. As critics have often pointed out, however, virtually all of the coastal conservation communities are exclusive gated enclaves that cater to the wealthiest (and whitest) segment of the population. The preserved land cannot be accessed by those who do not live there. Open space in environmental resorts does not always mean public space. As Vince Graham reflected in 2010, "Spring Island is a beautiful place, and Jim Chaffin and Jim Light, you know they work really hard and they're great stewards of the land, but I wonder sometime. Yeah, there's a place for it. I mean there's always been a place for people who want to have their retreats in the countryside." But he wondered if such "places aren't just a fad. Are they sustainable in the long term?"[60]

Such elite conservation communities represent only a small (but growing) percentage of new coastal neighborhoods. They collectively are not large enough (in terms of the number of residents and the amount of acreage) to redress the environmental damage inflicted by sprawl. But they are significant nonetheless. The effort to use innovative approaches to coastal development as a means of protecting more open space, enhancing community, and improving the quality of fragile ecosystems has strengthened the reach and appeal of the culture of conservation. Their symbolic visibility as well as their innovative features, communitarian ideals, and educational programs have made a powerful contribution to the conservation culture that transcends their actual size and scale. As models for green development, they have cascading consequences. A "green development," as one planning expert stressed, "can effect change far beyond its borders, helping to make environmental practitioners out of visitors, guests, and the surrounding community." Places such as Dewees Island, Spring, Island, and Sewee Preserve have changed the conversation about community planning in the lowcountry and across the United States. As Donald Lesh, a member of President Bill Clinton's Council on Sustainable Development, observed, "Dewees Island truly sets an international model for sustainability. I have not seen any development in my range of experience that so completely articulates sustainable practice."[61]

The new conservation resort enclaves in the lowcountry—those where large acreages of conserved space are protected through different schemes, designations, and forms of governance—remain within the control of a select few, often in close proximity to long-standing indigenous communities that once had access to the natural resources now enclosed by elegant gates and fences. Conservation communities have only recently begun to acknowledge that endangered minority groups and their traditional ways of life deserve preserving as well. The lowcountry conservation culture has thus emerged as a human ecosystem comprising a mosaic of institutional and governance regimes that foster conservation in distinctively different ways, for different motives, and with mixed success.

EIGHT

Weaving Tensions
into a Cultural Heritage

It was an incongruous scene. As the sun rose at luxurious Kiawah Island on July 12, 2007, thirty African Americans, mostly women, stooped to "pull" (harvest) long-stemmed blades of sweetgrass, a reedlike coastal plant named for its sweet taste. The harvesters had traveled for more than an hour south from their homes near Mount Pleasant, northeast of Charleston, to take advantage of a special opportunity to collect sweetgrass for making hand-woven baskets. The basket makers were engaging in a generations-old handicraft tradition within one of the nation's most exclusive resort communities, replete with championship golf courses, expensive condominiums, bicycle trails, and lush landscaping. Assisting the harvesters were the Kiawah Island Community Association (KICA) grounds crew, traffic engineers, and curious residents. A journalist and film crew documented the morning's activity (as did I in my role as a participant/observer). Local politicians were on hand as well. The only African American member of the Mount Pleasant Town Council, Thomasena Stokes-Marshall, had coordinated the harvest with KICA. Now she looked on with evident pride.[1]

The sweetgrass pulling on Kiawah Island marked a return of basket makers to a site where their ancestors had engaged in similar activities centuries earlier. The pulling of sweetgrass at Kiawah also highlighted how the island resort's landscaping practices have helped to preserve a native plant and sustain a local livelihood imbued with great cultural significance. The collection of sweetgrass on Kiawah Island also illuminated important issues involving land-use changes, diverse handicraft traditions, and new forms of conservation management in the lowcountry. The exclusive resort's support of an African American handicraft tradition revealed how the conservation ethic in the lowcountry has broadened over time to include the preservation of the region's ethno-cultural heritage as well as its physical landscape. "It's just like learning to play an instrument," said Henrietta Snype, a basket weaver. "It's part of us. It's our culture, our heritage."[2]

The image of basket makers, none of whom could afford to purchase property at Kiawah Island, pulling sweetgrass at the posh resort revealed how residential development in the lowcountry has often been a double-edged phenomenon. While accommodating population growth, facilitating the lucrative tourism industry, and generating new jobs and desired services, coastal resort development

Basket stand along Highway 17. Photograph by Angela Hallfacre.

has also threatened natural habitats, deeply embedded Gullah folkways derived from West Africa, and a cherished way of life. Ironically, both overdevelopment and its opposite—the creation of permanent natural preserves—can produce dispossession. Loss of habitat often means loss of home, for wildlife and for people, especially those living at the margins of social stature, economic status, and political power.

For example, both lowcountry real estate development and the contrasting efforts to conserve large parcels have displaced many historic African American communities that long relied on the land for their food, commerce, handicrafts— and cultural identity. Multigenerational extended families are the trademark of Gullah culture, a culture that is rooted in the land. Emory Campbell, a native of Hilton Head Island and Gullah community activist who became executive director of the Penn Center in Beaufort, described the Gullah commitment to land as a form of cultural preservation: "You have memories on that very land that you grew up on, memories of working the fields, stories told in the field or under a familiar oak tree, and memories of walking through your grandmother's yard. It is because of those memories that the Gullah/Geechee culture and its people have bonded to the land." Because the Gullah way of life—and self-identity— are so dependent upon land, issues of public welfare—environmental justice and social equity—have frequently collided with private property rights. As the African American photographer Vennie Deas Moore, a native of McClellanville, laments, "the Carolina lowcountry as I knew it as a child is being threatened." Sprawling development has put at risk the Gullah way of life in the lowcountry. "More and more, the people of the land are being displaced."[3]

Ecological science stresses the interconnectedness between and mutual dependence of flora and fauna. Yet ecologists too often ignore the connections between nature and people, whose fates are also intertwined. Likewise, community planners and government officials often focus on land-use issues without factoring in the significance of a community's heritage of land-based livelihoods. Just as diversity of species is beneficial to ecosystems, the diversity of people and livelihoods in a community enhances the quality of life. Coastal real estate development and rising property taxes have exerted unrelenting pressure on black (Gullah) land ownership. Many families who wanted to stay on their heirs' property have been uprooted because of high taxes or disputes within an extended family. "We have to avoid those situations," Campbell stressed. "We have to look at public policy to prevent families from being disrupted." He cited several examples of the Gullah culture "being disrupted by resort development through the sale of land, highways and planning laws that don't recognize traditions and customs of the culture."4

Until the late 1980s efforts to conserve the lowcountry environment focused more on protecting the physical landscape than addressing the needs of endangered folkways and traditional livelihoods. Yet the African American basket makers may be as endangered as the wood stork or the red-cockaded woodpecker. Basket making (the gathering of materials, sewing of baskets, and selling of products) is inextricably linked to the sprawling patterns of residential and commercial development as well as to the evolution of a conservation culture in the lowcountry. Over the last twenty years or so the conservation culture in the lowcountry has expanded conventional notions of conservation to include the preservation of historic folkways, some of which depend upon particular natural resources.5

Sweetgrass Basket Making—A Land-Based Livelihood

Basket making is an ancient handicraft practiced around the world. People have been weaving multicolored tightly coiled durable grass baskets for centuries on several continents. Enslaved Africans adapted their intricate ancestral basket-making practices to South Carolina plantation life by using materials that grew locally in the lowcountry: sweetgrass, bulrush, longleaf pine needles, and palmetto fronds. The basket-making tradition has since become the most visible element of the Gullah culture; according to Thomasena Stokes-Marshall, the Gullah community and sweetgrass basket makers go "hand in hand."6

The Gullah culture (also known as Geechee or Gullah-Geechee) includes distinctive forms of speech, family social units, religious beliefs and practices, music, dance, storytelling, arts and crafts, and the use of natural resources for the people's livelihoods. The word *Gullah* was probably derived from Gola, an African tribe. Gullah language is a particularly important aspect of the African American culture in the lowcountry because of its historic role in providing a confidential way for enslaved Africans from two dozen different tribal cultures to communicate with each other. Gullah is a creole language, a hybrid of West African and English speech patterns spoken with a Caribbean inflection. As cultural historian Alada D. Shinault-Smalls explained, Africans "came [to Carolina] with their own linguistic cultural baggage and were not allowed to read and write

English, and as a survival mechanism they developed their own language." Of course, Africans arriving in the Americas also came from many different tribes and spoke different dialects, so they gradually created Gullah as a form of universal communication.[7]

Today hundreds of African American basket makers in the lowcountry strive to sustain both the Gullah language and many of its folk practices. A basket maker in 2008 noted that "Gullah is actually *the* black language." The Gullah culture originated on the sea islands at the same time that West Africans put their transplanted skills to use making sweetgrass baskets, some flat and traylike, some bowl-shaped, some lidded. During the eighteenth and nineteenth centuries the baskets served both as implements for processing rice and as containers for shipping and storing agricultural products. Rice could not have been produced in such large quantities without the traditional coiled "fanner" basket used for separating the rice grains from the hulls.[8]

Two plant materials were originally used to make baskets: sweetgrass and black needlerush (also called bulrush). The strongest baskets were made of black needlerush bound with strips of white oak or palmetto. Because it is less durable, straw-colored sweetgrass was reserved for the more delicate "show baskets" that have become so popular with retail customers. Sweetgrass thrives naturally in clumps landward of the second dune line at beaches as well as in the boundaries between marsh and woods. It cannot grow in salty water or in the shade. Yet sweetgrass, like many other coastal plants, often benefits from disturbance caused by storms. Hurricanes, for example, clear the land and thereby stimulate the new growth of coastal grasses. Sweetgrass also benefits from being pulled. The regular thinning of clumps keeps the fast-growing plant from choking itself.

Although basket making has long been an important part of the household economies of African Americans in the lowcountry, its importance as a source of outside income is a more recent development. Since the early twentieth century members of the Gullah community have made baskets for sale to tourists as well as locals. During the agricultural depression following the hurricanes of the 1890s and early 1900s, and in the aftermath of the boll weevil infestation in 1918, "show" baskets provided a crucial source of income to impoverished sea islanders. For some, then and since, basket making was their primary vocation; for most, it is an important source of supplementary income. "My mother did it, and her mother, and her mother's mother, all the way back," recalled Adeline Mazyck, a lowcountry basket maker. But "if we don't watch out," she warned, "we are going to lose it."[9]

During the middle of the twentieth century the basket makers became a visible, valued element of the lowcountry tourist trade; the "majority of basketmakers [live in or] have their roots" in Mount Pleasant. They sold baskets at scores of roadside stands along U.S. Highway 17, the "Old Ocean Highway," just north of Mount Pleasant, and in the tourist areas of downtown Charleston, including the Market and the Four Corners of Law.

Modern-day sweetgrass harvest, Kiawah Island.
Courtesy of *Charleston City Paper.*

Baskets that were originally woven for agricultural use have since become prized works of art embellishing affluent homes and prestigious museums across the United States and around the world. In 1949, long before court-mandated racial integration, the editors of the *Charleston Post and Courier* expressed pride in the African American tradition of basket making. Tourists should "stop for a look at an importation of the artistry of African workers." The basket weavers' retail stands along six-lane U.S. Highway 17, the major north-south coastal artery, were an open-air museums of sorts, showcasing the "artists in their handiwork."[10]

Squeezing out Sweetgrass

By the late twentieth century the highly visible basket-making economy was in trouble. Hurricane Hugo destroyed most of the basket stands that lined Highway 17. Even more important, the hurricane necessitated coastal reconstruction that in turn stimulated waves of new development around Mount Pleasant that destroyed or restricted access to much of the sweetgrass. Many of the plant populations were declared off limits to the basketmakers because they were growing within exclusive new gated communities or on private property where the owners did not allow access to the reedy plant. The lack of access to sweetgrass forced basket makers to pay "gatherers" who venture well south—often into south Georgia and north Florida—to find sweetgrass. In the 1940s and 1950s a female basketmaker recalled, "my mom and [her friends] . . . used to . . . gather [the sweetgrass] themselves, and that kept the cost of the basket down, but as time progressed and people started building houses and condominiums and stores, they killed the sweetgrass. Now it's hard to find, so other people went out and got sweetgrass [outside the lowcountry] and . . . we have to pay them for their gas and time." Today a bundle of sweetgrass about three inches in diameter can cost about fifty dollars. The expense of paying gatherers has greatly complicated the handicraft tradition. Another basket maker, a male, explained that sweetgrass "grows near the rivers . . . and you could pull it [down by the rivers on islands such as] Daniel Island. . . . The pine needles, these drop off the pine tree on[to] the ground . . . [to] make fertilizer. . . . And you would go and rake it up, put it in plastic bags, and bring 'em home. . . . But, you know, these things a long time back was [mostly] free . . . but everything costs now."[11]

While basket makers acknowledge that the dramatic population growth in the lowcountry has brought more customers and higher prices for their baskets, it has also disrupted their ability to make and sell them. A basket maker explained that the dramatic changes in the lowcountry were threatening not only the basket-making tradition but also their distinctive community:

> Well, I went away when I was seven, and Mount Pleasant was a quiet place. You could actually go on that two-lane highway [U.S. Highway 17] out there and sit in the middle of it for hours . . . and you wouldn't see a car. And then all of the sudden, I started coming back home on . . . vacations, and these cars [were] zipping up and down the road. All that used to be woods, trees-trees-trees, nothing but trees, and they're now houses and businesses. The reason that I moved back home was for the peace and quiet, and now they've boxed me in completely. . . . Boxed in roads, roads, roads, and cars. Sometimes I sit in my driveway for 20 minutes waiting to get out because of the cars and all of our little private dirt roads that we had through here to get from place to place, they use them commercially. We had to put a log over that road to keep the cars from zipping off of [High-way] 17 and coming through here and the dust putting it in your face, messing up your hair.

Since 1990 the feverish development around Mount Pleasant has increasingly surrounded the historic African American neighborhoods. While none of the neighborhoods has disappeared, their autonomy has diminished.[12]

Conserving a Cultural Tradition

However ambivalent the basket makers are about the forces of modernity, their plight has garnered substantial local and national attention in recent years. Public officials, concerned citizens, and conservation organizations have repeatedly acknowledged the need to preserve the Gullah culture. In doing so they have stretched the conventional notion of conservation to include not only native plants but native handicraft traditions as well. As a journalist stressed, "the baskets are as much a part of Charleston as carriage rides past the city's pastel homes and the ring of church bells on a sultry July breeze. They are sold in the city's open-air market and on the stone steps of the federal building in the heart of the historic district. The true center of sweetgrass basket weaving, however, is a few miles to the east, across the sweeping Cooper River, in Mount Pleasant, the fastest-growing town in South Carolina."[13]

In 1987 basket makers met at Greater Goodwill AME Church in Mount Pleasant to organize the Sweetgrass Preservation Society. The following year the Mott Foundation and the National Endowment for the Arts sponsored the Charleston Sweetgrass Conference. Government officials, biologists, environmentalists, and basket makers converged to discuss the impact of public policies and development on lowcountry sweetgrass. The well-attended conference was the first concerted attempt to publicize the plight of basket makers and propose solutions. Richard Jones, then the mayor of Mount Pleasant, told the audience that the basket-making culture was "a very integral part of the culture and heritage of the town." He pledged to work with the state transportation department to protect the roadside basket stands. Dana Beach, then serving as special assistant to U.S. Representative Arthur Ravenel, attended the sweetgrass conference and urged the participants to include the basket-making tradition within the region's culture of conservation. He explained that "people come to this city to see history in context. When these things disappear—basketmaking and other indigenous industries like oystering and shrimping, due to encroaching development—If the city is simply a collection of beautiful old houses, it will make it less legitimate."[14]

The concerns expressed at the Charleston conference helped convince the U.S. Soil Conservation Service (SCS) to develop a comprehensive plan to begin growing sweetgrass near the African American neighborhoods around Mount Pleasant. Some sixteen groups and agencies collaborated on the sweetgrass restoration project. In the fall of 1989 SCS planted sweetgrass at the Clemson University Experiment Station near Charleston. The following year the Beaufort-Jasper Water and Sewer Authority offered SCS a five-and-one-half-acre tract of Palm Key, near Ridgeland, South Carolina, on which to plant sweetgrass. SCS staff members and volunteers transplanted sweetgrass being displaced by a new golf course at Kiawah Island to the Palm Key site.[15]

The Palm Key restoration project, however, was too far from Mount Pleasant to benefit most of the basketmakers. In 1993 the first of a series of sweetgrass restoration efforts began in the Charleston / Mount Pleasant area. Volunteers planted sweetgrass at several protected sites over the course of the mid-1990s, but the efforts had mixed results. Basket makers still encountered difficulties in gaining access to the privately owned sites. At the same time many of the test plantings were so poorly maintained that they were overrun by invasive plants. At those sites where populations still exist, the grass is sparse and not easily accessible.[16]

Since the mid-1990s, however, efforts to preserve and protect the sweetgrass basket-making culture have gained renewed momentum. New subdivisions in the Mount Pleasant area often include sweetgrass among their landscaping plants, although it is usually a different species from that used by basket makers. In these cases plantings may occur in or along parking lots in commercial areas, in the welcome areas to a community, or in the open spaces now included in many lowcountry subdivisions. In recent years basket makers have indicated that landscaping-related plantings have become increasingly commonplace, including within urban jurisdictions. In Mount Pleasant, for example, sweetgrass has not only become a common planting at strip malls and new businesses, but the plant also adorns the fringes of parking lots and highway median strips in the Charleston / Mount Pleasant area.[17]

In 1997 the Town of Mount Pleasant officially recognized the cultural significance of the sweetgrass basket-making tradition by placing a historical marker along U.S. 17 at the intersection of Hamlin Road. In 2002 researchers from the U.S. Department of Agriculture's Forest Southern Research Station and the College of Charleston, with funding from the South Carolina Sea Grant Consortium, began studying how to ensure that basket makers gained access to sweetgrass. The following year champions of the basket-making tradition founded the Sweetgrass Cultural Arts Festival Association (SCAFA). It is solely dedicated to promoting the historic African art of basket making. Two years later, in 2005, the South Carolina legislature and Governor Sanford designated sweetgrass basket making as the official state handicraft. That same year SCAFA launched a two-day annual Sweetgrass Cultural Arts Festival. In 2006 the state legislature officially named the stretch of U.S. 17 running north from Mount Pleasant the "Sweetgrass Basketmakers Highway." At the same time the Town of Mount Pleasant created the Sweetgrass Basket Overlay District, a 1.5 mile segment of U.S. 17 where the basket makers for generations had erected their retail stands. Creating the overlay district was a joint effort with Charleston County to protect the African American handicraft tradition from the continuing encroachment of residential and commercial development.[18]

Also in 2006 the federal government officially established the Gullah-Geechee Heritage Corridor running through the coastal regions of the Carolinas, Georgia, and Florida, a corridor that overlaps with the tradition of coiled basket making. The legislation provided one million dollars a year for ten years to create a federal commission to oversee efforts to preserve the Gullah culture in the lowcountry. It also established the Coastal Heritage Center at the Penn Center on St. Helena Island. U.S. Representative James Clyburn, who wrote the legislation creating the Gullah-Geechee Heritage Corridor, said it was intended to identify and preserve what remains of the unique fusion of African and European cultures. The Gullah tradition, he noted, was "slipping away in the wake of coastal development and pressures from a 'modern' world." Clyburn, whose wife is of Gullah origin, recalled that when he arrived as a new member of Congress, there were lots of bills being written to save "the marsh and prevent sprawl," but "no one was paying attention to this culture that, to me, was sort of just going away" and needed to be conserved.[19]

In 2007 the Town of Mount Pleasant and Charleston County agreed to limit development where sweetgrass still grows. Perhaps the most promising initiative related to the supply of sweetgrass was the 2007 purchase by the Sweetgrass Society of two parcels near the town of McClellanville. The properties total nearly seventy-one acres and border the Francis Marion National Forest. The project, funded by a $1.7 million grant from Charleston County, focuses on preserving and propagating sweetgrass for the use of the basket-making community. Sweetgrass is now being cultivated on the parcel, and the Sweetgrass Society coordinates annual lectures, demonstrations, classes, and festivals on the site. Also in 2007 the Highway 17 Corridor Task Force designated the segment of Highway 17 north of Mount Pleasant the Sweetgrass Basket Corridor, providing official recognition and protection of basket makers who have dozens of makeshift retail stands alongside the busy roadway. "Sweetgrass baskets will always be along Highway 17," declared task force member Richard Habersham, president of the Phillips Community Association. "Before, it was at the pleasure of the landowners, but now they're creating a right of way" for the basket sellers. A year later SCAFA gained the approval of the Mount Pleasant Waterworks to plant 1,200 sweetgrass clumps near the water tower as a pilot effort to propagate the grass. In 2009 the Town of Mount Pleasant constructed a Sweetgrass Cultural Arts Pavilion at the new Memorial Waterfront Park at the foot of the Arthur Ravenel Jr. Bridge. The open-air pavilion includes historical exhibits of sweetgrass basket making and space for basket sewers to sell their wares and demonstrate their weaving techniques. In 2010 the Sweetgrass Cultural Annual Arts Festival was held, for the first time, at the Sweetgrass Pavilion.[20]

Other efforts to sustain the basket-making cultural community have focused on creating collaborations or partnerships with landowners, community associations, and other organizations that manage land in the lowcountry. One basket maker shared her solution: "Well, if you have property, if we could plant it on the property . . . and let us come and pull the grass. As long as we pull it, it's not going to hurt it. . . . Let us harvest it—wouldn't hurt it at all." However, these collaborations have been wrought with tensions. Some communities have allowed basket makers to pull sweetgrass; others have prohibited it. Encouraging the private cultivation of sweetgrass has its challenges. As another basket maker acknowledged, "Well, I was given a plant at one of the shows we [went] to. I think it was on McLeod Plantation on James Island, and we were given a sample, and I took it home and planted it in the backyard and it grew, it became a part of the lawn. So, you can imagine how I felt about my husband *mowing* it! He didn't know how sweetgrass looked when it was green or in the growing stage. He only got a chance to see it when it was pulled out of the grove."[21]

For the most part, however, basket makers continue to be excluded from private and public sweetgrass sites. As one of them reported, "the sweetgrass name, to me, has been taken over more for the development [of new subdivisions] and not enough for the basket weavers! They have sweetgrass growing as decorations alongside the road and sweetgrass neighborhoods [and] sweetgrass corners, but there isn't enough being done for the people and persons that actually brought the name and the culture of sweetgrass basket[s] to Mount Pleasant and Charleston." Many of these sites include the residential communities spawned by upscale developments. Basket makers indicated that they could still find sweetgrass: "Right around this area—Seabrook and Kiawah—you could just actually go there to the marshland and get it. . . . But it's a resort now."[22]

Basket makers reported that for them to gain access to sweetgrass in gated or restricted communities usually required knowing someone with "clout" who could "open doors" for them. The terms and timing of access are controlled by the host community. The basket makers believe that the conservation-oriented gated communities must acknowledge that sweetgrass—and the baskets made from it—need to be conserved as much as the beaches and marshes. Some do. For example, developers of Dewees Island proclaim that "all of the rules of traditional beachfront real estate development were broken" because "the process was driven by restoration and preservation." The environmental community's conservation ethos extends to sweetgrass. The community's land manager has worked with local basket makers to arrange access to the grasses. In a 2002 interview a basket maker predicted that the approach used at Dewees Island might solve the situation—if it were mimicked at other exclusive communities. Efforts to arrange for the pulling of sweetgrass are gaining success in other gated communities such as Kiawah Island. However, sustaining the tradition of sweetgrass basket making is a community-wide challenge.[23]

The supply and availability of sweetgrass remain problematic. As one basket maker indicated, "when these new developments started coming over here . . . they [started] bulldozing all of our plants down. . . . Back in 1985, or 1986, we started noticing [the development], and then it just seemed like every time you turn around there's a new subdivision. And, every year, [the sweetgrass] has been declining. The thing is, as long as there's an edge of the river, marshland, [sweetgrass will grow there] . . . I think a lot of people don't even know that they have the sweetgrass on their property." Those habitats and plants that are not destroyed by new construction become the property of the new landowners, most of whom deny access to the gatherers. "When the property was untouched and undeveloped, no one bothered us when we went out there [to gather sweetgrass], and now the developers come in and develop the land, and, of course, it's private property now."[24]

Where sweetgrass still grows and can be accessed, it is often dangerous to collect. Many basket makers emphasized the risks associated with collecting plant materials in the lowcountry. "So far we've been pretty fortunate where an alligator has not attacked us or has not even come that close to us. On the other hand, snakes live in almost every area where we harvest the sweetgrass." Some basket makers have stopped gathering altogether because of the dangers and difficulties: "I will never go into the woods anymore to collect pine needles. I won't collect anything!" Weaving the materials into baskets is also arduous work. The basket makers use a modified spoon handle, called a bone or nail bone, to thread palmetto leaves into coiled rows of sweetgrass, bulrush, and pine needles. Their hands and fingers are often cut by the thin strands of grass.[25]

The dangers are along the highway as well as in the marsh. The fast-moving cars and trucks on Highway 17 pose mortal risks for those selling—and buying—the baskets. Road widening, numerous new access roads into new residential developments and retail shopping centers, and increased traffic have increased the risks of retailing. Since the destructive fury of Hurricane Hugo many of the roadside stands have disappeared. As a basket maker noted, the number of stands has dropped considerably in the last twenty-five years: "Well, . . . used to be you could walk from one basket stand to the other. Now because of all the [new] businesses, there are huge spaces where there are no baskets [sold]. . . . The basket stands used to be two, three, four of them right in one spot. Now with the [highway] dividers, the access has changed; cars can't get in and out. The traffic [on the highway] is so heavy that once they get in, they can't get out." From the new Arthur Ravenel Jr. Bridge to the 10 Mile Community (each rural neighborhood heading north on Highway 17 is named for the number of miles from the bridge), there are about eighty basket stands left along the highway, typically on the shoulders of the roadbed or on adjoining land belonging to a basket-making family, a church, or the state. Often the stands are on heirs' property.[26]

Heirs' Property, Sprawl, and Race

The multiracial cultural heritage of the lowcountry has been an important factor in enriching, complicating, and expanding the region's understanding of conservation and the land ethic undergirding it. Issues of environmental justice involving race and class are often embedded in disputes over land and natural resources. Poor people, people of color, and others with little or no political clout have often experienced discrimination and manipulation at the hands of developers, realtors, and land-use planners. And mainstream conservationists—usually affluent white people—have often devoted less attention to the environmental issues affecting the poor groups living at the margins of social status and economic influence. African Americans, especially those with multigenerational ties to the coastal region, have been greatly affected by the dynamics of residential and commercial growth and its impact on the natural environment.[27]

The irony of unintended consequences stalks the environmental movement. The efforts of conservation organizations to preserve large tracts of land can often conflict with the livelihoods and folkways of indigenous people—especially African Americans. As a journalist noted, "after all, what is left to preserve? The land that, once upon a time, those in power didn't want: remote rural areas, sandhills, tidal wetlands, swamps, sea islands. Who lives on this land? In South Carolina, mostly poor blacks." Penn Center executive director Emory Campbell explained that historically the Gullah people had been "insulated geographically as well as insulated from land speculators. But that has changed because the coast is no longer an inconvenient place for people to live. Bridges connect the islands [to the mainland]. The coast used to be an uncomfortable place to live in the summer, but the pests are being controlled, waterways are no longer a hindrance, and now we are threatened by other cultures."[28]

Examples abound of the ways in which both unrelenting development *and* land conservation efforts have impinged upon the lowcountry's ethno-cultural heritage, at times even physically dividing African American communities. At the end of the twentieth century, for instance, Charleston County's new land-use regulations sought to restrict the amount of new development in rural areas so as to impede exurban sprawl. On Wadmalaw Island, where black residents outnumbered white but white residents owned most of the land, tensions arose when the county's Unified Development Ordinance sought to reduce the amount of future development by restricting the number of houses per acre. African American residents, however, pointed out that such restrictions meant that as extended black families grew, descendants could not live on the property owned by their ancestors because of the new zoning densities. As on Hilton Head Island, black and white residents on Wadmalaw Island and throughout the lowcountry have different perspectives on environmental conservation. Efforts to restrict black property rights in the name of land conservation have fragmented both the conservation community and the black stakeholders.[29]

During the Civil War commercial agriculture in the lowcountry collapsed. After 1865 much of lowcountry agriculture reverted to subsistence cultivation in an increasingly impoverished area. At the same time land *ownership* patterns were dramatically transformed. As many of the lowcountry sea islands fell under the control of the Union Army early in the war, they became the site for various federal experiments to help long-enslaved workers make the transition to freedom. The freed slaves acquired land in a variety of ways: purchasing newly subdivided plantation lands, receiving lands directly from the Union Army through "special field orders" or by virtue of service in the Union Army or Navy or claiming areas that were abandoned by the white owners. More than sixteen thousand African American families acquired at least fifty thousand acres through federal and state government sales, as well as through private efforts that shaped Reconstruction-era land distribution policies.[30]

In the late 1970s about one-third of the land owned by African Americans in rural South Carolina was heirs' property. Today the acreage owned is much less, in part because some of the heirs' groups decided to sell the property to developers. In 2002 an estimated 2,000 land parcels in the Charleston area were heirs' property varying in size from one to 1,200 acres. Heirs' property is particularly vulnerable to exploitation because it frequently lacks legal documentation. Passed down through generations, usually without the benefit of a legal will, the land is owned "in common" by all the extended family members who are heirs, regardless of where they live. The heirs share fractional ownership rights as "tenants in common." All of the heirs, or co-tenants, often dozens or scores of siblings, cousins, nephews and nieces scattered across the country, share unity of possession. In some cases one hundred or more extended family members may own a single parcel. The law of partition governs the disposition of tenants-in-common property. Partition provides for the division of property, or its cash equivalent, according to the wishes of the owners. Any heir can seek to "cash out" a share, and because the land cannot be split into dozens or even hundreds of pieces, the courts often order the sale of the entire parcel at the request of a single co-owner. "There's a lot of disagreements among heirs, and like any other family, there is infighting," said Willie Heyward, an attorney for the nonprofit Center for Heirs Property Preservation. "But for these African American families, it is exacerbated because they are separated by mass migration up north. A lot of the heirs have never been to South Carolina and have no interest in the property. And all you need is one heir who wants to sell it to bring it to arbitration."[31]

Over the years developers and real estate attorneys have taken advantage of the ambiguous nature of heirs' property, usually by convincing a single family member to sell and then taking the entire extended family to court to force a sale. Family members rarely have the financial resources to fend off such legal efforts. Thousands of African American families in the former Confederate states have lost millions of acres through partition sales in the last thirty years. Of the 5.5 million acres of farmland owned by black families in the South in 1970, 80 percent has been lost, according to the U.S. Agricultural Census. Forced partition sales account for half of those losses.[32]

Ironically the lands originally given to freed slaves after the Civil War were largely property unwanted by white people—mosquito-infested parcels on barrier islands or in marshy areas. Today many heirs' properties are prized for coastal development. Much of the heirs' property "was considered malaria property. Now it has become prime real estate," noted Marquetta Goodwine, a native of St. Helena who has become known as Queen Quet, the chieftess of the Gullah-Geechee Nation. "In the 1950s, there started an onslaught of bridges [onto the barrier islands]. The bridges then brought the resorts. I call it destruction; other people call it development."[33]

Gullah is a land-based culture. Goodwine explained that she and her Gullah friends and neighbors view land as the hub of their Gullah heritage. To preserve their culture they believe they must preserve their land, for it has always provided the anchorage for extended families. Benjamin Dennis IV, an African American chef, talked about his great-great-grandfather's land on Daniel Island near Charleston. He had paid eleven dollars for twenty-two acres that he had farmed before passing it down to his son, sisters, and daughters, who in turn passed the land down through their extended family. "Now," however, "all we have is an acre and a half. . . . Every other week [we] have somebody come to my granddaddy's house and [ask]: 'When you going to sell the land? We'll give you $1,900,000 for the land.'" But his grandfather and his family were not swayed by dollars. "Money don't mean nothing. It's about heritage and where you're from. My great-great-grandfather was the one who left that [land] for his grandchildren. And my granddaddy is leaving that for his grandchildren. And I told my granddaddy I would never, ever sell." Land has always offered the Gullah community the possibility of self-reliance. Residents have grown their own food while sustaining their family bonds. "The reason we've been able to stay here," Goodwine observed, "is that we look out for each other." Keeping the land "is a priority," she stressed. "Yet we also need to keep our spirits intact, to nurture and restore minds, to remind ourselves what our language is, what our culture is."[34]

Northeast of Charleston, along the Wando River in Cainhoy, for instance, some 70 percent of heirs' property has been sold to developers. As a black property owner observed, "people want to come through with roads and they want to bring the road right through your house. You'd live in a place all your life and [then] they want . . . to do a road, and they want to bring it right through your house." On Warsaw Island, near Hilton Head, Gullah families continue to hold out against the lure of development. "This is our heritage," explained Henry Aiken. "We were born and raised here, and we are not going to . . . let anyone come and take it from us. This land is like a million dollars to us. And if one of us hurts, everyone hurts."[35]

Liz Hunt Alston, a former chair of the Charleston County School Board, belongs to a family of fifty or more relatives who own heirs' property in Dorchester County. She pointed out that heirs' property owners are often at a disadvantage in court because the burden of proving ownership is on them, yet they often do not have the conventional legal documents because many of their ancestors did not create wills or keep titles or deeds. As Stokes-Marshall observed, "people who own or live on heirs property, they don't want to talk about it." They are also burdened by interfamily squabbles over whether or not to sell land. Many family members were born and raised elsewhere, often in the Northeast or in Chicago, and they have little interest in their ancestral property in South Carolina. Those heirs' property owners who want to conserve their family lands often feel besieged. "I see land being developed by outsiders, [and as a result] a generation [of African Americans is] being displaced," Alston said in 2006. "It's a travesty of justice. I believe in cultural heritage. I believe in history. I believe in ancestors."[36]

Yet other owners of heirs' property resent the efforts of conservationists to keep them from selling their property for development. New zoning ordinances promoting smart-growth principles led one prominent Richland County black farmer in 2002 to dismiss such land conservation efforts as a new form of economic discrimination and racial exploitation: "It's robbery," said fifty-one-year-old South Carolina native Joe Neal. Why should he be forced to forego the profits he would make by selling his ninety-two-acre farm to developers? While he, too, cared about the environment, "people," he stressed, "are part of the environment, too." Neal, a Baptist minister who also was a Democratic state representative and chair of the Legislative Black Caucus, asserted that "state and county governments are pursuing conservation and antisprawl at the cost of the minority population that historically has been denied the opportunity to accumulate wealth."[37]

Jennie Stephens, the executive director of the Center for Heirs' Property Preservation in Charleston, summarized how rural African Americans view development and conservation in the lowcountry: "You've got yours, but you want to tell me I can't have mine." To the rural black property owners their right to sell to the highest bidder is a basic issue of fairness and justice. As Stephens explained, "you hear what the environmentalists are saying about wanting to protect land, but what about people who for so long protected land not valued and now have the opportunity to reap the benefits of their property?" In 2006 the General Assembly passed legislation designed to protect heirs' property owners by giving families the opportunity to purchase the property at its appraised value in the event a share owner tried to sell the property in a partition lawsuit. In signing the bill Governor Mark Sanford said that it would effectively give black families a "right of first refusal" when developers sought to purchase the tract.[38]

The pressures on multigenerational legacy property owned by African Americans have become intense since the 1980s. In 1996 Solomon Mazyck and his wife sold their cinder-block house on congested U.S. Highway 17, where they had lived for forty-six years, for nearly two hundred thousand dollars. Its appraised value for tax purposes was thirty-two thousand dollars. The two adjoining houses, owned by Mazcyck's siblings, were also sold. The extended Mazyck family had joined other black property owners in requesting that their properties fronting on U.S. 17 be rezoned by Charleston County from residential to commercial. Other African American property owners refused to sell. Florence Brown said she had no interest in selling her home that was built in 1965. "Where would I go?" she asked. "I'm not interested in selling, regardless of what. I have nieces to leave it to," she added, even though her property was being encircled by new businesses.[39]

Brown was the exception, however. The resolve of most of her neighbors to keep their property diminished over the years as the dollar offers from developers soared. Solomon Maczyk's sister Carolyn Rouse understood Brown's perspective, and she agreed that African Americans should keep their property as long as they could because selling leads to a loss of Gullah culture and history. But if people decided to sell, as she had done, they need to "get what you think the property is worth." Joe McCormick, the coordinator for technical services for land, environment, and education programs at the Penn Center, agreed that developers showed little or no understanding of the cultural and historical value of African American communities astride U.S. Highway 17. "All they're trying to do is get strip development along the highway. They don't understand what this does to community heritage and culture," McCormick stressed. "Our people don't understand zoning and what it means. They're going to take you for a ride," he warned the black property owners.[40]

The Racial Divide near Mount Pleasant

The efforts to preserve African American properties and honor the sweetgrass basket-making tradition have garnered national attention. Yet the future of basket making in the lowcountry remains in doubt—as does the survival of heirs' property. Other challenges remain, including overt racism. A basket maker encountered a landowner who did "not want any niggers on their property or walking by their property." Local land planners and policymakers lament the continuing lack of awareness among developers and new residents of the distinctive unique histories and cultures of African American communities in the greater Mount Pleasant area. This public ignorance has lingered in spite of significant attention in the local media.[41]

In 2004 Charleston County voters approved an additional half-cent sales tax that generated thirty-six million dollars for the creation of a greenbelt by limiting the expansion of the city into rural areas. Three important aspects of the greenbelt initiative intersected with the sweetgrass basket-making community. First, although a stated goal of the greenbelt program is to conserve "lowcountry natural resources" and "productive landscapes," there is no mention of sweetgrass. Second, the greenbelt advisory board in the early years of its existence did not include sweetgrass as an element of lowcountry life to be preserved. Finally public hearings emphasized the inclusion of "lowcountry natural resources" as a top priority. Yet among the several hundred comments received from citizens across the county, only two addressed the issue of sweetgrass. One of those comments specifically mentioned the need to conserve the plant and ensure that basket makers had access to it. "Well, I think that what should happen is they need to start designating some land and planting the stuff that we need to make the baskets."[42]

Race and class remain volatile topics in South Carolina. Lowcountry residents—both black and white—continue to suffer from the silence associated with the history of slavery and its lingering effects. True, the lowcountry now celebrates its unique racial and cultural heritage. Charleston mayor Joe Riley noted that "Charleston was Ellis Island for African Americans, and I think there's more African-ness here than you know any place in the country. . . . In this region, is more African-ness, presence of African Americans, but I mean, you know, the sounds, the baskets, the life, and so I think . . . that is why the sea islands are so important, and why the ACE Basin is so important. But to keep those [preserved] places, to continue to have the reality. . . . the preservation of the Gullah culture is [also] very important." However, sustaining the Gullah culture amid the region's rapid changes is a formidable challenge. In many respects African Americans are disproportionately impacted by sprawl. As a black member of the City of Charleston planning staff explained, "it's that you've never heard of a predominantly European-American neighborhood being adversely affected by development at the scale and the number of instances that it happens to African-American communities. And somewhere in your mind, you have to say, 'Why? Why? Why me again? Why I got to move again? Why? Why? Why?'"[43]

Rapid development around Mount Pleasant, a town whose motto is *cresco,* or "we grow," put the basket-making culture at risk during the 1990s. It has also increased the financial pressure on those with heirs' property to sell their land because of the difficulty of paying higher property taxes and the temptation to sell to aggressive developers. "It used to be a lot quieter here before all this development," Richard Habersham recollected in 2004. His family had lived in the Phillips Community since the 1870s, when his ancestors, freed slaves, purchased land along Horlbeck Creek near Mount Pleasant in what has remained an unincorporated area of Charleston County. But the relentless advance of suburban sprawl and the accompanying spike in property taxes threatened the historic African American community, half of whose lands are heirs' property. "When they build those high-dollar houses," Habersham noted, "the value of our property goes up, too, and it affects our taxes. When taxes get too high, some residents might have to sell and move away." Fending off the disrupting effects of sprawl on his historic community has become a constant necessity. "It seems there's always something coming up," he acknowledged. "A little battle here, a little battle there." It is in this context, then, that recent efforts to make clumps of sweetgrass more readily available to the basket makers are helping to conserve a distinctive way of life. In a very real sense basket making helps weave together a stronger community fabric.[44]

Mount Pleasant, the once quaint bedroom suburb of Charleston, has become South Carolina's fifth largest—and fastest growing—city. From 1950 to 1980 its population grew from 1,857 to 13,838, the largest percentage change of any community in South Carolina. From 1990 to 2010 the population soared, growing from 30,000 to almost 70,000. Mount Pleasant remains one of the state's fastest growing cities, with all of the attendant effects of rampant sprawl: traffic congestion, rising property values and taxes, and environmental degradation. Upscale gated communities, some with golf courses and many with waterfront parcels with private docks, now dominate the once rural community.

The Town of Mount Pleasant recently commissioned a population study as well as a one-hundred-thousand-dollar marketing campaign to attract even more residents to the area. As part of the marketing plan the town council approved a new logo featuring the majestic Arthur Ravenel Jr. Bridge connecting Charleston and Mount Pleasant with the slogan "Come on Over." The campaign focused on attracting younger families to the town because 40 percent of its residents will be fifty-five or older in 2025. As town administrator Mac Burdette observed: "A healthy community is a diverse community. We're going to need to recruit young folks in order to remain diverse." Racial diversity is not mentioned, however. In the marketing campaign the story of Mount Pleasant was conveyed in a two-and-one-half minute presentation festooned with bucolic images of the creeks, marshes, and ocean as well as local families. At one point, the narrator says:

To understand Mount Pleasant is to intimately know the water, the ebb and flow of the tide, the marsh creeks and rivers that surround us. Living here means measuring time enjoyed by the water. Here, water is sustenance. Shrimp boats at dawn, crabbing off the dock, the day's catch being hauled in. It's the taste that lingers on your lips after day is done. Mt. Pleasant is an idealist. Our strong neighborhoods are built from generations of strong neighbors: folks who work hard, whose children play with yours, who say 'hey' when they see you, gently guide even the most confused tourists to the beach. . . . Mt. Pleasant is born of the land and water. Protecting them is part of who we are, not just because our shrimp are caught in local waters or our tomatoes are grown on local vines not just so our children and grand-children have them to enjoy, but because this kind of raw beauty, this rich history and culture has a harmony we strive to emulate.

As it ends the marketing video shows a male basket maker, but there is no mention of the Gullah culture as part of Mount Pleasant's story.[45]

"Protecting" the land and water may have been the dominant theme of Mount Pleasant's marketing campaign, but ironically the community's rapid development was simultaneously threatening the survival of the sweetgrass culture. A basket maker noted that "the community is changing because the people are moving [here in large numbers], coming in from all over. They have different backgrounds, and [the new] people [are] just different." Tourists in Mount Pleasant rarely stray far from the intensively developed Highway 17. As a consequence they come and go without seeing African American neighborhoods (often named by their distance from the bridge connecting Mount Pleasant and Charleston), such as the four- or seven-mile communities, each of which has a distinctive rural character.[46]

Growth has also reconfigured the area's socioeconomic and racial demographics. The rapid development of Mount Pleasant has stimulated some portions of the economy more than others, much to the detriment of its African American population. More than a century ago black people comprised 70 percent of the population in South Carolina's coastal counties; white residents made up the remaining 30 percent. In 1990 the percentage of African Americans in Mount Pleasant had declined to 15.7 percent; today African Americans comprise just 7.3 percent of the population. The per capita income of African Americans is less than half that of white residents. As Mount Pleasant has grown, concern about the vulnerability of the basket-making economy and the sustainability of the basket making neighborhoods has soared.[47]

The development of new retail and residential areas along U. S. 17 has impeded the sale of sweetgrass baskets. A basket maker commented that "with so much development and the road widening, they're trying to push the basket makers off the highway." The same basket maker said that the recent plans to widen the road from four to six lanes is likely to have a similar impact to the earlier widening from two to four lanes. Each day some forty-five thousand cars traverse U.S. 17 (Johnnie Dodds Boulevard), and the number is projected to grow to seventy-thousand cars by 2030. For the basket makers the pressures of road widening and congested traffic on the roadside stands has degraded the quality of their social interaction and human fellowship: "I appreciate meeting the different people and the different nationalities when they come by the basket stand. . . . This is a place to gather for conversation."[48]

The Fraying of the Basket-making Culture

Conversations among the basket makers, however, are not as harmonious as they once were; the basket makers are more fragmented than ever. Such fragmentation is in part the result of the growth machine in the lowcountry. New roads built to support residential and commercial development have bisected several of the rural hamlets where basket-making families have lived for generations. In addition, the constant pressures of development and the competitive challenges of acquiring sweetgrass have exacerbated tensions among the basket makers. The basket makers also manifest the jealousies and self-interest common to all human groupings. Pride in their artistry often generates competition. When a black woman from a basket-making family published a book about the handicraft, she was roundly criticized by neighbors for promoting herself and her family at the expense of other basket makers and African Americans in Mount Pleasant.

The tensions among the basket makers often surface in the context of their collective efforts to nurture their handicraft. Two organizations promote the welfare of basketry and the basket makers: SCAFA and the Mount Pleasant Sweetgrass Basketmakers Association. There is some overlap between the two groups, but there are even more tensions. When public events and programs are launched, such as the sweetgrass basket makers' summer camp for children, some basket makers oppose the admission of white children. Others view the multiracial camp as an ideal way to educate the entire community about the Gullah heritage and the basket-making tradition. In part as a result of such divergent views and competitive pressures, the basket makers have not forged a cohesive alliance among themselves. As a result their relationship to the culture of conservation is ambivalent and inconsistent—and at times even counterproductive. In general, rural African Americans display a very different outlook toward environmental conservation from that of middle-class and wealthy white activists who predominate among the conservation organizations.

When asked about the concept of environmental conservation, basket makers emphasize their need to gain access to plant materials, preserve their ability to sell their basket at stands along busy U.S. 17, and fend off encroaching suburban and retail development. Few of them view environmental issues in the same terms as the mainstream conservation organizations do; nor do they often speak collectively for the group. Their focus is much more on preserving a way of life rather than preserving wetlands or wildlife habitat. There is a palpable tone of nostalgia in their reminiscences. "Mount Pleasant was a very peaceful area," said one basket maker. "Until development came in there, everybody knew each other and everybody looked out for each other, but now you don't know who your neighbor [is]."[49]

Basket makers readily suggest what needs to be done to preserve their traditional livelihood. They are eager to work with the growing number of people, organizations, and agencies interested in "designating some land [for growing sweetgrass] and planting the stuff that we need to make the baskets." But respondents felt that their voices were not being heard by local and state government: "Your views aren't recognized here. South Carolina is back in the eighteenth century. They ain't never got to the twentieth." Many of the respondents are so embittered and alienated that they have become disengaged from recent community initiatives intended to protect the roadside basket stands. Others have become very involved in basket-maker associations and participate actively in public meetings; however, few basket makers expect any meaningful assistance from government agencies or public officials (which may explain their relatively, as a group, limited participation).[50]

Livelihoods and Cultural Conservation

The efforts to save the sweetgrass basket-making culture demonstrate how the lowcountry culture of conservation has come to include efforts to preserve its heritage of land-based livelihoods. Long marginalized African American basket makers and their families are now adding new voices and new issues to the lowcountry conversation about conservation. The textured outlook of the basket makers centers on the logic and appeal of sustainability. As one of them stressed, "we're doing one craft that actually is good for the environment because we're not damaging anything." How the basket makers have gained credibility and clout reveals much about the growing depth and diversity of the region's conservation ethic. Yet the basket makers share a perception that the supply of resources needed to sustain their handicraft, and their way of life, remains in jeopardy. "It's just like learning to play an instrument," said basket maker Henrietta Snype in 2007, as she wove a basket. "It's part of us. It's our culture, our heritage." Such poignant reflections suggest why more and more lowcountry agencies and leaders have agreed that the sweetgrass basket-making culture must be sustained through protection, preservation, and conservation. There now is more than one voice for conservation operating in the lowcountry.[51]

The pride in their handicraft displayed by basket makers often leads them to expand the concept of what should be conserved to include age-old artistic techniques. "My great-great-grandfather was a basket maker, and my grandmother taught me [how to weave] when I was 4 or 5 years old," seventy-one-year-old Alma Washington said in 2007. "It's something I hope will never die." Many basket makers have tried to pass on their handicraft techniques to their children.

Girl weaving a sweetgrass basket. Courtesy of the Charleston Museum.

But it is not easy. Typically, young children learn how to weave baskets, then quit making them around adolescence, only to return to the handicraft as adults if they remain in the lowcountry. Basket makers fear that their children will see the troubles faced by their elders and abandon the art, leaving a potentially devastating cultural void. "My children don't have interest in the baskets whatsoever. They think I'm crazy." Another basket maker emphasized that "the [biggest] concern is that the [tradition] is going to die out."[52]

Listening to the basket makers enriches but also complicates the conversation about conservation in the lowcountry, for their voices are not always harmonious even though they are engaged in a common handicraft. The tensions and infighting among basket makers have at times weakened their effectiveness as an interest group within the umbrella of the culture of conservation. The recent efforts to ensure access to sweetgrass amid the dramatic development of the lowcountry illustrate the ironies and tensions between conserving natural resources and preserving a handicraft tradition and land-based livelihoods. A chorus with similarly varied voices is evident within the community of lowcountry farmers, whose livelihoods are another emergent thread in the fabric of the conservation culture.[53]

NINE

Conserving Agri*Culture*

The concerted efforts to preserve the lowcountry basket-making tradition demonstrate that the culture of conservation encompasses much more than conventional efforts to preserve and protect the natural environment. One of the most endangered elements of the coastal region's historic way of life is agriculture. In recent years South Carolina has been losing about thirty-five acres of farmland daily to residential and commercial development, and the lowcountry has experienced the greatest of those losses. Concern about the loss of farmlands has led the conservation coalition to focus more attention on the issue. Land trusts have been buying dormant farms and executing conservation easements to preserve others. The Charleston County Greenbelt Bank Board also purchases rural land to protect it from development. Saving farmland has become an urgent issue. As James Island attorney Margaret Fabri stressed in 2000, "we don't have many rural spaces left, and if we don't protect them now, we will have none left." She and others pointed to examples throughout the lowcountry of farmlands being gobbled up by suburban development. "If we don't keep the country in lowcountry, we don't have a lowcountry," said Jim Hare, coordinator of the Ashley River Conservation Coalition.[1]

Rockville, a quaint creekside town on rural Wadmalaw Island, south of Charleston, illustrates the pressures exerted by sprawling development on rural life in the lowcountry. That the hamlet's economy has long depended on the activity of shrimpers and farmers helps explain why year-round residents are so determined to preserve the rural way of life. Town dwellers emphatically oppose new development in the form of condominiums, gas stations, and bed-and-breakfast inns. "We don't want Wal-Mart, and we don't want McDonald's. We don't want paved streets and don't want stores. We don't need 'progress,' and we don't want it," said longtime resident Jimmie Davis in 2006. His neighbor Nancy Stafford agreed, asserting that "we hate development. We want Rockville to stay really, really rural."[2]

Sam Brownlee, a resident of Johns Island, shared such sentiments. In the late 1980s he decided to move across the Stono River to the rural island from suburban James Island. He wanted "to get away from the hustle and bustle" of traffic jams, crowds, radio towers, and litter so as to "increase our quality of life," he explained. By 2004, however, he saw the same forces threatening his rural serenity on Johns Island. "We're turning into another Mount Pleasant or James Island," he sighed. To fend off such "progress," Brownlee devoted about twenty hours a week to attending zoning hearings and public meetings. While acknowledging the right of property owners to develop their rural land, he affirmed the need for smart-growth planning and zoning.[3]

To protect and preserve rural areas county planning commissions across the lowcountry at the end of the twentieth century crafted new land-use regulations intended to slow the advance of sprawling development into rural areas by limiting the ability of property owners to subdivide their land, creating new setback requirements, tree protections, sign ordinances, and other guidelines for green development. The rationale for such restrictions was to keep the county's rural areas from being overrun by incompatible developments as well as by an influx of new residents. Such regulations intended to protect the rural character of the lowcountry, however, have collided with the rights of private property owners to dispose of their land as they see fit. Critics argued that the new land-use requirements had the effect of depriving owners of the ability to garner the highest possible profit. The rural zoning densities effectively prevented people from subdividing their land for sale or for family use. The most equitable proposed solution, as demonstrated in Beaufort County, is to create a county-managed fund to "buy" the development rights ("highest and best use") of rural property owners. In essence such a program compensates farmers for placing their lands in a conservation easement rather than selling the property to the highest bidder. Purchasing development rights is less expensive than buying property outright, and it does not encroach on private property rights. Such a voluntary program, said longtime Johns Island farmer Thomas Legare, would be "a win, win situation for everybody. We want to preserve our property as farmland, but we can't afford to give away a [conservation] easement." Few counties have created such funds, however. As a result, Adair McKoy, a Johns Island tomato farmer, lamented in 2004 that county planners were trying to "control land through zoning" alone, and planning commissions can change "zoning in a week" in response to public and political pressure. The "sad thing," McKoy added, is that the county planning commission in the late 1990s had an opportunity to make "agriculture a permanent part of the community." But it did not happen. "In the last ten years, agriculture has just about disappeared from the island."[4]

Agriculture—A Diminishing Resource

The challenge of developing equitable land-use regulations to preserve low-country farms reflects the complex history of the region's agricultural sector. The lowcountry's farming heritage is rooted in the former plantation system, but it has been transformed over the years in response to environmental, economic, political, and social changes. After the Civil War the long-dominant plantation system was in ruins. The physical destruction of farms and livestock during the war, the lack of investment capital and a stable currency, the emancipation of enslaved laborers, and the need to create a new pool of paid farmworkers after the Union victory threw the agricultural economy into turmoil. As a white planter asked, "how will we ever get our crops worked without slaves, and no money to hire laborers?"[5]

Eventually new types of farming filled the void created by the collapse of the plantation-slave system. By 1889 a farmer could report that "the old plantations are being cut up and rented or sold in small tracts for farming purposes." In the postwar South capital was scarce, and rural folk—both black and white—were desperate for livelihoods. The result was widespread tenantry and sharecropping, whereby the vast majority of farmers eked out a hand-to-mouth existence by working land they did not own. A typical post–Civil War labor contract entailed the landowner providing a minimum subsistence to the workers (clothing, shelter, seed, and tools) until they received a portion (usually half to one-third) of the harvest in exchange for their labor. Most postwar labor contracts specified restrictions on behavior, calling for workers to be "obedient" and "respectful"; banning "impertinence," insubordination, and weapons; and prohibiting the presence of noncontract persons on the property.[6]

Most African Americans who acquired heirs' property were similarly limited to a life of subsistence farming. One tangible result of the rise of tenant farming was the dramatic reduction in farm size throughout the southern states. In 1860 the average South Carolina farm contained 569 acres; by 1880 it had dropped to 143 acres, and by 1920 it was only 65 acres.

The distinctive geographic features of the lowcountry landscape, especially the prevalence of wetlands and the abundance of tidal and river systems that served to break up agricultural property into disconnected parcels, reinforced the prevalence of small-scale agriculture in the coastal region during the late nineteenth century. So-called pocket-farming, whereby farmers worked several small, non-contiguous properties, became commonplace.[7]

During the late nineteenth century the predominance of rice and cotton production in the lowcountry gave way to truck farming, which entails the commercial cultivation of seasonal vegetables for transport to local or distant markets. *Truck* does not refer to a vehicle but rather was a Middle English word meaning bartering, the exchange of commodities. The advent of refrigerated rail cars led to a year-round demand for fresh vegetables among city dwellers living along the Atlantic seaboard, and truck farms sprouted in the lowcountry to meet the demand. Some of the most common lowcountry truck crops include sweet corn, tomatoes, melons, strawberries, potatoes, and green vegetables. In Charleston County in 1938, for example, 10,000 acres were planted in Irish potatoes, 4,500 in cabbage, and 5,500 in beans, cucumbers, spinach, peas, lettuce, collards, and tomatoes. In 1929 the typical truck farmer in the lowcountry owned 88 acres, of which an average of 27 were planted at any one time. Many of the truck farmers supplemented their income by raising pigs, cows, and chickens.

During the mid-twentieth century more tomatoes were shipped through Charleston than any other part of the United States. Since then, however, farming in the lowcountry has faced stiffening competition from inexpensive produce imported from Florida, California, and Latin America. At the same time, fruits and vegetables imported from Mexico soared after the passage of the North American Free Trade Agreement (NAFTA) in 1994. Lowcountry farmers still growing row crops such as corn and soybeans found it difficult to compete with the industrial farms in Mexico, the Midwest, on the Great Plains, and in the Far West. Mechanization also transformed the agricultural sector after World War II. Then in 1989 Hurricane Hugo dealt a severe blow to lowcountry agriculture, already struggling with declining demand. The storm smashed barns and storage buildings and caused more than one hundred million dollars' worth of crop losses. Farmworkers also lost their jobs to machines. Agricultural machinery—tractors, harvesters, and combines—pushed many farmworkers off the land at the same time that cities and suburbs gobbled up surrounding farmlands. Other farmers could not survive without continuing federal crop subsidies. The majority of small farmers today are part-time farmers; they have to work others jobs to make ends meet.

Farming remains South Carolina's second-largest industry, contributing $36 billion worth of annual revenue and sustaining 460,000 jobs. Since 1960, however, the number of farms across the state has declined from 86,000 to 24,000. The most recent U.S. Agricultural Census documents a slight increase in agricultural activity in recent years. Of South Carolina's 19.27 million acres in total land area in 2007, 4.85 million acres, or 25.1 percent, were in farms. From 2002 to 2007 the number of farms across the state increased from 24,541 to 25,867, an average increase of about 1 percent annually. Even more worrisome is the fact that only 4 percent of the food consumed in South Carolina is grown in the state. Growers lack warehouses, marketing resources, and distribution networks to sell their produce effectively to local markets.[8]

Embedded within these statewide statistics, however, is a more complex landscape in the lowcountry. Seven of the coastal counties have more than 350,000 acres classified as farmland, with Berkeley County reporting the largest amount—just over 70,000 acres. The lowcountry's agricultural sector has been diminishing since the beginning of the twentieth century, however. In Charleston and Beaufort Counties, for example, the number of commercial truck crop farms has been steadily declining since 1990. In 1990 those two counties led the state in tomato production, producing annual crops worth thirty-five million and thirteen million dollars respectively. By 2007 the value of the tomato crop for all of South Carolina had plummeted to eleven million dollars. In 2002 there were 116 "farms" in Beaufort County totaling 44,373 acres. But only 47 of those farms representing 3,368 acres actually harvested any crops.[9]

Part of the problem with lowcountry agriculture is the nature of the land itself. The wetlands throughout the coastal region were once ideal for cash crops such as rice, indigo, and sea island cotton, but the marshy terrain is unsuitable for other crops. As a white male farmer explained, "we never had a lot of land in Charleston County; it's one of our problems. Small fields, lowlands, it was hard to get the production, it was ideal for vegetables 'cause the small fields would keep the wind down." A related challenge is the demography of the farm community. The average age of current growers in the lowcountry is fifty-nine. A few young adults are starting farm-related enterprises, but most children of farm families are abandoning rural life altogether.[10]

An even greater threat to the farming culture has been the residential and commercial growth along the South Carolina coast. Since the end of World War II many lowcountry plantations and farms have been converted to other uses: timber farms, hunting preserves, golf courses, and residential communities. Today the most profitable form of agriculture is selling farmland for development. "The landscape of coastal South Carolina is in a state of fluctuation," observed Gerry Cohn of the American Farmland Trust in 2008. "Where we once had tomato packing houses and open fields, we're seeing a new crop of houses going up for retirees and vacationers." Farms and plantations have been gobbled up by sprawl. "Everybody is selling out," lamented a farmer on Wadmalaw Island in 2008. "For many farmers, the prices offered by developers were difficult to turn down." The potential developed value of lowcountry farms has caused land prices to soar. Charleston County has the highest average per-acre value in the state at $6,929, three times the average value of rural land across the state. As Jack Queener, the Beaufort County extension agent observed, "why would anybody try to grow soybeans when they could sell or develop their property as a golf course?" A farmer on Wadmalaw Island acknowledged the recent efforts to preserve the culture of agriculture in the lowcountry, but he was not optimistic about the future. "It's just a matter of time" before shopping centers and neighborhoods replace farm fields, Whitt Russell sighed in 2004. "The handwriting is on the wall."[11]

Alan Ulmer Jr., for example, owned one of the largest farms in Beaufort County until the 1980s. He raised cattle and grew vegetables across from Moss Creek. He also planted corn, soybeans, and hay. But he reached a point where he could not afford to be a farmer. "I wish I was still planting [vegetables]; it's just not economical," he said with a hint of nostalgia in 2001. The rising costs of labor, fuel, pesticides, and fertilizer, as well as storage fees and out-of-state competition, led him to sell much of his property to developers. He added that for him and other area farmers, growing turf grass for the many golf courses in the area had become the most profitable form of agriculture. "We grow grass for people to knock balls on."[12]

The Next Conservation Frontier: Farming

Preserving the lowcountry's agricultural heritage has become the latest priority of the conservation culture. The current comprehensive plan for Charleston

County, for example, recognizes "the importance of preserving Charleston County's farming resources, including individual farms and areas of productive soils, as well as a way of life valued by the community." In a similar vein the Beaufort County Comprehensive Plan declares that the preservation "of farmland in the County is important to the maintenance and growth of local food production, the economic well being of area farmers, and maintenance of green space." Keeping farms operating is indeed an inexpensive way of preserving open space. Farms not only enhance the quality of life by producing food and generating tax revenues, but they also reduce the strain on local infrastructure. Enabling farm owners to fend off the temptation to sell their acreage to developers reduces the need for more roads, utilities, sewers, and government workers. Farms also help diffuse population density and limit traffic congestion.

Long-standing conservation organizations such as the Coastal Conservation League, Ducks Unlimited, the Lowcountry Open Land Trust, and the Nature Conservancy have always emphasized preserving rural lands. But now, as Lisa Turansky, the sustainable agriculture program director for the Coastal Conservation League, explained in 2010, "we all recognize that reviving the local agricultural economy is vital to rural land protection. There is also agreement that it is the local food economy that has the potential to rescue and revive the small community farmer. The local food movement has gained conservation traction in South Carolina like it has across the nation, and there are few who disagree about the value of buying local products."[13]

Conservationists, both individuals and organized groups, now explicitly promote sustainable agricultural activities. That is, they favor farms that cultivate produce, livestock, and aquaculture in ways that minimize damage to the region's ecosystem. Sustainable agriculture differs from conventional farming in that it uses less water, fertilizers and pesticides, fuel, and energy. It also reduces transportation costs (on average, the food purchased in lowcountry chain grocery stores has traveled 1,600 miles from where it was grown) by focusing on local markets, and it encourages protecting farmlands from being developed for residential, commercial, or recreational (golf course) use.[14]

A smaller but growing number of conservationists have been promoting a more expansive concept of sustainable agriculture that includes preserving the livelihoods of those engaged in agricultural activity. The most visible effort to preserve lowcountry farms has been an array of initiatives orchestrated by the burgeoning "buy-local" movement. In 2007 the *Charleston Post and Courier* reported that "the push to eat 'local' has come to a boil in the lowcountry. . . . Consumers are finding a basket full of reasons for eating what's closer to home: perceived advantages in taste and health, environmental concerns, fears of *E. coli* outbreaks and quality problems with imported goods. Nearly everyone says it's important to support the area's economy." Three years later, in 2010, the *Charleston City Paper* celebrated the "newfound reverence for local food" in the lowcountry, explaining that "when the trend turned toward sustainable agriculture,

"Off to Work." A farmer in Beaufort County headed to the fields.
Courtesy of Scott Hansen.

Charleston found itself in the right place at the right time, with the right people already evangelizing for a return to the dirt. What was a fad of sorts became a redefining trend that changed our restaurant culture for the better."[15]

In 2009 the *Charleston Post and Courier* applauded the emergence of Community Supported Agriculture (CSA) enterprises in the lowcountry. Nationwide the CSA movement emerged in the 1980s as an innovative way to support small farms, revive rural economies, and provide more wholesome foods to more people. CSAs decentralize the complex global commercial food system by connecting local farmers directly with consumers. They promote locally grown (and often organically produced) fruits, vegetables, and meats by creating cooperative purchasing associations. CSA members (often called subscribers) buy shares in the seasonal harvest of a farm or consortium of farms. Unlike shoppers at a conventional farmers' market, the members of a CSA cooperative share part of the farmers' risk. That is, they pay in advance for a portion of the total crop. If weather or insects or disease limit the crop, the shareowners receive less produce. If the crop is bountiful, the shareowners receive more than originally expected.[16]

CSAs appeared late in the lowcountry compared to other regions in the United States. The first CSA in the coastal region did not coalesce until 2007. By 2010, however, Community Supported Agriculture "had taken off" in Charleston County, according to the local extension agent. Not surprisingly many of the first subscribers to lowcountry CSAs were people who were already engaged in the region's culture of conservation. To promote the benefits and explain the concept of Community Supported Agriculture, the *Charleston Post and Courier* showcased an organic CSA coordinated by two Wadmalaw Island farms, Thackeray Farms and Rita's Roots. David Quick, the *Post and Courier* reporter, effusively described the varied delights of locally produced fruit and vegetables:

> Besides the purple carrots and delicate squash, we've received bok choy, summer and acorn squash, three kinds of beans (including purple!), edamame, Haikuri turnips, Italian heirloom green peppers, lots of arugula, Japanese eggplant, heirloom and cherry tomatoes, D'Avignon radishes, mustard greens, spinach, butterbeans, scallions, Swiss chard, kiwi, as well as cilantro, basil and dill. . . . Since college, I've been among those who have lamented the loss of the family farm and what it meant to the health and wellness of America, as well as the people who are brave and tough enough to choose farming as a profession. Most of us chalked it up as an inevitable side effect of the inevitable global economy. CSAs may be a tool for turning it all around for the better. I'll be a repeat customer and hope more of us will put our money where our mouths are.

Such publicity helped increase interest among consumers in locally produced food.[17]

Organic farmers in the lowcountry are a diverse group—young and old, newcomers and natives. Born and raised in the Midwest, Rita Bachman, the founder of Rita's Roots, arrived in the lowcountry as a freshman at the College of Charleston in 2000. After graduating four years later she participated in organic farming internships in the Catskill Mountains of New York state and in the central valley of California before returning in 2006 to the lowcountry, where she leased acreage at Ambrose Family Farms for her CSA. Pete Ambrose, the farm's owner for more than three decades, had been preparing to sell his land to a developer and give up agriculture altogether when he learned about Community Supported Agriculture and realized that buying "local is the new organic." Bachman agreed. "I keep everything as local as possible," she explained. "It's logical, it's usually less expensive, it supports the local economy, and it's less fuel polluting." One of her other goals was to show that "young people can and should be interested in agriculture." By 2010 Bachmann had come to be known as the lowcountry's "queen of veggies."[18]

Legare Farms on Johns Island also started a CSA in 2008 and sold all of the shares within thirty-six hours. "It gives us a way to get some money up front, without having to go to the bank," explained Thomas Legare, a ninth-generation lowcountry native who manages the 350-acre family farm and nursery with his sisters, Helen and Linda. "We wanted something new to try."[19]

The CSA programs in the lowcountry are symptomatic of a national trend: more and more people have become alienated by the distant, impersonal, unsustainable nature of the commercial agricultural network. Interest in locally grown (and often organically produced) meats, vegetables, and fruits has blossomed into a sophisticated revolution. "It's better when you pick it and put it right on the table and eat it," said Joyce Johnson of Johns Island. By 2002 "organic consumers" had come to comprise about one-third of all grocery shoppers. Farmers' markets have sprouted in virtually every town and city, and the sales of organically grown produce have soared. The lowcountry now has more certified organic farms than any other region of the state. Celeste Albers, who owns the Green Grocer Farm on Johns Island with her husband George, said in 2002 that the trend toward organically grown vegetables may be "the only way for people to survive in farming." Sustainability is her theme. Their approach "is to farm from nature and maintain a healthy soil." By doing so "you are not feeding the plant, you are feeding the soil, and it will reward you with a healthy plant." Restaurants have led the way in purchasing locally grown organic meats and produce. "People want to buy local; there's an eagerness to buy local if they can," explained Sarah Cothran, the coordinator of farmers' markets for the City of Charleston. "The state is pushing it, as well as local organizations, and the restaurants want to say the food is local because people want that."[20]

By reducing the dependence on conventional commercial food distribution process centered on huge industrial farms, global wholesalers, and chain grocery stores, CSAs eliminate the middlemen—food brokers, processors, and wholesalers. They also reduce transportation costs, provide fresher, more wholesome food for consumers as well as higher profits for farmers, and help foster ongoing relationships between growers and customers. "People are becoming more and more aware of the importance of eating locally," said Jamee Haley, executive director of Lowcountry Local First, a nonprofit organization that supports both independent businesses and farms. "People want to know where their food comes from, they feel like it's safer to eat local produce, and they want to reconnect with the land."[21]

Farmers' markets and CSAs also promote what is called civic agriculture. That is, they restore the direct relationships between farmers and consumers that prevailed in the preindustrial era. Such grassroots interactions cna help strengthen civic bonds. Organic grower Rita Bachman expressed in 2010 the nonpecuniary motives shared by many people engaged in sustainable farming when she revealed how proud she was "to have served this community. . . . It's not about the money, but the act of making a difference in the way we eat and view food and about being a steward to the Earth." She also noted that the buy-local emphasis in the lowcountry enabled her and other younger growers to "put a face with food, showing that young people can and should be interested in agriculture." The U.S. Department of Agriculture was so keen on fostering such civic agriculture that it created in 2009 a new program—Know Your Farmer, Know Your Food—to bring consumers and farmers together.[22]

The social dynamic of consumers engaging in face-to-face transactions with farmers is frequently cited as one of the most appealing aspects of the buy-local movement. Holly Herrick, a Charleston food writer, noted in 2007 that people liked "buying directly from the source, buying local and fresh." Why? "One of the things I think is going on," Herrick added, "is ecological, to support the health of the Earth. A big part of it, too, is to be a part of the community and to support the local economy and that of the farmers."[23]

Promoting such civic agriculture has become one of the priorities the low-country conservation culture. People living along the coast were going "nuts about farmers' markets," reported the *Charleston Post and Courier* in 2003. By 2010 the newspaper had become an outspoken advocate of the local-foods movement, declaring that "there's no excuse not to eat locally grown food." The buy-local efforts in the lowcountry have been facilitated by the proliferation of farmers' markets. The Charleston Farmers' Market, which opened in 1989, was the first in the lowcountry. It remains the area's largest, but now virtually every community in the coastal region hosts at least one weekly market. Bill Stanfield, the chief executive officer of the nonprofit Metanoia Development Corporation, which operates the Chicora farmers' market five miles from downtown Charleston, explained that "the market has a spiritual purpose as well. It's more than a market—a way to build community and a way for people to meet neighbors. The food is important, but the way it connects the community is really important as well."[24]

Small farmers usually generate more financial security from year-round CSA programs than from weekly farmers' markets. Since 2007 more than a dozen CSAs have emerged along the South Carolina coast as farmers strive to find creative ways to sustain their livelihood in the face of challenging circumstances. Agriculture has always been a difficult profession. Unpredictable weather, mercurial markets, fluctuating commodity prices and interest rates, and rising expenses create perennial challenges. In the lowcountry, however, other factors make farming even more difficult. The rising cost of land, machinery, fuel, and fertilizer; the difficulty of finding seasonal farmworkers; the aging of area farmers and the declining interest in farming among children; and the competition from commercial farms in Florida, California, and Latin America have combined to threaten the future of lowcountry agriculture.[25]

The numerous farmers' markets and CSA programs in the lowcountry represent an innovative effort to conserve the region's farming heritage and in the process create another bridge across the racial barrier that has historically divided the region's conservation coalition. Black farmers are disappearing faster in the lowcountry than white farmers. Joseph Fields, a multigeneration African American grower along River Road on Johns Island, is the exception. All six of his siblings were born on the farm. In 2008 he converted his fifty-acre Johns Island farm to the growing of certified chemical-free organic produce: melons, peaches, potatoes, sweet potatoes, squash, collard greens, tomatoes, onions, okra, peas, and butterbeans. He also took advantage of the buy-local movement in the lowcountry by organizing a CSA cooperative with his wife, Helen ("We work as a team."). He was motivated by his desire to sustain a family tradition and a cultural heritage. "I was born and raised on the farm," he stressed. "It was my grandparents' farm." Fields knew he would not grow rich from organic farming, but he would derive great satisfaction from tilling the soil. "I never thought of not being a farmer. You've got to be a farmer because you love to do it, because you love to watch things grow and make people smile when they get fresh vegetables." To be sure, organic farming is not easy. "It's a little more expensive," Fields explained. "It takes more [natural] fertilizer, more labor and working it, such as hoeing." It is labor-intensive work. "Everything has to be labeled and kept separately," added Helen Fields. "A lot of that stuff has to be hand-held; you have to pay somebody to go in and pull weeds." To Fields the contemporary concern for sustainable agriculture and locally grown food represents a throwback to the way he and his ancestors used to farm. "Back then, we spread out chicken and horse manure in the field. Then we went to commercial stuff [fertilizer] because it made crops grow faster. Now we're going back to manure. You know, the old way. The way God intended—natural." Fields lives on the property where all six of his siblings were born and still live as neighbors. And he sells his produce at four area farmers' markets and supplies several local Charleston restaurants, as well as his CSA shareholders.[26]

Lowcountry Local First

The efforts to support small farmers in the lowcountry received a boost in 2006, when a new organization was founded expressly for that purpose. Matt Bauer, a resident of Daniel Island, created Lowcountry Local First (LLF) to promote the region's small farms and independent businesses. The group is part of a national organization called Business Alliance for Local Living Economy. Its mission also includes encouraging "businesses and consumers to be environmentally sustainable and socially responsible." A year later, in the fall of 2007, LLF formed a Sustainable Agriculture Program in partnership with the Coastal Conservation League. The CCL had itself launched a new program earlier that year, called Sustainable Agriculture, focused on policy issues related to farming. The CCL provided funding to support LLF during its first eighteen months. One of LLF's first initiatives was a series of "Farm to Table" meetings intended to bring together— for the first time—the various members of the lowcountry food network: growers, consumers, restaurateurs, chefs, representatives of the state department of agriculture, and environmental conservation organizations. The meetings resulted in the creation of a structured food network centered on promoting the sustainable production and consumption of local food.[27]

LLF has become one of the largest local farm-advocacy groups in the Southeast. Jamee Haley credited the organization's immediate success to the region's powerful pride of place: "I think because there is such a strong sense of place here, that [it] has enabled us to grow faster than other networks." Agriculture also represents one of the most cost-effective ways to improve two of the lowcountry's most acute environmental challenges: water quality and climate change. By promoting farming practices and policies that are environmentally responsible yet economically practical, the sustainable agriculture movement has come to represent one of the newest—but also one of the most important—elements of the lowcountry culture of conservation: "I think the big picture for us . . . by supporting local we're strengthening our economy. The wonderful byproducts of that, we are also helping the environment, we are preserving historic and rural spaces and creating better jobs."[28]

The buy-local crusade is the most visible effort to conserve the region's rural heritage, but LLF and other lowcountry environmental organizations are also helping to create more conservation easements on rural lands, using county and municipal comprehensive plans to reduce the pressures on farmers to sell their lands to developers, and assisting heirs' property owners in their efforts retain control of their ancestral lands. In 2011 the Coastal Conservation League created a new program titled GrowFood Carolina. Like LLF it focuses on reviving the culture of small farms, strengthening the rural economy, and promoting the buy-local phenomenon. Its initial emphasis, however, has been facilitating the transportation of produce from lowcountry farms to a warehouse in downtown Charleston where it can readily be distributed to local restaurants and grocery stores.

Perceptions and Persistence of Farmers

Lowcountry farmers are keenly aware of the threats to their livelihood. In 2006 and 2007 a graduate student under my supervision interviewed a diverse group of twenty-one Charleston County farmers in an effort to gain their perspective on the changes transforming the region and threatening their livelihood. The farmers who participated in the survey primarily grew fruits and vegetables. Of the twenty-one respondents, seventeen were male and four were female. Seventeen were Caucasian and four were African American. The average age of those interviewed was fifty-one.[29]

Many of the growers highlighted the challenges of change—changes in the nature of farming and the farm economy, changes in the lowcountry caused by relentless development, and changes triggered by shifting land-use policies. "Development, development is coming and taking over," said one farmer. The result has been "inflated land prices" that have encouraged people to sell their property. Another grower agreed that the most powerful threat to lowcountry farming was "rising land prices" caused by the region's rapid growth. Many of the respondents dated the turning point for lowcountry agriculture as being some "thirty-five to forty years ago . . . [when conventional commercial] agriculture dried up." Mirroring these

Abandoned tractor in Beaufort County. Courtesy of Jason Taylor.

impressions, the acreage under production, the percentage of time working on the farm, and the value of crops grown declined from 2002 to 2007.[30]

One of the farmers characterized his situation as being analogous to the invasion of enterprising northerners after the Civil War:

> I tease people sometimes that we may have lost the Civil War, but we are going backwards with them [northerners] now; we are selling them our real estate. Until you look at it and realize that we are still selling it too cheap, and, because we do, we don't have the . . . ability to preserve it or take care of it. Because the people from out of town or the people who haven't been here can't, or won't [conserve the land], they don't look at it that way. They are used to urban sprawl, they don't understand [the value of a land ethic]. . . . Every time I think about the national parks it makes me want to cry because it [*sic*] used to be sort of a wonderful place. Not many people visited it, it was quiet, and you could go out there and get lost; I mean you could literally get lost.[31]

Such lamentations are common among multigenerational lowcountry farmers. They often blame "outsiders" for eroding the region's devotion to the land. "Yankees, Yankees, Yankees, Yankees, all from Ohio," groused one farmer. "They discovered that this is a nice place to live, and they are moving here in droves."[32]

Just as the African American sweetgrass basket makers have seen their traditional livelihoods threatened by coastal development while the prices for their baskets have risen, so too have lowcountry farmers been hurt *and* helped by the region's transformation since the end of World War II. On one hand residential and commercial development has increased the value of agricultural property. On the other hand rising property values have also increased taxes on local farms and the expense to growers of leasing farm acreage. Like the basket makers, farmers are not a homogenous group. Some own all of the land they cultivate; others lease most of the acreage. They display different attitudes toward land-management issues, private property rights, and the best ways to conserve natural resources and traditional ways of life in the face of unrelenting development. They regret the diminishing stature and viability of agriculture and often lament their marginalized situation: "I feel like an outsider, I feel like agriculture is not important in Charleston anymore."[33]

For those who love the land and revere the vocation of husbandry, it hurts to see so many farm fields converted into subdivisions and strip shopping centers. Said one farmer, "Developers find it easier to put houses in a field. It is less expensive than to clear the woods; it just seems a shame that land that has been producing for seven or eight generations be torn up and houses put on it." Yet it is hard to cast blame on those who chose to sell their land rather than continue to cultivate it amid the growing challenges facing farmers. One of the growers said that farmers would be "crazy" not to sell their farmland for the prices developers were offering. "Why would you even consider [continuing to farm] unless you just loved it?" Another wryly noted that the biggest cash crop in the low-country was tourists.[34]

Many of the respondents viewed real estate development and greed being as synonymous in the lowcountry: "You know, we are developing. I want to call Mount Pleasant, Mount Development and Greed, you know? We are developing and destroying all of the pretty areas, what people come here for. A lot of these golf courses, they are doing away with the golf courses and developing the property. We are going to be like Houston or Dallas or anywhere else, it is just going to be houses and, you know, outsource your food. . . . There won't be a place like this."[35]

Others predicted that tourism and development would eventually displace all of the land-based livelihoods along the coast: "The biggest threat is there won't be any land to farm, which is, well, we are not far from that now." The onslaught of real estate developers has created a sense of fatalism among some respondents. As one reflected, "We can't stop them, they are coming whether we like it or not, so we just have to deal with [them]. But it is going to take our way of life and that is the most important thing to me. [They are] taking our way of life away from us."[36]

Lowcountry Farming in a Land of Change

Lowcountry farmers have always had to be resilient; for centuries they have been forced to adjust their vocation to fluctuating market conditions. For example, until the 1980s in the greater Mount Pleasant area there were a number of large truck farms, which provided fresh seasonal produce to the national food market. "A lot of [farming] history [is] in this area; . . . a generation before was truck farming; it was Irish potatoes and cabbage. Then . . . we had to change to cucumbers and tomatoes. Before that, it was cotton and rice, so [there] is a long history [of adaptability] in the lowcountry.[37]

What will the future hold? A few growers paint a hopeless picture. One observed that farming is "an era . . . [that is] over." Despite the efforts of the "buy local" movement, the farming community in the coastal counties continues to shrink and grow more fragmented. Some respondents identify specific events that have threatened the sustainability of farming. "Since Hurricane Hugo," one of them said, "we haven't grown anything but field corn." The difficulty of finding seasonal farmworkers after the hurricane and the need to spend months making repairs prevented him from getting "back into vegetable crops. After that, we just stuck with grain."[38]

The most compelling theme emerging from the interviews was the persistence of lowcountry farmers in the face of competing demands and pressures. New practices and new people are emerging in lowcountry fields and farms. As one grower put it, "I have neighbors that are still farming commercially, and they are having to change, [they have to] clean up their farmsteads and present themselves in a more professional manner. I guess that is not a bad thing, but some people have been that way for generations, not willing to change, so they will be like the dinosaur with one foot in the tar pit I guess. In farming, if you are not willing to change, you're not [going to be] long in this business."[39]

Some farmers highlighted the difficulty of competing with large commercial growers in Florida and California. Others, like this one, bemoan the diminishing awareness among newcomers of the importance of land-based livelihoods:

Well, the people who actually enjoy getting out on a farm and picking their own vegetables and seeing the land how it used to be, that's going to be what's lost. The attachment to the land is lost. But that doesn't seem to be a problem for our society now. Our society is geared totally different than it was even thirty, forty years ago. The whole mindset is so different, so I don't know that there is going to be a big loss. The loss is going to come in the generation coming up now, who've never experienced it, have nothing to lose. And they've never known it, they've never experienced it. They don't know what it's like to go out and pick sweet corn for supper. They don't know what it's like to go out and find a ripe watermelon for dessert. Or dig up a potato. Or pick okra, how to pick it without getting all itchy. They don't know that it's completely lost. But I don't think the majority of people here miss it. If there wasn't a farm left on this island today, I guarantee you 90 percent of the people would not miss it. They wouldn't know any different.[40]

Perhaps more than any other vocation, farming displays the trade-offs and compromises inherent in the lowcountry's culture of conservation. It remains a delicate balancing act to decide what should be preserved and how best to address competing needs. One farmer reflected at length on the tensions between preserving the lowcountry's rural heritage and promoting modern development:

Well, historically it [agriculture] was extremely important. It is not anymore; Charleston County could do without agriculture now. Agriculture means nothing to Charleston County now, nothing. In fact, it is a deterrent to developers and it is a deterrent to people. I find that most people come down here, or the people who are moving down here who don't remember what this county was like when it was largely an agrarian society, who don't have that, they view a lot of my farm equipment as a hindrance to them, and I will give you a very good example. A lot of my fields are so far apart. I don't have the luxury of having one contiguous farm like a lot other places. . . . I have 10 acres here, I have 15 acres there, I have 50 acres there, 100 acres there. It is all in pieces here [and] there, scattered all around between Johns Island and Wadmalaw and that means I have got to travel up and down these highways [in farm equipment] to get from one to the other. I can't tell you how many times [people in passing cars have made] . . .

obscene gestures and [shouted] profanity, and I have even been hit with an egg salad sandwich because I am just a target; I am slowing people down.

In contrast, many of those same impatient commuters wax sentimental about the agrarian way of life. They betray a "nostalgic feeling; they want to see pretty crops and green space. They want that, but they don't want what comes with it. They don't want the hassle of farm equipment crawling down the road."[41]

Impatient drivers represent only one of the many challenges facing low-country farmers. Finding workers is an acute source of frustration. One farmer betrayed the exasperation felt by many: "I can't get high school kids for ten dollars an hour to help me stack hay. They've got a borrowed BMW or a new Honda car, and they're going to the beach." Yet for all of the challenges, farmers persist. One of them accentuated the need for flexibility: "Probably the best and only hope for agriculture in this area . . . is . . . high value specialty crops." Growers expressed appreciation for the efforts of various lowcountry organizations to help conserve the coastal region's agricultural heritage and its physical environment. As one of them stressed, "I admire the people that are trying to do something. I mean like the Open Land Trust. . . . The Nature Conservancy is [also] buying up additional land. The ACE Basin is fabulous, fabulous [in part because]. . . . it's done without penalizing the private individual."[42]

Others would expand the concept to include preventing severe or irreversible damage to the livelihoods of those most engaged in the economic activity. Sustainable agriculture, including practices such as integrated pest management, organic farming, and reduced water usage, has become a small, but growing, part of the culture of conservation and environmental stewardship in the region during the twenty-first century.[43]

Complex Collaborative Conservation

The Charleston County farmers who participated in the interviews for this book view conservation as involving much more than simply a concern for the environment. It also encompasses efforts to enable them to sustain their land-based livelihood. The growers often alluded to their cherished way of life and proud sense of place. And they expressed appreciation for recent efforts across the low-country to preserve their agri-*culture*. A gritty example of the spirit of agricultural preservation is the Reverend York Washington, a septuagenarian African American farmer who grew vegetables for forty years on a farm south of Charleston that he had inherited from his father. Although his children and grandchildren had all chosen other vocations, Washington remained dedicated to his calling as a cultivator. "I know one thing for sure," he said about vegetable farming. "You never grow hungry."[44]

Washington and other growers recognized that the burgeoning buy-local movement offered the best hope for the future of lowcountry agriculture. Attorney and restaurateur Richard Stoney noted how the current rage for local food represented the revival of an old tradition. When he was a child, he recalled, "eating local was ordinary, such as crab and shrimp from the lowcountry's waterways." Ironically, he added, the marketplace is now reverting to its old ways. "I do feel it's almost come full circle. This whole Slow Food movement is what life used to be 75 to 100 years ago when everything was local. . . . We're reverting back to a simpler time." The vogue for simpler living among affluent coastal residents and tourists is helping to sustain small-scale lowcountry farming in the twenty-first century.[45]

In 2010 the *Charleston City Paper* highlighted the rapid growth of the buy-local movement. "Awareness about eating locally has spread from restaurants to our homes in just a handful of growing seasons." Nikki Seibert, a staff member of Lowcountry Local First, said in 2010 that "now is the time . . . to really get your hands in and stake a claim in farming. It is a big, uphill battle, not necessarily against conventional farming, but learning how to overcome the barrier of educating people on the cost and value of organic and local farming." The *Charleston City Paper* concluded that "we just need more farmers. And despite all the romanticism about getting dirt under your fingernails and connecting with food at its source, it takes a special dedication to devote yourself to farm life." Such dedication is fostering a rising appreciation among the consuming public. "God bless our local farmers and fishermen for their work," said Baron Hanson of Charleston in 2011. "The fruits of their labor are ending up on more lowcountry minds and tables each week, thanks to their innovations in preparation, communication, and delivery."[46]

Conclusion

On July 16, 2005, the graceful new Arthur Ravenel Jr. Bridge, named for the prominent conservative Republican legislator from Mount Pleasant who had played the primary role in securing government funding for the project, was dedicated after a week-long series of special events and celebrations. The Ravenel Bridge (also called the Cooper River Bridge), overlooks scenic Charleston Harbor and spans the Cooper River and Town Creek, connecting the Town of Mount Pleasant with downtown Charleston via Highway 17. It took four years to build but was finished under budget and a year ahead of schedule. The eight-lane, three-and-one-half-mile-long "cable stayed" suspension bridge, the longest of its type in North America, is supported by two 572-foot-tall diamond-shaped towers. The award-winning bridge, the most expensive infrastructure project in the state's history ($632 million), replaced two antiquated bridges that had become inadequate and unsafe.

The opening of the Ravenel Bridge was a blessing for motorists and a boon to real estate developers. Controversial Florida-based golf resort developer E. R. "Bobby" Ginn viewed the Ravenel Bridge as a catalyst for a new wave of growth in Mount Pleasant and Charleston. A South Carolina native, Ginn had acquired Sea Pines Plantation in the mid-1980s, as well as several other commercial properties on Hilton Head Island before going bankrupt and finding a safe haven at the Wild Dunes resort on Isle of Palms. A few years later Ginn relocated to Florida, found new financial backing, and began developing resort properties again. Early in the twenty-first century the Ginn Company started investing in the lowcountry, spending thirty-five million dollars acquiring properties adjoining both sides of the Ravenel Bridge. "When they announced the [decision to construct the] bridge, we engaged," Ginn said. "We bought [development property] because of that bridge. . . . It gives a whole new dimension to the city." In the fall of 2008 Ginn announced plans for a large multiuse development on two hundred acres adjacent to the bridge. The "ritzy waterfront development" would include hundreds of high-end condominiums and townhouses, office space, retail shops, as many as three hotels, a ten-thousand-seat amphitheater, a golf course, and a public marina. But the project never materialized. The onset

Arthur Ravenel Jr. Bridge. Courtesy of Dustin K. Ryan Photography.

in 2008 of what came to be called the Great Recession put an end to Ginn's grandiose waterfront scheme.[1]

While the Ravenel Bridge stimulated Ginn and others to pursue new real estate deals, it also symbolized the maturing culture of conservation in the low-country. The bridge not only connected two vibrant communities and provided greatly increased capacity for the projected volume of traffic in coming decades; it also included a twelve-foot-wide biking/walking lane named "Wonders Way." Initially the bridge planners opposed the inclusion of the biking/walking lane, but conservation organizations and outdoor recreation groups, as well as concerned citizens, lobbied for its inclusion. The recreational lane has since become much more heavily used than originally projected. "People are exercising more because of the bridge's bike and pedestrian lane," reported the *Charleston Post and Courier* three years after the bridge opened. That the bridge had become so widely used for public recreation led the *New York Times* to announce that "the Ravenel Bridge has fundamentally altered Charleston's psychology. Nowhere is this more true than on the bridge's wide bike-and-pedestrian lane. Suburban moms from Mount Pleasant rub elbows with families from gritty downtown Charleston. And Lycra-wearing cyclists whiz past iPod-clutching joggers from the bustling Citadel and College of Charleston. It's a perfect symbol for Charleston, straddling the Old and New South."[2]

The Ravenel Bridge is more than a traffic connector. It is also a powerful symbol of the ways in which the ideological differences between conventional economic development and environmental concerns have been bridged in the lowcountry. From the start those responsible for the design of the new bridge were determined to align its construction and operation with the ideals associated with the lowcountry's culture of conservation. For example, the twenty-two acres on the Mount Pleasant side freed up by the demolition of the two old bridges were converted into Memorial Waterfront Park with a visitors' center and pavilion showcasing the history and art of sweetgrass basket making. The acreage on the City of Charleston side of the bridge was reconfigured as an urban renewal project that included affordable housing, parks, drainage improvements, and economic opportunities for the East Side neighborhood (although almost two dozen homes owned by African Americans had to be moved to accommodate the bridge). Foundations from one of the demolished bridges were reused to construct a public fishing pier. The steel from the old bridges was recycled, and the concrete was used to create artificial reefs offshore.[3]

The bridge dedication ceremony was an extraordinary spectacle. Navy jets roared overhead, flags snapped in a brisk breeze, and a band played patriotic music. Legislators and transportation officials delivered two hours of speeches. "We have created not only a bridge, but a thing of beauty," said Arthur Ravenel Jr. The architectural beauty of the bridge was intended to mimic the natural beauty surrounding it. Throngs of people, many of them in boats, filled the harbor to see the largest fireworks display ever in South Carolina. While most of the boats were motorized, kayaks transported other spectators (including the author) from nearby conservation-centered subdivisions, such as I'On. The kayakers paddled along floating islands of golden green spartina grass juxtaposed against the Ports Authority's massive container terminal.[4]

As evening enveloped the dedication ceremony, fireworks and the bridge's lights illuminated the night sky. But it would be the last time that the lights would burn after 10 P.M.—at least during turtle nesting season. U.S. Fish and Wildlife biologists argued that the bridge lights would confuse endangered loggerhead turtle hatchlings as they made their way to the ocean in the dark of night. Using the authority of the federal Endangered Species Act, officials requested that timers and dimmers be added to the bridge's lighting system. Environmental conservation and economic development were again yoked in an awkward embrace.

Just as the Ravenel Bridge has helped span the tensions between economic development and environmental concerns, the long-dominant culture of growth in the lowcountry has been joined to—and tempered by—a culture of conservation since the late 1980s. In 1998 Arthur Ravenel Jr., then a Republican state senator from Mount Pleasant, had marveled at the growing strength of "environmental sentiment" along the coast. By the twenty-first century that sentiment had mushroomed. As Charles Lane, a lifelong conservationist, reflected in 2010, "we've really changed what the lowcountry is going to look like. . . . It was all going to look like southern Beaufort County and Myrtle Beach. . . . And [now] that's not going to be the case. We changed the psychology of how people view the area, and it happened in the last twenty years." Lane recognized that a transformation of attitudes had occurred since the 1980s. The sense of urgency motivating the conservation culture had helped to change public perceptions about the relative importance of promoting development and preserving the environment. Over time the lowcountry has come to be viewed as a commons to be cherished and protected by all, not simply by "environmentalists."[5]

In 2006 the *Charleston Post and Courier* reported that the lowcountry "is starting to get a handle on how to grow." Two years later the Charleston County Council adopted changes to its comprehensive plan intended to combat suburban sprawl, protect rural areas from suburban encroachment, and promote infill redevelopment within existing communities. The revisions resulted from "growing consumer interest in driving less and living in town-like settings." Attitudes toward growth in the lowcountry have changed dramatically since 1989. In 2005 the editors of the *Charleston Post and Courier* acknowledged that "in the never-ending battle to preserve natural and historic resources in the lowcountry, there is a lot of credit to be shared." The culture of conservation has become broad and diverse. It has come to include nonprofit organizations and foundations, corporations, elected officials, Republicans and Democrats, planners, developers, realtors, and the media. But most of all it has come to include a growing number of concerned citizens willing to engage in the shaping of environmental policies. A naturalist on Hilton Head Island declared in 2006 that lowcountry residents were becoming "good stewards of the land. Development and environmental conservation do not have to be mutually exclusive. It's a win-win situation for everyone." In 2010 the Town of Hilton Head became the first community in the state to join the Audubon International's Sustainable Communities Program as a major step in the resort island's efforts to become the "premier destination for eco-tourists and green businesses."[6]

The effects of the culture of conservation have been quite tangible. Since the 1980s, as the *Charleston Post and Courier* noted in 2005, city and county governments as well as residents and conservation organizations have been "taking extraordinary steps" to protect the region "against any development or destruction that would sacrifice priceless natural and historic resources for the sake of maximizing profits." In the fall of 2007, for example, the Dorchester County Council became so concerned about the "ill effects" of rampant growth that it imposed a six-month moratorium on new residential development. A year later the editors of the *Charleston Post and Courier*, steadfast advocates of the culture of conservation, published a series of articles dealing with "growth and sprawl in the lowcountry." The lowcountry, they wrote, "is at a turning point. Will it sprawl out into rural areas as in the past, or are their other options?" The week-long series of articles delineated the major issues associated with controlling sprawl and encouraged citizens to become even more involved with the efforts of local governments to promote smarter growth and wiser conservation. The good news was that "developers, landowners, and local government planners" were "realizing the urgency of the growth problem."[7]

The newspaper series about sprawl documented the scope and depth of the culture of the conservation in the lowcountry. Many developers and residents of community associations now consider conservation protocols (for example, wetlands protection, land preservation, conservation easements, zoning restrictions, storm-water management, open-space commons) necessary elements of their communities. The African American community has also become increasingly vocal about the impact of sprawl on its handicraft heritage. One basket maker reported that her sense of place and community had been disrupted: "Mount Pleasant was a very peaceful area. Until development came in there, everybody knew each other and everybody looked out for each other, but now you don't know who your neighbor is."[8]

Farmers—old and new—are also participants in the debates over development. As one of them said, "I admire the people that are trying to do something. I mean like the Lowcountry Open Land Trust [and] the Nature Conservancy are buying up additional land. The ACE Basin is fabulous, fabulous." However, in their own fields and in their small rural communities, farmers tend to see conservation differently than many of the other people discussed in this book. While they often mention environmental concerns, their focus tends to be on the preservation of their agricultural way of life rather than the preservation of the region's ecology.[9]

The major conservation organizations—the Nature Conservancy, Coastal Conservation League, and the Lowcountry Open Land Trust—have provided structure, expertise, and energy to the culture of conservation. Yet despite the significant role played by such increasingly powerful organizations, the most important element of the culture of conservation is the residents themselves. They demonstrate day in and day out that grassroots concern is the lifeblood of a sustainable conservation culture. Such steadfast public involvement has become quite visible and potent. As an editorial in the *Charleston Post and Courier* declared in 2009, "developers should be under no illusions about the county's commitment to growth management." The lowcountry was now firmly committed to "limiting sprawl." Two years earlier the newspaper's editors had endorsed the idea of local governments restricting growth by new zoning ordinances and by refusing to fund new infrastructure requests from developers. They explained that "conservation sentiment" in the lowcountry had become the prevailing view among the citizenry.[10]

The Maturing Culture of Conservation

The evolution of the lowcountry's culture of conservation is a story of hope and passion, redemption and promise, all undergirded by hard work and resilience. A powerful pride of place remains the foundation of the conservation movement. As Louisa Moore, owner of a farmstead on a tidal creek close to the headwaters of the Wando River, said in 2010: "I have given my heart and my soul and my sweat and my tears to this place because I love it, and I want to—it's in my blood. This is all I do, and I love it."[11]

The passion displayed by Moore and others helps to explain the remarkable success of the conservation ethic in the lowcountry. What was once a monologue spoken by the domineering growth-for-growth's-sake culture has become a much more vital and diverse dialogue, vigorous and (mostly) balanced, animated by a growing sense of urgency and possibility. A robust culture of conservation is now in place, not yet dominant by any means, but steady in power and influence. Rand Wentworth, the president of the national Land Trust Alliance in Washington, D.C., visited the lowcountry in 2006 and reported after visiting with local officials that "the story here is that it is working. Conservation has gone mainstream." The process by which this has happened—and the ways that the concept of conservation has been deepened and expanded—represent tangible signs of a growing sense of civic engagement in the lowcountry.[12]

More and more people in the lowcountry are growing anxious about the velocity of growth and are determined to preserve the region's distinctive quality of life and its natural resources. Public interest in the stewardship of the environment has created a new vehicle for grassroots involvement. Since the late 1980s, residents from all walks of life have become much more engaged in addressing the implications of rampant development and promoting sustainable communities. Natives and newcomers in large numbers participate in the culture of conservation in the ways best suited to their concerns and abilities: they join conservation groups, organize to thwart poorly planned developments, embrace the use of land trusts and conservation easements, and engage in the ongoing policy debates related to smart growth. The *Charleston Post and Courier* emphasized in 2010 that the people living in the lowcountry "want to help make the decisions [about development and conservation] that will affect them directly." Social change works best when it occurs at the local level. Public activism, as the lowcountry has demonstrated, can exercise surprising power. As an editor of the *Charleston Post and Courier* asked in 2007, "Could it be that the citizens of regional Charleston are slowly but surely getting serious about the ravages of unbridled growth? Sure seems that way."[13]

The success of the conservation culture can be measured in many ways. Lowcountry conservation organizations have grown in number and variety since 1989, and their resources and membership rosters have risen. Conservation-oriented subdivisions, as well as land protected by conservation easements, have proliferated. Charleston County and Beaufort County voters, for example, have approved significant annual funding to enable purchases of undeveloped land for conservation. Hundreds of thousands of acres have been conserved throughout the lowcountry. At the same time populations of "endangered" or "threatened" species such as the wood stork, red-cockaded woodpecker, bald eagle, whooping crane, and osprey have rebounded. As a result of the "incessant" efforts of the land conservation coalition, the *Charleston Post and Courier* reported in 2007, a "remarkable ring of protected green space" now encircles the region, a protective greenbelt "of distinctive lowcountry territory that can't be gobbled up for growth."[14]

Other signs of the conservation culture abound. A flood of local growth-control initiatives has emerged across the lowcountry. Comprehensive land-use planning that explicitly promotes conservation principles is now in place across the lowcountry. For example, the Beaufort County Comprehensive Plan (1997) highlighted the "strong public outcry for conservation and preservation" as well as the role played by conservation efforts in strengthening the county's economic vitality. The county's "chief comparative advantage for its long-term development is the quality of its environment." The plan represented the county's effort to "facilitate growth in a rational manner" through "sustainable economic development." Leaders within all sectors (private, public, and nonprofit) have encouraged such comprehensive planning and have formed unlikely alliances in promoting various conservation initiatives. And they have acknowledged the need to balance private property interests with the welfare of the environment—in an inclusive and transparent way. As the Beaufort County Comprehensive Plan stated, "the County must find a *balance* between the private property rights and the rights of the neighbors and preserving and enhancing the natural and cultural environment and quality of life in the community. To do so, the County must work toward increasing accessibility to the planning process for all citizens."[15]

One example of the ways in which the planning process in the lowcountry has changed as a result of the efforts of the culture of conservation is the 2011 decision by land-use planners in the Town of Bluffton, near Hilton Head, to adopt progressive new "standards for the town's growth, pinpointing where development should and should not go and what form it should take." They overhauled the town's conventional car-dependent zoning ordinances, which had always segregated commercial and business areas from residential neighborhoods, to allow for mixed-use developments with high-density neighborhoods as well as low-density "edges that preserve rural character and open land." The new planning ordinance also included incentives for developers and builders who employed "green-building standards" and provided "affordable housing."[16]

Conservation-centered Communities

During the twenty-first century the number and quality of conservation-centered communities have also grown apace. Perhaps the most significant new community is East Edisto, a massive 78,600-acre mixed-use development west of Charleston on the eastern side of the Edisto River straddling Charleston and Dorchester Counties. It is the largest planned development ever launched on the southeastern coast of the United States—so large, in fact, that it may take as long as fifty years to build its three phases. The heavily wooded property was owned by one of the nation's largest timber companies, land-rich MeadWestvaco (now called MWV), which in 2008 created MVW Community Development and Land Management Company to oversee its real estate enterprises. In March 2008 the company, following extensive public forums and collaboration with the planning staffs of both counties, unveiled its fifty-year "conservation-inspired" master plan for East Edisto. The dozens of public hearings and surveys delivered a clear message to the developer: the lowcountry wanted East Edisto to be an exemplary conservation-oriented community that would preserve most of the tract's forest and farmland. The East Edisto planners and designers responded in kind. The centerpiece of the master plan is a commitment to preserve 75 percent of the acreage as green space, around which would be built a cluster of sustainable towns and villages, corporate parks, densely clustered multifamily and single-family walkable neighborhoods, schools, churches, medical offices, conserved lands, parks, lakes, and rural areas. Residents would live near their workplaces, thereby minimizing automobile traffic. Planned outdoor amenities include natural areas, recreational areas, interconnected greenways, trails for hiking, biking, and horseback riding, an Edisto River interpretive and education center, and buffers that protect the river and other precious natural resources. No homes would be allowed along the river itself.[17]

The widely acclaimed master plan for East Edisto provided tangible witness to the impact of the conservation culture on lowcountry real-estate development. The development's self-described "green" and "smart growth-centered" mission statement encapsulated the guiding principles of the culture of conservation: "to respect community heritage; to preserve and protect natural resources; to preserve rural character and avoid creating additional financial burden on taxpayers; to create affordable, diverse and balanced housing options; to enhance life-long learning opportunities; and to develop walkable communities and avoid congestion." MWC highlighted its desire not only to make a profit but also to create an "unprecedented" conservation community that would serve the needs of the growing lowcountry community. MWC wanted "to be part of a planning process that helps manage the Charleston region's growth, while creating new sustainable communities that remain true to the beauty and character of the lowcountry."[18]

Roadblocking

Perhaps the most important accomplishment of the culture of conservation is its ability to blunt the momentum and change the dynamics of sprawl. Today, unlike a generation ago, any proposed residential or commercial development must pass through a cordon of environmental scrutiny. The Coastal Conservation League has developed such clout, credibility, and negotiating savvy that developers often come to there first before presenting plans to a planning board or zoning commission. "We're a stakeholder, as they would see it," noted Executive Director Dana Beach in 2010. CCL staff members spend more time at the negotiating table than organizing protests at public hearings. Their emphasis on smart growth has helped bridge the adversarial distance between conservation advocates and developers and realtors. As Beach explained, "We do a lot more than just say, 'No,'" to proposed developments across the region. "We say, 'No, but . . . [let's talk].'"[19]

The same is true for major infrastructure projects intended to ease traffic congestion and foster new development. In 2010, for example, the Federal Highway Administration, the South Carolina Department of Transportation, and Charleston County created a proposal to complete the eight-mile-long final section (the "unconstructed corridor") of Interstate 526, also called the Mark Clark Expressway, from its terminus at U.S. Highway 17 in the West Ashley area across Johns Island to James Island before tying into the James Island Connector leading into downtown Charleston. The planned highway, which would twice cross the Stono River, provoked a firestorm of opposition. Hundreds of people signed petitions opposing the extension, and thousands attended numerous public hearings to voice their concerns, especially the fear that the new highway would in fact encourage more development and exacerbate already congested traffic. A group called the Concerned Citizens of the Sea Islands (made up of property owners on Johns, James, Wadmalaw, Kiawah, and Seabrook Islands) organized to stop the project. Their explicit goal was to work together to improve "the quality of life, sense of place and rural character of our shared home." The Town of James Island, Historic Charleston Foundation, Coastal Conservation League, Nature Conservancy, Southern Environmental Law Center, *Charleston Post and Courier*, National Marine Fisheries Service, and South Carolina Department of Natural Resources joined the opposition to the proposed new road. The controversy over the $489 million interstate extension revealed how quickly—and effectively—the diverse elements making up the region's conservation coalition could mobilize to address new projects. Such civic engagement among an interconnected group of activists and officials, most of whom know each other well and interact often, is a valuable form of "social capital" that provides cascading benefits to the quality of life in the lowcountry.[20]

The idea of extending the Mark Clark Expressway onto the sea islands had been simmering since the 1970s. No sooner had the original expressway opened in June 1992 than discussions had begun about "completing" the highway across rural Johns Island to James Island. In 2007 the Charleston County Council passed a resolution endorsing the completion of the final segment of the espressway, and the State Infrastructure Bank awarded Charleston County ninety-nine million dollars for the project. But public criticism of the highway extension prompted the county council to ask the department of transportation to consider other options. By 2008 more than a dozen possible routes had been developed for the proposed extension. Public hearings and feedback from stakeholders increased the number of suggested alternates to thirty-nine, which were eventually winnowed to seven. Finally, in 2010, the South Carolina Department of Transportation recommended its new preferred route. It reflected public concerns

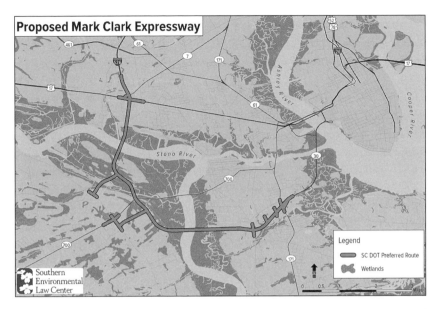

Map of proposed I-526 Mark Clark Expressway. Courtesy of Jovian Sackett and Southern Environmental Law Center.

by changing the extension from an interstate highway to a four-lane "parkway" with posted speed limits from thirty-five to forty-five miles per hour. It also included a pedestrian/bicycle lane.[21]

Supporters of the project argued that the revamped extension plan would improve traffic congestion in the metropolitan Charleston region, facilitate hurricane-related evacuations, enable tourists and property owners to get more quickly from Charleston to the popular resorts on Kiawah and Seabrook Islands, and boost economic development. Opponents countered that the expensive project would transform the rural character of Johns Island while reducing drive time to Charleston by only a few minutes. The construction of the highway would also displace two dozen homes and damage or destroy one hundred acres of salt marsh wetlands. The extension connecting to Johns Island, for example, would include four major bridges within a five-mile segment. "Building new highways," maintained the Concerned Citizens of the Sea Islands, "induces new development which brings more traffic and creates even more congestion." They and others argued that the traffic congestion could be eased by creating a network of smaller roads at much less expense to the taxpayers and the environment.[22]

In 2006, as engineers and surveyors were developing the probable routing of the highway, residents of Johns Island formed the Johns Island Preservation Coalition to stop the project. Johns Island farmer Thomas Legare expressed the determination of those opposed to the highway project when he vowed: "We're not going to roll over and play dead on this. I think we do have a chance [to stop it]." Louise Maybank, who was a tenacious advocate for tighter zoning rules designed to keep Wadmalaw Island's rural nature and chaired Charleston County's Greenbelt Advisory Group, also opposed the highway.[23]

By the summer of 2010, when the South Carolina Department of Transportation began holding a new round of public hearings about the proposed routes for the interstate extension, the opposition had blossomed into a mass movement. Of the 1,550 people who spoke at the public hearings, more than one thousand opposed the extension project. The town councils of Folly Beach and James Island passed resolutions opposing it. They argued that the completion of the eastern half of the Mark Clark Expressway across the Cooper River in 1992 had triggered a tsunami of new residential and commercial development that had transformed Mount Pleasant. New roads, bridges, and sewer lines accelerate rather than ameliorate sprawl. "Growth follows infrastructure," said Jane Lareau of the Coastal Conservation League. "Ninety percent of traffic on a new road is generated by the road itself." In July 2010 a project consultant for the South Carolina Department of Transportation responded to the growing criticism by proposing to the Charleston County Council an alternative to the extension of I-526: a low-speed, four-lane parkway with a fifteen-foot center median and a pedestrian/bicycle lane. But the controversy continued. In September 2010 the U.S. Environmental Protection Agency announced that it opposed the highway project. By October 2010 Buck Limehouse, the state transportation secretary, conceded that "we've certainly got to deal with the objections if we're going to move forward."[24]

The prolonged—and very public—debate about the extension of the Mark Clark Expressway saw members of the conservation coalition on opposite sides. Mayor Joe Riley of Charleston, for example, endorsed the parkway scheme (in large part because it would be a "quieter, more appropriately scaled road") while lowcountry conservation organizations vehemently opposed any extension of the expressway. Yet the conservation coalition opposing the interstate expansion displayed its maturity by not simply saying no. Instead they went to great expense to organize a team of transportation consultants who held their own public hearings before recommending an alternative plan at half the cost that would improve existing roadways and add parallel secondary routes to alleviate traffic congestion. Conservationists in the lowcountry have learned that they must do more than simply prevent change; they must try to shape change. NIMBYISM alone does not constitute a civic vision. The interstate extension controversy revealed that promoting conservation on a regional scale often involves contentious trade-offs, compromises, and differences of opinion. By 2011 Buck Limehouse admitted that there was "substantial opposition and substantial cost" to the project. "We have got to resolve whether to build it or not. It's costing money every day. The funds [$420 million from the South Carolina Transportation Infrastructure Bank] could be used somewhere else if we decide not to do it." The controversy over extending I-526 onto Johns and James Islands reached a dramatic climax on the evening of April 14, 2011, when the Charleston County Council unanimously voted to cancel the project. It took the additional step of declaring that the state department of transportation could not even consider alternative extension plans until "enhancements to the existing transportation infrastructure to accomplish the project goals."[25]

The debate over the interstate extension displayed yet again the diversity and vitality of the culture of conservation by revealing how major infrastructure and development projects are now subject to layers of environmental scrutiny and grassroots opposition. The culture of conservation now exercises persistent leverage over land use and development decisions, heralding a new era of grassroots activism that is centered on a steadfast quest for sustainability. As Tom Bradford, director of Charleston Moves, a nonprofit organization promoting alternative forms of transportation, wrote in 2010, "the Mark Clark [Expressway] controversy is a sign that we are nearing the limit for road building in the lowcountry." In fact, he added, "we are reaching the limit for traditional kinds of development, the single-story, big-box variety that crowds our suburbs." The "helter-skelter development" associated with sprawl had "blighted our vistas" and "depressed" the lowcountry "quality of life." Penn Center's executive director, Emory Campbell, opposes the I-526 extension. He argued it "would devastate an already regrettably threatened Gullah Geeche cutlure that has become a national treasure." Historically, economic growth and ecological health have usually been in conflict; now they are more often considered in tandem.[26]

Lessons Learned

For all of its distinctive historical and social elements, the culture of conservation in the lowcountry suggests several lessons that are applicable to other regions of the nation. Growth is inevitable—especially along the coast. How the lowcountry responds to the imperatives of growth remains a matter of choice, however. "To build a better motor," the noted conservationist Aldo Leopold wrote, "we tap the uttermost powers of the human brain; to build a better countryside, we throw dice." Gambling on the future quality of the environment is risky business. A community can allow its future to be dictated by chaotic market forces or, as the conservation culture has shown, the lowcountry can grow more intentionally. That is, the region can take the long view—taking into consideration the fragility of ecosystems, the limits of natural resources, and the virtues of cultural and historic heritage. This requires that the lowcountry region establish its priorities about what really matters. In the end a community's quality of life or "livability" is a function of what it most values. There is a powerful lesson in the coastal region's embrace of conservation and its growing skepticism of the growth-for-growth's sake mentality. Natural resources are limited and often fragile; they should not be heedlessly exploited. The lowcountry environment can only accommodate so much growth; it has a limited carrying capacity. As a consequence, conservation culture is not as much about managing the environment or regulating growth as it is about changing human behavior—activities, appetites, expectations, and habits.[27]

Sustaining a *culture* of conservation requires sensitivity to the history, psychology, aspirations, and circumstances of a community. Such a comprehensive approach is required to balance the imperatives of growth with the long-term welfare of the environment and the coastal region's unique cultural heritage of land-based livelihoods (basket making and farming) and recreational hunting and fishing. Taking the long view is never easy; it requires constant attention, abiding engagement, and deferred gratification. But such prospective thinking is what distinguishes humans from other species. In 1903 Republican president Theodore Roosevelt reminded Americans of their obligation to be good environmental stewards—for the ages. "We are not building this country of ours for a day," he said. "It is to last through the ages." Taking the long view involves a balancing act that is not only delicate; it is essential. As Mayor Riley emphasized in 2010, balancing the imperatives of growth with the health of the environment requires strenuous persistence. "It's not a dainty balance," he said in an interview, "but it is . . . a delicate thing."[28]

The evolution of a conservation ethic in the lowcountry has also demonstrated the importance of understanding the cultural dimensions of environmental issues. The complex realities of individual community contexts make suspect any effort to generalize about the dynamics undergirding the formation of conservation cultures. The lowcountry example illustrates how such complexities, nuances, and ironies make generalizations across a region a treacherous exercise. Environmental research has traditionally distinguished between human concerns and environmental concerns. Yet human culture and the environment cannot be so easily separated; they are entwined in a reciprocal and often interdependent relationship. The perceptions people have of the natural environment are complex but real; they guide human behavior that often reshapes or degrades the environment—or restores it. Just as the historical preservation movement has discovered that it must take into consideration local sentiment and economic realities (as well as an awareness of potential "elitism" influencing such preservation efforts), the culture of conservation has come to recognize the same valuable lessons. Protecting the lowcountry environment cannot be done solely through the efforts of a few prominent activists. Nor can it be imposed from above. It must continue to engage the support of those who, black or white, rich or poor, live on and love the land—and identify their own cultural heritage and pride of place with its fate. To such residents the environment is more than the land and its resources. It is their legacy, their heritage, their nexus of meaning. The development of an intangible but still powerful pride of place involves deeply engrained traditions and multiple layers of meaning that create what might be termed a shared ethnoecology.[29]

The lowcountry remains especially fertile ground for exploring the intersection of culture and conservation, ethnography and environment. A powerful emotional attachment to the symbolic value of the coastal landscape continues to shape human behavior in a region awash in cultural heritage. Scientists, natural resource managers, planners, elected officials, and activists have, in varying degrees, stretched the boundaries of conservation to include attentiveness to a region's ethno-cultural traditions and folkways. A region's cultural fabric and heritage are crucial factors in understanding—and improving—its environmental quality. Issues of race, class, and geodemography have been powerful undercurrents shaping the environmental landscape. In the lowcountry, people of all races and classes, newcomers and natives, outsiders and insiders, have been powerful actors on the conservation stage. Cultural and natural scientists as well as conservation advocates need to continue to incorporate cultural concerns into their efforts by pursuing an inclusive strategy that educates the public about environmental concerns—and options.

The example of the lowcountry culture of conservation also reinforces the need to pursue conservation efforts on a regional and multijurisdictional basis rather than a piecemeal and local approach. By necessity, effective growth management and land-use practices transcend municipal boundaries. The natural environment does not abide by city limits or county maps; the social and environmental costs of unregulated growth trespass across civic borders.

The conservative lowcountry social and political tradition—as well as the close-knit, informal "insiders'" circle of elite, wealthy, and virtually all white natural-resource conservationists—have shaped the conservation community's strategic decision to focus on the preservation of land through outright acquisition or the purchase (or donation) of easements. As sociologist Caroline W. Lee has written, "a deeply conservative region with entrenched elites" has surprisingly managed "to support conservation instead of [unrestrained] growth." One member of the conservation elite acknowledged in 2001 that the leadership of the lowcountry "conservation community is in fact fairly small. You get a lot of overlap in boards, a lot of overlap different people have in where they're putting their conservation energies." At the same time that such a tradition of "backstage networking" has facilitated important deal making and strategic decision making, it has also tended to limit the scope and effectiveness of efforts to promote social justice in an environmental context. The coalition of property owners that combined to help create the ACE Basin, for example, was led by prominent members of affluent multigenerational lowcountry families. However successful the ACE Basin project was from the point of view of preserving natural resources, it did not address what Lee has termed the "stark" racial and class inequalities embedded in the demography of the ACE Basin.[30]

Finally, as is often the case, a virtue can become a vulnerability. The distinctive strength of the culture of conservation in coastal South Carolina has been its informal network of associations, collaborations, and partnerships connected by a shared desire to preserve the region's cultural heritage. The close-knit personal relationships among the conservation community have facilitated efforts to preserve land, protect habitat and natural resources, and stop or modify development projects that would degrade the environment. Such a close-knit, socially homogeneous network, however, can unravel over time as participants die or move, lose interest or change roles. Will the conservation culture be able to find replacements for Dana Beach, Elizabeth Hagood, Charles Lane, Joe Riley, and Thomasena Stokes-Marshall as they retire from their longtime roles? As the conservation culture has evolved, it has also become more diverse and complex. For example, the recent debates over the proposed extension of I-526 has found members of the conservation coalition on opposing sides. This is a sign of maturation. Sustaining a conservation coalition is labor-intensive; it requires frequent communication, interaction, maintenance, and renewal. The hard work of belonging to a place and nurturing its future is never over. Permanence cannot be taken for granted. In reflecting on the conservation culture in the lowcountry, Dana Beach said in 2009 that there are only "a handful of places in the country like this, unique landscapes that are truly irreplaceable." The conservation coalition had enjoyed great success since the 1980s, but "there is still so much to be done."[31]

The Conservation Culture amid the Great Recession

Calamities sometimes provide unintended benefits. Hurricane Hugo generated a rebuilding boom along the coast that had the unexpected effect of heightening concerns about the environmental effects of sprawl and creating a sense of urgency about the need for a more robust culture of conservation. In a similarly ironic way, the so-called Great Recession of 2008–2010 benefited the culture of conservation by dramatically slowing the rate of population growth and new development in the lowcountry. The bursting of the national real estate bubble generated a concussive shock wave that turned an overheated economy into the worst recession since the Great Depression of the 1930s. Across the nation and throughout the lowcountry, unemployment skyrocketed, bankruptcies soared, and foreclosures multiplied. Grossly inflated prices for real estate plummeted, as did the number of tourists visiting the coast.[32]

Yet amid the prolonged slowdown and its harrowing miseries, there was a silver lining in the lowcountry. The recession accidentally provided environmental dividends. "It brought sanity back to the real estate market," Dana Beach observed in 2010. "Everything up to the crash [in 2008] was a fiction, a Ponzi scheme, a collective delusion. People sincerely believed that simply buying a piece of real estate guaranteed a doubling of value in a year, and if the buyer put 10 percent down, that translated into a 1,000 percent return on investment. And everyone was doing it." The recession punctured the inflated real estate valuations in the lowcountry and brought new development to a standstill. Garrett Budds, the director of the Beaufort office of the Coastal Conservation League, noted that the economic collapse was allowing the region "to consider how to manage growth better when it inevitably resumes." Public officials reported that the "flaws inherent in how we were growing were at least identified [as a result

Egret taking flight. Photograph by Angela C. Halfacre.

of the recession]." The runaway development of the lowcountry, Budds added, "was a lot of disjointed growth." He predicted that the Great Recession had changed the way people view real estate development. "I think folks are sitting back and taking stock. People aren't waiting out the recession to resume what they were doing. It may be the end of an era. We aren't going back to the way we were doing things. It's not sustainable."[33]

Of course, a recession does not provide a long-term environmental strategy. The Great Recession was beneficial to the extent that it raised public awareness by validating many of the concerns about runaway growth that conservationists had been voicing for decades. The economic slowdown, said a reporter for *The Beaufort Gazette*, might enhance the lowcountry's culture of conservation by helping people adopt "a new way of looking at the environment and development— not as competing goals but as complementary elements that must remain in balance."[34]

Maintaining Balance

Maintaining that delicate balance between the imperatives of growth and the quality of the environment remains the region's foremost challenge. The ability of the lowcountry environment and its quality of life to absorb the effects of per-petual development brings to mind the story of a young martial arts student who, after watching O Sensei, the founder of Aikido, sparring with another fighter, asked him why he never lost his balance. "You are wrong," O Sensei replied. "I am constantly losing my balance. My skill lies in my ability to regain it." The future of the lowcountry holds significant challenges, but a culture of conservation— centered on the evolving concept of sustainable development—has coalesced to allow the region to regain its balance—over and over again.

Bridge over marsh on Pawleys Island. Courtesy of Robert Donovan.

A viable culture of conservation is a dynamic endeavor that is never finished; it assumes new dimensions as it generates new ideas and deals with unexpected challenges. No sooner is one crisis or opportunity addressed than another emerges. Jane Lareau acknowledged the need for perpetual vigilance when she said: "As long as there is something beautiful, pure and natural out there, there's somebody who wants to build on it, dam it, run a road through it, and make a buck off it. When you lose something, you lose it finally. When you win to protect something, you simply protect it long enough to go back and defend it another time."[35]

During early 1998 U.S. Secretary of the Interior Bruce Babbitt visited the lowcountry on three separate occasions to bestow conservation awards and give major public addresses. At a press conference at Drayton Hall, an Ashley River antebellum plantation on the National Register of Historic Places, Babbitt highlighted the remarkable success of the culture of conservation in the lowcountry. He told the audience that the lowcountry "is farther ahead than anyone in the nation. For whatever reason, there is a spirit [of environmental conservation and historic preservation] here. It is very important that you keep at it." In documenting the region's "extraordinary progress" over the previous decade in environmental conservation, he highlighted the ACE Basin as a powerful example of what can be accomplished when federal, state, and local agencies and conservation organizations creatively work together with property owners for a common preservation goal.

Bestowing awards on lowcountry environmentalists, Babbitt said, "is becoming a habit." The interior secretary then acknowledged the challenge facing not only the lowcountry but the nation as well: planning for a sustainable future that includes development and preservation. There remains much more to be done, since growth is inevitable, and opinions will always differ about how best to manage the tensions between development and conservation. "Can a balance be found?" Based on what he had learned about the lowcountry, Babbitt said that the "answer to that question must be—must be—yes."[36]

Introduction

1. Archdale, "A New Description of that Fertile and Pleasant Province of South Carolina," 295; Cushman, "South Carolinians Nurture a Little Cause That Could." Wise, "Holy City Displaces San Francisco as No. 1 on Condé Nast List." Charleston is called the "holy city" because of the prevalence of church steeples on its cityscape.

2. Behre, "Forum to Look at Projects"; "Forum to Address Changes in the City."

3. Allen, "Another Day, Another Project"; "It's All about Balance"; Berry, "Preserving Wildness," 139. On the concept of social ecology, see Cohen et al., "Environmental Orientations."

4. For an examination of the unique nature of human culture, see Tomasello, "The Human Adaptation for Culture." Assessing which people in a community participate in the decision-making process and which are being "marginalized" is a crucial concern of environmental perception studies. The individual is often viewed as "one voice"; in practice, however, how a person interacts within society influences individual perception. See Merchant, *Radical Ecology*, 1–2. For a sampling of the debates about how conservation and development are conceptualized, see Cronon, "The Trouble with Wilderness"; Duncan and Duncan, "The Aestheticization of the Politics of Landscape Preservation"; K. Brown, "Innovations for Conservation and Development"; Berkes, "Rethinking Community-based Conservation"; Oldekop et al., "Understanding the Lessons and Limitations of Conservation and Development"; and Gruber, "Key Principles of Community-Based Natural Resource Management." See also Zimmerer, "The Reworking of Conservation Geographies." Political scientists have long viewed a robust sense of community as the best setting in which to meet the requirements of legitimate government, especially in democratic regimes. See Dahl, *Democracy and Its Critics*. One author defines a political community as "a group of people who live under the same political rules and structure of governance and share status as citizens" and defines a cultural community as "a group of people who share a culture and draw their identities from common language, history, and traditions" (Stone, *Policy Paradox*, 19). Communities of place are connected to a physical space; communities of identity may transcend place and be bound by social characteristics, and communities of interest are defined by how they interact with resources or ecosystems. See Duane, *Shaping the Sierra*. In practice each community constitutes a heterogeneous entity rather than fits completely within a single classification. See Agrawal and Gibson, "Enchantment and Disenchantment," and Johnson and Halfacre, "Resident Place Identities in Rural Charleston County, South Carolina."

5. Davis, "A Sense of Place," 2, and O'Connor, "The Partridge Festival," 426. On the concept of "pride of place," see B. Allen, "The Genealogical Landscape and the Southern Sense of Place"; Hiss, *The Experience of Place;* Jacobson, *Place and Belonging in America;* Low, "Cultural Conservation of Place."

6. Leland, *Porcher's Creek,* 6, and Conroy, *The Prince of Tides,* 5.

7. Leland, *Porcher's Creek,* xii, 114; Conroy, *The Water Is Wide,* 5; Humphries, "A Disappearing Subject Called the South," 214.

8. Bruce, *Transfer of Grace,* 24; Dolah et al., *The Condition of South Carolina's Estuarine and Coastal Habitats,* 2004.

9. Morgan quoted in "South Carolina Preserves Sandy Island." Tourism is South Carolina's most important industry, and just three lowcountry counties—Horry, Charleston, and Beaufort—account for nearly 60 percent of the state's total tourism-related income. See Collins, "Climate Change." For a textured first-person account of the lowcountry, see Cuthbert and Hoffius, *Northern Money, Southern Land.* A more general overview of the region is Zepke, *Coastal South Carolina.*

10. Slade, "S.C. Population Growth in Top Ten." See also R. Johnson, "New Frontier in Waterfront"; Schmidt, "Beaufort, S.C.," and Charleston Regional Development Alliance, "Market Profile" (website). On the concept of growth machines, see Logan and Molotch, *Urban Fortunes.* Growth data for the lowcountry are available in Allen and Lu, "Modeling and Predicting Future Urban Growth in the Charleston Area" (website), and Phillips, "S.C. Residents Flock to Urban Areas, Coast." For growth projection maps, see Strom Thurmond Institute, "Charleston Urban Growth Project 1973–2030" (website). See also "Lowcountry among Nation's Top 100 Fastest-Growing Areas"; London and Hill, *Land Conversion in South Carolina;* and Urban Land Institute, *Growing by Choice or Chance.*

11. Wilson and Fischetti, "Coastline Population Trends in the United States."

12. Elmendorf and Luloff, "Using Ecosystem-based and Traditional Land-use Planning to Conserve Greenspace." There are few published scholarly studies of lowcountry environmental history. A useful source is H. Smith, "Watersheds of Control."

13. Hagood, e-mail message to the author, February 24, 2011.

14. See Lee, "Conservation as a Territorial Ideology," and Huffman, "Defining the Origins of Environmentalism in Wisconsin."

15. On the relationship between the environment and culture, see Kottak, "The New Ecological Anthropology"; Low, "Cultural Conservation of Place."

16. Coastal Conservation League (website, 2010); TopRetirements.com website, "South Carolina Low Country Popular with Boomers"; "Lowcountry among Nation's Top 100 Fastest-growing Areas"; Fretwell, "Study Shows South Carolina Lost 142,000 Acres of Forests between 1993–2000." On development and growth trends in South Carolina, see Urban Land Institute, *Growing by Choice or Chance,* and the Charleston Regional Development Alliance, "Market Profile" (website). For an overview of southern environmental history, see Stewart, "Southern Environmental History."

17. Mills, quoted in Chamberlain, "Trying for Balance in Rural Development"; Caldwell, quoted in Cushman, "South Carolinians Nurture a Little Cause That Could," and in Maze, "Some Affluent Arrivals Seek Out Ways to Become Involved with Charleston Groups." See also Johnson and Zipperer, "Culture, Place, and Urban Growth in the U.S. South."

18. See Cohen et al., "Environmental Orientations."

19. Original data that inform this book come from a range of ethnographic and archival sources. Focus-group and individual interviews were conducted with a range of citizens in the lowcountry. One hundred eighty-one individuals were interviewed through twenty

focus groups from 2006 to 2008. These groups included home owners' association representatives, conservation groups, rural residents in the Sewee to Santee area, and municipal planners. Surveys were conducted with local elected officials (2000), residents (2003), community association residents and managers (2006–2007), farmers (2006–2008), sweetgrass basket makers (2002–2003, 2004–2005, 2006–2008). Individual interviews were conducted with those identified as key informants (2000–2010; with several in-depth interviews with key leaders in the region in 2010) through a snowball sample technique. I observed a multitude of public hearings and events related to conservation and growth in the region. Local newspapers, government documents, websites of interest, and other archival materials have also been examined. For a ten-year period I collaborated with hundreds of undergraduate and graduate students on research projects examining environmental perceptions, conservation, development, and community in the region. Throughout this period I collaborated and published case-based research studies with other scholars in the disciplines of political science, sociology, geography, geology, history, biology, ecology, psychology, engineering, economics, botany, public policy, and anthropology. Verbatim transcriptions were made of all individual and group interviews. Most interviews were conducted in confidentiality, and the names of the interviewees are withheld by mutual agreement.

20. On ethnography and its research methods, see Wolcott, *Ethnography,* and Richardson, "Evaluating Ethnography." The challenges of ethnographic research are many: "While ethnography is essentially descriptive in intent, the process of describing the activities and realities of other people is not as straightforward a task as we often assume. First, there are problems inherent in the description of even the most commonplace or 'obvious' of events and activities.

Second are perhaps more vexing problems which derive from the ethnographer's interest not simply in 'events' and 'activities' themselves—if there be such—but in the ways in which they are engaged in, guided, described, and generally assigned significance by group members." (Emerson, *Contemporary Field Research,* 19). See also Patton, *Qualitative Research and Evaluation Methods.* Environmental perception as a field of study is surveyed in Saarinen et al., *Environmental Perception and Behavior.* For a good example of a study of shifting environmental perceptions in a particular community, see Brehm and Eisenhauer, "Environmental Concern in the Mormon Culture Region."

21. Cronon, "In Search of Nature," 52.

22. Coastal Conservation League staff member, focus group interview with the Donnelly Foundation, 2007.

23. Weathers, quoted in "South Carolina Preserves Sandy Island." For an examination of the Sandy Island case, see Halfacre et al., "Environmental Decision-making and Community Involvement."

24. For a sophisticated analysis of the elusive and often ironic nature of how people perceive "nature" and "conservation," see Cronon, "The Trouble with Wilderness."

25. Horry County is on the northern edge of the lowcountry region. Because of the concentrated tourist industry around Myrtle Beach, it is more exceptional than representative of the other eight counties.

26. Monroe, quoted in Brinson, "Nature and Nurture."

Chapter 1: The Lowcountry Environment—Past and Present

1. "An Old Letter, (About March 1671)," 308. Some observers refer to the lowcountry as encompassing those coastal counties south of and including Charleston; others consider

the lowcountry to be all of South Carolina's coastal counties below Horry; and still others prefer a broader definition that incorporates all eleven counties below the fall line (change in gradient).

For the purposes of this book I have included those coastal counties north and east of the fall line south of Murrells Inlet, including Horry County, and down to the Savannah River and its border with Georgia. This area falls almost entirely within the boundaries of what environmental geographers have labeled the Middle Atlantic Coastal Plain, or Inner Coastal Plain, as well as the Southern Coastal Plain, or Outer Coastal Plain, ecoregions.

2. New South Associates, *A Cultural Resources Management Plan,* 8.

3. For a breezy overview of the lowcountry, see Zepke, *Coastal South Carolina.*

4. Adams, "Marshes of the Lowcountry" (website).

5. Travel Industry Association, *The Economic Impact of Travel on South Carolina Counties 2006.*

6. Meriwether, *The Expansion of South Carolina,* 4.

7. Griffith et al. "Ecoregions of North Carolina and South Carolina" (website), and Blagden and Beasley, *The Rivers of South Carolina.* See also "Old Rice Fields Spawn Controversy."

8. For a comprehensive guide to the environmental habitats of the lowcountry, see Lippson and Lippson, *Life along the Inner Coast.* Also useful is Vileisis, *Discovering the Unknown Landscape.*

9. Laurie and Chamberlain, *The South Carolina Aquarium,* 80–85, 92–106, 107–27, 150–60, 164–81.

10. F. Nelson, *Lower Santee River Environmental Quality Study.*

11. Kovacik and Winberry, *South Carolina* (1987). See National Park Service, *Low Country Gullah Culture;* Coakley, *Sweegrass Baskets;* F. Nelson, *The Cooper River Environmental Quality Study;* Marcy et al., *Fishes of the Middle Savannah River Basin;* and Able and Horan, *Paddling South Carolina.*

12. Edgar, *South Carolina.*

13. Kovacik and Winberry, *South Carolina.* See also Nicholls, *Paradise Found;* Silver, *A New Face of the Countryside,* 1–66.

14. C. Hudson, *The Southeastern Indians,* and Brickell, *The Natural History of North Carolina,* 273. On the effects of fire, see Pyne, *Fire in America,* and Cronon, *Changes in the Land,* 49–51.

15. Blagden and Beasley, *Rivers of South Carolina.*

16. See Steinberg, *Down to Earth.*

17. Edgar, *South Carolina,* 21–34.

18. Ibid., 49–52. See also Weir, *Colonial South Carolina.*

19. See W. Fraser, *Charleston! Charleston!* On the displacement of Native Americans, see J. Wright, *The Only Land They Knew.*

20. S. Wilson, "An Account of the Province of Carolina, 1682," 174–75. On the Huguenots, see Hirsch, *The Huguenots in Colonial South Carolina,* 3–46.

21. Archdale, "A New Description of That Fertile and Pleasant Province of Carolina." See Duffy, *Epidemics in Colonial America,* 164–77, 186–88, 197–200. See also Wood, "The Changing Population of the Eighteenth-century South," 57–132.

22. W. Marshall, *Assessing Change;* Glen, "An Attempt towards an Estimate of the Value of South Carolina," 178.

23. Morse, quoted in Chaplin, *An Anxious Pursuit,* 79.

24. Drayton, *A View of South Carolina*, 147. On the rice economy in South Carolina, see Carney, *Black Rice*; Chaplin, *An Anxious Pursuit*; Coclanis, *The Shadow of a Dream*; Edelson, *Plantation Enterprise in Colonial South Carolina*; Joyner, *Down by the Riverside*; Littlefield, *Rice and Slaves*; Tuten, *Lowcountry Time and Tide*; and Wood, *Black Majority*. A more comprehensive study is Dethloff, *A History of the American Rice Industry*. Useful articles include Clifton, "The Rice Industry in Colonial America"; Coclanis, "The Rise and Fall of the South Carolina Low Country"; and Stewart, "Rice, Water, and Power." For a contemporary tour of antebellum rice plantations, see Ward, "Historic Rice Plantations of South Carolina."

25. Minnix and Cowley, *Black Cargoes,* plates following 146. See also Dusinberre, *Them Dark Days,* 31–35.

26. Drayton, *A View of South Carolina*, 116.

27. Edelson, *Plantation Enterprise in Colonial South Carolina*, 141; and Doar, *Rice and Rice Planting*, 8. See also Ferguson, *Uncommon Ground*.

28. Blagden, *Lowcountry;* Garden, quoted inTibbetts, "Riches to Ruin," 4. The shift from upland to tidal rice planting accelerated after the Revolutionary War. See Chaplin, "Tidal Rice Cultivation."

29. Apple, "A Southern Legacy and a New Spirit"; Quincy, *Memoir of the Life of Josiah Quincy,* 72–73. Because rice production remained the most labor-intensive form of agriculture, it also required the heaviest concentration of slaves. There were four times as many slaves on rice plantations as on sugar plantations and ten times as many as were employed in cotton or tobacco production. See Olwell, *Masters, Slaves, and Subjects.*

30. Chaplin, "Tidal Rice Cultivation."

31. On the rise of the cotton culture in South Carolina, see L. Ford, *Origins of Southern Radicalism*, and L. Gray, *History of Agriculture.*

32. Wright, *Old South, New South.* See also Trimble, *Man-induced Soil Erosion.*

33. During the Civil War some five thousand Confederate troops were dispatched to protect the Edisto River Basin because of its strategic economic significance. See Reynolds, *Reconstruction in South Carolina,* and Lareau et al., *Lowcountry.*

34. Hayne, quoted in Channing, *Crisis of Fear,* 291, and Jenkin, quoted in Leifermann, "An Out-of-the-Way Isle in South Carolina."

35. Charleston," *New York Times*, March 9, 1865; Williamson, *After Slavery,* 43.

36. Simkins and Woody, *South Carolina during Reconstruction*, 282. See also J. Moore, "The Lowcountry in Economic Transition."

37. W. Fraser, *Charleston! Charleston!*, 275, 291; "Affairs in South Carolina."

38. "Southern Jottings and Journeyings"; Williamson, *After Slavery,* 106; and Carlton, "The Piedmont and Waccamaw Regions." See also McCurry, *Masters of Small Worlds*, and Edgar, *South Carolina*, 372–76.

39. "Great Damage Caused by Storms"; "The Charleston Cyclone"; "Ruined by the Floods"; "The Path of the Storm"; "In the Wrecked Territory"; "On the Way to Beaufort"; "Sea Islands Overwhelmed"; "Gov. Tillman's Anxiety"; "The Cotton Crop"; "The Sea Islands Suffer"; "Big Storm in the South"; "Charleston in Grip of Fatal Hurricane"; and Tuten, "Bad Storms Rising."

40. Williamson, *After Slavery,* 142. See also Clifton, "Twilight Comes to the Rice Kingdom," 151. On black land ownership patterns, see Schweniger, *Black Property Owners in the South.*

41. See Rose, *Rehearsal for Reconstruction,* and Pollitzer, *The Gullah People and Their African Heritage.*

42. Pinchot, "Southern Forest Products and Forest Destruction and Conservation."

43. *New York Lumber Trade Journal* 68 (May 16, 1887), cited in Earley, *Looking for Long-leaf,* 204. See also Cowdrey, *This Land, This South,* 111–14; Gates, "Federal Land Policy in the South"; and M. Williams, *Americans and Their Forests,* 238–88.

44. See Clark, *The Greening of the South,* 14–25.

45. Harrison, *How to Get Rich in the South,* 189–92.

46. Cooper and Terrill, *American South,* 128.

47. Watson, *Handbook of South Carolina,* 548, 549, and Clark, *The Greening of the South,* 49.

48. Shick and Doyle, "The South Carolina Phosphate Boom."

49. See Tibbetts, "The Bird Chase."

50. Cuthbert and Hoffius, *Northern Money, Southern Land,* xxii. On the hunting culture in the Carolinas, see Marks, *Southern Hunting in Black and White.*

51. Clayton, *Mill and Town in South Carolina.* See also Daniel, *Breaking the Land.*

52. Tindall, *The Emergence of the New South,* 121–22. See also "Why the Deadly Boll Weevil?"

53. Petty, *Twentieth-century Changes in South Carolina Population,* 160, 180.

54. C. Brown, "Modernizing Rural Life."

55. Rutledge, "What Price Power?"; Rutledge, "Night Is in the Pinelands." See also Hart, "The Santee-Cooper Landscape."

56. See Edgar, *History of Santee Cooper,* and Bostick, *Sunken Plantations.*

57. Porcher and Fick, *The Story of Sea Island Cotton,* 108, 131.

58. Byrnes, quoted in Grantham, *The South in Modern America,* 267. See also Cobb, *The Selling of the South* and *Industrialization and Southern Society.*

59. On the pulp/paper industry in the South, see Clark, *The Greening of the South.*

60. Data about the timber industry in South Carolina are available at the South Carolina Forestry Commission website, http://www.state.sc.us/forest/ (accessed 2 August 2009). On the importance of longleaf pine in the Carolinas, see Earley, *Looking for Long Leaf.* The environmental effects of the southern pulpwood industry are summarized in M. Williams, *Americans and Their Forests,* 238–330.

61. Goldfield, *Promised Land,* 197.

62. Faulkner, "On Fear," 98. See also Schulman, *From Cotton Belt to Sunbelt.*

63. Moore, "The Lowcountry in Economic Transition"; Frady, "Mendel Rivers, the Military Congressman"; R. D. Johnson, *Congress and the Cold War,* 159. See also King, "Federal Funds Pour into Sunbelt States."

64. A. Porter, "South Carolina Industries," and Monk and Fretwell, "DHEC under Fire." See also Fretwell, "South Carolina Environmental Board's Rules Get Tough on Polluters."

65. Edgar, *South Carolina,* 583, and Coley, "The Road to Urban Sprawl?" See also Bass and Poole, *The Palmetto State.* For similar trends across the nation, see Rome, *The Bulldozer in the Countryside.*

66. Riddle, "As Hilton Head Grows, What of the Environment?"

67. See Austin, "Resident Perspectives"; Elmendorf and Luloff, "Using Key Informant Interviews"; Luloff, "The Doing of Rural Community Development Research."

68. Berkeley-Charleston-Dorchester Council of Governments, *Berkeley County Comprehensive Plan* (1999), 7. See also Dolah et al., *The Condition of South Carolina Estuarine and Coastal Habitats during 1999–2000.*

69. Peirce and Johnson, "A Powerful Wave of Growth"; Marshall, *Ashley Scenic River Management Plan,* 2; Petersen, "Tale of Two Cities Highlights Charleston's Growth Concerns." See also Petersen, "Westvaco in Transition."

70. South Carolina Budget and Control Board, "Data about South Carolina and Its People." Wilbert, "Coastal Area Explodes with Growth Woes"; London and Hill, *Land Conversion in South Carolina;* and Menchaca, "Foundation Grants $4 Million to Protect Forests on South Carolina Coast."

71. London and Hill, *Land Conversion in South Carolina;* Coastal Conservation League website, "Regions: South Coast." The Nature Conservancy reports in its website's "About Us" section that the state is "the 40th largest in the nation and the 10th fastest growing. South Carolina has one of the highest rural-to-urban land conversion rates of all 50 states." See also Allen and Lu, "Modeling and Predicting Future Urban Growth in the Charleston Area" (website); Riddle, "South Carolina Confronts Urban Sprawl."

72. Travel Industry Association, *The Economic Impact of Travel on South Carolina Counties 2006.*

73. Berkeley-Charleston-Dorchester Council of Governments, *Berkeley County Comprehensive Plan,* 18; Beach, "The Greening of South Carolina."

Chapter 2: The Emergence of a Conservation Culture

1. "Land Conservation Adds to Value of Lowcountry Life"; "Support Sanford Conservation Plan."

2. Tibbetts, "New Visions for Growth." See Lee, "Is There a Place for Private Conversation in Public Dialogue?" In addition to ways in which the conventional media have promoted the conservation culture, *Coastal Heritage* magazine, a quarterly publication of the South Carolina Sea Grant Consortium, has been a highly visible and in-depth source of information about the status of the lowcountry's natural environment and its cultural heritage. The consortium is a public-university-based "network supporting research, education, and outreach to conserve coastal resources and enhance economic opportunity for the people of South Carolina." See the South Carolina Sea Grant Consortium's *Changing Face of South Carolina.*

3. Property Rights Foundation of America website, *Biography: Mark Nix;* Behre, "Rezoning Hot Topic of Debate." By 2005 Nix was insisting that the South Carolina Landowners Association was not simply "promoting unbridled growth but rather well-planned growth geared towards the benefit of the entire community." Nix, "Land Restrictions Costly." See also Petersen, "The Gobbling Up of the Lowcountry."

4. See Vig and Kraft, *Environmental Policy for the Twenty-first Century;* Vig and Faure, *Green Giants?;* Klyza and Sousa, *American Environmental Policy;* Rosenbaum, *Environmental Politics and Policy;* Rome, "'Give Earth a Chance.'"

5. See Kingdon, *Agendas, Alternatives, and Public Policies;* Sabatier, *Theories of the Policy Process.* On punctuated equilibrium as a descriptive hypothesis in biology, see Gould and Eldridge, "Punctuated Equilibria," and Gould, *The Structure of Evolutionary Theory.*

6. Repetto, *Punctuated Equilibrium,* 4. See also Baumgartner and Jones, *Agendas and Instability in American Politics;* True et al., "Punctuated-Equilibrium Theory"; Jones, *Reconceiving Decision-making in Democratic Politics.*

7. Prominent environmentalist, quoted in Lee, "Conservation as a Territorial Ideology," 312.

8. South Carolina Coastal Zone Management Act, *Congressional Findings,* U.S. Code 16 (2010) § 1451 et seq., and *Report of the South Carolina Blue Ribbon Committee on Beachfront Management,* i.

9. *Report of the South Carolina Blue Ribbon Committee on Beachfront Management,* i.

10. Repetto, *Punctuated Equilibrium,* 9; Woman 2 (Department of Planning, City of Charleston), focus group interview with the author. The following focus group interviews informed Tracy Duffy's 2007 master's thesis, "Planners' Response to Environmental Change in the Lowcountry of South Carolina." Staff (Department of Planning, City of Charleston) and Neighborhoods (City of Charleston), focus group interviews with the author, 2007; Department of Planning (Town of Mount Pleasant), focus group interview with the author, 2007; Community Association focus group interview with the author, 2006–2007; Staff (Coastal Conservation League, the Nature Conservancy, Ducks Unlimited, Lowcountry Open Land Trust, Southern Environmental Law Center), focus group interviews with the Donnelly Foundation, 2006–2007. All interviews were conducted in confidentiality, and the names of the interviewees are withheld by mutual agreement.

11. See Duane, *Shaping the Sierra.*

12. Fulton, *Who Sprawls Most?*

13. Schneider, "The Suburban Century Begins"; Flint, *This Land,* 1; Ford, quoted in Petersen, "Sprawl, Traffic Arising from a Surprising Source."

14. See also Baxandall and Ewen, *Picture Windows;* Donaldson, *The Suburban Myth;* Duany et al., *Suburban Nation;* Fishman, *Bourgeois Utopias;* Jackson, *Crabgrass Frontier;* Kruse and Sugrue, *The New Suburban History;* Rome, *The Bulldozer in the Countryside;* Ullman, *The Suburban Economic Network.* See also Tucker, "The Battle over Sprawl," and C. Schmidt, "The Specter of Sprawl."

15. See Garreau, *Edge City,* and Teaford, *Post-Suburbia.*

16. Rouse, quoted in "Cities: Hope for the Heart"; Robert Reich, quoted in Blakely and Snyder, *Fortress America,* 24; "The City: Starting from Scratch."

17. Weaver, quoted in "Cities: Hope for the Heart." Suburbia has become more inclusive and diverse. There are now blue-collar and minority-centered suburbs. See also Berger, *Working-Class Suburb;* Kruse, *White Flight;* B. Williams, *Black Workers in an Industrial Suburb.*

18. Duany et al., *Suburban Nation,* x; "The New American Land Rush"; "Environment: The Costs of Sprawl"; Parris Glendenning, quoted in Thompson, "Asphalt Jungle." For a less sympathetic view of the new urbanism and more positive views of sprawl, see Bruegman, *Sprawl;* Cox, *War on the Dream;* A. Marshall, *How Cities Work;* Postrel, "The Pleasantville Solution."

19. McPhee, *Encounters with the Archdruid,* 121; W. Marshall, *Ashley Scenic River Management Plan,* 2; R. Brinson, "Looks Like We're Getting Serious about Controlling Growth." See also Wyche, "The Fiscal Impact of Sprawl in South Carolina."

20. Petersen, "Tale of Two Cities Highlights Charleston's Growth Concerns"; Menchaca, "A Conversation with Joe Riley"; Hardin, "Report Advises S.C. to Rein in Sprawl." In 2001 a Rutgers University study ranked South Carolina as the fifth fastest-sprawling state in the nation. See Tibbetts, "The Freeway City." On the pulp/paper industry in the South, see Clark, *The Greening of the South.*

21. Lessard, "The World Turned Inside Out."

22. See "Timber Giant May Sell Land"; McDermott, "MeadWestvaco's 70,000 Acre Plan." See also "Study: S.C. to Lose Forests to Sprawl."

23. Menchaca and Hicks, "MeadWestvaco to Sell 6,600 Acre Tract"; Petersen and Menchaca, "Art of the Deal"; "Great Prospect for Poplar Grove"; Petersen and Munday, "Lender Foreclosing on Watson Hill."

24. Riley, quoted in Hardin, "Report Advises S.C. to Rein in Sprawl"; Beach, quoted in Bartelme, "Sell-off Talk Prompts Thrills, Chills"; Peirce and Johnson, "A Powerful Wave of

Growth." See also Petersen, "MeadWestvaco in Transition"; Barringer, "Deals Turn Swaths of Timber Company Land into Development-Free Areas"; Department of Planning Staff (Town of Mount Pleasant), focus group interview with the author, 2007; Staff (Department of Planning, City of Charleston), focus group interview with the author, 2007; Staff (Low Country Open Land Trust, Coastal Conservation League, the Nature Conservancy, Southern Environmental Law Center, and Ducks Unlimited), focus group interviews with the Donnelly Foundation, 2006–2007.

25. South Carolina Budget and Control Board, "Data about South Carolina and Its People"; Passandre, quoted in Wilbert, "Coastal Area Explodes with Growth Woes"; London and Hill, *Land Conversion in South Carolina;* Menchaca, "Foundation Grants $4 Million to Protect Forests on South Carolina Coast"; Porter, "Studies Project Growth." See also Behre, "Imagining Charleston 100 Years from Now."

26. Bartelme, "Sell-off Talk Prompts Chills, Thrills"; London and Hill, *Land Conversion in South Carolina;* W. Wise, "Sprawl Called Biggest Threat to Forests." The Nature Conservancy's website reports the state is "the 40th largest in the nation and the 10th fastest growing. South Carolina has one of the highest rural-to-urban land conversion rates of all 50 states." See also Nemirow and Baugh, "Nature Conservancy Grows Its Presence in Upstate"; Coastal Conservation League focus group interview with the Donnelly Foundation, 2006. See Allen and Lu, "Modeling and Predicting Future Urban Growth in the Charleston Area" (website).

27. Bartelme, "Tri-County Growth Binge 'Not a Good Pattern'"; Behre, "Imagining Charleston 100 Years from Now"; Lane, quoted in Petersen, "The Gobbling Up of the Lowcountry"; Waldo, "Sprawl Biggest Issue"; Riley quoted first in Menchaca, "A Conversation with Joe Riley," and second in A. Porter, "Studies Project Growth." See also Hardin, "Report Advises S.C. to Rein in Sprawl"; Porter, "Studies Project Growth"; Wyche, "The Fiscal Impact of Sprawl in South Carolina."

28. "Poplar Grove Conservation Victory." See also, for example, K. Smith, "South Carolina: How Shall We Grow?"; Ramsey, "Study Finds South Carolina Land Development Increased Faster than Population."

29. Conroy, "Don't Destroy Beaufort, Lowcountry." Conroy's letter to the editor, reprinted in the *Island Packet* (Hilton Head-Bluffton, S.C.), generated numerous responses. See, for example, "Novelist Decries Sprawl."

30. "A County in Crisis."

31. Swindell, "Residents Seek State Growth Laws"; Hicks, "Growth Takes Toll on South Carolina's Coastal Culture." See also Quick, "Mount Pleasant Struggles with Sprawl," and Fretwell, "Study Shows South Carolina Lost 142,000 Acres of Forests between 1993–2000."

32. Hicks, "Growth Takes Toll on South Carolina's Coastal Culture"; "Charleston-Area Traffic Woes Get Worse"; "Lowcountry among Nation's Top 100 Fastest-Growing Areas."

33. Behre, "Imagining Charleston 100 Years from Now."

34. "Report Links Sprawl to Declining Coastal Health." See also "Sprawl Ruining Coastal Waters, Report Says." One tangible indicator of shifting attitudes toward development was displayed by MeadWestvaco. In 2007 the company decided to quit selling large tracts of land to developers so as to ensure that its remaining holdings were developed with an emphasis on environmental conservation and preservation. See "MeadWestvaco's Extraordinary Land Challenge and Commitment." See also Barkes, "Water Quality Protection in Local Communities."

35. Wentworth, quoted in "Development Booms in Hurricane Zones." On the complex dynamics of Hurricane Hugo, see Lennon et al., *Living with the South Carolina Coast.*

36. Commission on Engineering and Technical Systems, *Hurricane Hugo*.

37. Parker, "Hurricane Gave Insurance Industry a Wakeup Call." On Hugo's impact on lowcountry forests, see "South Carolina Forest Shows Nature's Ability to Take Storms in Stride"; Gruson, "Healing Comes Slowly to Woods and Streams Where Hurricane Left Death."

38. Man 5 (Department of Planning, City of Charleston), focus group interview with the author, 2007; "Constant Peril of Overflow." See also Behre, "How We've Changed."

39. Staff (Department of Planning, Town of Mount Pleasant), focus group interview with the author, 2007; Luloff, "The Doing of Rural Community Development Research"; Austin, "Resident Perspectives"; Elmendorf and Luloff, "Using Key Informant Interviews." On the notion of recovery machines, see Pais and Elliott, "Places as Recovery Machines."

40. "A Hurricane's Fury Fast Forgotten"; Cochrane, quoted in Hagenbaugh, "Economic Growth from Hurricanes Could Outweigh Costs."

41. Applebome, "Hugo's 3-year Wake"; Mullener, "A Sister City Flourishes."

42. Man 4 (Georgetown Community Associations), focus group interview with the author, 2006.

43. Group 4 (Sewee to Santee residents), focus group interview with the author, January 2007; Johnson and Halfacre, "Resident Place Identities in Rural Charleston County, South Carolina"; Minis, "Changing Character."

44. Group 4 (Sewee to Santee residents), focus group interview with the author, January 2007.

45. Applebome, "Hugo's 3-year Wake"; Tullos, "Taking on the Wheels of Change"; Tullos, "Taking Another Look at the 701 Corridor and Suburban Sprawl." On trends in post-Hugo development, see Chamberlain, "Trying for Balance in Rural Development"; "Lowcountry among Nation's Top 100 Fastest-Growing Areas"; Minis, "Changing Character." Of course it is very difficult to document an exact cause-effect relationship between the hurricane and the surge of development in the lowcountry during the 1990s and since. There are other reasons why development surged after 1989, including the growing popularity of Spoleto, the spring arts festival in Charleston that attracts thousands of visitors from across the country and the globe. But as is true in fire-ravaged southern California, the threat of natural disasters does not deter hordes of people from moving to an area. On the economic impact of hurricanes and Hurricane Hugo in particular, see Guimaraes et al., *Wealth and Income Effects of Natural Disasters*. See also Burton et al., *The Environment as Hazard*, and the 2004 newspaper article "Development Booms in Hurricane Zones." On the role of natural disasters in American history, see Rozario, *The Culture of Calamity*, and Steinberg, *Acts of God*. The concept of creative destruction was first introduced by German sociologist Werner Sombart and later elaborated on and popularized by the Hungarian economist Joseph Schumpeter.

46. Hagood, in interview with the author, February 25, 2011.

47. Behre, "How We've Changed"; Harness and Pilkey, quoted in Applebome, "After Hugo."

48. Tibbetts, "Disaster Resilience."

49. Walsh, "Newcomers Interested in Growth Issues."

50. Dawe, "Hugo's Legacy"; Glover, "Ground Zero." See also Applebome, "Outlook Risky."

51. Piacente, "As Earth Warms, Seas May Rise." See also Langley, "Climate Forecast Ominous"; Langley, "Two-foot Rise in Sea Level Predicted This Century"; Munday, "Two Lowcountry Cities Start Effort to Curb Global Warming"; Jakubiak, "Study: Global Warming Will Impact Carolina Coast"; Slade, "S.C. Lawmakers Deem Threat of Global Warming

Serious"; Stock, "A Chilling View of Warming"; Slade, "Poll Says Global Warming Is Growing Concern in S.C."; Slade, "Concerns Rise with the Seas"; Slade, "Global Fever"; Slade, "Mayor Riley Wants City to Get Greener"; Slade, "Coalition Takes Aim at Emissions"; Peterson, "Climate Change Could Hurt Fort Sumter"; Behre, "Climate Change Is Hot Topic Today"; Tibbetts, "Sea-Level Rise."

52. See "Miles of South Carolina Coastline at Stake." See also Intergovernmental Panel on Climate Change, *Fourth Assessment Report.*

53. See Wyche, "Beach Erosion"; "Opposition to Beach Regulation Mounting"; "Sellout Beach Pact Protested"; "Out with the Tide"; "Law to Stem S.C. Beach Erosion Called Too Little, Too Late by Some"; Mitchell, "Scientists."

54. Lucas v. South Carolina Coastal Council. See also Platt, "Life after Lucas"; Lennon et al., *Living with the South Carolina Coast.* The Lucas case gained widespread national attention, but it did not eviscerate the major provisions of the Beachfront Management Act. All new homes must be set back from the ocean, and no new seawalls can be constructed. In 2011 wealthy property owners on Hilton Head Island challenged new more-restrictive state guidelines related to beachfront construction. The new guidelines resulted in part from concern about long-term sea-level rise along the South Carolina coast.

55. Behre, "Imagining Charleston 100 Years from Now"; Slade, "Charleston Makes Pledge to Cut Emissions"; "Heed Consensus on Warming." See also Koob, "Under the Sea."

56. Sanford, "A Conservative Conservationist?"; Slade, "Mayor Riley Wants City to Get Greener." See also Petersen, "Area-Defining Marshes Drowning."

57. Frost, "Mayors Urging Action on Climate Change"; "Groups to Sponsor Forum on Global-Warming Issues"; "Gov. Sanford Names Climate Change Group"; Sanford, "A Conservative Conservationist?"

58. "Miles of South Carolina Coastline at Stake."

59. Behre, "Sprawl Summit Makes Dialogue Its Main Focus"; Behre, "Summit Urges Smart Growth." See also Waldo, "County Greenbelt Plan Wins '06 Planning Award."

Chapter 3: Leveraged Leadership

1. On the development of the Coastal Conservation League, see Cushman, "South Carolinians Nurture a Little Cause That Could"; Quick, "South Carolina Coastal Conservation League's Long Crusade"; Petersen, "CCL: From Small Time to Big Deal"; Fretwell, "Dana Beach Is King of Conservation."

2. Beach, in interview with the author, April 9, 2010.

3. Speth, quoted in Quick, "South Carolina Coastal Conservation League"; Cushman, "South Carolinians Nurture a Little Cause That Could." I served on the board of directors of the Coastal Conservation League from 2001 to 2007.

4. Beach, quoted in Riddle, "South Carolina Confronts Urban Sprawl"; Forrester, quoted in Quick, "South Carolina Coastal Conservation League."

5. Beach, in interview with the author, April 9, 2010; Lareau, quoted in Quick, "South Carolina Coastal Conservation League."

6. Quick, "South Carolina Conservation League."

7. Beach, "The Greening of South Carolina."

8. Petersen, "CCL: From Small Time to Big Deal"; Quick, "South Carolina Coastal Conservation League."

9. "Twenty Years of Coastal Protection"; Lee, "Conservation as a Territorial Ideology," 313; "Twenty Years of Coastal Protection." See also Margerum, "A Typology of Collaboration Efforts"; Wondolleck and Yaffee, *Making Collaboration Work.*

10. Lee, "Conservation as a Territorial Ideology"; Ravenel, quoted in Quick, "South Carolina Coastal Conservation League."

11. Northouse, *Leadership: Theory and Practice;* Manolis et al., "Leadership: A New Frontier in Conservation Science." See also Burns, *Leadership,* and Bass, *Leadership and Performance beyond Expectations.* For a brief overview of the transformational (and transactional) leadership models, see Northouse, *Leadership:Theory and Practice,* 175–79. Bass, *Leadership and Performance beyond Expectations;* and Bass and Riggio, *Transformational Leadership;* Bass and Avolio, "The Implications of Transactional and Transformational Leadership"; Bass and Avolio, *Improving Organizational Effectiveness.* See also Bennis and Nanus, *Leaders;* Kouzes and Posner, *The Leadership Challenge.*

12. Christensen, "Foreword," in Gordon and Berry, *Environmental Leadership,* x. See also Redekop. "Introduction: Connecting Leadership and Sustainability"; Manolis et al., "Leadership"; Greenleaf, *The Servant as a Leader,* and Greenleaf, *On Becoming a Servant Leader;* Ferdig, "Sustainability Leadership"; Conger, "Charismatic and Transformational Leadership in Organizations"; Conger and Kanungo, *Charismatic Leadership in Organizations;* Snow, *Voices from the Environmental Movement,* and Snow, *Inside the Environmental Movement;* The Conservation Fund, "Conservation Leadership Network" (website). National Conservation Leadership Institute, "NCLI 2008–09 Cohort 3 Annual Report" (website); Dietz et al., "Defining Leadership in Conservation."

13. These researchers developed a model of environmental leadership that identified personal values (openness to change, self-transcendence, and ecocentrism), personality characteristics (need for achievement, need for affiliation, emotional maturity, self-confidence, and need for power), and leadership skills (interpersonal, technical, conceptual, and political) as being the drivers for the leadership behaviors (transformational, or innovator, facilitator, mentor, broker; transactional, or producer, coordinator, director, monitor). Ecocentric management or a focus on adaptive, sustainable organizational and societal well-being and ecologically sustainable relationships (systems including natural, social, and global/environmental as well as individual and interorganizational) are affected by the leadership behaviors and influence them. See Egri and Herman, "Leadership in the North American Environmental Sector." See also Shin and Zhou, "Transformational Leadership Conservation, and Creativity"; Meyerson and Kline, "Psychological and Environmental Empowerment." For the connections between personality and transformational leadership see Judge and Bono, "Five-factor Model of Personality and Transformational Leadership."

14. Gordon and Berry, *Environmental Leadership,* 104. Gordon and Berry identify the six ingredients crucial to environmental leadership: 1) prepare to be a leader and a follower; 2) think frequently and positively about change; 3) strive to develop the capacity to think broadly and flexibly; 4) learn to listen effectively; 5) know and practice your values/ethics; and 6) be a lifelong learner.

15. See Rooke and Tobert, "Seven Transformations of Leadership."

16. See Boiral et al., "The Action Logics of Environmental Leadership"; Byrne and Bradley, "Culture's Influence on Leadership Efficiency"; Repetto, *Punctuated Equilibrium;* Baumgartner, "Strategies of Political Leadership in Diverse Settings."

17. Hagood, in interview with the author, February 25, 2011. See also Gallup Poll results: Gallup website, "State of the States: Midyear 2009." For example, in a mid-2009 poll, South Carolina is the sixth most conservative state in the United States (46 percent of those participating in the poll self-identify as "conservative"). In this same analysis Gallup provides a "net conservative" statistic (defined as the total percentage calling themselves conservative

minus the total percentage defining themselves as liberal). South Carolina is one of twelve states identified as "most conservative" in the United States.

18. Hambrick, "The Big Prize and the Art of Compromise"; Petersen and Menchaca, "Art of the Deal."

19. Beach, in interview with the author, April 9, 2010.

20. For Riley's background, see the City of Charleston official website.

21. Apple, "A Southern Legacy and a New Spirit."

22. Riley, in interview with the author, July 29, 2010.

23. Menchaca, "A Conversation with Joe Riley"; Riley, in interview with the author, July 29, 2010.

24. Hardin, "Respected Charleston, S.C., Newspaper Chairman Dies"; Lee, "Conservation as a Territorial Ideology," 313–14.

25. Lee, "Is There a Place for Private Conversation in Public Dialogue?," 72.

26. Over the last decade of data collection I repeatedly asked prominent activists in the region to share their lists of conservation leaders across sectors, especially elected officials, nonprofit organization contributors, real estate developers, and private citizens. I also used participant observation and documentary evidence to identify the leaders profiled in this chapter; Sanford, "A Conservative Conservationist?"

27. Lane, in interview with the author, and Riley, in interview with the author, July 29, 2010.

28. Campsen, in interview with the author, July 28, 2010; Campsen, quoted in Hicks, "Islands in the Lowcountry Marshes Face Fierce Development Pressure"; Campsen, in interview with the author, July 28, 2010.

29. Campsen, in interview with the author, July 28, 2010.

30. Sanford, in interview with the author, July 27, 2010; Langley, "Brighter Day Seen for Earth."

31. Langley, "Brighter Day Seen for Earth."

32. Ibid.

33. Graham, in interview with the author, July 29, 2010.

34. Ibid.

35. Lane, in interview with the author, and Campsen, in interview with the author, July 29, 2010.

36. Campsen, in interview with the author, July 28, 2010.

37. Lane, in interview with the author, July 29, 2010.

38. Ibid.

39. Lane, in interview with the author, July 29, 2010, and Campsen, in interview with the author, July 28, 2010.

40. Findlay, "There is a Lot of History There"; Stokes-Marshall, "Where I Stand on Important Issues" (personal blog). On efforts to preserve the Gullah-Geechee culture, see Pollitzer, *The Gullah People and Their African Heritage*; Tibbets, "Living Soul of Gullah," and Tibbetts, "Gullah's Radiant Light."

41. Stokes-Marshall, in interview with the author, July 28, 2010.

42. Ibid.

43. See, for example, White, "Seven Mile Relies on Basketry and Heritage to Keep History Alive."

44. Ravenel, "Sweetgrass"; "Sewing the Seeds for Future Generations."

45. Stokes-Marshall and Wigfall, quoted in Greene, "Readers' Choice, 2008 Giving Back Awards" (website).

46. In discussions with individuals in the region, several people were identified as leaders and/or important allies. For example, in state government: Robert Brown, Bill Dresher, David Thomas, Larry Martin, and Sally Murphy. In the conservation nonprofit sector: Ann Timberlake and Ben Gregg. In the private sector: Charles Fraser, Ted Turner, and Gaylord Donnelly.

Chapter 4: The Primacy of Land and Partnerships

1. Campsen, in interview with the author, July 29, 2010.
2. Leopold, "Land Pathology," in *"The River of the Mother of God,"* 212–13; Leopold, "Conservation: In Whole or In Part," in *"The River of the Mother of God,"* 311, 318. See also Freyfogle, *Why Conservation Is Failing.*
3. Hagood, "Lowcountry Open Land Trust."
4. Parks, e-mail message to the author, July 26, 2010. The counties included in these data are Jasper, Beaufort, Colleton, Charleston, Dorchester, Berkeley, Georgetown, and Horry.
5. Beach, in interview with the author, April 9, 2010.
6. Nixon, "Special Message to the Congress Outlining the 1972 Environmental Program" (website). See also Beatley, *Habitat Conservation Planning;* Burgess, *Fate of the Wild;* Keiter, *Keeping Faith with Nature.*
7. Center for Biological Diversity, "Our Story" (website); Taugher, "Activists' Suits Stir Talk of Species Act Changes"; Humes, *Eco Barons,* 97, 136. For an analysis of environmental advocacy organizations, see Bosso, *Environment, Inc.*
8. Hagood, e-mail message to the author, February 24, 2011. For sophisticated analyses of very different regional conservation strategies, see DeLeon, *Left Coast City;* Duane, *Shaping the Sierra;* Press, *Saving Open Space.*
9. Rivers, "Expand Hugh Lane's Bold Idea."
10. Leopold, "A Biotic View of Land," in *"The River of the Mother of God,"* 266–73.
11. Barringer, "Deals Turn Swaths of Timber Company Land into Development-free Areas"; Bartelme, "S.C. Weighs Laws to Acquire Large Swaths of Land"; Faraci, quoted in Barringer, "Deals Turn Swaths of Timber Company Land into Development-Free Areas." See also "Nature Conservancy, Westvaco to Preserve Endangered Habitats"; "Timely Land-preservation Bill."
12. Land Trust Alliance website, "Land Trust Alliance Fact Sheet"(2010).
13. Brewer, *Conservancy.*
14. Byers and Ponte, *The Conservation Easement Handbook.* On easements see Gustanski and Squires, *Protecting the Land.* On the influence of federal tax incentives on land trusts, see McLaughlin, "Increasing the Tax Incentives for Conservation Easement Donations." Freyfogle provides an eloquent argument against paying for preserves in *Why Conservation Is Failing.* See also Langley, "Tax Incentives Boost Lowcountry Conservation Easements."
15. Schofield, quoted in Fretwell, "Special Report."
16. "Raymond," comment on website of the *Beaufort (S.C.) Gazette* on story titled "County to Buy Parcels Near Okatie River to Prevent Their Development"; Hagood, e-mail message to the author, February 24, 2011.
17. The results of the study funded by the Donnelly Foundation were shared only with the organizations. I was given access to the interviews conducted with staff members. Focus group interviews (six ninety-minute focus group interviews; each group had from six to twelve participants) conducted for Donnelly Foundation Grant Project with Lowcountry Open Land Trust, Coastal Conservation League, the Nature Conservancy, Southern Environmental Law Center, and Ducks Unlimited staff members, 2006 and 2007. All focus

group interviews were conducted by a professional moderator. The Donnelly Foundation Project interviews informed Voelker's master's thesis "Applicability of Convergence Hypothesis at the Organizational Level." All interviews were conducted in confidentiality, and the names of the interviewees are withheld by mutual agreement.

18. Man 1 (Ducks Unlimited) and Woman 2 (Coastal Conservation League), focus group interviews with the Donnelly Foundation, 2006.

19. Woman 4 (the Nature Conservancy), focus group interview with the Donnelly Foundation.

20. Quick, "South Carolina Governor Pushes Land Conservation Bank at Summit"; Langley, "Tax Incentives Boost Lowcountry Conservation Easements." See also B. Kline, *A Brief History of the U.S. Environmental Movement.* A more extensive history of environmentalism can be found in Gottlieb, *Forcing the Spring.* For an overview of public policies, see Z. Smith, *The Environmental Policy Paradox,* and Rosenbaum, *Environmental Politics and Policy.*

21. Baysden, quoted in Stevens, "Keeping Development from Devouring Plantations"; Lee, "Conservation as a Territorial Ideology," 313.

22. Beach, discussion; Hagood, e-mail message to the author, February 24, 2011. See also Weir, *Colonial South Carolina.*

23. Woman 3 and Woman 1 (both from Ducks Unlimited), focus group interview with the Donnelly Foundation, 2006 .

24. Man 1 (Lowcountry Open Land Trust), focus group interview with the Donnelly Foundation, 2006, and Beach, in interview with the author, April 9, 2010.

25. Beach and Lane, quoted in Stevens, "Keeping Development from Devouring Plantations."

26. Land trusts often collaborate with developers to promote conservation-centered developments. See Fairfax et al., *Buying Nature.*

27. "Lessons We've Learned from the Land Boom."

28. One reference list for lowcountry environmental and conservation organizations available is the South Carolina Information Highway (SCIWAY) website. For environmental and conservation groups by region (coastal), see SCIWAY, "Coastal SC Environmental and Conservation Organizations." The coastal region has more groups than the midlands or upstate regions. For all groups registered on this site, see SCIWAY, "South Carolina Environmental Organizations—By Region."

29. The Nature Conservancy website, "About Us," "South Carolina 6/09 Update," and "Places We Protect." See also Langley, "Conservancy Puts Protecting Nature First"; "Land Purchase to Help Save Wildlife Habitat in South Carolina"; and Barringer, "Deals Turn Swaths of Timber Company Land into Development-Free Areas."

30. Dewig, "Protecting the Lowcountry"; Williams, quoted in Langley, "Conservancy Puts Nature First." See also Nemirow and Baugh, "Nature Conservancy Grows Its Lowcountry Presence."

31. Langley, "Saving Scenery"; Petersen, "Humble Island Leads to Conservation Legacy"; Lowcountry Open Land Trust website, "Land Protection." See also "25 Years of Conservation."

32. Southern Environmental Law Center website.

33. Southern Environmental Law Center website, "SELC's Long-term Strategic Action Plan" and "SELC's Greatest Hits."

34. Menchaca, "Foundation Grants $4 Million," and Wilbert, "Coastal Area Explodes with Growth Woes."

35. Nix, "Land Restrictions Costly." On Charleston County's Greenbelt program, see A. Porter, "County's Future Depends on Sales Tax, Leaders Told."

36. Ducks Unlimited website, "2009 State Conservation Report"; Ducks Unlimited website, "Lowcountry Initiative: Conservation Easements"; Robertson, "New Leader Has Ducks Unlimited Expanding Reach."

37. See Ron Nixon, "Cultures in Conflict."

38. J. Porter, "Building Diverse Communities."

39. Ibid. On Emory Campbell, see Minis, "Emory Campbell."

40. Staff members, quoted in Lee, "Is There a Place for Private Conversation in Public Dialogue?," 82–83; Lane, discussion. As Lee notes, not all coalition efforts at collaboration are successful. Pulling together numerous partners can be labor-intensive. See also three articles by Petersen, "Ex-Regulator Seeks Public-Private Alliances"; "Green Corridor"; "Preserving Our Coastal Forests."

41. Leopold, *The River of the Mother of God,"* 227.

42. Laurie, "ACE Basin 1988–1998." See also Blagden, *South Carolina's Wetland Wilderness.*

43. Leonard, quoted in Paras, "Wildlife Preserve or Tourist Destination?"

44. Lane, quoted in Ford, "Love of the Lowcountry"; Lane, quoted in Petersen, "ACE Basin at 20"; Lane, quoted in Paras, "Wildlife Preserve or Tourist Destination?"

45. Ford, "Love of the Lowcountry," 4.

46. Frampton, quoted in Paras, "Wildlife Preserve or Tourist Destination?" See also Humphries, "Roaming Carolina Low Country"; Stevens, "Keeping Development from Devouring Plantations"; Lee and Lee, "Rice Fields Cultivate Old Ways." On the racial and class issues in the ACE Basin, see Vollmer, "Sustainable Land-use Planning for the Ashepoo-Combahee-Edisto (ACE) Basin Region"; Lee, "Conservation as a Territorial Ideology"; Lee, "Is There a Place for Private Conversation in Public Dialogue?"

47. See Jeff Miller, "A River Runs around It"; Agee, "Best Known for Its Eco-system, Sandy Island Holds Historic Trove"; Bartelme, "Shifting Sands."

48. Castles Consulting Engineers, *A Conceptual Plan for Sandy Island.* See Paulsen, "Special Report: The Quiet Battle for Bull Creek."

49. Paulsen, "Special Report: The Quiet Battle for Bull Creek."

50. See "Residents of Island Find Bridge Threatening"; Pratt, quoted in Paulsen, "Special Report: A Different World on Sandy Island"; Weathers, quoted in Wilson, "South Carolina Preserves Sandy Island."

51. Farren, quoted in Smothers, "Proposal for a Bridge Intrudes on Island Life"; Jeff Miller, "An Education in Cultural Preservation."

52. Wall, "Sandy Island Developers Will Destroy Area's Resources." For the investigative series in the *State* newspaper, see Paulsen, "Special Report: A Handful of Powerful Families Hold Region's Fate"; Paulsen, "Special Report: A Different World on Sandy Island"; Paulsen, "Special Report: The Quiet Battle for Bull Creek"; Paulsen, "Three Roads, One Intersection: E. Craig Wall Jr."; Fretwell, "Special Report: Coalition is Fighting to Save Slice of S.C. Wilderness." See also Smothers, "Proposal for a Bridge Intrudes on Island Life."

53. "Coastal Council to Hear Sandy Island Development"; "What to Do with Sandy Island?"

54. Langley, "Sandy Island Bridge Plan Torn Down Again." See also Paulsen, "Failure of Bridge Plan Irks Sandy Island Owners"; Smothers, "Environment Fight Kills Plan for Bridge to Carolina Island."

55. See Langley, "Lowcountry Banking on Wetlands Savings Pays Off."

56. Halfacre et al., "Environmental Decision-making and Community Involvement."

57. Director, Coastal Management Division, South Carolina Ocean and Coastal Resource Management, and regional officer, United States Fish and Wildlife Service, quoted in Halfacre et al., "Environmental Decision-making and Community Involvement."

58. Chepesiuk, "Saving Sandy Island" (website); "State Closes Deal to Buy Sandy Island." See also Langley, "Refuge Plan Wins Wildlife Agency's OK."

59. Langley, "Refuge Plan Wins Wildlife Agency's OK"; "State Closes Deal to Buy Sandy Island." See also Soraghan, "State Owns Major Part of Island Property"; Fretwell, "Agency's Wetland-Tradeoff Policy Raises Questions."

60. Eckstrom and Larson, quoted in Wilson, "Ceremony Marks Island's Last Change"; "Treat Idyllic Island with Fitting Regard"; "This Deal Pleases Everyone"; Dayton, "Island Bargain Wins Award." See also Smothers, "Land on South Carolina Island Is Sold to State"; Langley, "Lowcountry Banking on Wetlands Savings Pays Off."

61. Staff member, South Carolina Department of Transportation, quoted in Halfacre et al., "Environmental Decision-making and Community Involvement"; Chepesiuk, "Saving Sandy Island" (website).

62. Holleman, "Conservationists Find Ways to Pay for Land Preservation." In late 2010 the Federal Highway Administration awarded the South Carolina Department of Transportation a sixty-foot ferry boat to serve the residents of Sandy Island. See G. Smith, "Sandy Island to Get Ferry."

63. South Carolina Conservation Bank website, "The S.C. Conservation Bank Act." See also "Conservation Bank: Wise Investment"; Hicks, "Conservation Bank Keeping Land Untouched." In 1976 the South Carolina General Assembly created the Heritage Trust Act which created the Heritage Trust, a nonprofit legal entity to purchase and protect special "irreplaceable" properties across the state. It was a major step for the conservation effort, but its funding and its scope were much more limited than those of the Conservation Bank. See Davis, "Preserving Our Natural Wealth."

64. See Beach, "Local Voices." On the mapping project, see Carswell and Robinson, *Conserving South Carolina.*

65. Roman, "Mayor Plants Bipartisan Seed."

66. Ibid.

67. Campsen, in interview with author, July 28, 2010. See also Quick, "South Carolina Governor Pushes Land Conservation Bank at Summit."

68. Quick, "South Carolina Governor Pushes Land Conservation Bank at Summit"; Campsen, quoted in Wenger, "Sanford Proposes Adding $20M to State Land Bank"; Peeler, quoted in "South Carolina Bill Would Create Land Bank."

69. "Conservation Bank Act Passed by S.C. Legislature." See also Holleman, "Conservationists Find Ways to Pay for Land Preservation"; Fretwell, "South Carolina Governor Signs Bill to Allow Protection of Wild Lands"; B. Marshall, "S.C. Must Get Serious about Conservation"; Robertson, "S.C. Desperately Needs Conservation Bank Act"; Robertson, "Land Initiative Year's Top Story"; "Saving the Conservation Bank."

70. "Saving the Conservation Bank"; Isham, quoted in Fretwell, "South Carolina Governor Signs Bill to Allow Protection of Wild Lands." See also Quick, "South Carolina Governor Pushes Land Conservation Bank at Summit."

71. On the Issues website, "Mark Sanford on Environment"; "Gov. Sanford's Budget to Add $20 Million to Conservation Bank." See also "Conservation Success Story"; "'Great Day' for Conservation"; "Gov. Sanford's Budget to Add $20 Million to Conservation Bank."

72. The Trust for Public Land website, "Beaufort County Land Acquisition Program"; district officer, National Marine Fisheries Service, quoted in Halfacre et al., "Environmental

Decision-making and Community Involvement." In 2010, 70 percent of Dorcester County referendum voters approved a greenbelt land purchasing program. See "Heed Voters on Green Space"; Greenways, Inc., website; and Waldo, "County Greenbelt Plan Wins '06 Planning Award." On the Charleston County Greenbelt program, see "Champion for Conservation."

73. In 2010 more than 70 percent of Dorchester County voters endorsed a referendum proposal to allocate money from property tax revenues to purchase and preserve rural lands. See "Heed Voters on Green Space."

74. Beach, in interview with the author, April 9, 2010; Petersen, "Tale of Two Cities Highlights Charleston's Growth Concerns."

75. Hicks, "Conservation Bank Keeping Land Untouched"; Petersen, "Tale of Two Cities Highlights Charleston's Growth Concerns." See also Freyfogle, "What is Land?; Freyfogle, "Goodbye to the Public-Private Divide."

Chapter 5: Growing by Choice: Community Planning

1. Johnson, Halfacre, and Hurley, "Resident Place Identities in Rural Charleston County, South Carolina."

2. Walinchus, "Tiny Town of Awendaw Feels Growing Pains."

3. Findlay, "Another Rural Battle Brews."

4. Jessica Johnson, "Election Splits Awendaw."

5. Findlay, "Awendaw Likely to OK Development"; Minutes of the Awendaw Town Council Meeting, December 7, 2006. See also Walinchus, "Town OKs 400–Home Subdivision"; Green, "Race Has No Part in Awendaw Development Debate."

6. Graham, in interview with the author, July 29, 2010.

7. Man 2 (Lowcountry Open Land Trust), focus group interview with the Donnelly Foundation, 2006.

8. Findlay, "Another Rural Battle Brews"; Chaffin, "Foreword," in Wilson et al., *Green Development*. The tools developed to better manage growth in the lowcountry did not stop growth, but they did improve the quality and reduce the damage of growth. The public benefits of growth have improved. In a similar vein social scientist Harvey Molotch has demonstrated that "the primary thrust of growth control has probably been to alter the ratio of public to private benefits from the projects that are built." See Molotch, "Urban Deals in Comparative Perspective," 184.

9. Blacklocke, "Comprehensive Land-Use Planning in South Carolina: Addressing New Challenges in Allocating Resources."

10. NIMBYISM is often portrayed in a critical light, but in fact the activities are not always a manifestation of self-interested negativism. See Kraft and Clary, "Citizen Participation and the Nimby Syndrome."

11. Man 1 (Lowcountry Open Land Trust), focus group interview with the Donnelly Foundation, 2006. For an overview of the literature regarding possible comprehensive conservation approaches, see Gruber, "Key Principles of Community-based Natural Resource Management." See also Knight and White, *Conservation for a New Generation;* Oldekop et al., "Understanding the Lessons and Limitations of Conservation and Development." For management (by scale and system) perspectives and ramifications, see Robbins, *Lawn People;* Layzer, *Natural Experiments;* and Scheffer, *Critical Transitions in Nature and Society.* Some economists have focused on assessing the financial advantages of conservation. See DiNapoli. *Economic Benefits of Open Space Preservation* (Office of the State Comptroller website); Groves et al., "Planning for Biodiversity Conservation." To view the resulting

map, see "South Carolina: A Conservation Vision," *S.C. Landscape Land Trust* (Lowcountry Open Land Trust website).

12. "S.C. Leaders See the Need for Growth Blueprint."

13. On the Comprehensive Planning Act, see Municipal Association of South Carolina, *Comprehensive Land Planning for Local Governments*, and Wyche, "Land Use Planning and Regulation."

14. South Carolina Local Government Comprehensive Planning Enabling Act. More recently the General Assembly has added "priority investment areas" and "transportation" to the required elements of comprehensive plans. On the role of such long-range plans in promoting more sustainable development, see Conroy and Berke, "What Makes a Good Sustainable Development Plan?"; Elmendorf and Luloff, "Using Ecosystem-based and Traditional Land-use Planning to Conserve Greenspace."

15. Lovettt, "Development Brings Challenges."

16. See Ramsey, "Sierra Club Wants Growth Plan Review."

17. Tibbetts, "Coastal Growth Hits Home."

18. "A County in Crisis"; Segal, "Hispanics Outnumber Blacks on Hilton Head."

19. "A County in Crisis"; Gioielli, "Developer Says Urban Sprawl Driven by Market." For insights into how a West Coast community adopted a more region-wide planning philosophy, see DeLeon, *Left Coast City,* 139–42.

20. Hagood, "New Planning Requirements Should Reduce Haphazard Development and Sprawl."

21. A. Porter, "Charting County's Future."

22. County of Charleston Zoning and Planning Department, "Part 2: Vision," in *Charleston County Comprehensive Plan Update* (website).

23. A. Porter, "Citizens Speak Out on Development"; A. Porter, "Land Use Plan Draws Suit Threat." See also A. Porter, "Land Use Plan Draws Support"; A. Porter, "Council's Landmark Decision."

24. A. Porter, "County Approves Plan to Control Rural Growth." County of Charleston Planning Department, *County of Charleston Comprehensive Plan, As Adopted by the Charleston County Council April 20, 1999.* Updated and adopted November 18, 2008; amended December 22, 2009.

25. Templeton, quoted in Tibbetts, "Coastal Growth Hits Home," 9. See also A. Porter, "Comprehensive Plan to Have a Big Impact"; and A. Porter, "Stay Solid on Comprehensive Plan."

26. Quick, "Planning Board Will Make Its Final Land Use Proposal"; Quick, "Urbanism Growth Part of Plan."

27. Quick, "Development Border Touches Nerve"; Quick, "Mt. Pleasant Considers Cap on Growth."

28. "No Sprawling Allowed."

29. Skalskie, "County Planners Envision Village to Help Tame Sprawl in Okatie."

30. Shapiro, "Okatie River Development Plan Gets Initial OK."

31. Shapiro, "1,252 New Homes Proposed for Land between S.C. 170 and the Okatie River"; and "Okatie Village: Osprey Point Planned United Development Agreement" (website).

32. Shapiro, "Planning Commission Says It Needs More Information on Okatie Village."

33. Beaufort County Planning Commission Minutes, February 4, 2008.

34. Shapiro, "Planning Commission Votes Down Okatie Village," and Shapiro, "Okatie Village Developers Agree to Pay County $10.7 Million."

35. Beaufort County Planning Commission Minutes, February 4, 2008.

36. Hilton Head Real Estate Report, "Here's a Classic Case of the TIME LINE!!" (blog).

37. Wilkinson, "South Carolina Residents Want Limits on Land Development."

38. Maki, "Charleston, S.C. Mayor Touts Smart Growth for Memphis."

Chapter 6: Conservation Communities

1. *I'On Homeowners Association Newsletter,* June 2, 2007.

2. On environmental amenities, see Johnston et al., "Rural Amenity Values and Length of Residency."

3. Survey discussed in *Retirement Living Newsletter,* February 2006.

4. Analysis covers data collected from a number of sources, including previous studies that examined subdivision conservation in the lowcountry. See Shuler, "Conserving Subdivided Nature."

5. Findlay and Slade, "Cities Battle Sprawl by Filling in the Holes"; Froelich, "Smart Growth."

6. Wilson et al., *Green Development,* 11.

7. Smart Growth America website.

8. Researchers have documented numerous negative ecological consequences induced by rapid growth and sprawling development. For more on the loss of open space and wildlife habitat from direct conversion and associated fragmentation, see Bastian et al., "Environmental Amenities and Agricultural Land Values"; Perlman and Milder, *Practical Ecology;* Ryan, "Comparing the Attitudes of Local Residents, Planners, and Developers"; Blinnikov et al., "Gated Communities of the Moscow Green Belt"; and Kaplan and Austin, "Out in the Country." See Cho et al., "Measuring Rural Homeowners' Willingness to Pay for Land Conservation Easements"; Elmendorf and Luloff, "Using Ecosystem-based and Traditional Land-use Planning to Conserve Greenspace"; Gobster and Rickenbach, "Private Forestland Parcelization and Development in Wisconsin's Northwoods"; Johnson and Klemens, *Nature in Fragments;* Smart Growth America website.

9. See Arendt, *Conservation Design for Subdivisions;* Bullard, *Growing Smarter;* Downs, "What Does 'Smart Growth' Really Mean?" Smart Growth has generated criticism as well as support. See Cox, "The Dangers of Smart Growth Planning"; Pozdena, *Smart Growth and Its Effects on Housing Markets.*

10. Wilkinson, "South Carolina State, Local Governments Split on Fixing Urban Sprawl"; "Loose Lips" (website). See also Burris, "Senator Pitches Planned Growth Legislation."

11. Behre, "Sprawl vs. Growth Debate to Move On."

12. "Unrealistic Expectations."

13. Swindell, "Residents Seek State Growth Laws."

14. Wilkinson, "Critics Blast Smart Growth Plan."

15. Surratt, "Critics Voice Views at Public Hearing on South Carolina Growth Bill"; Swindell, "Residents Seek State Growth Laws."

16. Hardin, "Harnessing Growth Portrayed as Vital."

17. B. Smith, "An Extra Million People Will Mean Big Growth."

18. Urban Land Institute, South Carolina Growth Initiative,"Growing by Choice or Chance: State Strategies for Quality Growth in South Carolina."

19. Hardin, "Report Advises S.C. to Rein in Sprawl"; "Growing by Choice or Chance: State Strategies for Quality Growth in South Carolina."

20. Hardin, "Report Advises S.C. to Rein in Sprawl."

21. Bozarth, "Citizens Should Demand Agency Restructuring, Sanford Says."

22. Sanford, "2008 State of the State Address" (website).

23. "Charleston-Area Realtors Launch Smart Growth Website and Advocacy Campaign" (website); Duany and Plater-Zyberk, "The Second Coming of the American Small Town," 21; Duany, quoted in Flint, *This Land*, 65.

24. See Gordon, "New Urbanism and Smart Growth"; Duany et al., *Suburban Nation*; Devlin, *What Americans Build and Why.*

25. Katz, quoted in Guilfoil, "New Urbanism Upscale Exercise in Nostalgia." See also Katz, *The New Urbanism*; Lynch, *A Theory of Good City Form*; Calthorpe, *The Next American Metropolis*; Duany et al., *Suburban Nation*; McCann, "Neotraditional Developments," 225; Congress for the New Urbanism website, *Charter.*

26. Padgett, "Saving Chapel Hill"; Bjelland et al., "The Quest for Authentic Place"; Reynolds, quoted in Tibbetts, "The Beauty of Sprawl," 7. See also Dover, *Charter of the New Urbanism*; Katz, *The New Urbanism.*

27. For critical views of the antisprawl movement, see Moore and Henderson, "Plan Obsolescence"; Postrel, "The Pleasantville Solution."

28. Duany, quoted in Flint, *This Land*, 66; Bartling, "The Magic Kingdom Syndrome." Although new-urbanist ideology seeks to mitigate the shortcomings of a shifting urban economy through architectural social engineering, it is often described as an ocularcentric (vision-centered) theory of normative city planning, skirting the deeper problems that it seeks to address.

29. A. Marshall, "A More Benevolent Sprawl," review of Duany et al., *Suburban Nation* (website).

30. Gordon, "New Urbanism and Smart Growth." See also Anderson, "Is Seaside Too Good to be True?"; Beauregard, "New Urbanism"; Bressi, *The Seaside Debates*; Grant, *Planning the Good Community*; Plas and Lewis, "Environmental Factors and Sense of Community in a Planned Town"; Ross, *The Celebration Chronicles*; Southworth, "Walkable Suburbs?"; Veninga, "Spatial Prescriptions and Social Realities," 480; Krieger, "The Costs—and Benefits?—of Sprawl"; Randolph, *Environmental Land Use Planning and Management.*

31. Wilkinson, "Sanford Wants to End Sprawl." See also "Growth at Tipping Point, Sanford Tells Conference."

32. See Pejchar et al., "Evaluating the Potential for Conservation Development."

33. Arendt, *Conservation Design*; Arendt, *Growing Greener.*

34. Arendt, *Conservation Design*, 2–3.

35. Ibid., 9. See also Mohammed, "The Economics of Conservation Subdivisions"; Frankston, "Nature as a Neighbor"; Arendt, "Linked Landscapes"; Austin and Kaplan, "Resident Involvement in Natural Resource Management"; Arendt, *Conservation Design.*

36. Arendt, *Conservation Design*, xvii; Arendt, quoted in Phua, "A Fight to Save the Special Things."

37. Phua, "A Fight to Save the Special Things"; Herring, in interview with the author, 2005, 2006, 2007.

38. Franklin, quoted in National Park Service, *Guiding Principles of Sustainable Design.*

39. On the emergence and nature of conservation developments, see Bjelland et al., "The Quest for Authentic Place"; Duerksen and Snyder, *Nature-friendly Communities*; Elmendorf and Luloff, "Using Ecosystem-based and Traditional Land-use Planning to Conserve Greenspace"; J. Kline, "Public Demand for Preserving Local Open Space"; McHarg, *Design with Nature*; Milder, "A Framework for Understanding Conservation Development"; Milder and Perlman, *Practical Ecology*; and Zimmerer, "The Reworking of Conservation Geographies."

40. See Aberly, *Futures by Design;* Lopez Barnett, *A Primer on Sustainable Building;* Calthorpe, *The Next American Metropolis;* Langdon, *Better Place to Live;* Lyle, *Regenerative Design for Sustainable Development;* Mantell et al., *Creating Successful Communities;* Roelofs, *Greening Cities.*

41. Bellah et al., *The Good Society,* 262.

42. See Nelson, *Private Neighborhoods;* Kabii and Horwitz, "A Review of Landholder Motivations and Determinants"; Foldvary, "Proprietary Communities and Community Associations," 258–88. Kennedy, "Residential Associations as State Actors"; MacCallum, "The Case for Land Lease Versus Subdivision," 371–400.

43. Kennedy, "Residential Associations as State Actors"; MacCallum, "The Case for Land Lease versus Subdivision"; Blandy and Lister, "Gated Communities"; Chen and Webster, "Homeowners Associations." See also Austin and Kaplan, "Resident Involvement in Natural Resource Management."

44. McDermott, "Project Forsakes Convention for Conservation"; Avery, quoted in Bucher, "Life in Harmony with Nature" (website); and Avery, "Proper Development Can Advance Cause of Conservation."

45. Avery, "Proper Development Can Advance Cause of Conservation."

46. Ibid.

47. Haltiwanger, "Developments Like Sewee Preserve Don't Really Help the Environment."

48. McDermott, "Project Forsakes Convention for Conservation."

49. Remax Island Realty, 2008 (website).

50. Boudoulf, "Sewee Preserve" (website).

51. Palmetto Bluff website.

52. Palmetto Bluff website, "Conservation"; Simon Hudson, interview with Donna London, *Your Day,* NPR, June 3, 2010; Reed, quoted in Shipnuck, "Growing Pains." In South Carolina, golf "generates more income than any entertainment or recreation activity in the state" and employs roughly thirty thousand people. There are more golf courses per capita in the lowcountry than anywhere else in the world. For more on the nature of golf trends and the industry of golfing, including a profile of the Kiawah Island Golf Resort, see Hudson and Hudson, *Golf Tourism.*

53. Shuler, "Conserving Subdivided Nature." Using Geographic Information Systems, document analysis, focus group interview content analysis, participant observation, and survey research, Shuler developed a typology for her master's thesis that highlighted each community's environmental design, management, and governance. Marketing analysis was conducted by students in my graduate Environmental Studies Case Studies course (2007) and reanalyzed for this book by the author. A cautionary note is needed, however, as these data include two locations with additional phases of development planned. Palmetto Bluff and Daniel Island were less than 50 percent built-out when I did the compilation, so at the time they included large parcels of land slated for future development. Still, using information gathered from developer representatives reveals that at completion 39 percent of Palmetto Bluff is to be open space, as is 10 percent of Daniel Island. While this number represents a rather dramatic drop in typical new urbanist or conservation development planning for Daniel Island, this project is based on principles of smart growth and new urbanism, suggesting a commitment to density and land-use efficiency rather than specifically to conserving particular island habitats or ecologies.

54. Shuler, "Conserving Subdivided Nature." Shuler identified four types of conservation-oriented communities: 1) open space conservationist; 2) developed nature conservationist;

3) natural amenity producer; and 4) man-made amenity producer. See her thesis for her interpretation of these categories. This book uses an alternative analysis.

55. Shuler, "Conserving Subdivided Nature." An earlier trend analysis is more carefully explored in Shuler's thesis. Data collection (GIS, focus group interviews, survey interviews) was funded through grants obtained by the author of this book who then was serving as Shuler's thesis adviser. In this book Shuler's data is reexamined to explore the role of development in the emergence of a conservation culture.

56. Kaplan and Austin, "Out in the Country"; Kearney, "Residential Development Patterns and Neighborhood Satisfaction"; Bastian et al., "Environmental Amenities and Agricultural Land Values"; and Kaltenborn and Bjerke, "Associations between Environmental Value Orientations and Landscape Preferences." See R. Nelson, *Private Neighborhoods;* Glasze, "Some Reflections on the Economic and Political Organisation of Private Neighbourhoods"; Blandy and Lister, "Gated Communities"; McCabe, "The Rules Are Different Here"; and Chen and Webster, "Homeowners Associations."

57. Stedman, "Is it Really Just a Social Construction?" See also Petersen, "Kiawah Island Tests Aim to Restore Wetlands"; Breffle et al., "Using Contingent Valuation"; Austin and Kaplan, "Resident Involvement in Natural Resource Management"; and Brody et al., "Exploring the Mosaic of Perceptions."

58. On Daniel Island, see Riddle, "Charleston, S.C."

Chapter 7: Sustainable Subdivisions, Conservation Communities

1. "Kiawah Island Gateway." See also Petersen, "Kiawah Neighbors Spark New Preservation Program." Of course some people argue that barrier islands should never be developed.

2. Riddle, "Upscale Homes for South Carolina Woods." See the Palmetto Bluff website. See Shuler, "Conserving Subdivided Nature." On the phenomenon of conservation communities, see Arendt, *Conservation Design for Subdivisions;* Austin and Kaplan, "Resident Involvement in Natural Resource Management"; Austin, "Resident Perspectives"; Barr and Gilg, "Sustainable Lifestyles"; Bastian et al., "Environmental Amenities and Agricultural Land Values"; Berkes, "Rethinking Community-based Conservation"; Brunn, "Gated Minds and Gated Lives"; Elmendorf and Luloff, "Using Ecosystem-based and Traditional Landuse Planning"; Hamlin, "Reading (Conservation Subdivision) Plans"; Kaltenborn and Bjerke, "Associations between Environmental Value Orientations and Landscape Preferences"; Kaplan and Austin, "Out in the Country"; James Miller, "Restoration, Reconciliation, and Reconnecting with Nature Nearby"; Kaplan et al., "Open Space Communities"; Kearney, "Residential Development Patterns"; J. Kline, "Public Demand"; Mohammed, "The Economics of Conservation Subdivisions"; and Zimmerman, "The 'Nature' of Urbanism."

3. Yablonski, "Marketing the Wealth of Nature."

4. Greer, *The Sands of Time.*

5. "The Little Emperor of Hilton Head," and Hilton, "Islander: Charles E. Fraser."

6. Hilton, "Islander: Charles E. Fraser."

7. "Deflated Developer."

8. Danielson, *Profits and Politics in Paradise,* 31.

9. On the challenges of sustaining environmental management protocols over time, see Langholz and Krug, "New Forms of Biodiversity Governance." On the problems at Hilton Head associated with overdevelopment and bankruptcies, see Scardino, "A Gust of Bankruptcy and Scandal," and Riddle, "Hilton Head, S.C.: With Expansion, What of Ecology?"

10. Danielson, *Profits and Politics,* 32. (Emphasis added.)

11. C. Fraser, "Basic Data on the Sea Pines Development."

12. Stuart, "Hilton Head Seen as Island Paradise."

13. Chris Schmitt, quoted in Tibbetts, "The Beauty of Sprawl," 10.

14. Danielson, *Profits and Politics in Paradise,* 72.

15. Lauderdale, "Fraser's Model Proved Beauty Can Trump All."

16. C. Phillips, "Let's Not Blow Up the Bridge—Yet," and Bowers and Bowers, "What Does the Future Hold for Hilton Head Island?"

17. Riddle, "As Hilton Head Grows, What of the Environment?"

18. Campbell, "'Comyas' Forever Changed the Heirs of Mitchelville."

19. Bowie, "Zoning Hearings Create Much Heat, Little Light."; "Hilton Head Islanders Split Racially over Incorporation Vote." See also Reed, "Blacks in South Struggle to Keep the Little Land They Have Left," and Applebome, "Tourism Enriches an Island Resort, but Hilton Head Blacks Feel Left Out." On the general issue of affluent new conservation communities complicating and compromising the quality of life for poor residents, see Ghose, "Big Sky or Big Sprawl?," and Walker and Fortmann, "Whose Landscape?"

20. Pinckney, quoted in Shipnuck, "Growing Pains."

21. Gale, "Hilton Head: The Canopy View."

22. "Troubled Little Island."

23. Ballentine, "Cut Future Population"; Joseph Fraser, quoted in Danielson, *Profits and Politics in Paradise,* 280.

24. Chris Schmitt, quoted in Tibbetts, "The Beauty of Sprawl,"10.

25. Frady, "The View from Hilton Head," 105.

26. "BASF Backs Off from a Beachhead."

27. "Hilton Head Takes on a Chemical Company."

28. deVere, "A Town is Born" (website); Hilton Head Town Council, *Town of Hilton Head Island Comprehensive Plan,* 47; Stock, "Playing in Paradise," 229.

29. Chaffin, "Foreword," in Wilson et al., *Green Development,* ix.

30. Nesmith, "Under the Spell of Spring Island."

31. Riddle, "Spring Island, S.C."

32. Ibid.

33. Wilson et al., *Green Development,* 131.

34. "Spring Island Developers Downsize Project."

35. Chaffin/Light website, "Environmental Stewardship."

36. Chaffin, foreword, in Wilson et al., *Green Development,* ix, and Martin, "Neighbors with Nature."

37. "South Carolina Developers Make a Difference in Island's Development."

38. Spring Island Realty website, "The Spring Island Philosophy"; "Spring Island Journal" (blog); Man 2, Spring Island focus group, discussion with the author, 2007. See also Stern, "Avoiding Pendulum Ecologies."

39. Spring Island focus group, discussion with the author, 2007; Wilson et al., *Green Development,* 209.

40. Beach, quoted in Riddle, "Spring Island, S.C."; Graham, "Thoughts on Spring Island Master Plan," interoffice memorandum, August 1989.

41. Graham, "Thoughts on Spring Island Master Plan," interoffice memorandum, August 1989.

42. Duke, "Graham's Promised Land." See also Quick, "Vince Graham."

43. Quick, "Vince Graham."

44. Jacobs, *The Death and Life of Great American Cities,* 37.

45. I'On Realty website, "Inside I'On." The author bought a house in I'On in 2006.

46. Graham, in interview with the author, July 29, 2010.

47. Quick, "Vince Graham," and Graham, in interview with the author, July 29, 2010.

48. See Binkley, "Developers Discover Old Values Can Bring Astonishing Returns," and Behre, "Newpoint Boasts Sense of Community."

49. Graham, in interview with the author, July 29, 2010. For insights into the politics and procedures of approving neo-traditional developments, see Rybczynski, *Last Harvest.*

50. Quick, "Old Ideas Put to Work in New Community Plans." See also Behre, "Kind of Development Seen as a Key Issue in Growth."

51. Graham, in interview with the author, July 29, 2010.

52. Ibid.; Fennell, "Jordan Tract Vote Stalled for 120 Days."

53. Fennell, "Zoning Battle Heats Up."

54. Quick, "Jordan Tract Plan Is Rejected"; Meggett, "Jordan Tract Developers Scale Down Plan"; Meggett, "Jordan Tract Gets Council's First OK"; and Meggett, "Jordan Tract Rezoning OK'd."

55. Behre, "I'On Subdivision Takes Shape." On the appreciation in property values, see Stech, "Amid Market Slowdown, I'On Holds Its Own."

56. Quick, "Vince Graham"; I'On Realty website, "Inside I'On."

57. On the public transit factor, see N. Ross, "New Urbanism Stalls without Public Transit."

58. Quick, "Vince Graham"; Graham, quoted in Heavens, "Blueprint 2000," and Kendrick, quoted in "Award-Winning Subdivision."

59. Duany, quoted in Tibbetts, "The Beauty of Sprawl," 10.

60. Graham, in interview with the author, July 29, 2010. See Hamlin, "Reading (Conservation Subdivision) Plans."

61. Wilson et al., *Green Development,* 373, 381.

Chapter 8: Weaving Tensions into a Cultural Heritage

1. B. Smith, "Development Threatens Basket-making Tradition." See also Petersen, "Kiawah Neighbors Spark New Preservation Program." The Kiawah Island harvest spurred interest in having other organizations and entities provide harvesting sites that were closer to basket makers' homes. For example, the Mount Pleasant Waterworks identified a site that is scheduled for harvest through the Sweetgrass Cultural Arts Festival Association (SCAFA). This is one of seven sites that SCAFA coordinates. Basket makers sign up for participation at one of two luncheons hosted by SCAFA per year. Basket makers pay twenty-five dollars to cover travel and driver costs. The basket makers are selected on a first-come, first-served basis via sign-up sheets from the luncheons. Each participant is required to wear a nametag distributed through SCAFA (and cannot participate without these). Other harvesting sites include Charlestowne Landing. Kiawah was a harvest site in 2007 and 2008, but the other closer sites have been the focus of SCAFA more recently. Stokes-Marshall, in interview with the author, July 28, 2010.

2. Three specific studies of basket makers, conducted in collaboration with faculty and graduate student colleagues, inform this chapter. A 2002–2003 study included interviews with a total of twenty-three Charleston-area basket makers, including those from the three main locations in the Charleston area: the Four Corners of Law where Meeting and Broad Streets intersect and the Old City Market between East Bay and Meeting Streets, both located in downtown, peninsular Charleston, and from the basket stands found in Mount

Pleasant along the Old Ocean Highway (also known as U.S. Highway 17). Another set of interviews conducted in summer 2003 included fifteen respondents from the same locations, and the 2006–2008 data collection efforts included interviews with twenty-six basket makers from the same three sales locations as well as a newer basket stand site at the local farmers' market (located at Marion Square in downtown Charleston). In all three studies participants were identified using both convenience and snowball sampling, with most identified specifically through field excursions to basket stands and additional interviews coming from referrals by participants. In the notes that follow to document interview quotations, some basket makers desired anonymity (these are numbered by interviewee), while others desired that their names be shared. For additional documentation of the environmental ethnographic methods in this chapter and for resulting theses and publications, see T. R. Hart, "Stakeholder Participation"; Hart et al., "Community Participation"; Grabbatin, "Sweetgrass Basketry"; B. Smith, "Development Threatens Basket-making Tradition." All interviews were conducted in confidentiality, and the names of interviewees are withheld by mutual agreement.

3. Campbell, quoted in H. Frazier, *"Behind God's Back,"* 214; Moore, *Home: Portraits from the Carolina Coast.* On the Gullah heritage see Tibbetts, "Gullah's Radiant Light," and Tibbetts, "Living Soul of Gullah." On the dramatic loss of farmlands owned by black families in the South, see T. Johnson, "Blacks Press Struggle to Retain Farmland"; Robinson, "Developer Land Rush Divides Black Families."

4. Campbell, quoted in H. Frazier, *"Behind God's Back,"* 214.

5. See Miller et al., "Biodiversity Conservation in Local Planning." For an overview of much of the literature regarding possible comprehensive conservation approaches, see Gruber, "Key Principles of Community-based Natural Resource Management." For additional discussions about the complexity of conservation in theory and practice, see Knight and White, *Conservation for a New Generation;* Oldekop et al., "Understanding the Lessons and Limitations of Conservation Development"; Layzer, *Natural Experiments;* and Scheffer, *Critical Transitions in Nature and Society.*

6. Stokes-Marshall, in interview with the author, July 28, 2010.

7. White, "Gullah: An Inventive Form of Survival in the New World." See also Pollitzer, *The Gullah People and Their African Heritage,* 1; Carney, *Black Rice;* Opala, *The Gullah;* Derby, "Black Women Basketmakers"; Coakley, *Sweetgrass Baskets and the Gullah Tradition;* Tibbetts, "Gullah's Radiant Light"; National Park Service website, *Low Country Gullah Geechee Culture Special Resources Study Draft.*

8. Basket maker 2, interview. 2002; National Park Service website, *Low Country Gullah Geechee Culture Special Resources Study Draft;* Carney, *Black Rice.*

9. Derby, "Black Women Basketmakers"; Coakley, *Sweetgrass Baskets and the Gullah Tradition;* Yuhl, *A Golden Haze of Memory;* "Sweetgrass Basketry: A Tradition Under Fire," College of Charleston workshop sponsored by the Avery Research Center for African-American History and Culture, December 12, 2005; Mazyck, quoted in Donna St. George, "Artform of Making Sweetgrass Baskets Threatened."

10. Stokes-Marshall, in interview with the author, July 28, 2010; Jack Leland, "Basket Weaving: African Art Survival?"

11. Jack Leland, "Basket Weaving: African Art Survival?"; Hunt, "Save Our Sweetgrass"; Hurley et al., "Finding a 'Disappearing' Non-timber Forest Resource"; basket maker Linda Blake, interview with Brian Grabbatin, August 14, 2006; basket maker John Simons, interview with Grabbatin, 2006.

12. Basket maker Mae Hall, interview with Grabbatin, July 18, 2006.

13. B. Smith, "Centuries-old Basket-weaving Tradition in S.C. Is Threatened"; Grabbatin, "Sweetgrass Basketry."

14. Harrell, "The Sweetgrass Basket Case."

15. "Conference on Access to Sweetgrass," McKissick Museum, University of South Carolina, Columbia, 1988; Edwards, "Saving the Sweetgrass."

16. Hart et al., "Community Participation in Preservation of Lowcountry South Carolina Sweetgrass (*Muhlenbergia filipes*) Basketry." See M. Frazier, "A Struggle for Sweetgrass"; McDowell, "In Search of Sweetgrass for Basketmakers."

17. Harrell, "The Sweetgrass Basket Case"; Danny J. Gustafson, in interview with the author.

18. See Behre, "Time Has Come to Save Basket Stands"; Findlay, "Weaving History into a Growing Area."

19. Findlay, "Weaving History into a Growing Area."; Waldo, "Nearly 4000 Acres Protected"; Coakley, *Sweetgrass Baskets;* Tibbetts, "Gullah's Radiant Light"; Peterson, "Local Students Are Heard"; Lawrence, "Mount Pleasant's Sweetgrass Basketmakers"; Sweetgrass Festival website, "The Festival: Details and Locations"; Lawrence, "Mount Pleasant's Sweetgrass Basket Makers"; Town of Mount Pleasant, South Carolina, website, "Town Co-sponsors Sweetgrass Cultural Event"; J. Johnson, "Sweetgrass Pavilion to be Dedicated"; Dangerfield, "Summertime for Gershwin."

20. Findlay, "Weaving History into a Growing Area"; Walinchus, "Highway 17 Panel Points to Progress." See also "Sweetgrass Harvest to Benefit Local Basketmakers."

21. Basket makers Elizabeth Mazyck and Middleton (first name not available), interviews with Grabbatin, 2007.

22. Basket maker 4, interview with Zachary Hart, 2002.

23. Basket makers 5 and 3, interviews with Hart, 2002; Since 2006 an ecology professor at the Citadel, the state's military college, has been test growing various strands of sweetgrass on Apron Island, an eighteen-acre barrier island near Folly Beach. The intent of his research is to determine which variety of sweetgrass is the native cultivar to the South Carolina coast and use that information to help expand the dwindling population. He is concerned that planting nonnative sweetgrass species could actually harm the native variety and further decrease the supply available for sweetgrass basket makers. See Gustafson et al., "Practical Seed Source Selection."

24. Basket makers 4 and 18, interviews with Hart, 2002.

25. Jones-Jackson, *When Roots Die;* Dufault et al., "Sweetgrass: History, Basketry, and Constraints to Industry Growth"; Basket makers 11 and 12, interview with Grabbatin, 2006; interview with Grabbatin; basket maker Nakia Wigfall, interview with Grabbatin, July 20, 2008. See also Ravenel, "Wildlife Comes with the Territory Where Sweetgrass Is Involved."

26. Basket maker, interview with Grabbath, 2006.

27. All of the interviews, public events, local news stories, government and other documentary sources, field notes, photographs, participant survey, and/or audio recordings were analyzed following guidance from Clifford, "Notes on (Field)notes," and Berg, *Qualitative Methods for the Social Sciences.* Coakley, "History" (Sweetgrass Festival website.) Personal communications with basket-making community members indicate that there are 250 to 300 active (to varying degrees) weavers in the region. In total the three sets of interviews include about 20 percent of those active. A variety of data and analysis techniques inform this chapter. The methods used rely primarily on semistructured in-depth interviews, document analysis, participant observation, field research, and attendance at key community

events. Over the course of several years of observations of local government meetings, visits with basket makers in their homes and stands, tours of local communities with residents, and field visits to numerous local subdivisions, I gained valuable insight. By analyzing government documents related to land-use decision making, community workshops associated with planning processes, community governance in area subdivisions, websites and marketing materials for these same subdivisions, and newspaper stories and popular-magazine articles about growth and sweetgrass basket making, an ethnographic understanding of dynamics can be documented.

28. C. Brinson, "Crossing a Great Divide"; Campbell, quoted in H. Frazier, *"Behind God's Back,"* 214.

29. A. Porter, "Land Use Fight Keys on Race, Rights"; A. Porter, "Land Use Rules Vital, Backers Say"; "Resisting the Road to Extinction."

30. F. Rivers, "Restoring the Bundle of Rights." See also Jonsson, "Preserve or Let Go"; "Preserving the Family Homes"; Glanton, "Ex-slaves' Land Heirs Struggle to Keep Property in Family Hands."

31. F. Rivers, "The Public Trust Debate"; Glanton, "Ex-slaves' Land Heirs Struggle to Keep Property in Family Hands." See also White, "Seven Mile Relies on Basketry and Heritage to Keep History Alive."

32. For poignant examples of how heirs' property has been lost, see H. Frazier *"Behind God's Back."* According to the Coastal Community Foundation of South Carolina (CCF), a large amount of land is held as heirs' property: 2,000 tracts in Charleston County and 1,300 tracts (representing 17,000 acres) in Berkeley County. The CCF study reported that on Wadmalaw Island there were 111 tracts in 1999. According to Fred Lincoln, president of the Cainhoy Huger Community Development Corporation, "85 percent of the property [on the Cainhoy peninsula in 1999] is owned as heirs' property" (no recent comprehensive data exist). Brinson, "Crossing a Great Divide." See also Lewan and Barclay, "Torn from the Land"; Ogawa, "Wando-Huger"; "Preserving the Family Homes."

33. Goodwine, quoted in Dangerfield, "Summertime for Gershwin"; Dennis, quoted in Frazier, *"Behind God's Back,"* 216. See also Fennell, "Fighting to Save a Heritage."

34. Dangerfield, "Summertime for Gershwin"; Tibbetts, "Gullah's Radiant Light," 8; Tibbetts, "Living Soul of Gullah," 10.

35. Basket maker Marilyn Dingle, interview with Grabbatin, 2006; Aiken, quoted in Glanton, "Ex-slaves' Land Heirs Struggle to Keep Property in Family Hands."

36. Stokes-Marshall, in interview with the author, July 28, 2010; Alston, quoted in Petersen, "Heirs' Property Owners' Hold on Land Often Delicate."

37. Neal, quoted in "Smart-Growth Plan Riles Black Farmers."

38. Stephens, quoted in Brinson, "Crossing a Great Divide." See also Parker, "Director Jennie Stephens Helps Preserve Heirs' Property."

39. Meggett, "Development Hits Highway 17."

41. Basket maker 6, interview with Hart, 2002; Knich, "South Carolina Sweetgrass Basketmakers"; Basket maker 4, interview with Hart, 2002. Fennell, "Keeping Gullah Culture Alive."

42. Basket maker 11, interview with Grabbatin; basket maker Emily Johnson, interview with Grabbatin, August 10, 2008.

43. Riley, in interview with the author, July 29, 2010.

44. Habersham, quoted in Tibbetts, "Gullah's Radiant Light," 3. Still another factor affecting the viability of the sweetgrass basket-making community is the impact of rapidly rising

property taxes as a result of coastal real estate development. A basket maker explained how escalating property values were pinching their meager incomes. "Property taxes are just ridiculous. . . . When developers come and they put up all the houses that are worth about $500,000 or $600,000, you know. Our tax should not be the same as their tax. . . . I'm thinking people are being forced off of their land." See basket maker Nakia Wigfall, interview with Grabbatin, July 20, 2008, and basket maker Helen Simmons, interview with Grabbatin, July 17, 2007.

45. Mount Pleasant community website, "Home: Mount Pleasant named 2010 All-America City." See models and projections for the town, county, and state in a report By McKibben commissioned by the Town of Mount Pleasant. His estimates have been conservative. In his report, from 2005 to 2015 the Town of Mt. Pleasant population is projected to increase by 8,760, or 14.8 percent, to 67,860. From 2015 to 2025 the population is projected to continue to increase by an additional 5,440 persons or 8 percent to 73,300. McKibben, "Town of Mount Pleasant Population Forecasts: 2005–2025."

46. Ohlandt, "Where the Sweetgrass Grows"; Kovacik and Winberry, *South Carolina: A Geography;* U.S. Census Bureau, Population Estimates, 2000; basket maker Nakia Wigfall, interview with Grabbatin, July 20, 2008.

47. U.S. Census Bureau, Population Estimates, 1990, 2000, 2007.

48. Basket maker Linda Blake, interview with Grabbatin, August 14, 2006; Findlay and Slade, "Making over Johnnie Dodds."

49. Basket maker Vera Manigault, interview with Grabbatin, April 8, 2006.

50. Basket maker Mae Hall, interview with Grabbatin, July 18, 2006; basket maker 27, interview with Grabbatin, 2008.

51. Henrietta Snypes, quoted in Associated Press, "Development Shakes Centuries-old Tradition of Grass Basket-weaving Tradition."

52. Washington, quoted in B. Smith, "Centuries-old Basket-weaving Tradition in S.C. Is Threatened"; Basket maker 26, interview with Grabbatin, 2007; Basket maker 14, interview with Hart, 2003; basket maker Barbara McCormik, interview with Grabbatin, 2007.

53. Basket maker Nakia Wigfall, interview with Grabbatin, July 20, 2008; basket maker Mae Hall, interview with Grabbatin, July 18, 2006; B. Smith, "Centuries-old Basket-weaving Tradition in S.C. Is Threatened." See also Zimmerer, "The Reworking of Conservation Geographies."

Chapter 9: Conserving AgriCulture

1. Behre, "Whose Island Is Johns Island? The Farmer Who Is Fed Up with It All." See also Lawrence, "The Dirt on Dirt."

2. Fennel, "Development Increase Worries Rockville, S.C. Residents."

3. Behre, "Whose Island Is Johns Island? The Many Battles of One Resident."

4. Legare, quoted in Tibbetts, "Investing in Open Space," 8; McKoy, quoted in Behre, "Agriculture Slowly Disappears from Johns Island, S.C." On the idea of a county purchasing "development rights," see "Rural Preservation Innovation"; "Greenbelt Success Will Require Focusing on the 'Big Picture.'" On the broader efforts to use land-use restrictions to preserve rural areas, see A. Porter, "County Planners Define Land-Use Categories"; Hicks, "Residents Plan to Battle Wadmalaw Density Plan"; Porter, "Board Steadfast on Island Density"; Porter, "Growing Pains for Wadmalaw Development"; Behre, "Wadmalaw Just the Start of Land-Use Debate"; Porter, "County Approves Plan to Control Rural Growth"; Porter, "Land-Use Rules Vital, Backers Say"; Porter, "Changes to Land-use Rules";

Porter, "Chaos Concludes Wadmalaw Meeting"; Porter, "Land Use Fight Keys on Race, Rights"; Porter, "County Passes Wadmalaw Zoning Map"; Graham, "Drawing the Line"; Hicks, "Our Changing Coast"; Behre, "Zoning Idea Draws Critics"; Chamberlain, "Trying for Balance in Rural Development"; Waldo, "Wadmalaw Plan Spurs Big Outcry."

5. American Farmland Trust website, "South Carolina"; *A Little History of St. Andrews Parish,* 7; and Murray, *This Our Land,* 151.

6. See Schwalm, *A Hard Fight for We.*

7. Halfacre-Hitchcock et al., "Latino Migrant Farmworkers in Lowcountry South Carolina."

8. "Growing and Eating Food—Locally and Sustainably." See also K. Wise, "Down on the Farm"; L'Heureux, "Family Farms Remain Predominant in South Carolina." The U.S. Census defines a farm as "any place from which $1,000 or more of agricultural products were produced and sold, or normally would have been sold, during the census year." The definition has changed nine times since it was established in 1850. The current definition was first used for the 1974 Census of Agriculture and has been used in each subsequent agriculture census. This definition is consistent with the definition used for current USDA surveys.

9. Crop data was provided by Roger Francis, senior extension agent with Clemson University Cooperative Extension, Charleston County Office, in an e-mail message to the author, November 3, 2010. See also Hsieh, "A Farming Renaissance?"

10. Farmer 4, interview with Alan Moore, 2007. Twenty-one interviews were conducted by graduate student Alan Moore for his master's thesis titled "Is There a Future for Local Food?" Names are withheld in compliance with the research protocols of the thesis data collection. Farm sizes vary greatly in the lowcountry. In Beaufort County, for example, very large farms (greater than 2,000 acres) comprised 28,013 acres in 2002 and 32,442 acres in 2007. Berkeley and Colleton Counties show an increase in very large farms, too (in Berkeley from 12,439 in 2002 to 16,752 in 2007; in Colleton 47,683 in 2002 to 90,679 in 2007; in Georgetown 15,004 in 2002 to 19,948 in 2007; in Dorchester 9,958 to 18,247). Some counties experiences decreases: Jasper (57,054 to 32,022) and Williamsburg (42,674 to 34,382) and Hampton (65,619 to 55,743). Data were not available for Charleston County.

11. Gerry Cohen, quoted in "Growing New Farmers for the Lowcountry"; "Wadmalaw farmer," quoted in Taylor, "Wadmalaw Couple Find Niche in Farming"; Behre, "Agriculture Slowly Disappears from Johns Island, S.C." On land values see the U.S. Department of Agriculture Census (2007).

12. Buntain, "Lowcountry Farms Give Way to Homes and Golf-Course Turf."

13. Turansky, e-mail message to the author, November 17, 2010.

14. Gold, *Sustainable Agriculture;* J. Allen, "Why Charleston is the Right Place to Eat Right Now."

15. Taylor, "Taste, Health, Quality and Ecology." See also Quick, "Earth Day at 40"; Weisul, "Consumers Buy into 'Buy Local.'"

16. Lowcountry Local First website, "Community Supported Agriculture (CSA)"; Ostrom, "Community Supported Agriculture as an Agent of Change?," 99; On the CSA movement, see Schnell, "Food with a Farmer's Face," and Vileisis, *Kitchen Literacy.*

17. Quick, "CSA's Great Way to Get Veggies." The CSA formed by Thackeray Farms and Rita's Roots was unusual in that few of the vegetables and fruits they grew were native to the lowcountry. In addition Rita Bachman, the creator of Rita's Roots (and one of my

former graduate students), featured organically grown produce. She also is a white woman who was then in her mid-twenties, a rare demographic combination in the traditionally male-dominant lowcountry farming community. In 2010, three years after the *Charleston Post and Courier* article, Bachman grew so frustrated at the challenges of finding reasonably priced land to lease for her farming operation in the lowcountry that she relocated to Virginia. See Lawrence, "Rita's Roots Ends Its Run on Wadmalaw."

18. Lawrence, "Keeping it Rural"; Bachman, e-mail message to the author, November 5, 2010; Lawrence, "Rita's Roots Ends Its Run on Wadmalaw."

19. Francis, e-mail message to the author, November 3, 2010; Lawrence, "Harvest of Plenty." See also Lawrence, "Sidi Limehouse."

20. Hicks, "When It Comes to Produce, Many Say Fresh Is Best"; McDermott, "South Carolina Farming Industry Profits from 'Organic' Movement"; J. Allen, "People of the Earth"; Taylor, "Buying Close to Home." On the commercialization of the American food economy, see Vileisis, *Kitchen Literacy.*

21. Stech, "Plan Cultivates Love for Local Crops." As an environmental historian notes, such grassroots food networks make local agriculture more sustainable by "the decommodification of food and land, which opens up an economic space where social divisions can be eroded rather than accentuated. This is an alternative agriculture of substance, because it provides an alternative not only to production inputs and methods but also to the entire system of industrial farming." See Guthman, *Agrarian Dreams,* 184–85.

22. Lawrence, "Keeping It Rural"; Lawrence, "Rita's Roots Ends Its Run on Wadmalaw"; Bachman, e-mail message to the author, November 5, 2010; Forrester, e-mail message to the author, November 10, 2010.

23. Taylor, "Buying Close to Home," and Quick, "To Market, to Market."

24. Taylor, "Buying Close to Home," and Quick, "Earth Day at 40."

25. Wise, "Down on the Farm."

26. Quick, "Organic Farmer Cultivates Movement"; Lawrence, "Keeping It Rural"; Taylor, "Farmer Driven by Love of the Land." See also Agnew, "Homegrown Charleston."

27. Lowcountry Local First website.

28. Taylor, "Leader Puts Local Business First."

29. Farmers 13 and 18, interviews with Moore, 2007.

30. Farmer 14, interview with Moore, 2007.

31. Farmer 15, interview with Moore, 2007.

32. Farmers 13, 8, and 5, interviews with Moore, 2007.

33. Farmer 1, interview with Moore, 2007.

34. Farmers 2, 6, and 10, interviews with Moore, 2007.

35. Farmer 3, interview with Moore, 2007.

36. Farmers 4 and 5, interviews with Moore, 2007.

37. Farmer 2, interview with Moore, 2007.

38. Farmers 20 and 16, interviews with Moore, 2007.

39. Farmer 2, interview with Moore, 2007.

40. Farmer 12, interview with Moore, 2007.

41. Ibid.

42. Farmers 1 and 8, interviews with Moore, 2007; Gold, *Sustainable Agriculture.*

43. Blair, "The Friction between the Fair-Trade and Local-First Movements."

44. Washington, quoted in J. Parker, "Market a Boon to Growers, Buyers."

45. Stoney, quoted in Taylor, "Buying Close to Home."

46. Lawrence, "Cultivating Future Lowcountry Growers"; Hanson quoted on Low-country Local First website.

Conclusion

1. Scardino, "A Gust of Bankruptcy and Scandal"; McDermott, "Ginn Sees Land of Opportunity"; M. Parker, "Developer Shopping 'Promenade' to Maritime Industry"; Slade, "Plans for Ginn Company's Promenade Take Shape."

2. Quick, "Pathway to Fitness"; Dixon, "36 Hours in Charleston, South Carolina." "Wonders Way" was named in memory of Garett Wonders, a young navy officer stationed in Charleston who was training for the 2004 Olympics when he was killed in a bicycle-vehicle collision.

3. Findlay, "Park Plans to Outdo Piers." See also Slade, "City Would Get $3M, Land in Bridge Agreement."

4. Ravenel, quoted in "North America's Longest Cable Bridge Dedicated in South Carolina."

5. Ravenel, quoted in Langley, "Area Makes Progress but Many See More to Do"; Lane, in interview with the author, July 29, 2010.

6. Petersen, "The Gobbling Up of the Lowcountry"; Findlay and Slade, "Cities Battle Sprawl by Filling in the Holes"; "Conservation Fight"; "A Desire for Green"; Barton, "Hilton Head Emphasizing Green." See also McDermott, "Industries Find That Corporate Conservation is Good Business."

7. "Conservation Fight"; Slade and Knich, "Mapping the Future"; "Residents Can Guide Growth"; "Maintain Rural Protections"; "Consider Conservation Option for Westvaco's East Edisto."

8. Basket maker Vera Manigault, interview with Brian Grabbatin, April 8, 2006.

9. Farmer 8, interview with Alan Moore, 2007.

10. "Residents Can Guide Growth"; "Maintain Rural Protections"; "Consider Conservation Option for Westvaco's East Edisto." On the greenbelt program, see Bartelme's articles "Greenbelt Hits Brakes on Sprawl" and "Recognizing Greenbelt Success."

11. McLeod, "At Home on the Farm."

12. Petersen, "Easements Likely Next Conservation Battlefield."

13. "Balance Growth, Livability"; R. Brinson, "Looks Like We're Getting Serious." See also Lee, "Is There a Place for Private Conversation in Public Dialogue?" Lee labeled grass-roots activism "empowered deliberative democracy."

14. Peirce and Johnston, "A Powerful Wave of Growth." See Schiffman, *Alternative Techniques for Managing Growth.* On the status of various species, see "More Osprey Found along SC's South Coast"; "Symbol of Nation, Nature"; Petersen, "Wood Storks Stage Comeback"; "Whoop It Up for Nature." A related indication of improving ecologies is the resurgence of the beaver population. See Petersen, "Beavers Create Problems for Human Habitat."

15. "Beaufort County Comprehensive Plan" (website). Emphasis added.

16. Stice, "Bluffton to Unveil Development Standards."

17. "MeadWestvaco Unveils East Edisto Preliminary Master Plan" (website). See also Petersen, "Westvaco in Transition"; Stech, "Massive East Edisto Tract Could One Day Be New Town"; "Plotting East Edisto's Course"; Petersen, "East Edisto Master Plan Introduced."

18. "MeadWestvaco Unveils East Edisto Preliminary Master Plan" (website); "East Edisto" (website). See also Slade, "East Edisto Plan Hits Milestone"; McDermott, "MeadWestvaco's 3-year-Old Real Estate Unit Looks to Cover All Bases"; "Make Green Protections Official."

19. Hambrick, "The Big Prize and the Art of Compromise." Beach, quoted in Stech, "Fighting Green's Red Tape."

20. Concerned Citizens of the Sea Islands (Johns Island, South Carolina) website. The phrase *social capital* comes from social scientist Robert Putnam's influential study of civic engagement titled *Bowling Alone*.

21. Slade, "I-526 Expansion Still Not Settled."

22. Slade, "I-526 Proposal Draws Fire at Public Hearing"; Concerned Citizens of the Sea Islands (Johns Island) website, "Current Initiatives." See also Lawrence, "Public Meetings Begin Comment Period on Mark Clark Extension"; Hambrick, "Public Pans I-526 Parkway"; "I-526 'Parkway' Is a Non-Starter."

23. Behre, "'What Do We Want the Future of Johns Island to Be?'"

24. Coley, "The Road to Urban Sprawl?"; Limehouse, quoted in Findlay and Slade, "SCDOT Pushes for Decision on I-526." For the South Carolina Department of Transportation's responses to such criticisms, see Mark Clark Expressway website (South Carolina Department of Transportation), "Frequently Asked Questions." See also Waldo, "I-526 Foes to Talk about Alternatives"; Hankla, "Engineers Offer Alternatives to I-526 Extension"; Waldo, "Group Hits Cost of I-526."

25. Findlay, "Objections to I-526 Expansion Increasing"; Fretwell, "Charleston Project Holds Up Columbia Road Work." See also Knich, "Coastal Conservation Proposes Alternative to I-526 Extension"; Knich, "Parkway Would Complete I-526"; Slade, "I-526 Resolution Still Out of Reach"; Findlay, "'Silent Majority' Backs I-526"; Slade, "Plan for I-526 Rejected."

26. Bradford, "I-526 Debate Shows Local Road Building Has Reached End Game." See Hambrick, "The Big Prize and the Art of Compromise." On the concept of sustainable development, see *Sustainable America*. Campbell, quoted in Findlay, "Talks on Extension of I-526 Ongoing."

27. Leopold, "The Conservation Ethic." In its original sense the term *carrying capacity* referred to the capacity of a habitat to support a particular species. Populations that exceed the carrying capacity begin degrading the habitat to the point that the carrying capacity is reduced. Although scholars dispute whether the concept of carrying capacity can be applied to human social systems, it does apply to issues of growth management and land-use planning/policies.

28. Roosevelt, quoted in Turner, *Rediscovering America*, 328; Riley, in interview with the author, July 29, 2010. See also Thomas Power, *Lost Landscapes and Failed Economies*.

29. Cohn, "Culture and Conservation."

30. On the role of white elite conservationists in the lowcountry, see Lee, "Conservation as a Territorial Ideology"; Lee, "The Politics of Localness"; and, Lee, "Is There a Place for Private Conversation in Public Dialogue?"

31. Yarian, "United They Stand."

32. S. Gray, "Southeastern States Are Hit Hard by Recession."

33. Beach, e-mail message to the author, October 30, 2010; Covington, "When the Race Resumes"; Mitchell, "Does the Recession Offer an Opportunity to Scale Back Growth, Benefit the Environment?" As early as 2006 some people in the lowcountry were predicting

that the dramatic increase in home values was a bubble bound to burst. The region's real estate market was "overpriced and overbuilt." Petersen, "Sprawl, Traffic Arising from Surprising Source."

34. Covington, "When the Race Resumes."

35. Lareau, quoted in Quick, "South Carolina Coastal Conservation League's Long Crusade Earns Friends, Foes."

36. "Conservation Kudos."

Books, Sections of Books, and Letters

Aberly, Doug. *Futures by Design: The Practice of Ecological Planning*. Philadelphia: New Society, 1994.

Able, Gene, and Jack Horan. *Paddling South Carolina: A Guide to Palmetto State River Trails*. Orangeburg, S.C.: Sandlapper, 2001.

Allen, Barbara. "The Genealogical Landscape and the Southern Sense of Place." In *Sense of Place*, edited by Barbara Allen and Thomas J. Schlereth. Lexington: University Press of Kentucky, 1990.

Anderson, Kurt. "Is Seaside Too Good to be True?" In *Seaside: Making a Town in America*, edited by David Mohney and Keller Easterling. Princeton, N.J.: Princeton Architectual Press, 1996.

Archdale, John. "A New Description of that Fertile and Pleasant Province of South Carolina." In Alexander S. Salley Jr., *Narratives of Early Carolina*. 1911. Reprint, New York: Barnes and Noble, 1967.

Arendt, Randall G. *Conservation Design for Subdivisions: A Practical Guide to Creating Open Space Networks*. Washington, D.C.: Island Press, 1996.

———. *Growing Greener: Putting Conservation into Local Plans and Ordinances*. Washington, D.C.: Island Press, 1999.

Bass, Bernard M. *Leadership and Performance beyond Expectations*. New York: Free Press, 1985.

Bass, Bernard M., and Bruce J. Avolio. *Improving Organizational Effectiveness through Transformational Leadership*. Thousand Oaks, Calif.: Sage Publications, 1994.

Bass, Bernard M., and Ronald E. Riggio. *Transformational Leadership*. 2nd ed. Mahuah, N.J.: Lawrence Erlbaum Associates, 2006.

Bass, Jack, and Scott Poole, *The Palmetto State: The Making of Modern South Carolina*. Columbia: University of South Carolina Press, 2009.

Baumgartner, Frank R. "Strategies of Political Leadership in Diverse Settings." In *Leadership and Politics: New Perspectives in Political Science*, edited by Bryan Jones. Lawrence: University Press of Kansas, 1989.

———, and Bryan D. Jones. *Agendas and Instability in American Politics*. Chicago: University of Chicago Press, 1993.

Baxandall, Rosalyn, and Elizabeth Ewen. *Picture Windows: How the Suburbs Happened*. New York: Basic Books, 2000.

Beatley, Timothy. *Habitat Conservation Planning: Endangered Species and Urban Growth*. Austin: University of Texas Press, 1994.

Bellah, Robert N., Richard Madsen, William M. Sullivan, Ann Swidler, and Steven M. Tipton. *The Good Society.* New York: Knopf, 1991.

Bennis, Warren, and Burt Nanus. *Leaders: The Strategies for Taking Charge.* New York: Harper and Row, 1985.

Berg, Bruce. *Qualitative Methods for the Social Sciences.* Boston: Allyn and Bacon, 2001.

Berger, Bennett. *Working-class Suburb: A Study of Auto Workers in Suburbia.* Berkeley: University of California Press, 1968.

Berry, Wendell. "Preserving Wildness." In *Home Economics: Fourteen Essays.* San Francisco: North Point, 1987.

Blagden, Tom. *Lowcountry: The Natural Landscape.* Greensboro, N.C.: Legacy, 1999.

————. *South Carolina's Wetland Wilderness: The ACE Basin.* Englewood, Colo.: Westcliffe, 1992.

————, and Barry Beasley, *The Rivers of South Carolina.* Englewood, Colo.: Westcliffe, 1999.

Blakely, Edward, and Mary Gail Snyder, *Fortress America: Gated Communities in the United States.* Washington, D.C.: Brookings, 1997.

Bosso, Christopher J. *Environment, Inc.: From Grassroots to Beltway.* Lawrence: University Press of Kansas, 2005.

Bostick, Douglas W. *Sunken Plantations: The Santee Cooper Project.* Charleston, S.C.: History Press, 2008.

Bressi, Todd, ed. *The Seaside Debates: A Critique of the New Urbanism.* New York: Rizzoli, 2002.

Brewer, Richard. *Conservancy: The Land Trust Movement in America.* Hanover, N.H.: Dartmouth University Press, 2003.

Brickell, John. *The Natural History of North Carolina.* Murfreesboro, N.C.: Johnson, 1737, 1968.

Bruce, Teresa. *Transfer of Grace: Images of the Lowcountry.* Charleston, S.C.: Joggling Board, 2007.

Bruegman, Robert. *Sprawl: A Compact History.* Chicago: University of Chicago Press, 2005.

Bullard, Robert D., ed. *Growing Smarter: Achieving Livable Communities, Environmental Justice, and Regional Equity.* Cambridge: MIT Press, 2007.

Burgess, Bonnie. *Fate of the Wild: The Endangered Species Act and the Future of Biodiversity.* Athens: University of Georgia Press, 2001.

Burns, James MacGregor. *Leadership.* New York: Harper and Row, 1978.

Burton, Ian, Robert Kates, and Gilbert White. *The Environment as Hazard.* New York: Oxford University Press, 1978.

Byers, Elizabeth, and Karin Marchetti Ponte. *The Conservation Easement Handbook.* San Francisco: Trust for Public Land and the Land Trust Alliance, 2005.

Calthorpe, Peter. *The Next American Metropolis: Ecology, Community, and the American Dream.* New York: Princeton Architectural Press, 1993.

Carney, Judith A. *Black Rice: The African Origins of Rice Cultivation in the Americas.* Cambridge: Harvard University Press, 2001.

Carswell, Lisa, and Pam Robinson, eds. *Conserving South Carolina: Sustaining and Protecting Our Natural Resources.* Columbia: South Carolina Nature Conservancy, 1999.

Castles Consulting Engineers. *A Conceptual Plan for Sandy Island.* Myrtle Beach, S.C.: Castles Engineering, 1990.

Chaffin, James J., Jr. "Foreword." In *Green Development: Integrating Ecology and Real Estate,* edited by Alex Wilson, Jennifer L. Uncapher, Lisa McManigal, L. Hunter Lovins, Maureen Cureton, and William D. Browning. New York: Wiley, 1998.

Channing, Steven A. *Crisis of Fear: Secession in South Carolina.* New York: Norton, 1970.

Chaplin, Joyce E. *An Anxious Pursuit: Agricultural Innovation and Modernity in the Lower South, 1730–1815.* Chapel Hill: University of North Carolina Press, 1993.

Christensen, Norman L., Jr. Foreword in John C. Gordon and Joyce K. Berry. *Environmental Leadership Equals Essential Leadership: Redefining Who Leads and How.* New Haven: Yale University Press, 2006.

Clark, Thomas D. *The Greening of the South: The Recovery of Land and Forest.* Lexington: University Press of Kentucky, 1984.

Clayton, David L. *Mill and Town in South Carolina, 1880–1920.* Baton Rouge: Louisiana State University Press, 1982.

Clifford, James. "Notes on (Field)notes." In *Fieldnotes: The Makings of Anthropology,* edited by Roger Sanjek. Ithaca: Cornell University Press, 1990.

Coakley, Joyce V. *Sweetgrass Baskets and the Gullah Tradition.* Charleston, S.C.: Arcadia, 2005.

Cobb, James C. *Industrialization and Southern Society, 1877–1984.* Lexington: University of Kentucky Press, 1984.

———. *The Selling of the South: The Southern Crusade for Industrial Development, 1936–1980.* Baton Rouge: Louisiana State University Press, 1982.

Coclanis, Peter A. *The Shadow of a Dream: Economic Life and Death in the South Carolina Low Country, 1670–1920.* New York: Oxford University Press, 1988.

Conger, Jay A., and Rabindra N. Kanungo. *Charismatic Leadership in Organizations.* Thousand Oaks, Calif.: Sage Publications, 1998.

Conroy, Pat. *The Prince of Tides.* New York: Houghton Mifflin Harcourt, 1986

———. *The Water Is Wide.* New York: Houghton Mifflin, 1972.

Cooper, William J., Jr., and Thomas Terrill. *American South: A History.* 2 vols. Plymouth, U.K.: Rowman & Littlefield, 2009.

Cowdrey, Albert E. *This Land, This South: An Environmental History.* Lexington: University Press of Kentucky, 1983.

Cox, Wendell. *War on the Dream: How Anti-Sprawl Policy Threatens the Quality of Life.* New York: Universe, 2006.

Cronon, William. *Changes in the Land: Indians, Colonists and the Ecology of New England.* New York: Hill and Wang, 1983.

———. "In Search of Nature." In *Uncommon Ground: Toward Reinventing Nature,* edited by William Cronon. New York: Norton, 1995.

———. "The Trouble with Wilderness; or, Getting Back to the Wrong Nature." In *Uncommon Ground: Toward Reinventing Nature,* edited by William Cronon. New York: Norton, 1995.

Cuthbert Robert B., and Stephen G. Hoffius, eds. *Northern Money, Southern Land: The Lowcountry Plantation Sketches of Chlotilde R. Martin.* Columbia: University of South Carolina Press, 2009.

Dahl, Robert. *Democracy and Its Critics.* New Haven: Yale University Press, 1989.

Daniel, Pete. *Breaking the Land: The Transformation of Cotton, Tobacco, and Rice Cultures since 1880.* Urbana: University of Illinois Press, 1985.

Danielson, Michael. *Profits and Politics in Paradise.* Columbia: University of South Carolina Press, 1995.

Danielson, Michael, and Patricia R. F. Danielson. *Profits in Paradise: The Development of Hilton Head Island.* Columbia: University of South Carolina Press, 1995.

DeLeon, Richard E. *Left Coast City: Progressive Politics in San Francisco, 1975–1991.* Lawrence: University Press of Kansas, 1992.

Dethloff, Henry C. *A History of the American Rice Industry, 1685–1985.* College Station: Texas A & M University Press, 1988.

Devlin, Ann Sloan. *What Americans Build and Why: Psychological Perspectives.* New York: Cambridge University Press, 2010.

Doar, David. *Rice and Rice Planting in the South Carolina Low Country.* 1936. Reprint, Charleston: Charleston Museum, 1970.

Donaldson, Scott. *The Suburban Myth.* New York: Columbia University Press, 1969.

Dover, Victor. *Charter of the New Urbanism.* New York: McGraw-Hill, 2000.

Drayton, John. *A View of South Carolina as Respects Her Natural and Civil Concerns.* 1802. Reprint, Spartanburg, S.C.: Reprint Co., 1972.

Duane, Timothy P. *Shaping the Sierra: Nature, Culture, and Conflict in the Changing West.* Berkeley: University of California Press, 1999.

Duany, Andres, Elizabeth Plater-Zyberk, and Jeff Speck. *Suburban Nation: The Rise of Sprawl and the Decline of the American Dream.* New York: North Point Press, 2000.

Duerksen, Christopher, and Cara Snyder. *Nature-friendly Communities: Habitat Protection and Land-use Planning.* Washington, D.C.: Island Press, 2005.

Dufault, Robert J., Mary Jackson, and Stephen K. Salvo. "Sweetgrass: History, Basketry, and Constraints to Commercialization." In *Proceedings of the Second National Symposium New Crops: Exploration, Research, Commercialization,* edited by Jules Janick and James E. Simon. New York: Wiley, 1993.

Duffy, John. *Epidemics in Colonial America.* Baton Rouge: Louisiana State University Press, 1953.

Dusinberre, William. *Them Dark Days: Slavery in the American Rice Swamps.* New York: Oxford University Press, 1996.

Earley, Lawrence S. *Looking for Long Leaf: The Fall and Rise of an American Forest.* Chapel Hill: University of North Carolina Press, 2004.

Edelson, S. Max. *Plantation Enterprise in Colonial South Carolina.* Cambridge: Harvard University Press, 2006.

Edgar, Walter. *History of Santee Cooper, 1934–1984.* Columbia, S.C.: R. L. Bryan, 1984.

———. *South Carolina: A History.* Columbia: University of South Carolina Press, 1998.

Emerson, Robert M., ed. *Contemporary Field Research: A Collection of Readings.* Prospect Heights, Ill.: Waveland, 1983.

Fairfax, Sally K., Lauren Gwin, Mary Ann King, Leigh Raymond, and Laura A. Watt. *Buying Nature: The Limits of Land Acquisition as a Conservation Strategy, 1780–2004.* Cambridge: MIT Press, 2005.

Faulkner, William. "On Fear." In *Essays, Speeches, and Public Letters by William Faulkner,* edited by James Meriwether. New York: Random House, 1965.

Ferguson, Leland. *Uncommon Ground: Archaeology and Early African America, 1650–1800.* Washington, D.C.: Smithsonian, 1992.

Fishman, Robert. *Bourgeois Utopias: The Rise and Fall of Suburbia.* New York: Basic Books, 1971.

Flint, Anthony. *This Land: The Battle over Sprawl and the Future of America.* Baltimore: Johns Hopkins University Press, 2006.

Foldvary, Fred E. "Proprietary Communities and Community Associations." In *The Voluntary City: Choice, Community, and Civil Society,* edited by David T. Beito, Peter Gordon, and Alexander Tabarrok. Ann Arbor: University of Michigan Press, 2002.

Ford, Lacy K., Jr. *Origins of Southern Radicalism: The South Carolina Upcountry, 1800–1860.* New York: Oxford University Press, 1988.

Fraser, Walter J. *Charleston! Charleston! The History of a Southern City*. Columbia: University of South Carolina Press, 1989.

Frazier, Herb. *"Behind God's Back": Gullah Memories*. Charleston, S.C.: Evening Post Books, 2011.

Freyfogle, Eric T. *Why Conservation Is Failing and How It Can Regain Ground*. New Haven: Yale University Press, 2006.

Fulton, William. *Who Sprawls Most? How Growth Patterns Differ across the U.S.* Washington, D.C.: Brookings, 2001.

Garreau, Joel. *Edge City: Life on the New Frontier*. New York: Random House, 1991.

Glen, James. "An Attempt towards an Estimate of the Value of South Carolina." In *The Colonial South Carolina Scene: Contemporary Views, 1697–1744*, edited by H. Roy Merrens. Columbia: University of South Carolina Press, 1977.

Gold, Mary V. *Sustainable Agriculture: Definitions and Terms*. Beltsville, Md.: National Agriculture Library, 1999.

Goldfield, David R. *Promised Land: The South since 1945*. Arlington Heights, Ill.: Harlan Davidson, 1986.

Gordon, John C., and Joyce K. Berry. *Environmental Leadership Equals Essential Leadership: Redefining Who Leads and How*. New Haven: Yale University Press, 2006.

Gottlieb, Robert. *Forcing the Spring: The Transformation of the American Environmental Movement*. Washington, D.C.: Island Press 1993.

Gould, Stephen Jay. *The Structure of Evolutionary Theory*. Cambridge, Mass.: Belknap, 2002.

Grant, Jill. *Planning the Good Community: New Urbanism in Theory and Practice*. New York: Routledge, 2006.

Grantham, Dewey. *The South in Modern America: A Region at Odds*. New York: Harper Collins, 1994.

Gray, Louis C. *History of Agriculture in the Southern United States to 1860*. 2 vols. Clifton, 1932. Reprint, N.J.: Englewood, 1973.

Greenleaf, Robert K. *On Becoming a Servant Leader*. San Francisco: Jossey-Bass, 1996.

———. *The Servant as a Leader*. Indianapolis: Greenleaf Center, 1970.

Greer, Margaret. *The Sands of Time: A History of Hilton Head Island*. Hilton Head Island: SouthArt, 1988.

Guimaraes, Paulo, Frank L. Hefner, and Douglas P. Woodward. *Wealth and Income Effects of Natural Disasters: An Econometric Analysis of Hurricane Hugo*. Columbia: Division of Research, College of Business Administration, University of South Carolina, 1992.

Gustanski, Julie Ann, and Roderick H. Squires, eds. *Protecting the Land: Conservation Easements Past, Present, and Future*. Washington, D.C.: Island Press, 2000.

Guthman, J. *Agrarian Dreams: The Paradox of Organic Farming in California*. Berkeley: University of California Press, 2004.

Harrison, William H., Jr. *How to Get Rich in the South: Telling What to Do, How to Do It, and the Profits to Be Realized*. Chicago: Harrison, 1888.

Hirsch, Arthur Henry. *The Huguenots in Colonial South Carolina*. London: Archon, 1962.

Hiss, Tony. *The Experience of Place*. New York: Random House, 1990.

Hudson, Charles M. *The Southeastern Indians*. Knoxville: University of Tennessee Press, 1976.

Hudson, Simon, and Louise Hudson. *Golf Tourism*. Oxford, U.K.: Goodfellow, 2010.

Humes, Edward. *Eco Barons: The New Heroes of Environmental Activism*. New York: Ecco, 2009.

Humphries, Josephine. "A Disappearing Subject Called the South." In *The Prevailing South: Life & Politics in a Changing Culture,* edited by Dudley Clendenin. Atlanta: Longstreet, 1988.

Jackson, Kenneth T. *Crabgrass Frontier: The Suburbanization of the United States.* New York: Oxford University Press, 1985.

Jacobs, Jane. *The Death and Life of Great American Cities.* New York: Modern Library, 1993.

Jacobson, David. *Place and Belonging in America.* Baltimore: Johns Hopkins University Press, 2002.

Johnson, Elizabeth A., and Michael W. Klemens, eds. *Nature in Fragments.* New York: Columbia University Press, 2005.

Johnson, Robert David. *Congress and the Cold War.* New York: Cambridge University Press, 2006.

Jones, Bryan. *Reconceiving Decision-making in Democratic Politics: Attention, Choice, and Public Policy.* Chicago: University of Chicago Press, 1994.

Jones-Jackson, Patricia. *When Roots Die: Endangered Traditions on the Sea Islands.* Athens: University of Georgia Press, 1987.

Joyner, Charles. *Down by the Riverside: A South Carolina Slave Community.* Urbana: University of Illinois Press, 1984.

Katz, Peter. *The New Urbanism: Toward an Architecture of Community.* New York: McGraw-Hill, 1994.

Keiter, Robert B. *Keeping Faith with Nature: Ecosystems, Democracy, and America's Public Lands.* New Haven: Yale University Press, 2003.

Kingdon, John. *Agendas, Alternatives, and Public Policies.* Boston: Little, Brown, 1984.

Kline, Benjamin. *A Brief History of the U.S. Environmental Movement.* San Francisco: Acadia Books, 2000.

Klyza, Christopher McGrory, and David Sousa. *American Environmental Policy, 1990–2006.* Cambridge: MIT Press, 2008.

Knight, Richard L., and Courtney White, eds. *Conservation for a New Generation: Redefining Natural Resources Management.* Washington, D.C.: Island Press, 2009.

Kouzes, James M., and Barry Z. Posner, *The Leadership Challenge: How to Get Extraordinary Things Done in Organizations.* San Francisco: Jossey-Bass, 1987.

Kovacik, Charles F., and John J. Winberry. *South Carolina: A Geography.* Boulder, Colo.: Westview Press, 1987.

———. *South Carolina: The Making of a Landscape.* Columbia: University of South Carolina Press, 1989.

Krieger, Alex. "The Costs—and Benefits?—of Sprawl." In *Sprawl and Suburbia,* edited by William Saunders. Minneapolis: University of Minnesota Press, 2005.

Kruse, Kevin M. *White Flight: Atlanta and the Making of Modern Conservatism.* Princeton: Princeton University Press, 2005.

———, and Thomas J. Sugrue, eds. *The New Suburban History.* Chicago: University of Chicago Press, 2006.

Langdon, Phillip. *Better Place to Live: Reshaping the American Suburb.* Amherst: University of Massachusetts Press, 1994.

Lareau, Jane, Tom Blagden, and Richard D. Porcher. *Lowcountry: The Natural Landscape.* Charleston, S.C.: Legacy Publications, 1988.

Laurie, Peter B., and David Chamberlain. *The South Carolina Aquarium Guide to Aquatic Habitats of South Carolina.* Columbia: University of South Carolina Press, 2003.

Layzer, Judith A. *Natural Experiments: Ecosystem-based Management and the Environment.* Cambridge: MIT Press, 2008.

Leland, John. *Porcher's Creek: Lives between the Tides.* Columbia: University of South Carolina Press, 2002.

Lennon, Jered, William J. Neal, David M. Bush, Orrin H. Pilkey, Matthew Stutz, and Jane Bullock. *Living with the South Carolina Coast.* Durham: Duke University Press, 1996.

Leopold, Aldo. *"The River of the Mother of God" and Other Essays by Aldo Leopold,* edited by Susan L. Flader and J. Baird Callicott. Madison: University of Wisconsin Press, 1991.

Lippson, Robert, and Alice Jane Lippson. *Life along the Inner Coast: A Naturalist's Guide to the Sounds, Inlets, Rivers, and Intracoastal Waterway from Norfolk to Key West.* Chapel Hill: University of North Carolina Press, 2009.

A Little History of St. Andrews Parish and Its Adaptability to Early Truck Farming, Dairy Farming, and Stock Raising. Charleston: Charleston Bridge Company, 1889.

Littlefield, Daniel C. *Rice and Slaves: Ethnicity and the Slave Trade in Colonial South Carolina.* Baton Rouge: Louisiana State University Press, 1981.

Logan, John R., and Harvey L. Molotch, *Urban Fortunes: The Political Economy of Place.* Berkeley: University of California Press, 1987.

London, James B., and Nicole L. Hill. *Land Conversion in South Carolina: State Makes the Top 10 List.* Clemson, S.C.: Jim Self Center on the Future, 2000.

Lopez Barnett, Dianna. *A Primer on Sustainable Building.* Snowmass, Colo.: Rocky Mountain Institute, 1995.

Low, Setha. "Cultural Conservation of Place." In *Conserving Culture,* edited by Mary Hufford. Urbana: University of Illinois Press, 1994.

Lyle, John Tillman. *Regenerative Design for Sustainable Development.* New York, Wiley, 1994.

Lynch, Kevin. *A Theory of Good City Form.* Cambridge: MIT Press, 1981.

MacCallum, Spencer Heath. "The Case for Land Lease versus Subdivision: Homeowners' Associations Reconsidered." In *The Voluntary City,* edited by David T. Beito, Peter Gordon, Alexander Tabarrok. Ann Arbor: University of Michigan Press, 2002.

Mantell, Michael, Stephen F. Harper, and Luther Propst. *Creating Successful Communities: A Guidebook to Growth Management Strategies.* Washington, D.C.: Island Press, 1990.

Marcy, Barton C., Jr., Dean E. Fletcher, F. Douglas Martin, Michael H. Paller, and Marcel J. M. Reichert. *Fishes of the Middle Savannah River Basin: With Emphasis on the Savannah River Site.* Athens: University of Georgia Press, 2005.

Marks, Stuart A. *Southern Hunting in Black and White.* Princeton: Princeton University Press, 1991.

Marshall, Alex. *How Cities Work: Suburbs, Sprawl, and the Roads Not Taken.* Austin: University of Texas Press, 2001.

McCurry, Stephanie. *Masters of Small Worlds: Yeoman Households, Gender Relations, and the Political Culture of the Antebellum South Carolina Low Country.* New York: Oxford University Press, 1997.

McHarg, Ian. *Design with Nature.* New York: Wiley, 1969.

McPhee, John. *Encounters with the Archdruid.* New York: Farrar, Straus and Giroux, 1971.

Merchant, Carolyn. *Radical Ecology: The Search for a Livable World.* New York: Routledge, 2005.

Meriwether, Robert Lee. *The Expansion of South Carolina, 1729–1765.* Kingsport, Tenn.: Southern Publishers, 1940.

Milder, Jeffrey C., and D. L. Perlman. *Practical Ecology for Planners, Developers, and Citizens*. Washington, D.C.: Island Press, 2005.

Minnix, Daniel P., and Malcolm Cowley. *Black Cargoes: A History of the Atlantic Slave Trade, 1518–1865*. New York: Viking, 1962.

Molotch, Harvey. "Urban Deals in Comparative Perspective." In *Beyond the City Limits: Urban Policy and Economic Restructuring in Comparative Perspective*, edited by John R. Logan and Todd Swanstrom. Philadelphia: Temple University Press, 1990.

Moore, Vennie Deas, with William Baldwin. *Home: Portraits from the Carolina Coast*. Charleston, S.C.: History Press, 2006.

Murray, Chalmers S. *This Our Land: The Story of the Agricultural Society of South Carolina*. Charleston, S. C.: Carolina Art Association, 1949.

National Park Service, *Guiding Principles of Sustainable Design*. Denver, Colo.: National Park Service, 1993.

Nelson, Robert H. *Private Neighborhoods and the Transformation of Local Government*. Washington, D.C.: Urban Institute Press, 2005.

New South Associates. *A Cultural Resources Management Plan for the Cooper River Drainage in Berkeley County, South Carolina*. Stone Mountain, Ga.: New South Associates, 2004.

Nicholls, Steve. *Paradise Found: Nature in America at the Time of Discovery*. Chicago: University of Chicago Press, 2009.

Northouse, Peter Guy. *Leadership: Theory and Practice*. 4th ed. Thousand Oaks, California: Sage, 2007.

O'Connor, Flannery. "The Partridge Festival." In *The Complete Stories*. New York: Fararr, Straus and Giroux, 1971.

"An Old Letter, (About March 1671)." In *The Shaftesbury Papers and Other Records Relating to Carolina and Its First Settlement on the Ashley River Prior to the Year 1676*, edited by Langdon Cheves. Collections of the South Carolina Historical Society, vol. 5 (Charleston, S.C., 1897).

Olwell, Robert. *Masters, Slaves, and Subjects: The Culture of Power in the South Carolina Low Country, 1740–1790*. Ithaca: Cornell University Press, 1998.

Opala, Joseph A. *The Gullah: Rice, Slavery, and the Sierra-Leone Connection*. Washington D.C.: U.S. Department of State, 2001.

Ostrom, Marcia Ruth. "Community Supported Agriculture as an Agent of Change: Is It Working?" In *Remaking the North American Food System: Strategies for Sustainability*, edited by C. Clare Hinrichs and Thomas A. Lyson. Lincoln: University of Nebraska Press, 2007.

Patton, Michael Quinn. *Qualitative Research and Evaluation Methods*. Thousand Oaks, Calif.: Sage Publications, 2002.

Perlman, Dan L., and Jeffrey Milder. *Practical Ecology: For Planners, Developers, and Citizens*. Washington, D.C.: Island Press, 2005.

Petty, Julian. *Twentieth-century Changes in South Carolina Population*. Columbia: Bureau of Economic Research, University of South Carolina, 1962.

Pinchot, Gifford. "Southern Forest Products and Forest Destruction and Conservation since 1865." In *The South in the Building of the Nation*, edited by Walter Lynwood Fleming. 13 vols. Richmond, Va.: Southern Historical Publication Society, 1909.

Pollitzer, William S. *The Gullah People and Their African Heritage*. Athens: University of Georgia Press, 1999.

Porcher, Richard D., and Sarah Fick. *The Story of Sea Island Cotton.* Salt Lake City: Gibbs Smith, 2005.

Power, Michael. *Lost Landscapes and Failed Economies: The Search for a Value of Place.* Washington, D.C.: Island Press, 1996.

Pozdena, Randall J. *Smart Growth and Its Effects on Housing Markets: The New Segregation.* Washington, D.C.: National Center for Public Policy Research, November 2002.

Press, Daniel M. *Saving Open Space: The Politics of Local Preservation in California.* Berkeley: University of California Press, 2002.

Putman, Robert. *Bowling Alone: The Collapse and Revival of American Community.* New York: Simon & Schuster, 2000.

Pyne, Stephen J. *Fire in America: A Cultural History of Wildland and Rural Fire.* Princeton: Princeton University Press, 1982.

Quincy, Susan, ed. *Memoir of the Life of Josiah Quincy, Junior of Massachusetts: 1744–1775.* Boston: John Wilson and Son, 1874.

Randolph, John. *Environmental Land Use Planning and Management.* Washington, D.C.: Island Press, 2004.

Redekop, Benjamin W. "Introduction: Connecting Leadership and Sustainability." In *Leadership for Environmental Sustainability.* New York: Routledge, 2010.

Repetto, Robert, ed. *Punctuated Equilibrium and the Dynamics of U.S. Environmental Policy.* New Haven: Yale University Press, 2006.

Reynolds, John S. *Reconstruction in South Carolina: 1865–1877.* Columbia, S.C.: State Publishing, 1905.

Robbins, Paul. *Lawn People: How Grasses, Weeds, and Chemicals Make Us Who We Are.* Philadelphia: Temple University Press, 2007.

Roelofs, Joan. *Greening Cities: Building Just and Sustainable Communities.* New York: Bootstrap Press, 1996.

Rome, Adam. *The Bulldozer in the Countryside: Suburban Sprawl and the Rise of American Environmentalism.* Cambridge, U.K.: Cambridge University Press, 2001.

Rose, Willie Lee. *Rehearsal for Reconstruction: The Port Royal Experiment.* Indianapolis: Bobbs-Merrill, 1964.

Rosenbaum, Walter A. *Environmental Politics and Policy.* Washington, D.C.: CQ Press, 2008.

Ross, Andrew. *The Celebration Chronicles: Life, Liberty, and the Pursuit of Property Value in Disney's New Town.* New York: Ballantine, 2006.

Rozario, Kevin. *The Culture of Calamity: Disaster & the Making of Modern America.* Chicago: University of Chicago Press, 2007.

Rybczynski, Witold. *Last Harvest: From Cornfield to New Town.* New York: Scribner, 2007.

Saarinen, Thomas F., David Seamon, and James L. Sell, eds. *Environmental Perception and Behavior: An Inventory and Prospect.* Chicago: University of Chicago Press, 1984.

Sabatier, Paul A., ed. *Theories of the Policy Process.* Boulder, Colo.: Westview Press, 1999.

Salley, Alexander S., Jr. *Narratives of Early Carolina.* 1911. Reprint, New York: Barnes and Noble, 1967.

Scheffer, Marten. *Critical Transitions in Nature and Society.* Princeton: Princeton University Press, 2009.

Schiffman, Irving. *Alternative Techniques for Managing Growth.* Berkeley, Calif.: Institute of Governmental Studies Press, 1989.

Schulman, Bruce J. *From Cotton Belt to Sunbelt: Federal Policy, Economic Development, and the Transformation of the South, 1938–1980.* New York: Oxford University Press, 1991.

Schwalm, Leslie A. *A Hard Fight for We: Women's Transition from Slavery to Freedom in South Carolina.* Urbana: University of Illinois Press, 1997.

Schweniger, Loren. *Black Property Owners in the South, 1790–1915.* Urbana: University of Illinois Press, 1990.

Silver, Timothy. *A New Face of the Countryside: Indians, Colonists, and Slaves in South Atlantic Forests, 1500–1800.* Cambridge, U.K.: Cambridge University Press, 1990.

Simkins, Francis Butler, and Robert Hilliard Woody. *South Carolina during Reconstruction.* Chapel Hill: University of North Carolina Press, 1932.

Smith, Zachary A. *The Environmental Policy Paradox.* Upper Saddle River, N.J.: Pearson/Prentice Hall, 2009.

Snow, Donald, ed. *Inside the Environmental Movement: Meeting the Leadership Challenge.* Washington D.C.: Island Press, 1992.

———. *Voices from the Environmental Movement: Perspectives for a New Era.* Washington D.C.: Island Press, 1992.

Steinberg, Ted. *Acts of God: The Unnatural History of Natural Disaster in America.* New York: Oxford University Press, 2000

———. *Down to Earth: Nature's Role in American History.* New York: Oxford University Press, 2002.

Stewart, Mart A. "Rice, Water, and Power: Landscapes of Domination and Resistance in the Lowcountry, 1790–1880." In *Out of the Woods: Essays in Environmental History,* edited by Char Miller and Hal Rothman. Pittsburgh: University of Pittsburgh Press, 1997.

———. "Southern Environmental History." In *A Companion to the American South,* edited by John B. Boles. Malden, Mass.: Blackwell, 2002.

Stone, Deborah. *Policy Paradox: The Art of Political Decision Making.* New York: Norton, 2001.

Sustainable America: A New Consensus for Prosperity, Opportunity, and a Healthy Environment for the Future. Washington, D.C.: President's Council on Sustainable Development, 1996.

Teaford, Jon. *Post-Suburbia: Government and Politics in the Edge Cities.* Baltimore: Johns Hopkins University Press, 1997.

Tindall, George. *The Emergence of the New South, 1913–1945.* Baton Rouge: Louisiana University Press, 1968.

Trimble, Stanley W. *Man-induced Soil Erosion on the Southern Piedmont, 1700–1970.* Ankeny, Iowa: Soil and Water Conservation Society of America, 1974.

True, James L., Bryan D. Jones, and Frank Baumgartner. "Punctuated-Equilibrium Theory." In *Theories of the Policy Process,* edited by P. Sabatier. Boulder, Colo.: Westview Press, 1999.

Turner, Frederick. *Rediscovering America: John Muir in His Time and Ours.* New York: Viking, 1985.

Tuten, James H. *Lowcountry Time and Tide: The Fall of the South Carolina Rice Kingdom.* Columbia: University of South Carolina Press, 2010.

Ullman, John E., ed. *The Suburban Economic Network: Economic Activity, Resource Use, and the Great Sprawl.* New York: Praeger, 1977.

Urban Land Institute. *Growing by Choice or Chance: State Strategies for Quality Growth in South Carolina.* Washington, D.C.: Urban Land Institute, 2003.

Vig, Norman J., and Michael G. Faure. *Green Giants? Environmental Policies of the United States and the European Union.* Cambridge: MIT Press, 2004.

Vig, Norman J., and Michael E. Kraft. *Environmental Policy for the Twenty-first Century.* Washington, D.C.: CQ Press, 2009.

Vileisis, Ann. *Discovering the Unknown Landscape: A History of America's Wetlands.* Washington, D.C.: Island Press, 1997.

———. *Kitchen Literacy: How We Lost Knowledge of Where Food Comes from and Why We Need to Get It Back.* Washington, D.C.: Island Press, 2008.

Weir, Robert M. *Colonial South Carolina: A History.* Columbia: University of South Carolina Press, 1983.

Williams, Bruce B. *Black Workers in an Industrial Suburb.* New Brunswick, N.J.: Rutgers University Press, 1987.

Williams, Michael. *Americans and Their Forests: A Historical Geography.* New York: Cambridge University Press, 1989.

Williamson, Joel. *After Slavery: The Negro in South Carolina during Reconstruction, 1861–1877.* New York: Norton, 1965.

Wilson, Alex, Jennifer L. Uncapher, Lisa McManigal, L. Hunter Lovins, Maureen Cureton, and William D. Browning, eds. *Green Development: Integrating Ecology and Real Estate.* New York: Wiley, 1998.

Wilson, Samuel. "An Account of the Province of Carolina, 1682." In Alexander S. Salley Jr., *Narratives of Early Carolina, 1650–1708.* New York: Scribner's, 1911.

Wolcott, Harry F. *Ethnography: A Way of Seeing.* Lanham, Md.: Alta Mira, 1999.

Wondolleck, Julia M., and Steven L. Yaffee. *Making Collaboration Work: Lessons from Innovation in Natural Resource Management.* Chicago: University of Chicago Press, 2000.

Wood, Peter H. *Black Majority: Negroes in Colonial South Carolina.* New York: Norton, 1974.

———. "The Changing Population of the Eighteenth-century South: An Overview." In *Powhatan's Mantle: Indians in the Colonial Southeast,* ed. Gregory A. Waskelov and Thomas Hatley. Lincoln: University of Nebraska Press, 2006.

Wright, Gavin. *Old South, New South: Revolutions in the Southern Economy since the Civil War.* Baton Rouge: Louisiana State University Press, 1996.

Wright, J. Leitch, Jr. *The Only Land They Knew: The Tragic Story of the American Indians in the Old South.* Lincoln: University of Nebraska Press, 1981.

Wyche, Bradford W. "Land Use Planning and Regulation." In *Environmental Law in South Carolina* (Columbia, S.C.: South Carolina Bar Association, 2011).

Yuhl, Stephanie E. *A Golden Haze of Memory: The Making of Historic Charleston.* Chapel Hill: University of North Carolina Press, 2005.

Zepke, Terrance. *Coastal South Carolina: Welcome to the Lowcountry.* Sarasota: Pineapple Press, 2006.

Newspapers

"Affairs in South Carolina." *New York Times,* October 11, 1867.

Agee, J. "Best Known for Its Eco-system, Sandy Island Holds Historic Trove." *Pawleys Island (S.C.) Coastal Observer,* November 6, 1997.

Allen, Jeff. "People of the Earth: Growing Good Food on the New Family Farm." *Charleston City Paper,* May 17, 2006.

———. "Why Charleston is the Right Place to Eat Right Now." *Charleston City Paper,* August 11, 2010.

"Another Day, Another Project." *Charleston Post and Courier,* February 6, 2010.

Apple, R. W., Jr. "A Southern Legacy and a New Spirit." *New York Times,* November 26, 1999.

Applebome, Peter. "After Hugo, a Storm over Beach Development." *New York Times,* September 24, 1989.

————. "Hugo's 3-year Wake: Lessons of a Hurricane." *New York Times,* September 18, 1992.

————. "Outlook Risky: Storm Cycles and Coastal Growth Could Make Disaster a Way of Life." *New York Times,* August 30, 1992.

————. "Tourism Enriches an Island Resort, but Hilton Head Blacks Feel Left Out." *New York Times,* September 2, 1994.

Associated Press. "Development Shakes Centuries-old Tradition of Grass Basket-Weaving Tradition." *Augusta (Ga.) Chronicle,* July 28, 2007.

Avery, Dennis. "Proper Development Can Advance Cause of Conservation." *State,* February 24, 2003.

"Award-winning Subdivision in Mount Pleasant, S.C., Moved beyond Obstacles." *State,* December 26, 2000.

"Balance Growth, Livability." Editorial. *Charleston Post and Courier,* January 10, 2010.

Ballantine, Todd. "Cut Future Population," *Island Packet* (Hilton Head–Bluffton, S.C.), February 11, 1991.

Barringer, Felicity. "Deals Turn Swaths of Timber Company Land into Development-free Areas." *New York Times,* April 2, 2006.

Bartelme, Tony. "Greenbelt Hits Brakes on Sprawl." *Charleston Post and Courier,* August 31, 1997.

————. "Recognizing Greenbelt Success." *Charleston Post and Courier,* March 14, 2010.

————. "S.C. Weighs Laws to Acquire Large Swaths of Land." *Charleston Post and Courier,* January 21, 2006.

————. "Sell-off Talk Prompts Chills, Thrills." *Charleston Post and Courier,* September 22, 2006.

————. "Shifting Sands: Pristine Sandy Island Keeps Its Spirit in Face of Change." *Charleston and Courier,* February 9, 1997.

————. "Tri-County Growth Binge 'Not a Good Pattern.'" *Charleston Post and Courier,* September 11, 1997.

Barton, Tom. "Hilton Head Emphasizing Green." *Island Packet* (Hilton Head–Bluffton, S.C.), December 27, 2010.

Beach, Dana. "Local Voices: South Carolina Conservation Bank Essential Investment in the Future." *Beaufort (S.C.) Gazette,* April 28, 2001.

Behre, Robert. "Agriculture Slowly Disappears from Johns Island, S.C." *Charleston Post and Courier,* June 8, 2004.

————. "Climate Change Is Hot Topic Today." *Charleston Post and Courier,* November 28, 2007.

————. "Forum to Look at Projects." *Charleston Post and Courier,* January 1, 2010.

————. "How We've Changed: Hurricane Left Deep, Indelible Imprint on Lowcountry." *Charleston Post and Courier,* September 22, 2009.

————. "Imagining Charleston 100 Years from Now." *Charleston Post and Courier,* December 31, 1999.

————. "I'On Subdivision Takes Shape." *Charleston Post and Courier,* March 15, 1999.

————. "Kind of Development Seen as a Key Issue in Growth." *Charleston Post and Courier,* April 2, 2001.

————. "Newpoint Boasts Sense of Community." *Charleston Post and Courier,* January 20, 1997.

————. "Rezoning Hot Topic of Debate." *Charleston Post and Courier,* March 7, 2006.

————. "Sprawl Summit Makes Dialogue Its Main Focus." *Charleston Post and Courier,* March 26, 2000.

———. "Sprawl vs. Growth Debate to Move On." *Charleston Post and Courier*, March 29, 2000.

———. "Summit Urges Smart Growth." *Charleston Post and Courier*, March 28, 2000.

———. "Time Has Come to Save Basket Stands, and the Communities That Create Them." *Charleston Post and Courier*, June 5, 2006.

———. "Wadmalaw Just the Start of Land-Use Debate." *Charleston Post and Courier*, March 15, 1999.

———. "'What Do We Want the Future of Johns Island to Be?'" *Charleston Post and Courier*, August 16, 2006.

———. "Whose Island Is Johns Island? The Farmer Who Is Fed Up with It All." *Charleston Post and Courier*, June 8, 2004.

———. "Whose Island Is Johns Island? The Many Battles of One Resident." *Charleston Post and Courier*, June 7, 2004.

———. "Zoning Idea Draws Critics." *Charleston Post and Courier*, April 26, 2006.

"Big Storm in the South." *New York Times*, October 3, 1898.

Binkley, Christina. "Developers Discover Old Values Can Bring Astonishing Returns." *Wall Street Journal*, December 4, 1996.

Blair, Eric. "The Friction between the Fair-Trade and Local-First Movements." *Charleston City Paper*, April 30, 2008.

Bowers, Doris, and Seward Bowers. "What Does the Future Hold for Hilton Head Island?" *Island Packet* (Hilton Head–Bluffton, S.C.), January 4, 1973.

Bowie, Jack. "Zoning Hearings Create Much Heat, Little Light." *Island Packet* (Hilton Head–Bluffton, S.C.), May 4, 1972.

Bozarth, Bennett E. "Citizens Should Demand Agency Restructuring, Sanford Says." *Daniel Island (S.C.) News*, May 31, 2007.

Bradford, Tom. "I-526 Debate Shows Local Road Building Has Reached End Game." *Charleston Post and Courier*, September 25, 2010.

Brinson, Claudia Smith. "Crossing a Great Divide: Chapter 7: Black, White and Green: Southern Conservation Has a Problem: The Inhabitants of Remaining Natural Areas often Are Poor, Rural Blacks Longing for Development." *State*, May 17, 2007.

———. "Nature and Nurture: Author Mary Alice Monroe Reaps Rich Stories from the Lowcountry's Landscape—But She Also Works to Preserve It." *State*, December 11, 2005.

Brinson, Ron. "Looks Like We're Getting Serious about Controlling Growth." *Charleston Post and Courier*, May 6, 2007.

Buntain, Rex. "Lowcountry Farms Give Way to Homes and Golf-Course Turf." *Beaufort (S.C.) Gazette*, April 20, 2001.

Burris, Roddie. "Senator Pitches Planned Growth Legislation." *State*, July 31, 1999.

Campbell, Emory S. "'Comyas' Forever Changed the Heirs of Mitchelville." *State*, February 20, 2011.

Chamberlain, Lisa. "Trying for Balance in Rural Development." *New York Times*, April 29, 2007.

"Champion for Conservation." Editorial. *Charleston Post and Courier*, November 29, 2010.

"Charleston-Area Traffic Woes Get Worse." *Charleston Post and Courier*, September 9, 2004.

"The Charleston Cyclone." *New York Times*, August 27, 1885.

"Charleston in Grip of Fatal Hurricane." *New York Times*, August 29, 1911.

"Coastal Council to Hear Sandy Island Development." *State*, June 17, 1993.

Coley, Jill. "The Road to Urban Sprawl? Growth Followed I-526." *Charleston Post and Courier*, January 14, 2007.

Conroy, Pat. "Don't Destroy Beaufort, Lowcountry." *Beaufort (S.C.) Gazette,* April 20, 2006.

"Conservation Bank: Wise Investment." Editorial. *Charleston Post and Courier,* April 10, 2004.

"Conservation Fight." Editorial. *Charleston Post and Courier,* April 6, 2005.

"Conservation Kudos: State's Efforts Impress Babbitt." Editorial. *Charleston Post and Courier,* April 21, 1998.

"Conservation Success Story." Editorial. *Charleston Post and Courier,* April 20, 2003.

"Constant Peril of Overflow: Why Should Men Build Cities Where Danger Is Always Imminent." *New York Times,* September 17, 1900.

"The Cotton Crop." *New York Times,* September 11, 1893.

"A County in Crisis." Editorial. *Beaufort (S.C.) Gazette,* October 21, 2001.

"A County in Crisis." *Island Packet* (Hilton Head–Bluffton, S.C.), October 21, 2001.

"County to Buy Parcels Near Okatie River to Prevent Their Development." *Beaufort (S.C.) Gazette,* January 27, 2010.

Covington, Marti. "When the Race Resumes: Recession Gives Environment a Break." *Beaufort (S.C.) Gazette,* January 30, 2010.

Cushman, John H., Jr. "South Carolinians Nurture a Little Cause That Could." *New York Times,* November 20, 2000.

Dayton, Kathleen. "Island Bargain Wins Award." *Myrtle Beach (S.C.) Sun News,* August 28, 1997.

"A Desire for Green." *Island Packet* (Hilton Head–Bluffton, S.C.), September 24, 2006.

"Development Booms in Hurricane Zones." *Dubuque (Iowa) Telegraph-Herald,* May 16, 2004.

Dewig, Rob. "Protecting the Lowcountry: Conservation Efforts Gaining Ground." *Carolina Morning News* (Bluffton, S.C.), August 4, 2003.

Dixon, Chris. "36 Hours in Charleston, South Carolina." *New York Times,* March 11, 2007.

Duke, A. B. "Graham's Promised Land." *Charleston Post and Courier,* May 11, 1997.

Fennell, Edward C. "Development Increase Worries Rockville, S.C. Residents." *Charleston Post and Courier,* August 15, 2006.

———. "Fighting to Save a Heritage: Preserving the Gullah Culture Is Challenged by Land Development Throughout the Lowcountry." *Charleston Post and Courier,* July 16, 2009.

———. "Jordan Tract Vote Stalled for 120 Days." *Charleston Post and Courier,* October 11, 1995.

———. "Keeping Gullah Culture Alive." *Charleston Post and Courier,* July 2, 2009.

———. "Zoning Battle Heats Up." *Charleston Post and Courier,* October 30, 1995.

Findlay, Prentiss. "Another Rural Battle Brews." *Charleston Post and Courier,* August 6, 2006.

———. "Talks on Extension of I-526 Ongoing: Country Seeks New Contract with DOT, State Bank." *Charleston Post and Courier,* October 5, 2011.

———. "Awendaw Likely to OK Development."*Charleston Post and Courier,* August 16, 2006.

———. "Objections to I-526 Expansion Increasing." *Charleston Post and Courier,* September 30, 2010.

———. "Park Plans to Outdo Piers." *Charleston Post and Courier,* July 9, 2007.

———. "'Silent Majority' Backs I-526." *Charleston Post and Courier,* February 11, 2011.

———. "There is a Lot of History There." *Charleston Post and Courier,* July 12, 2010.

———. "Weaving History into a Growing Area." *Charleston Post and Courier,* December 13, 2006.

———, and David Slade. "Cities Battle Sprawl by Filling in the Holes." *Charleston Post and Courier,* October 16, 2008.

———. "Making over Johnnie Dodds: Project to Improve Traffic, Livability Will Start This Year." *Charleston Post and Courier,* May 10, 2010.

———. "SCDOT Pushes for Decision on I-526." *Charleston Post and Courier,* October 13, 2010.

"Forum to Address Changes in the City." *Charleston Post and Courier,* January 4, 2010.

Frankston, Janet. "Nature as a Neighbor: With the Rise of 'Conservation Subdivisions,' Developers Discover Green Spaces Make Economic Sense." *Atlanta Journal and Constitution,* July 29, 2002.

Frazier, Marjorie. "A Struggle for Sweetgrass." *Charleston Post and Courier,* September 13, 1999.

Fretwell, Sammy. "Agency's Wetland-Tradeoff Policy Raises Questions." *State,* March 16, 1996.

———. "Charleston Project Holds Up Columbia Road Work." *State,* January 23, 2011.

———. "Dana Beach Is King of Conservation." *State,* May 30, 2010.

———. "South Carolina Environmental Board's Rules Get Tough on Polluters." *State,* December 15, 2000.

———. "South Carolina Governor Signs Bill to Allow Protection of Wild Lands." *State,* April 19, 2002.

———. "Special Report: Coalition is Fighting to Save Slice of S.C. Wilderness."*State,* February 25, 1995.

———. "Study Shows South Carolina Lost 142,000 Acres of Forests between 1993–2000." *State,* November 27, 2001.

"From Charleston. Condition of the City Reports from Sherman: The Negroes Enlisting." *New York Times,* March 9, 1865.

Frost, Peter. "Mayors Urging Action on Climate Change." *Island Packet* (Hilton Head-Bluffton, S.C.), November 6, 2007.

Gioielli, Rob. "Developer Says Urban Sprawl Driven by Market." *Island Packet* (Hilton Head-Bluffton, S.C.), March 12, 2001.

Glanton, Dahleen. "Ex-slaves' Land Heirs Struggle to Keep Property in Family Hands." *Chicago Tribune,* July 17, 2006.

Glover, Kerri. "Ground Zero: Hugo's Night of Terror Leave Lowcountry in Ruins." *Charleston Post and Courier,* September 21, 2009.

"Gov. Sanford Names Climate Change Group." *U.S. Federal News Service,* February 16, 2007.

"Gov. Sanford's Budget to Add $20 Million to Conservation Bank." *U.S. Federal News Service,* November 27, 2006.

"Gov. Tillman's Anxiety." *New York Times,* September 3, 1893.

Graham, Denesha. "Drawing the Line." *Charleston Post and Courier,* October 14, 2003.

"Great Damage Caused by Storms." *New York Times,* August 26, 1885.

"'Great Day' for Conservation." Editorial. *Charleston Post and Courier,* December 12, 2004.

"Great Prospect for Poplar Grove." *Charleston Post and Courier,* November 5, 2004.

Green, Dwayne. "Race Has No Part in Awendaw Development Debate."*Charleston City Paper,* May 29, 2009.

"Greenbelt Success Will Require Focusing on the 'Big Picture.'" Editorial. *Charleston Post and Courier,* July 23, 2005.

"Groups to Sponsor Forum on Global-warming Issues." *Charleston Post and Courier,* February 20, 2003.

"Growing by Choice, Not by Chance: South Carolina Smart Growth Initiative Explores Options." *P.R. Newswire*, September 26, 2002.

"Growing New Farmers for the Lowcountry." *U.S. Federal News Service*, March 10, 2008.

"Growth at Tipping Point, Sanford Tells Conference." *Charleston Post and Courier*, March 27, 2007.

Gruson, Kerry. "Healing Comes Slowly to Woods and Streams Where Hurricane Left Death." *New York Times*, November 12, 1989.

Guilfoil, Michael. "New Urbanism Upscale Exercise in Nostalgia, or Best Hope for Handling Growth and Rekindling Sense of Community." *Spokesman* (Spokane, Wash.), May 21, 1996.

Hagenbaugh, Barbara. "Economic Growth from Hurricanes Could Outweigh Costs." *USA Today*, September 27, 2004.

Hagood, Elizabeth M. "Lowcountry Open Land Trust Preserves Our 'Common Heritage.'" *Charleston Post and Courier*, February 15, 2011.

Haltiwanger, Will. "Developments Like Sewee Preserve Don't Really Help the Environment." *State*, March 17, 2003.

Hambrick, Greg. "The Big Prize and the Art of Compromise: Let's Make a Deal." *Charleston City Paper*, March 24, 2010.

———. "Public Pans I-526 Parkway." *Charleston City Paper*, September 14, 2010.

Hankla, Kristen. "Engineers Offer Alternatives to I-526 Extension." *Charleston Post and Courier*, January 4, 2008.

Hardin, Jason. "Harnessing Growth Portrayed as Vital." *Charleston Post and Courier*, October 14, 2001.

———. "Report Advises S.C. to Rein in Sprawl." *Charleston Post and Courier*, May 5, 2004.

———. "Respected Charleston, S.C., Newspaper Chairman Dies." *Charleston Post and Courier*, June 15, 2004.

Harrell, Bob. "The Sweetgrass Basket Case." *Atlanta Journal and Constitution*, April 24, 1988.

Heavens, Alan J. "Blueprint 2000: Many Prefer Tradition to Futuristic." *News & Record* (Piedmont Triad, N.C.), April 11, 1999.

"Heed Consensus on Warming." *Charleston Post and Courier*, February 7, 2007.

"Heed Voters on Green Space." *Charleston Post and Courier*, November 10, 2010.

Hicks, Brian. "Conservation Bank Keeping Land Untouched." *Charleston Post and Courier*, February 20, 2005.

———. "Growth Takes Toll on South Carolina's Coastal Culture." *Charleston Post and Courier*, November 28, 2003.

———. "Islands in the Lowcountry Marshes Face Fierce Development Pressure." *Charleston Post and Courier*, August 21, 2005.

———. "Our Changing Coast." *Charleston Post and Courier*, November 28, 2003.

———. "Residents Plan to Battle Wadmalaw Density Plan." *Charleston Post and Courier*, January 28, 1999.

———. "When It Comes to Produce, Many Say Fresh Is Best." *Charleston Post and Courier*, July 30, 2007.

"Hilton Head Islanders Split Racially over Incorporation Vote." *New York Times*, May 10, 1983.

Holleman, Joey. "Conservationists Find Ways to Pay for Land Preservation." *State*, November 19, 2000.

Hsieh, Jeremy. "A Farming Renaissance?" *Beaufort (S.C.) Gazette*, October 8, 2007.

Humphries, Josephine. "Roaming Carolina Low Country." *New York Times,* March 3, 1991.

"A Hurricane's Fury Fast Forgotten." *Washington Post,* April 9, 1990.

"I-526 'Parkway' Is a Non-Starter." Editorial. *Charleston Post and Courier,* February 1, 2011.

"In the Wrecked Territory." *New York Times,* September 1, 1893.

"It's All about Balance." *Charleston Post and Courier,* March 7, 2010.

Jakubiak, David. "Study: Global Warming Will Impact Carolina Coast." *Beaufort (S.C.) Gazette,* June 24, 2001.

Johnson, Jessica. "Election Splits Awendaw." *Charleston Post and Courier,* October 31, 2009.

———. "Sweetgrass Pavilion to be Dedicated." *Charleston Post and Courier,* July 2, 2009.

Johnson, Robert. "New Frontier in Waterfront: Swamps." *New York Times,* October 31, 2004.

Johnson, Thomas A. "Blacks Press Struggle to Retain Farmland." *New York Times,* July 13, 1980.

Jonsson, Patrik. "Preserve or Let Go: Blacks Debate Fate of Their Landmarks." *Christian Science Monitor,* January 31, 2007.

"Kiawah Island Gateway to Go into Conservation Protection." *P.R. Newswire,* January 21, 2004.

King, Wayne. "Federal Funds Pour into Sunbelt States." *New York Times,* February 9, 1976.

Knich, Diane. "Coastal Conservation Proposes Alternative to I-526 Extension." *Charleston Post and Courier,* January 25, 2009.

———. "Parkway Would Complete I-526." *Charleston Post and Courier,* July 29, 2010.

———. "South Carolina Sweetgrass Basketmakers Depend on the Hard-To-Find Plants, Researcher Hopes to Help Grow More." *Charleston Post and Courier,* July 6, 2006.

Koob, Lindsay. "Under the Sea: Greetings from Charleston's Underwater Future." *Charleston City Paper,* September 12, 2007.

"Land Conservation Adds to Value of Lowcountry Life." *Island Packet* (Hilton Head-Bluffton, S.C.), December 12, 2007.

"Land Purchase to Help Save Wildlife Habitat in South Carolina." *Charleston Post and Courier,* June 15, 2004.

Langley, Lynne. "Area Makes Progress but Many See More to Do." *Charleston Post and Courier,* April 22, 1998.

———. "Brighter Day Seen for Earth." *Charleston Post and Courier,* April 22, 1996.

———. "Climate Forecast Ominous." *Charleston Post and Courier,* April 20, 1995.

———. "Conservancy Puts Protecting Nature First." *Charleston Post and Courier,* November 1, 1998.

———. "Lowcountry Banking on Wetlands Savings Pays Off." *Charleston Post and Courier,* March 26, 1996.

———. "Refuge Plan Wins Wildlife Agency's OK." *Charleston Post and Courier,* June 11, 1995.

———. "Sandy Island Bridge Plan Torn Down Again." *Charleston Post and Courier,* September 22, 1995.

———. "Saving Scenery: The Lowcountry Open Land Trust." *Charleston Post and Courier,* May 15, 1995.

———. "Tax Incentives Boost Lowcountry Conservation Easements." *Charleston Post and Courier,* April 28, 2003.

———. "Two-foot Rise in Sea Level Predicted This Century." *Charleston Post and Courier,* March 1, 2000.

Lauderdale, David. "Fraser's Model Proved Beauty Can Trump All." *Island Packet* (Hilton Head-Bluffton, S.C.), September 3, 2006.

"Law to Stem S.C. Beach Erosion Called Too Little, Too Late by Some." *Atlanta Journal and Constitution,* June 5, 1988.

Lawrence, Stratton. "Cultivating Future Lowcountry Growers: Farming's New Wave." *Charleston City Paper,* April 21, 2010.

———. "The Dirt on Dirt." *Charleston City Paper,* April 2, 2008.

———. "Harvest of Plenty: Farmers Share Abundance with Community-Supported Agriculture Initiatives." *Charleston City Paper,* March 26, 2008.

———. "Keeping It Rural: The Plight of Small Farmers on Johns Island." *Charleston City Paper,* November 22, 2006.

———."Mount Pleasant's Sweetgrass Basketmakers Go Further Afield to Obtain Materials Grass Shortage." *Charleston City Paper,* July 30, 2008.

———. "Public Meetings Begin Comment Period on Mark Clark Extension." *Charleston City Paper,* November 19, 2008.

———. "Rita's Roots Ends Its Run on Wadmalaw." *Charleston City Paper,* January 22, 2010.

Lee, Matt, and Ted Lee. "Rice Fields Cultivate Old Ways." *New York Times,* February 25, 2001.

Leifermann, Henry. "An Out-of-the-Way Isle in South Carolina." *New York Times,* April 3, 1994.

Leland, Jack. "Basket Weaving: African Art Survival?" *Charleston News and Courier,* March 27, 1949.

"Lessons We've Learned from the Land Boom." *Bluffton (S.C.) Today,* December 14, 2007.

Lewan, Todd, and Dolores Barclay, "Torn from the Land: Today, Developers and Lawyers Use a Legal Maneuver to Strip Black Families of Their Lands." *Authentic Voice,* December 9, 2001.

L'Heureux, Dave. "Family Farms Remain Predominant in South Carolina." *State,* February 4, 2004.

"The Little Emperor of Hilton Head." *Atlanta Journal Constitution,* June 24, 1979.

Lovett, Megan. "Development Brings Challenges." *Beaufort (S.C.) Gazette,* July 29, 2007.

"Lowcountry among Nation's Top 100 Fastest-growing Areas." *Charleston Post and Courier,* April 5, 2007.

"Maintain Rural Protections." Editorial. *Charleston Post and Courier,* June 19, 2009.

"Make Green Protections Official." Editorial. *Charleston Post and Courier,* February 6, 2011.

Maki, Amos. "Charleston, S.C. Mayor Touts Smart Growth for Memphis." *Memphis Commercial Appeal,* September 22, 2005.

Marshall, Bill. "S.C. Must Get Serious about Conservation." *State,* January 29, 2002.

Maze, Jonathan. "Some Affluent Arrivals Seek Out Ways to Become Involved with Charleston Groups." *Charleston Post and Courier,* July 26, 2006.

McDermott, John P. "Ginn Sees Land of Opportunity." *Charleston Post and Courier,* February 12, 2006.

———. "Industries Find That Corporate Conservation is Good Business." *Charleston Post and Courier,* January 13, 1997.

———. "MeadWestvaco's 70,000 Acre Plan." *Charleston Post and Courier,* May 2, 2007.

———. "MeadWestvaco's 3-year-Old Real Estate Unit Looks to Cover All Bases." *Charleston Post and Courier,* January 24, 2011.

———. "Project Forsakes Convention for Conservation." *Charleston Post and Courier,* September 15, 2003.

————. "South Carolina Farming Industry Profits from 'Organic' Movement." *Charleston Post and Courier,* April 29, 2002.

McDowell, Elsa. "In Search of Sweetgrass for Basketmakers." *Charleston Post and Courier,* December 10, 2000.

"MeadWestvaco's Extraordinary Land Challenge and Commitment." *Charleston Post and Courier,* May 6, 2007.

Meggett, Linda L. "Development Hits Highway 17." *Charleston Post and Courier,* August 5, 1996.

————. "Jordan Tract Developers Scale Down Plan." *Charleston Post and Courier,* January 23, 1997.

————. "Jordan Tract Gets Council's First OK." *Charleston Post and Courier,* February 19, 1997.

————. "Jordan Tract Rezoning OK'd." *Charleston Post and Courier,* March 12, 1997.

Menchaca, Ron. "A Conversation with Joe Riley." *Charleston Post and Courier,* September 28, 2000.

————. "Foundation Grants $4 Million to Protect Forests on South Carolina Coast." *Charleston Post and Courier,* November 25, 2003.

————, and Brian Hicks. "MeadWestvaco to Sell 6,600 Acre Tract." *Charleston Post and Courier,* August 4, 2004.

"Miles of South Carolina Coastline at Stake: Sea Level Rise Threatening the Lowcountry." *Save the Lowcountry Campaign* news release, February 10, 2009.

Miller, Jeff. "An Education in Cultural Preservation: School Teaches Sea Islanders to Cope." *State,* October 25, 1993.

————. "A River Runs around It: Sandy Islanders Don't Feel Cut Off." *State,* April 27, 1993.

Miller, Jessica. "Taking a Stand for Heritage: Town Eyes Incentive for Businesses to Build Places for Basketmakers." *Charleston Post and Courier,* March 24, 2011.

Minis, Wevonneda. "Changing Character: The Old Cottages on the Isle of Palms Are Being Demolished and Replaced by Huge Homes, All Part of the Town's Evolution That Began in the Aftermath of Hurricane Hugo." *Charleston Post and Courier,* September 12, 2004.

————. "Emory Campbell: Keeping Penn Alive." *Charleston Post and Courier,* February 18, 1995.

Mitchell, Liz. "Does the Recession Offer an Opportunity to Scale Back Growth, Benefit the Environment?" *Beaufort (S.C.) Gazette,* August 22, 2009.

————. "Scientists: Rising Sea Levels Threaten Hilton Head, Fripp, and Parris Islands." *Island Packet* (Hilton Head-Bluffton, S.C.), March 29, 2009.

Monk, John, and Sammy Fretwell. "DHEC under Fire." *State,* November 16, 2008.

"More Osprey Found along SC's South Coast." *State,* October 11, 2010.

Mullener, Elizabeth. "A Sister City Flourishes." *New Orleans Times-Picayune,* December 14, 2005.

Munday, Dave. "Two Lowcountry Cities Start Effort to Curb Global Warming." *Charleston Post and Courier,* February 24, 2001.

Nemirow, Arnold, and Bob Baugh. "Nature Conservancy Grows Its Lowcountry Presence." *Charleston Post and Courier,* November 7, 2009.

Nix, Mark. "Land Restrictions Costly." *Charleston Post and Courier,* March 1, 2005.

"No Sprawling Allowed: County Planners Want Proposed Osprey Point Development to Be More Like a Village." *Island Packet* (Hilton Head-Bluffton, S.C.), June 14, 2007.

"North America's Longest Cable Bridge Dedicated in South Carolina." *Charleston City Paper,* March 24, 2010.

"Novelist Decries Sprawl." *Beaufort (S.C.) Gazette,* April 20, 2006.

"Old Rice Fields Spawn Controversy." *Charlotte (N.C.) Observer,* December 15, 1985.

"On the Way to Beaufort." *New York Times,* September 2, 1893.

"Opposition to Beach Regulation Mounting." *State,* January 17, 1988.

"Out with the Tide: S.C. Beaches in Danger." *State,* May 22, 1988.

Paras, Andy. "Wildlife Preserve or Tourist Destination?" *Charleston Post and Courier,* May 1, 2005.

Parker, Adam. "Director Jennie Stephens Helps Preserve Heirs' Property." *Charleston Post and Courier,* February 19, 2011.

Parker, Jim. "Hurricane Gave Insurance Industry a Wakeup Call." *Charleston Post and Courier,* September 21, 1999.

———. "Market a Boon to Growers, Buyers." *Charleston Post and Courier,* June 17, 1996.

"The Path of the Storm." *New York Times,* August 30, 1893.

Paulsen, Monte. "Failure of Bridge Plan Irks Sandy Island Owners." *State,* June 27, 1995.

———. "Special Report: A Different World on Sandy Island." *State,* February 19, 1995.

———. "Special Report: A Handful of Powerful Families Hold Region's Fate." *State,* February 19, 1995.

———. "Special Report: The Quiet Battle for Bull Creek." *State,* February 19, 1995.

———. "Three Roads, One Intersection: E. Craig Wall Jr." *State,* February 19, 1995.

Peirce, Neal, and Curtis Johnson. "A Powerful Wave of Growth: Trying to Balance Growth, Conservation." Editorial. *Charleston Post and Courier,* September 9, 2007.

Petersen, Bo. "ACE Basin at 20." *Charleston Post and Courier,* December 14, 2009.

———. "Area-Defining Marshes Drowning." *Charleston Post and Courier,* September 12, 2010.

———. "Beavers Create Problems for Human Habitat." *Charleston Post and Courier,* October 19, 2010.

———. "CCL: From Small Time to Big Deal." *Charleston Post and Courier,* September 27, 2009.

———. "Climate Change Could Hurt Fort Sumter." *Charleston Post and Courier,* July 12, 2007.

———. "Easements Likely Next Conservation Battlefield." *Charleston Post and Courier,* December 2, 2006.

———. "East Edisto Master Plan Introduced." *Charleston Post and Courier,* December 10, 2009.

———. "Ex-Regulator Seeks Public-Private Alliances."*Charleston Post and Courier,* March 14, 2005.

———. "The Gobbling Up of the Lowcountry." *Charleston Post and Courier,* October 15, 2006.

———. "Green Corridor." *Charleston Post and Courier,* July 28, 2009.

———. "Heirs' Property Owners' Hold on Land Often Delicate." *Charleston Post and Courier,* August 14, 2006.

———. "Humble Island Leads to Conservation Legacy." *Charleston Post and Courier,* February 15, 2011.

———. "Kiawah Island Tests Aim to Restore Wetlands." *Charleston Post and Courier,* March 1, 2004.

———. "Kiawah Neighbors Spark New Preservation Program." *Charleston Post and Courier,* April 27, 2004.

———. "Local Students Are Heard: We Now Have a State Handicraft." *Charleston Post and Courier,* February 24, 2006.

———. "Preserving Our Coastal Forests." *Georgetown (S.C.) Times,* December 12, 2003.

———. "Sprawl, Traffic Arising from a Surprising Source." *Charleston Post and Courier,* February 19, 2006.

———. "Tale of Two Cities Highlights Charleston's Growth Concerns." *Charleston Post and Courier,* October 4, 2005.

———. "The Gobbling Up of the Lowcountry." *Charleston Post and Courier,* October 15, 2006.

———. "Westvaco in Transition." *Charleston Post and Courier,* December 19, 2003.

———. "Wood Storks Stage Comeback." *Charleston Post and Courier,* July 27, 2010.

———, and Ron Menchaca. "Art of the Deal." *Charleston Post and Courier,* August 14, 2005.

———, and Dave Munday. "Lender Foreclosing on Watson Hill." *Charleston Post and Courier,* January 3, 2009.

Phillips, Noelle. "S.C. Residents Flock to Urban Areas, Coast," *State,* March 24, 2011.

Phua, Chelsea. "A Fight to Save the Special Things." *Providence Journal,* February 26, 2006.

Piacente, Steve. "As Earth Warms, Seas May Rise—Coastal Flooding Forecast." *Charleston Post and Courier,* July 10, 1997.

"Plotting East Edisto's Course." Editorial. *Charleston Post and Courier,* April 23, 2008.

"Poplar Grove Conservation Victory." *Charleston Post and Courier,* April 2, 2005.

Porter, Arlie. "Board Steadfast on Island Density." *Charleston Post and Courier,* January 29, 1999.

———. "Changes to Land-use Rules Would Allow More Development on Wadmalaw." *Charleston Post and Courier,* December 29, 2000.

———. "Chaos Concludes Wadmalaw Meeting." *Charleston Post and Courier,* July 11, 2001.

———. "Charting County's Future." *Charleston Post and Courier,* March 17, 1997.

———. "Citizens Speak Out on Development." *Charleston Post and Courier,* October 15, 1997.

———. "Comprehensive Plan to Have a Big Impact." *Charleston Post and Courier,* October 25, 1999.

———. "Council's Landmark Decision." *Charleston Post and Courier,* April 6, 1999.

———. "County Approves Plan to Control Rural Growth." *Charleston Post and Courier,* April 21, 1999.

———. "County Planners Define Land-Use Categories." *Charleston Post and Courier,* August 5, 1998.

———. "County's Future Depends on Sales Tax, Leaders Told." *Charleston Post and Courier,* August 18, 2000.

———. "County Passes Wadmalaw Zoning Map." *Charleston Post and Courier,* October 17, 2001.

———. "Growing Pains for Wadmalaw Development." *Charleston Post and Courier,* March 10, 1999.

———. "Land Use Fight Keys on Race, Rights." *Charleston Post and Courier,* July 20, 2001.

———. "Land Use Plan Draws Suit Threat." *Charleston Post and Courier,* March 26, 1999.

———. "Land Use Plan Draws Support." *Charleston Post and Courier,* January 26, 1999.

———. "Land Use Rules Vital, Backers Say." *Charleston Post and Courier,* October 27, 2000.

———. "South Carolina Industries, Utilities Ordered to Cut Cooper River Pollution." *Charleston Post and Courier,* May 30, 2002.

———. "Stay Solid on Comprehensive Plan." *Charleston Post and Courier,* November 17, 2003.

———. "Studies Project Growth." *Charleston Post and Courier,* October 3, 1999.

"Preserving the Family Homes: Southern Blacks Work Together to Keep Ancestral Lands." *Charleston Gazette,* October 16, 2006.

Quick, David. "CSA's Great Way to Get Veggies." *Charleston Post and Courier,* November 17, 2009.

———. "Development Border Touches Nerve." *Charleston Post and Courier,* June 18, 1998.

———. "Earth Day at 40." *Charleston Post and Courier,* April 20, 2010.

———. "Jordan Tract Plan Is Rejected." *Charleston Post and Courier,* December 13, 1995.

———. "Mount Pleasant Struggles with Sprawl." *Charleston Post and Courier,* December 27, 1999.

———. "Mt. Pleasant Considers Cap on Growth." *Charleston Post and Courier,* January 7, 2000.

———. "Old Ideas Put to Work in New Community Plans." *Charleston Post and Courier,* May 11, 1995.

———. "Organic Farmer Cultivates Movement." *Charleston Post and Courier,* July 31, 2010.

———. "Pathway to Fitness." *Charleston Post and Courier,* May 12, 2008.

———. "Planning Board Will Make Its Final Land Use Proposal." *Charleston Post and Courier,* September 17, 1998.

———. "South Carolina Coastal Conservation League's Long Crusade Earns Friends, Foes." *Charleston Post and Courier,* September 29, 2004.

———. "South Carolina Governor Pushes Land Conservation Bank at Summit." *Charleston Post and Courier,* March 13, 2001.

———. "To Market, to Market." *Charleston Post and Courier,* June 7, 2003.

———. "Urbanism Growth Part of Plan." *Charleston Post and Courier,* April 30, 1998.

———. "Vince Graham: Man behind I'On Promotes Traditional Development." *Charleston Post and Courier,* October 25, 2003.

Ramsey, Mike. "Sierra Club Wants Growth Plan Review." *State,* August 29, 2000.

———. "Study Finds South Carolina Land Development Increased Faster than Population." *State,* March 9, 2001.

Ravenel, Helen. "Sweetgrass: More Than a Basket—A Weave of Tradition." *Moultrie News* (Mt. Pleasant, S.C.) February 6, 2008.

———. "Wildlife Comes with the Territory Where Sweetgrass Is Involved." *Moultrie News* (Mt. Pleasant, S.C.), December 11, 2008.

Reed, Roy. "Blacks in South Struggle to Keep the Little Land They Have Left." *New York Times,* December 7, 1972.

"Report Links Sprawl to Declining Coastal Health." *US Newswire,* April 17, 2002.

"Residents Can Guide Growth." Editorial. *Charleston Post and Courier,* October 18, 2008.

"Residents of Island Find Bridge Threatening." *State,* April 12, 1993.

"Resisting the Road to Extinction: As Developers Move In and a Coastal Highway Grows Wider, Some Determined South Carolinians Try to Save a Roadside Trade Traced to Slave Ancestors—Fashioning Baskets Made of Sweetgrass." *Chicago Tribune,* June 7, 2006.

Riddle, Lyn. "As Hilton Head Grows, What of the Environment?" *New York Times,* July 28, 1991.

————. "Charleston, S.C.: A Village Proposed for a Pastoral Island." *New York Times*, December 13, 1992.

————. "Hilton Head, S.C.: With Expansion, What of Ecology?" *New York Times*, July 28, 1991.

————. "South Carolina Confronts Urban Sprawl." *New York Times*, December 26, 1999.

————. "Spring Island, S.C.: Development with an Environmental Bent." *New York Times*, June 28, 1992.

————. "Upscale Homes for South Carolina Woods." *New York Times*, October 14, 2001.

Rivers, John M., Jr. "Expand Hugh Lane's Bold Idea."*Charleston Post and Courier,* June 4, 2007.

Robertson, Pat. "Land Initiative Year's Top Story." *State,* December 27, 2001.

————. "New Leader Has Ducks Unlimited Expanding Reach." *State,* July 2, 2006.

————. "S.C. Desperately Needs Conservation Bank Act." *State,* January 13, 2002.

Robinson, Tatsha. "Developer Land Rush Divides Black Families." *Boston Globe,* November 23, 2002.

Roman, Dave. "Mayor Plants Bipartisan Seed." *Jacksonville Florida Times-Union,* January 15, 1999.

"Ruined by the Floods." *New York Times,* September 15, 1885.

"Rural Preservation Innovation." Editorial. *Charleston Post and Courier,* September 10, 1999.

Sanford, Mark. "A Conservative Conservationist? Why the Right Needs to Get Invested in the Search for Climate Change Solutions." *Washington Post,* February 23, 2007.

"Saving the Conservation Bank." *Charleston Post and Courier,* May 23, 2004.

Scardino, Albert. "A Gust of Bankruptcy and Scandal Rattles Elegant Hilton Head Island." *New York Times,* March 15, 1987.

"S.C. Leaders See the Need for Growth Blueprint: Forum Participants Push for Guidelines." *State,* July 22, 1993.

Schmidt, William E. "Beaufort, S.C.: The Rise of the Low Country." *New York Times,* June 1, 1986.

"Sea Islands Overwhelmed." *New York Times,* September 3, 1893.

"The Sea Islands Suffer." *New York Times,* October 2, 1896.

Segal, Jon. "Hispanics Outnumber Blacks on Hilton Head." *Beaufort (S.C.) Gazette,* March 16, 2001.

"Sellout Beach Pact Protested." *State,* March 8, 1988.

"Sewing the Seeds for Future Generations." *Moultrie News* (Mt. Pleasant, S.C.), July 10, 2010.

Shapiro, Michael. "Okatie River Development Plan Gets Initial OK." *Island Packet* (Hilton Head-Bluffton, S.C.), January 11, 2008.

————. "Okatie Village Developers Agree to Pay County $10.7 Million." *Island Packet* (Hilton Head-Bluffton, S.C.), September 5, 2008.

————. "1,252 New Homes Proposed for Land between S.C. 170 and the Okatie River." *Island Packet* (Hilton Head-Bluffton, S.C.), January 10, 2008.

————. "Planning Commission Says It Needs More Information on Okatie Village." *Island Packet* (Hilton Head-Bluffton, S.C.), February 5, 2008.

————. "Planning Commission Votes Down Okatie Village." *Island Packet* (Hilton Head-Bluffton, S.C.), March 4, 2008.

Skalskie, Ginny. "County Planners Envision Village to Help Tame Sprawl in Okatie." *Island Packet* (Hilton Head-Bluffton, S.C.), July 17, 2007.

Slade, David. "Charleston Makes Pledge to Cut Emissions." *Charleston Post and Courier,* April 23, 2006.

———. "City Would Get $3M, Land in Bridge Agreement." *Charleston Post and Courier,* May 10, 2005.

———. "Coalition Takes Aim at Emissions." *Charleston Post and Courier,* February 10, 2009.

———. "Concerns Rise with the Seas." *Charleston Post and Courier,* December 7, 2006.

———. "East Edisto Plan Hits Milestone." *Charleston Post and Courier,* January 22, 2011.

———. "Global Fever." *Charleston Post and Courier,* February 3, 2007.

———. "I-526 Debate Coming to Head." *Charleston Post and Courier,* April 6, 2011.

———. "I-526 Expansion Still Not Settled." *Charleston Post and Courier,* January 13, 2011.

———. "I-526 Proposal Draws Fire at Public Hearing." *Charleston Post and Courier,* September 1, 2010.

———. "I-526 Resolution Still Out of Reach." *Charleston Post and Courier,* January 30, 2011.

———. "Mayor Riley Wants City to Get Greener." *Charleston Post and Courier,* April 17, 2007.

———. "Plan for I-526 Rejected." *Charleston Post and Courier,* April 15, 2011.

———. "Plans for Ginn Company's Promenade Take Shape." *Charleston Post and Courier,* July 29, 2008.

———. "Poll Says Global Warming Is Growing Concern in S.C." *Charleston Post and Courier,* May 18, 2006.

———. "S.C. Lawmakers Deem Threat of Global Warming Serious." *Charleston Post and Courier,* January 22, 2006.

———. "S.C. Population Growth in Top Ten: In-Migration Gives State Biggest Boost." *Charleston Post and Courier,* December 23, 2008.

———, and Diane Knich. "Mapping the Future: All about the Big Picture." *Charleston Post and Courier,* October 15, 2008.

"Smart-Growth Plan Riles Black Farmers." *Insight on the News,* September 16, 2002.

Smith, Bruce. "An Extra Million People Will Mean Big Growth." *State,* September 26, 2002.

———. "Centuries-old Basket-weaving Tradition in S.C. Is Threatened." *Savannah (Ga.) Morning News,* July 27, 2007.

———. "Development Threatens Basket-making Tradition." *Oakland Tribune* (California), July 29, 2007.

Smith, Glenn. "Sandy Island to Get Ferry." *Charleston Post and Courier,* December 8, 2010.

Smothers, Ronald. "Environment Fight Kills Plan for Bridge to Carolina Island." *New York Times,* December 13, 1995.

———. "Land on South Carolina Island Is Sold to State." *New York Times,* March 24, 1996.

———. "Proposal for a Bridge Intrudes on Island Life." *New York Times,* May 6, 1995.

Soraghan, Mike. "State Owns Major Part of Island Property." *Myrtle Beach (S.C.) Sun News,* December 17, 1996.

"South Carolina Bill Would Create Land Bank." *Knight Ridder / Tribune Business News,* January 17, 2001.

"South Carolina Developers Make a Difference in Island's Development." *State,* May 29, 2001.

"South Carolina Forest Shows Nature's Ability to Take Storms in Stride." *Knight Ridder / Tribune Business News,* September 20, 1999.

"South Carolina Preserves Sandy Island." *Knight Ridder / Tribune Business Service,* March 14, 1996.

"Southern Jottings and Journeyings." *New York Times*, April 1, 1866.

"Sprawl Ruining Coastal Waters, Report Says." *Charleston Post and Courier*, April 16, 2002.

"Spring Island Developers Downsize Project 10–Fold and Form Environmental Trust to Protect Natural Resources and Ensure Land's Preservation." *P.R. Newswire*, May 19, 1992.

"State Closes Deal to Buy Sandy Island." *State*, December 18, 1996.

Stech, Katy. "Amid Market Slowdown, I'On Holds Its Own." *Charleston Post and Courier*, August 1, 2008.

———. "Fighting Green's Red Tape." *Charleston Post and Courier*, March 23, 2007.

———. "Massive East Edisto Tract Could One Day Be New Town." *Charleston Post and Courier*, March 26, 2008.

———. "Plan Cultivates Love for Local Crops." *Charleston Post and Courier*, January 9, 2008.

Stevens, Kimberley. "Keeping Development from Devouring Plantations." *New York Times*, January 2, 2005.

St. George, Donna. "Artform of Making Sweetgrass Baskets Threatened by Development and a Disinterested Younger Generation." *State*, August 25, 1993.

Stice, Allison. "Bluffton to Unveil Development Standards." *Island Packet* (Hilton Head-Bluffton, S.C.), February 21, 2011.

Stock, Kyle. "A Chilling View of Warming." *Charleston Post and Courier*, May 26, 2006.

Stuart, Reginald. "Hilton Head Seen as Island Paradise, Is Straining under Big-City Problems." *New York Times*, December 14, 1982.

"Study: S.C. to Lose Forests to Sprawl." *Island Packet* (Hilton Head-Bluffton, S.C.), June 1, 2002.

"Study Shows South Carolina Lost 142,000 Acres of Forests between 1993–2000." *Knight Ridder / Tribune Business News*, December 5, 2001.

"Support Sanford Conservation Plan." Editorial. *Charleston Post and Courier*, January 20, 2008.

Surratt, Clark. "Critics Voice Views at Public Hearing on South Carolina Growth Bill." *State*, January 26, 2000.

"Sweetgrass Harvest to Benefit Local Basketmakers." *Moultrie News* (Mt. Pleasant, S.C.), August 10, 2010.

Swindell, Bill. "Residents Seek State Growth Laws." *Charleston Post and Courier*, August 25, 2000.

"Symbol of Nation, Nature." *Charleston Post and Courier*, October 19, 2010.

Taugher, Mike. "Activists' Suits Stir Talk of Species Act Changes." *Albuquerque Journal*, August 24, 1997.

Taylor, Teresa. "Buying Close to Home." *Charleston Post and Courier*, April 2, 2008.

———. "Farmer Driven by Love of the Land." *Charleston Post and Courier*, September 24, 2008.

———. "Leader Puts Local Business First." *Charleston Post and Courier*, May 8, 2010.

———. "Taste, Health, Quality and Ecology Are Some of the Reasons for Eating 'Local.'" *Charleston Post and Courier*, September 26, 2007.

———. "Wadmalaw Couple Find Niche in Farming." *Charleston Post and Courier*, March 26, 2008.

"This Deal Pleases Everyone: Owners, Residents, Activists." *State*, March 23, 1996.

"Timber Giant May Sell Land." *Charleston Post and Courier*, September 21, 2006.

"Timely Land-preservation Bill." Editorial. *Charleston Post and Courier*, March 20, 2006.

"Treat Idyllic Island with Fitting Regard." *Myrtle Beach (S.C.) Sun News*, March 16, 1997.

"25 Years of Conservation." Editorial. *Charleston Post and Courier,* February 15, 2011.

Tullos, Jesse. "Taking Another Look at the 701 Corridor and Suburban Sprawl." *Georgetown (S.C.) News,* April 4, 2003.

———. "Taking on the Wheels of Change." *Georgetown (S.C.) News,* April 4, 2002.

Tuten, James. "Bad Storms Rising: The End of Lowcountry Rice Culture." *Charleston Post and Courier,* October 19, 2010.

"Twenty Years of Coastal Protection." *Charleston Post and Courier,* October 17, 2009.

"Unrealistic Expectations: Pursuing Smart Growth Won't Be Easy, Painless, or without Controversy." *Spartanburg (S.C.) Herald-Journal,* December 12, 2000.

Waldo, Tenisha. "County Greenbelt Plan Wins '06 Planning Award." *Charleston Post and Courier,* December 11, 2006.

———. "Group Hits Cost of I-526." *Charleston Post and Courier,* February 24, 2008.

———. "I-526 Foes to Talk about Alternatives." *Charleston Post and Courier,* January 2, 2008.

———. "Nearly 4000 Acres Protected." *Charleston Post and Courier,* August 2, 2007.

———. "Sprawl Biggest Issue." *Charleston Post and Courier,* October 29, 2006.

———. "Wadmalaw Plan Spurs Big Outcry." *Charleston Post and Courier,* October 3, 2007.

Walinchus, Lucia. "Highway 17 Panel Points to Progress." *Charleston Post and Courier,* March 18, 2007.

———. "Tiny Town of Awendaw Feels Growing Pains." *Charleston Post and Courier,* October 22, 2006.

———. "Town OKs 400–Home Subdivision." *Charleston Post and Courier,* September 8, 2006.

Wall, Tom. "Sandy Island Developers Will Destroy Area's Resources." Letter to the Editor. *State,* March 21, 1995.

Walsh, Sandra. "Newcomers Interested in Growth Issues." *Island Packet* (Hilton Head-Bluffton, S.C.), October 11, 2005.

Ward, Logan. "Historic Rice Plantations of South Carolina." *New York Times,* October 20, 1996.

Wenger, Yvonne M. "Sanford Proposes Adding $20M to State Land Bank." *Charleston Post and Courier,* November 28, 2006.

"What to Do with Sandy Island?" *State,* October 10, 1993.

White, Sully. "Gullah: An Inventive Form of Survival in the New World." *Moultrie News* (Mt. Pleasant, S.C.), February 25, 2008.

———. "Seven Mile Relies on Basketry and Heritage to Keep History Alive." *Moultrie News* (Mt. Pleasant, S.C.), March 9, 2010.

"Whoop It Up for Nature." *Charleston Post and Courier,* February 19, 2011.

"Why the Deadly Boll Weevil?" *New York Times,* January 9, 1910.

Wilbert, Lauren. "Coastal Area Explodes with Growth Woes." *Charleston Post and Courier,* June 24, 2004.

Wilkinson, Jeff. "Critics Blast Smart Growth Plan." *State,* December 13, 2000.

———. "Sanford Wants to End Sprawl." *State,* March 27, 2007.

———. "South Carolina Residents Want Limits on Land Development." *State,* March 28, 2000.

———. "South Carolina State, Local Governments Split on Fixing Urban Sprawl." *State,* March 21, 2000.

Wilson, Zane. "Ceremony Marks Island's Last Change." *Myrtle Beach (S.C.) Sun News,* March 8, 1997.

———. "South Carolina Preserves Sandy Island." *State,* March 14, 1996.

Wise, Kris. "Down on the Farm." *Charleston Post and Courier,* April 18, 2005.

Wise, Warren. "Holy City Displaces San Francisco as NO. 1 on Conde Nast List." *Charleston Post and Courier,* October 11, 2001.

———. "Sprawl Called Biggest Threat to Forests." *Charleston Post and Courier,* December 5, 2001.

Journals, Magazines, Online Publications

Agnew, Patricia. "Homegrown Charleston." *Charleston Magazine* (April 2008): 170–81.

Agrawal, Arun, and Clark C. Gibson. "Enchantment and Disenchantment: The Role of Community in Natural Resource Conservation." *World Development* 27 (April 1999): 629–49.

Arendt, Randall G. "Linked Landscapes: Creating Greenway Corridors through Conservation Subdivision Design Strategies in the Northeastern and Central United States." *Landscape and Urban Planning* 68 (May 2004): 241–69.

Austin, Maureen E. "Resident Perspectives of the Open Space Conservation Subdivision in Hamburg Township, Michigan." *Landscape and Urban Planning* 69 (August 15, 2004): 245–53.

———, and Rachel Kaplan. "Resident Involvement in Natural Resource Management: Open Space Conservation Design in Practice." *Local Environment* 8, no. 2 (2003): 141–53.

Barr, Stewart, and Andrew Gilg. "Sustainable Lifestyles: Framing Environmental Action in and Around the Home." *Geoforum* 37 (November 2006): 906–20.

Bartling, Hugh. "The Magic Kingdom Syndrome: Trials and Tribulations of Life in Disney's Celebration." *Contemporary Justice Review* 7, no. 4 (2004): 375–93.

"BASF Backs Off from a Beachhead." *Business Week,* April 11, 1970.

Bass, Bernard M., and Bruce J. Avolio. "The Implications of Transactional and Transformational Leadership for the Individual, Team, and Organizational Development." *Research in Organizational Change and Development* 4 (1990): 231–72.

Bastian, Chris T., Donald M. McLeod, Matthew J. Germino, William A. Reiners, and Benedict J. Blasko. "Environmental Amenities and Agricultural Land Values: A Hedonic Model Using Geographic Information Systems Data." *Ecological Economics* 40 (March 2002): 337–49.

Beach, Dana. "The Greening of South Carolina." *Coastal Guardian Newsletter* 18 (Winter 2007): 2.

Beauregard, Robert A. "New Urbanism: Ambiguous Certainties." *Journal of Architecture and Planning Research* 19 (Autumn 2002): 181–94.

Berkes, Fikret. "Rethinking Community-based Conservation." *Conservation Biology* 18 (June 2004): 621–30.

Bjelland, Mark D., Michelle Maley, Lane Cowger, and LisaBeth Barajas. "The Quest for Authentic Place: The Production of Suburban Alternatives in Minnesota's St. Croix Valley." *Urban Geography* 27 (April 1–May 15, 2006): 253–70.

Blandy, Sarah, and Diane Lister. "Gated Communities: (Ne)gating Community Development?" *Housing Studies* 20, no. 2 (2005): 287–301.

Blinnikov, Mikhail, Andrey Shanin, Nikolay Sobolev, and Lyudmila Volkova. "Gated Communities of the Moscow Green Belt: Newly Segregated Landscapes and the Suburban Russian Environment." *GeoJournal* 66 (November 2006): 65–81.

Boiral, Olivier, Mario Cayer, and Charles M. Brown. "The Action Logics of Environmental Leadership: A Developmental Perspective." *Journal of Business Ethics* 85 (April 2009): 479–99.

Breffle, William S., Edward R. Morey, and Tymon S. Lodder. "Using Contingent Valuation to Estimate a Neighborhood's Willingness to Pay to Preserve Undeveloped Urban Land." *Urban Studies* 35 (April 1998): 715–27.

Brehm, Joan M., and Brian W. Eisenhauer. "Environmental Concern in the Mormon Culture Region." *Society and Natural Resources* 19, no. 5 (2006): 393–410.

Brody, Samuel D., Wes Highfield, and B. Mitchell Peck. "Exploring the Mosaic of Perceptions for Water Quality across Watersheds in San Antonio, Texas." *Landscape and Urban Planning* 73 (October 15, 2005): 200–14.

Brown, Clayton. "Modernizing Rural Life: South Carolina's Push for Public Rural Electrification." *South Carolina Historical Magazine* 99, no. 1 (1998): 66–85.

Brown, Katrina. "Innovations for Conservation and Development." *Geographical Journal* 168, no. 1 (2002): 6–17.

Brunn, Stanley. "Gated Minds and Gated Lives as Worlds of Exclusion Fear." *GeoJournal* 66 (November 2006): 5–13.

Byrne, Gabriel J., and Frank Bradley. "Culture's Influence on Leadership Efficiency: How Personal and National Cultures Affect Leadership Style." *Journal of Business Research* 60 (February 2007): 168–75.

Carlton, David L. "The Piedmont and Waccamaw Regions: An Economic Comparison." *South Carolina Historical Magazine* 88 (April 1987): 83–100.

Chaplin, Joyce E. "Tidal Rice Cultivation and the Problem of Slavery in South Carolina and Georgia, 1760–1815." *William and Mary Quarterly* 49 (January 1992): 29–61.

Chen, Simon C. Y., and Chris J. Webster. "Homeowners Associations: Collective Action and the Costs of Private Governance." *Housing Studies* 20, no. 2 (2005): 205–20.

Cho, Seong-Hoon, David H. Newman, and J. M. Bowker. "Measuring Rural Homeowners' Willingness to Pay for Land Conservation Easements." *Forest Policy and Economics* 7 (August 2005): 757–70.

"Cities: Hope for the Heart." *Time*, March 4, 1966.

"The City: Starting from Scratch." *Time*, March 7, 1969.

Clifton, James M. "The Rice Industry in Colonial America." *Agricultural History* 55, no. 3 (1981): 266–83.

———. "Twilight Comes to the Rice Kingdom: Postbellum Rice Culture on the South Carolina Coast." *Georgia Historical Quarterly* 62 (Summer 1978): 146–54.

Coclanis, Peter A. "The Rise and Fall of the South Carolina Low Country: An Essay in Economic Interpretation." *Southern Studies* 24 (Summer 1985): 143–66.

Cohen, Eric, David F. Aberle, Leopoldo J. Bartolomé, Lynton K. Caldwell, Aristide H. Esser, Donald L. Hardesty, Riaz Hassan, H. Dieter Heinen, Jiro Kawakita, Olga F. Linares, Partha Pratim Majumder, Albyn Knight Mark, Harald Tambs-Lyche. "Environmental Orientations: A Multidimensional Approach to Social Ecology." *Current Anthropology* 17 (March 1976): 49–70.

Cohn, Jeffrey P. "Culture and Conservation: A Greater Sensitivity to Local Culture Could Increase the Success of Both Conservation and Development Projects." *BioScience* 38 (July–August 1988): 450–53.

Collins, Jan. "Climate Change: An Environmental *and* Business Issue." *Business & Economic Review* 53 (October–November–December 2006): 3–10.

Conger, Jay A. "Charismatic and Transformational Leadership in Organizations: An Insider's Perspective on These Developing Streams of Research." *Leadership Quarterly* 10 (Summer 1999): 145–79.

Conroy, Maria, and Philip Berke. "What Makes a Good Sustainable Development Plan? An Analysis of Factors That Influence Principles of Sustainable Development." *Environment and Planning* 36, no. 8 (2004): 1381–96.

Dangerfield, Whitney. "Summertime for Gershwin: In the South, the Gullah Struggle to Keep Their Traditions Alive." *Smithsonian*, June 1, 2007.

Davis, John E. "Preserving Our Natural Wealth." *South Carolina Wildlife* 48 (January–February 2001): 1–57.

———. "A Sense of Place." *South Carolina Wildlife* 47 (January 2000): 2.

Dawe, Nancy Anne. "Hugo's Legacy: Ten Years Later, Charleston, South Carolina, Finds the Hurricane that 'Changed Everybody's Life,' Changed Its Forest—for the Better." *American Forests* 105 (Autumn 1999): 40–43.

"Deflated Developer." *Time*, May 24, 1976.

Dietz, James M., Rina Aviram, Sophia Bickford, Karen Douthwaite, Amy Goodstine, Jose-Luis Izursa, Stephanie Kavanaugh, Katie MacCarthy, Michelle O'Herron, and Keri Parker. "Defining Leadership in Conservation: A View from the Top." *Conservation Biology* 18 (February 2004): 274–78.

Downs, Anthony. "What Does 'Smart Growth' Really Mean?" *Planning* 67 (April 2001): 20–26.

Duany, Andres, and Elizabeth Plater-Zyberk. "The Second Coming of the American Small Town." *Wilson Quarterly* 16 (Winter 1992): 19.

Duncan, James S., and Nancy G. Duncan. "The Aestheticization of the Politics of Landscape Preservation." *Annals of the Association of American Geographers* 91, no. 2 (2001): 387–409.

Edwards, S. "Saving the Sweetgrass." *Soil and Conservation News* 12 (January–February 1992): 15.

Egri, Carolyn P., and Susan Herman. "Leadership in the North American Environmental Sector: Values, Leadership Styles, and Contexts of Environmental Leaders and their Organizations." *Academy of Management Journal* 43, no. 4 (2000): 571–604.

Elmendorf, William F., and A. E. Luloff. "Using Ecosystem-based and Traditional Land-use Planning to Conserve Greenspace." *Journal of Arboriculture* 25 (September 1999): 264–73.

———. "Using Key Informant Interviews to Better Understand Open Space Conservation in a Developing Watershed." *Journal of Arboriculture and Urban Forestry* 32 (March 2006): 54–61.

"Environment: The Costs of Sprawl." *Time*, November 4, 1974.

Ferdig, Mary A. "Sustainability Leadership: Co-creating a Sustainable Future." *Journal of Change Management* 7, no. 1 (2007): 25–35.

Ford, Gary D. "Love of the Lowcountry." *Southern Living Magazine* (October 2005). http://www.southernliving.com/travel/south-east/slide-show-love-loucounry-00400000009160.

Frady, Marshall. "Mendel Rivers, the Military Congressman." *Life*, February 27, 1970, 52–61.

———. "The View from Hilton Head," *Harper's Magazine*. May 1970, 105.

Freyfogle, Eric. "Goodbye to the Public-Private Divide." *Environmental Law* 50 (Winter 2006): 101–18.

———. "What Is Land? A Broad Look at Private Rights and Public Power." *Planning & Environmental Law* 58 (June 2006): 3–9.

Froelich, Maryann. "Smart Growth: Why Local Governments Are Taking a New Approach to Managing Growth in their Communities." *Public Management* 80 (May 1998): 5–9.

Gale, Bob. "Hilton Head: The Canopy View," *American Forests,* November 1, 1990.

Gates, Paul Wallace. "Federal Land Policy in the South, 1866–1888." *Journal of Southern History* 6 (August 1940): 303–30.

Ghose, Rina. "Big Sky or Big Sprawl? Rural Gentrification and the Changing Cultural Landscape of Missoula, Montana." *Urban Geography* 25, no. 6 (2004): 528–549

Glasze, Georg. "Some Reflections on the Economic and Political Organisation of Private Neighbourhoods." *Housing Studies* 20, no. 2 (2005): 221–33.

Gobster, Paul H., and Mark G. Rickenbach. "Private Forestland Parcelization and Development in Wisconsin's Northwoods: Perceptions of Resource-oriented Stakeholders." *Landscape and Urban Planning* 69 (August 15, 2004): 165–82.

Gordon, David. "New Urbanism and Smart Growth: Twins Separated at Birth?" *Places: Forum of Design for the Public Realm* 15, no. 3 (2003): 68–70.

Gould, Stephen Jay, and Niles Eldridge. "Punctuated Equilibria: The Tempo and Mode of Evolution Reconsidered." *Paleobiology* 3 (April 1, 1977): 115–51.

Gray, Steven. "Southeastern States Are Hit Hard by Recession." *Time,* April 18, 2009.

Groves, Craig R., Deborah B. Jensen, Laura L. Valutis, Kent H. Redford, Mark L. Shaffer, J. Michael Scott, Jeffery V. Baumgartner, Jonathan V. Higgins, Michael W. Beck, and Mark G. Anderson. "Planning for Biodiversity Conservation: Putting Conservation Science into Practice." *BioScience* 52 (June 2002): 499–512.

"Growing and Eating Food—Locally and Sustainably: Conservation League Launches Sustainable Agriculture Initiative." *Coastal Conservation League* 19, no. 2 (Summer 2008).

Gruber, James S. "Key Principles of Community-based Natural Resource Management: A Synthesis and Interpretation of Identified Effective Approaches for Managing the Commons." *Environmental Management* 45 (January 2010): 52–66.

Gustafson, Danny J., Angela C. Halfacre, and Roger C. Anderson. "Practical Seed Source Selection for Restoration Projects in an Urban Setting: Tallgrass Prairie, Serpentine Barrens, and Coastal Habitat Examples." *Urban Habitats* 5 (May 2008): 7–24.

Hagood, Ben. "New Planning Requirements Should Reduce Haphazard Development and Sprawl." *South Carolina Business Journal* (September 2007).

Halfacre, Angela C., Jeremy Browning, and Brian Ballard. "Environmental Decision-making and Community Involvement: The Case of Sandy Island, South Carolina." *Southeastern Geographer* 41 (May 2001): 136–52.

Halfacre-Hitchcock, Angela C., Deborah McCarthy, Tracy Burkett, and Alicia Carvajal. "Latino Migrant Farmworkers in Lowcountry South Carolina: A Demographic Profile and an Examination of Pesticide Risk Perception and Protection in Two Pilot Case Studies." *Human Organization* 65 (Spring 2006): 55–71.

Hamlin, Elisabeth M. "Reading (Conservation Subdivision) Plans." *Planning Theory* 5 (July 2006): 147–72.

Hart, Zachary H., Angela C. Halfacre, and Marianne K. Burke. "Community Participation in Preservation of Lowcountry South Carolina Sweetgrass (*Muhlenbergia filipes*) Basketry." *Economic Botany* 58, no. 2 (2004): 161–71.

Hilton, Mary Kendall. "Islander: Charles E. Fraser." *Islander,* December 1966.

Huffman, Thomas R. "Defining the Origins of Environmentalism in Wisconsin: A Study in Politics and Culture." *Environmental History Review* 16 (Fall 1992): 47–69.

Hunt, S. "Save Our Sweetgrass." *Charleston Magazine* (October 2006): 139–45.

Hurley, Patrick T., Angela C. Halfacre, Norm S. Levine, and Marianne K. Burke. "Finding a 'Disappearing' Non-timber Forest Resource: Using Rounded Visualization to Explore

Urbanization Impacts on Sweetgrass Basketmaking in Greater Mt. Pleasant, South Carolina." *Professional Geographer* 60 (November 2008): 1–23.

Johnson, Cassandra Y., and Angela C. Halfacre. "Resident Place Identities in Rural Charleston County, South Carolina: Cultural, Environmental, and Racial Politics in the Sewee to Santee Area." *Human Ecology Review* 16, no. 1 (2009): 1–16.

Johnson, Cassandra Y. and Wayne C. Zipperer. "Culture, Place, and Urban Growth in the U.S. South." *Urban Ecosystems* 10, no. 4 (2007): 459–74.

Johnston, Robert J., Stephen K. Swallow, Timothy J. Tyrrell, and Dana Marie Bauer. "Rural Amenity Values and Length of Residency." *American Journal of Agricultural Economics* 85 (November 2003): 1000–15.

Judge, Timothy A., and Joyce E. Bono. "Five-factor Model of Personality and Transformational Leadership." *Journal of Applied Psychology* 85 (October 2000): 751–65.

Kabii, Thomas, and Pierre Horwitz. "A Review of Landholder Motivations and Determinants for Participation in Conservation Covenanting Programmes." *Environmental Conservation* 33, no. 1 (2006): 11–20.

Kaltenborn, Bjørn P., and Tore Bjerke. "Associations between Environmental Value Orientations and Landscape Preferences." *Landscape and Urban Planning* 59 (March 1, 2002): 1–11.

Kaplan, Rachel, and Maureen E. Austin. "Out in the Country: Sprawl and the Quest for Nature Nearby." *Landscape and Urban Planning* 69 (August 15, 2004): 235–43.

Kaplan, Rachel, Maureen E. Austin, and Stephen Kaplan. "Open Space Communities: Resident Perceptions, Nature Benefits, and Problems with Terminology." *Journal of the American Planning Association* 70, no. 3 (2004): 300–12.

Kearney, Anne R. "Residential Development Patterns and Neighborhood Satisfaction: Impacts of Density and Nearby Nature." *Environment and Behavior* 38 (January 2006): 112–39.

Kennedy, David J. "Residential Associations as State Actors: Regulating the Impact of Gated Communities on Nonmembers." *Yale Law Journal* 105 (December 1995): 761–93.

Kline, Jeffrey D. "Public Demand for Preserving Local Open Space." *Society and Natural Resources* 19, no. 7 (2006): 645–59.

Kottak, Conrad P. "The New Ecological Anthropology." *American Anthropologist* 101, no. 1 (1999): 23–35.

Kraft, Michael E., and Bruce B. Clary. "Citizen Participation and the Nimby Syndrome: Public Response to Radioactive Waste." *Western Political Quarterly* 44 (June 1991): 299–328.

Langholz, Jeffrey A., and Wolf Krug. "New Forms of Biodiversity Governance: Non-State Actors and the Private Protected Area Action Plan." *Journal of International Wildlife Law and Policy* 7, no. 1–2 (2004): 9–29.

Laurie, Pete. "ACE Basin 1988–1998: A Decade of Unparalleled Land Protection." *ACE Basin Current Events* (S.C. Dept. of Natural Resources): 1–8.

Lawrence, Stratton. "Sidi Limehouse." *Charleston Magazine* (November 2009): 72.

Lee, Caroline W. "Conservation as a Territorial Ideology." *City & Community* 8 (September 2009): 301–28.

———. "Is There a Place for Private Conversation in Public Dialogue? Comparing Stakeholder Assessments of Informal Communication in Collaborative Regional Planning." *American Journal of Sociology* 113 (July 2007): 41–96.

———. "The Politics of Localness: Scale-Bridging Ties and Legitimacy in Regional Resource Management Partnerships." *Society & Natural Resources* 24, no. 5 (2011): 439–54.

Leopold, Aldo. "The Conservation Ethic." *Journal of Forestry* 31 (October 1933): 189.

Lessard, Suzannah."The World Turned Inside Out." *Wilson Quarterly* 25 (Summer 2001): 10.

"Loose Lips." *POINT* (South Carolina's Independent Newsmonthly) (Summer 2000), http://www.scpronet.com/point/0006/lips.html.

Luloff, A. E. "The Doing of Rural Community Development Research." *Rural Society Journal*, 9, no. 1 (1999): 313–27.

Manolis, Jim C., Kai M. Chan, Myra E. Finkelstein, Scott Stephens, Cara R. Nelson, Jacqueline B. Grant, and Michael P. Dombeck. "Leadership: A New Frontier in Conservation Science." *Conservation Biology* 23, no. 4 (August 2009): 879–86.

Margerum, Richard D. "A Typology of Collaboration Efforts." *Environmental Management* 41 (January 2008): 487–500.

Martin, Robert. "Neighbors with Nature." *Bay Ledger* (February 2005) http://www.blnz.com/news/2008/4/23/Neighbors_with_Nature_6686.html.

McCabe, Barbara C. "The Rules Are Different Here: An Institutional Comparison of Cities and Homeowners Associations." *Administration and Society* 37, no. 4 (2005): 404–25.

McCann, Eugene J. "Neotraditional Developments: The Anatomy of a New Urban Form." *Urban Geography* 16 (April 1–May 15, 1995): 210–33.

McLaughlin, Nancy A. "Increasing the Tax Incentives for Conservation Easement Donations." *Ecology Law Quarterly* 31, no. 1 (2004): 1–115.

McLeod, Harriet. "At Home on the Farm." *Charleston Home Magazine* (Fall 2010): 54–61.

Meyerson, Shauna L., and Theresa J. B. Kline. "Psychological and Environmental Empowerment: Antecedents and Consequences." *Leadership and Organizational Development* 29 (July 10, 2008): 444–60.

Milder, Jeffrey C. "A Framework for Understanding Conservation Development and Its Ecological Implications." *Bioscience* 57 (October 2007): 757–68.

Miller, James R. "Restoration, Reconciliation, and Reconnecting with Nature Nearby." *Biological Conservation* 127 (January 2006): 356–61.

———, Martha Groom, George R. Hess, Toddi Steelman, David L. Stokes, Jan Thompson, Troy Bowman, Laura Fricke, Brandon King, and Ryan Marquardt. "Biodiversity Conservation in Local Planning." *Conservation Biology* 23 (February 2009): 53–63.

Mohammed, Rayman. "The Economics of Conservation Subdivisions: Price Premiums, Improvement Costs, and Absorption Rates." *Urbanism Affairs Review* 41 (January 2006): 376–99.

Moore, Adrian, and Rick Henderson. "Plan Obsolescence." *Reason* 30 (June 1998): 42–47.

Moore, Jamie W. "The Lowcountry in Economic Transition: Charleston since 1865." *South Carolina Historical Magazine* 80 (April 1979): 156–71.

"Nature Conservancy, Westvaco to Preserve Endangered Habitats." *South Carolina Business Journal* (December 1, 1999).

Nesmith, Lynn. "Under the Spell of Spring Island." *Southern Living Magazine,* October 1996.

"The New American Land Rush." Special Section, *Time,* October 1, 1973.

Nixon, Ron. "Cultures in Conflict: Sea Island Communities Are Fighting for Their Survival, Stirring New Hopes along the Coast of South Carolina." *Southern Exposure* 21 (Fall 1993): 53–56.

Oldekop, Johan A., Anthony J. Bebbington, Dan Brockington, and Richard F. Preziosi. "Understanding the Lessons and Limitations of Conservation and Development." *Conservation Biology,* 24 (April 2010): 461–69.

Pais, Jeremy F., and James R. Elliott. "Places as Recovery Machines: Vulnerability and Neighborhood Change after Major Hurricanes." *Social Forces* 86 (June 2008): 1415–53.

Padgett, Tom. "Saving Chapel Hill." *Time,* August 16, 1999.

Parker, Molly. "Developer Shopping 'Promenade' to Maritime Industry." *Charleston Regional Business Journal,* April 24, 2010.

Pejchar, Liba, Peter M. Morgan, Margaret R. Caldwell, Carl Palmer, and Gretchen C. Daily. "Evaluating the Potential for Conservation Development: Biophysical, Economic, and Institutional Perspectives." *Conservation Biology* 21 (February 2007): 69–78.

Phillips, Cabell. "Let's Not Blow Up the Bridge—Yet." *Islander,* May 1973.

Plas, Jeanne M., and Susan E. Lewis. "Environmental Factors and Sense of Community in a Planned Town." *American Journal of Community Psychology* 24 (February 1996): 109–43.

Platt, Rutherford H. "Life after Lucas: The Supreme Court and the Downtrodden Coastal Developer." *Natural Hazards Observer* 17, no. 1 (1992).

Porter, Jeanne L. "Building Diverse Communities: A Case Study of the Penn School for Preservation, Sea Islands, South Carolina." *Pew Partnership for Civic Change, Leadership Collaboration Series* (Fall 1995), http://www.cpn.org/topics/community/builddiverse .html (accessed October 25, 2011).

Postrel, Virginia. "The Pleasantville Solution." *Reason,* March 1999, 4–11.

Richardson, Laurel. "Evaluating Ethnography." *Qualitative Inquiry* 6 (June 2000): 253–55.

Rivers, Faith R. "The Public Trust Debate: Implications for Heirs' Property along the Gullah Coast." *Southeastern Environmental Law Journal* 15, no. 1 (2007–2008): 1–22.

———. "Restoring the Bundle of Rights: Preserving Heirs' Property in Coastal South Carolina." *American Bar Association Section of Real Property, Probate and Trust Law* (2006). http://www.vermontlaw.edu/emplibrary/faithpropertypreservationextract.pdf (accessed February 4, 2007).

Rome, Adam. "'Give Earth a Chance': The Environmental Movement and the 1960s." *Journal of American History* 90 (September 2003): 525–54.

Rooke, David, and William R. Tobert. "Seven Transformations of Leadership." *Harvard Business Review* 83 (April 2005): 66–76.

Ross, Nicola. "New Urbanism Stalls without Public Transit." *Alternatives Journal* 29 (Summer 2003), 14.

Rutledge, Archibald. "Night Is in the Pinelands." *Nature* 27 (February 1936): 73–77.

———. "What Price Power?" *Nature* 27 (March 1936): 173–74.

Ryan, Robert L. "Comparing the Attitudes of Local Residents, Planners, and Developers about Preserving Rural Character in New England." *Landscape and Urbanism Planning* 75 (February 2006): 5–22.

Schmidt, Charles W. "The Specter of Sprawl." *Environmental Health Perspectives* 106 (June 1998): 274–79.

Schneider, William. "The Suburban Century Begins." *Atlantic Monthly,* July 1992, 33.

Schnell, S. "Food with a Farmer's Face: Community-supported Agriculture in the United States." *Geographical Review* 97 (October 2007): 550–64.

Shick, Tom W., and Don H. Doyle. "The South Carolina Phosphate Boom and the Stillbirth of the New South, 1867–1920." *South Carolina Historical Magazine* 86 (January 1985): 1–31.

Shin, Shung Jae, and Jing Zhou. "Transformational Leadership Conservation, and Creativity: Evidence from Korea." *Academy of Management Journal* 46 (December, 2003): 703–14.

Shipnuck, Alan. "Growing Pains: As Sprawling Golf Communities Devour South Caro-lina's Lowcountry, Some Residents Ask, How Much is Too Much?" *Sports Illustrated* 96 (April 29, 2002). http://sportsillustrated.cnn.com/vault/article/magazine/MAG10245647 /index.htm.

Smith, Kit. "South Carolina: How Shall We Grow?" *Business and Economic Review* 47 (October–December 2000), 9–14.

Southworth, Michael. "Walkable Suburbs? An Evaluation of Neotraditional Communities at the Urban Edge." *Journal of the American Planning Association* 63, no. 1 (1997): 28–44.

Stedman, Richard C. "Is it Really Just a Social Construction? The Contribution of the Physical Environment to Sense of Place." *Society and Natural Resources* 16, no. 8 (2003): 671–85.

Stock, Kyle. "Playing in Paradise," *USAIRWAYS Magazine,* March 2006, 229.

Thompson, Dick. "Asphalt Jungle." *Time* 155, special issue (Spring 2000): 50.

Tibbetts, John H. "The Beauty of Sprawl." *Coastal Heritage* 15 (Fall 2000): 7–10.

———. "The Bird Chase." *Coastal Heritage* 15 (Spring 2001): 3–13.

———. "Coastal Growth Hits Home." *Coastal Heritage* 16 (Fall 2001): 8–9.

———. "Disaster Resilience: 20 Years after Hugo." *Coastal Heritage* 23 (Spring 2009): 3–10.

———. "The Freeway City." *Coastal Heritage* 17 (Winter 2002–3): 6.

———. "Gullah's Radiant Light." *Coastal Heritage* 19 (Winter 2004–2005): 3–13.

———. "Investing in Open Space." *Coastal Heritage* 12 (Spring 1998): 8.

———. "Living Soul of Gullah." *Coastal Heritage* 14 (Spring 2000): 3–13.

———. "New Visions for Growth: Investing in Open Space." *Coastal Heritage* 12 (Spring 1998): 3–9.

———. "Riches to Ruin: Pharaohs of the New World." *Coastal Heritage* 14 (Fall 1999): 4.

———. "Sea-Level Rise: Adapting to a Changing Coast." *Coastal Heritage* 24 (Summer 2009): 3–7.

Tomasello, Michael. "The Human Adaptation for Culture." *Annual Review of Anthropology* 28 (October 1999): 509–29.

"Troubled Little Island." *Time* 95 (January 26, 1970). http://www.time.com/time/magazine /article/0,9171,878739,00.html.

Tucker, Patrick. "The Battle over Sprawl: Has the Suburban Model Lost Its Allure?" *Futur-ist* (July–August 2006): 6–8.

Veninga, Catherine. "Spatial Prescriptions and Social Realities: New Urbanism and the Production of Northwest Landing." *Urban Geography* 25 (July 1–August 15, 2004): 458–82.

Walker, Peter, and Louise Fortmann, "Whose Landscape? A Political Ecology of the 'Exur-ban' Sierra." *Cultural Geographies* 10 (October 2003): 469–91.

Weisul, Kimberly. "Consumers Buy into 'Buy Local.'" *Small Business (Bloomberg Business-Week),* February 18, 2010.

Wyche, Bradford W. "Beach Erosion: A Growing Crisis." *Business & Economic Review* 34 (March 1988): 3–7.

———. "The Fiscal Impact of Sprawl in South Carolina." *Business & Economic Review* 53 (April–May–June 2007): 3–10.

Yablonski, Brian. "Marketing the Wealth of Nature." *PERC Reports* 23 (Fall 2005), http:// www.perc.org/articles/article587.php.

Yarian, Jon. "United They Stand." *Charleston Magazine* (February 2009). www.charleston mag.com/Charleston_magazine/feature/united_they_stand.

Zimmerer, Karl S. "The Reworking of Conservation Geographies: Non-equilibrium Landscapes and Nature-Society Hybrids." *Annals of the Association of American Geographers* 90, no. 2 (2000): 356–69.

Zimmerman, Jeffrey. "The 'Nature' of Urbanism on the New Urbanist Frontier: Sustainable Development, or Defense of the Suburban Dream?" *Urban Geography* 22 (April 1–May 15, 2001): 249–67.

Government Publications

"Beaufort County Comprehensive Plan." http://www.co.beaufort.sc.us/about-beaufortcounty/administration/beaufort-county-council/comprehensive-plan/index.php, (accessed April 15, 2011).

Berkeley-Charleston-Dorchester Council of Governments, *Berkeley County Comprehensive Plan* (1999).

Blacklocke, Sean. "Comprehensive Land-Use Planning in South Carolina: Addressing New Challenges in Allocating JResources." *Strom Thurmond Institute of Government & Public Affairs Opinion Page* (May 3, 1999). http://sean-blocklocke.com/articles/a008.pdf.

Commission on Engineering and Technical Systems. *Hurricane Hugo, Puerto Rico, the Virgin Islands, and Charleston, South Carolina, September 17–22, 1989.* Washington, D.C.: National Academy of Sciences, 1994.

"Conservation Bank Act Passed by S.C. Legislature." South Carolina Department of Natural Resources news release, April 1, 2002.

County of Charleston Planning Department, *County of Charleston Comprehensive Plan, As Adopted by the Charleston County Council April 20, 1999.* Amended plan adopted November 18, 2008. http://www.charlestoncounty.org/departments/planning/comp_plan.htm.

County of Charleston Zoning and Planning Department. "Part 2: Vision." *Charleston County Comprehensive Plan Update,* http://www.charlestoncounty.org/departments/Planning/Comp_Plan.htm (accessed October 19, 2010).

Cox, Wendell. "The Dangers of Smart Growth Planning." Testimony before the Senate Committee on Environment and Public Works, Heritage Foundation, May 15, 2002.

DiNapoli, Thomas P. *Economic Benefits of Open Space Preservation,* http://www.osc.state.ny.us/press/releases/mar10/032510.htm (accessed May 24, 2010).

Dolah, Robert F. Van, P. C. Jutte, G. H. M. Riekerk, M. V. Levisen, L. E. Zimmerman, J. D. Jones, A. J. Lewitus, D. E. Chestnut, W. McDermott, D. Bearden, G. I. Scott, M. H. Fulton. *The Condition of South Carolina Estuarine and Coastal Habitats during 1999–2000: Summary Report.* Charleston: South Carolina Marine Resources Division, 2002.

Dolah, Robert F. Van, George Riekerk, Martin Levisen, Lynn Zimmerman, John Jones, David Chestnut, William McDermott, Dan Bearden, Geoff Scott, and Mike Fulton. *The Condition of South Carolina's Estuarine and Coastal Habitats during 2001–2002.* Charleston: South Carolina Marine Resources Division, 2004.

Hilton Head Town Council, *Town of Hilton Head Island Comprehensive Plan* (March 16, 2004).

Intergovernmental Panel on Climate Change, *Fourth Assessment Report,* April, 2007, Working Group II. "Climate Change 2007: Impacts, Adaptation, and Vulnerability." §14.4.3, http://www.ipcc.ch/pdf/assessment-report/ar4/wg2/ar4–wg2–chapter14.pdf.

Lucas v. South Carolina Coastal Council, 304 S.C. 376, 404 S.E. 2d 895 (1991); revised, 505 U.S. 1003 (1992).

Marshall, William D. *Ashley Scenic River Management Plan.* Columbia: South Carolina Department of Natural Resources, 2003.

————, ed. *Assessing Change in the Edisto River Basin: An Ecological Characterization.* Columbia: South Carolina Water Resources Commission, 1993.

Municipal Association of South Carolina, *Comprehensive Land Planning for Local Governments* (2010).

National Park Service. *Low Country Gullah Culture Special Resources Study and Final Environmental Impact Statement.* Atlanta, Ga.: NPS Southeast Regional Office, 2005.

————. *Low Country Gullah Geechee Culture Special Resources Study Draft.* http://www.nps.gov/sero/planning/gg_srs/ggsrsindex.htm (accessed October 25, 2011).

Nelson, Frank P., ed. *Lower Santee River Environmental Quality Study.* Columbia: South Carolina Department of Natural Resources, 1976.

————. *The Cooper River Environmental Quality Study.* Columbia: South Carolina Department of Natural Resources 1974.

Report of the South Carolina Blue Ribbon Committee on Beachfront Management (March 1987).

South Carolina Budget and Control Board. "Data about South Carolina and Its People." http://www.bcb.sc.gov/BCB/BCB-sc-data.phtm (accessed August 2, 2009).

South Carolina Coastal Zone Management Act. *Congressional Findings,* U.S. Code 16 (2010) § 1451 et seq., http://www.law.cornell.edu/uscode/16/1451.html (accessed April 4, 2010).

South Carolina Local Government Comprehensive Planning Enabling Act (5 April 1994), sec. 6–29–510.

Travel Industry Association. *The Economic Impact of Travel on South Carolina Counties 2006: A Study Prepared for the S.C. Department of Parks, Recreation, and Tourism.* Washington, D.C.: Travel Industry Association, 2007.

U.S. Census Bureau, Population Estimates, 1990, 2000, 2007, 2011.

Watson, Ebbie Julian. *Handbook of South Carolina: Resources, Institutions, and Industries of the State.* Columbia: Department of Agriculture, 1907.

Wilson, Steven G., and Thomas R. Fischetti. "Coastline Population Trends in the United States: 1960–2008: Population Estimates and Projections." *Current Population Reports,* U.S. Department of Commerce, Economics and Statistics Administration, US Census Bureau, May 2010.

Theses and Dissertations

Barkes, Megan. "Water Quality Protection in Local Communities: Experiences with Creating Wetland Buffer Ordinances in the Lowcountry, South Carolina." Master's thesis, College of Charleston, 2006.

Derby, Doris Adelaide. "Black Women Basketmakers: A Study of Domestic Economy in Charleston County, South Carolina." Ph.D. diss., University of Illinois at Urbana-Champaign, 1980.

Duffy, Tracy. "Planners' Response to Environmental Change in the Lowcountry of South Carolina." Master's thesis, College of Charleston, 2007.

Grabbatin, Brian. "Sweetgrass Basketry: The Political Ecology of an African-American Art in the South Carolina Lowcountry." Master's thesis, College of Charleston, 2009.

Hart, T. Robert, Jr. "The Santee-Cooper Landscape: Culture and Environment in the South Carolina Lowcountry." Ph.D. diss., University of Alabama, 2004.

Hart, Zachary. "Stakeholder Participation in Management of Lowcountry South Carolina Sweetgrass (*Muhlenbergia Filipes*) Supplies." Master's thesis, College of Charleston, 2003.

Moore, Alan. "Is There a Future for Local Food? Small-Scale Farming in Lowcountry South Carolina and an Initiative to Strengthen a Local Food System." Master's thesis, College of Charleston, 2010.

Ogawa, Terry Yasuko. "Wando-Huger: A Study of the Impacts of Development on the Cultural Role of Black Land Communities of the South Carolina Lowcountry." Master's thesis, University of Michigan, 2008.

Ohlandt, K. F. "Where the Sweetgrass Grows: The Restoration of a Maritime Wet Grassland, Incorporating Harvesting of *Muhlenbergia filipes*." Master's thesis, University of Georgia, 1992.

Shuler, Jessi Ruth Adair. "Conserving Subdivided Nature: A Typology of Residential Development Practices in the South Carolina Lowcountry." Master's thesis, College of Charleston, 2007.

Smith, Hayden. "Watersheds of Control: An Environmental History of the South Carolina Lowcountry 1760–1860." Master's thesis, College of Charleston and The Citadel, 2002.

Stern, Marissa L. "Avoiding Pendulum Ecologies: Resident Perceptions of Environmental Management on Spring and Callawassie Islands in Lowcountry, South Carolina." Honors bachelor's essay, College of Charleston, 2007.

Voelker, Aaron. "Applicability of Convergence Hypothesis at the Organizational Level." Master's thesis, College of Charleston, 2007.

Websites and Other Electronic Sources

Adams, Dennis. "Marshes of the Lowcountry." http://www.beaufortcountylibrary.org/htdocs-sirsi/marshes.htm (accessed April 17, 2010).

Allen, Jeffery, and Kang Shou Lu. "Modeling and Predicting Future Urban Growth in the Charleston Area." http://www.strom.clemson.edu/teams/dctech/urban.html# (accessed August, 2 2009).

American Farmland Trust. "South Carolina." http://www.farmland.org/programs/states/sc/default.asp (accessed April 17, 2011).

Boudoulf, Ed. "Sewee Preserve." http://discoversewee.com/preserve.htm (accessed April 17, 2011).

Bucher, Patra. "Life in Harmony with Nature: Sewee Preserve: Mount Pleasant S.C." http://www.charlestonbuilders.com/sewee_preserve_sc.asp (accessed July 20, 2010).

Center for Biological Diversity. "Our Story." http://www.biologicaldiversity.org/about/story/index.html (accessed October 27, 2010).

Chaffin/Light. "Environmental Stewardship." http://www.chaffinlight.com/enviornmental stewardship.html (accessed August 11, 2010).

"Charleston-Area Realtors Launch Smart Growth Website and Advocacy Campaign." *Charleston Regional Business Journal.* http://www.preserveourlowcountry.com/about/ (accessed February 3, 2009).

Charleston Regional Development Alliance. "Market Profile." http://www.crda.org/business/market_profile/index.html (accessed July 24, 2009).

Chepesiuk, Ron. "Saving Sandy Island." http://www.americanprofile.com/articles/saving-sandy-island/ (accessed April 17, 2011).

City of Charleston official website. http://www.charlestoncity.info/dept/content.aspx?nid=495 (accessed November 7, 2010).

Coakley, Joyce V. "History" (Sweetgrass Festival). http://www.sweetgrassfestival.org/history.html (accessed April 17, 2011).

Coastal Conservation League. http://coastalconservationleague.org/ (accessed April 17, 2011).

———. "Regions: South Coast." http://coastalconservationleague.org/regions/south-coast/ (accessed April 17, 2011).

Concerned Citizens of the Sea Islands (Johns Island, South Carolina). http://concerned citizensoftheseaislands.org/ (3 November 3, 2010).

———. "Current Initiatives." http://concernedcitizensoftheseaislands.org/current-initiatives /i-526–extension (accessed November 3, 2010).

Congress for the New Urbanism. *Charter.* http://www.cnu.org/charter (accessed April 12, 2010).

Conservation Fund. "Conservation Leadership Network." http://www.conservationfund .org/training_education (accessed June 13, 2010).

deVere, Paul. "A Town Is Born." *Celebrate Hilton Head,* February 2008. http://www .celebratehiltonhead.com/article/723/a-town-is-born (accessed December 20, 2009).

Ducks Unlimited. "Lowcountry Initiative: Conservation Easements." http://www.ducks .org/South_Carolina/SouthCarolinaConservation/1478/LowcountryInitiative ConservationEasements.html (accessed June 7, 2010).

———. "2009 State Conservation Report." http://www.ducks.org/media/conservation /reports/southcarolina.pdf (accessed June 7, 2010).

"East Edisto." http://www.eastedisto.com/about/ (accessed April 17, 2011).

Gallup. "State of the States: Midyear 2009." http://www.gallup.com/poll/122333/political -ideology-conservative-label-prevails-south.aspx (accessed June 3, 2010).

Greene, Harlan. "Readers' Choice, 2008 Giving Back Awards." *Charleston Magazine,* September 2008–August 2009. http://www.charlestonmag.com/charitableeventscalendar /readers.html.

Greenways, Inc. http://www.greenways.com/charleston.html (accessed June 10, 2010).

Griffith, Glenn E., James M. Omernik, Jeffrey A. Comstock, Michael P. Schafale, W. Henry McNab, David R. Lenat (NCDENR), Trish F. MacPherson, James B. Glover, and Victor B. Shelburne. "Ecoregions of North Carolina and South Carolina" (color poster, Reston, Va.: U.S. Geological Survey, 2002). http://www.epa.gov/wed/pages/ecoregions/ncsc_eco .htm (accessed August 2, 2009).

Hilton Head Real Estate Report. "Here's a Classic Case of the TIME LINE!!" http://hilton headrealestatereport.blogspot.com/2008/10/heres-classic-case-of-time-line-process.html (accessed April 17, 2011).

I'On Realty. "Inside I'On." http://www.ionrealty.com/pdf/newsletter/375091410721201.pdf (accessed April 17, 2011).

Land Trust Alliance. "Land Trust Alliance Fact Sheet" (2010). http://www.landtrust alliance.org/conservation/.../what-is-land-trust.pdf (accessed April 12, 2011).

Lowcountry Local First. http://www.lowcountrylocalfirst.org/ (accessed October 8, 2010).

———. "Community Supported Agriculture (CSA)." http://www.Lowcountrylocalfirst.org /program/Community_Supported_Agriculture.php (accessed September 12, 2010).

Lowcountry Open Land Trust. "Land Protection." http://www.lolt.org/landprotection (accessed June 10, 2010).

Mark Clark Expressway. "Frequently Asked Questions." South Carolina Department of Transportation. http://www.dot.state.sc.us/i526/questions.shtml (accessed April 17, 2011).

Marshall, Alex. "A More Benevolent Sprawl." Book review of Duany et al., *Suburban Nation.* http://www.alexmarshall.org/index.php?pageId=79 (accessed August 25, 2010).

McKibben, Jerome N. "Town of Mount Pleasant Population Forecasts: 2005–2025." http://
www.townofmountpleasant.com/downloads/McKibben_Report-2007.pdf (accessed
October 31, 2010).

"MeadWestvaco Unveils East Edisto Preliminary Master Plan." http://www.meadwestvaco
.com/NewsEvents/PressReleases/ReleasesReplacableContent/MWV004048 (accessed
April 17, 2011).

Mount Pleasant community website. "Home: Mount Pleasant named 2010 All-American
City." http://www.townofmountpleasant.com/index.cfm?section=1 (accessed April 17,
2011).

National Conservation Leadership Institute. "NCLI 2008–09 Cohort 3 Annual Report."
http://www.conservationleadership.org/joomla/content/view/64/80/ (accessed June 8,
2010).

Nature Conservancy. "About Us." http://www.nature.org/aboutus/ (accessed April 2, 2010).

———. "Places We Protect." http://www.nature.org/ourinitiatives/regions/northamerica/
unitedstates/southcarolina/placesweprotect/index.htm (accessed June 7, 2010).

———. "South Carolina 6/09 Update." http://www.nature.org/ourinitiatives/regions/north
america/unitedstates/southcarolina/explore/sc_update_6_09.pdf (accessed June 7,
2010).

———. South Carolina website. http://www.nature.org/ourinitiatives/regions/northamerica
/unitedstates/southcarolina/index.htm (accessed August 2, 2009).

Nixon, Richard. "Special Message to the Congress Outlining the 1972 Environmental Program." www.presidency.ucsb.edu/ws/index.php?pid=3731 (accessed November 10, 2010).

"Okatie Village: Osprey Point Planned United Development Agreement." http://www
.bcgov.net/councilcentral/DevelopmentAgreementandPUDs/PUDs/OspreyPoint.pdf
(accessed August 23, 2010).

On the Issues. "Mark Sanford on Environment." http://www.ontheissues.org/governor
/Mark_Sanford_Environment.htm (accessed November 7, 2010).

Palmetto Bluff. http://www.palmetto-bluff.com/) (accessed July 22, 2009).

———. "Conservation." http://www.palmetto-bluff.com/conservation.asp (accessed July
20, 2010).

Property Rights Foundation of America. *Biography: Mark Nix*. http://prfamerica.org
/biography/Biography-Nix-Mark.html (accessed April 10, 2010).

Remax Island Realty, 2008, http://ww.remaxbeaufort.com (accessed July 20, 2010).

Sanford, Mark. "2008 State of the State Address." http://www.wistv.com/global/story.asp
?s=7710520 (accessed April 13, 2011).

S.C. Landscape Land Trust (Lowcountry Open Land Trust). http://www.lolt.org/land
protection/landscaping-mapping-project (accessed June 20, 2010).

Smart Growth America. http://www.smartgrowthamerica.org/whoweare.html (accessed
July 18, 2010).

South Carolina Budget and Control Board. "Data about South Carolina and Its People."
http://www.bcb.sc.gov/BCB/BCB-sc-data.phtm (accessed August 2, 2009).

South Carolina Conservation Bank. "The S.C. Conservation Bank Act." http://sccbank.sc
.gov/ (accessed June 10, 2010).

South Carolina Sea Grant Consortium. *The Changing Face of South Carolina: Valuing
Resources, Adapting to Change: Strategic and Implementation Plan 2010–2013*. http://www
.scseagrant.org/pdf_files/SCSGC_Strat_Plan_2010–13.pdf (accessed October 25, 2011).

"Spring Island Journal." http://springisland-sc.com/_blog/Spring_Island_Journal/post
/June_2010/ (accessed August 11, 2010).

Spring Island Realty. "The Spring Island Philosophy." http://springisland-sc.com/philosophy.html (accessed August 11, 2010).

South Carolina Growth Initiative. "Growing by Choice or Chance: State Strategies for Quality Growth in South Carolina." *Urban Land Institute,* 2003, PDF online document, http://southcarolina.uli.org/~/media/DC/South%20Carolina/SC%20Documents/Quality_Growth_Report.ashx (accessed August 13, 2010).

South Carolina Information Highway (SCIWAY). "Coastal S.C. Environmental and Conservation Organizations." http://www.sciway.net/org/environmental-coastal.html (accessed June 10, 2010).

———. "South Carolina Environmental Organizations – By Region." http://www.sciway.net/org/environmental.html (accessed June 10, 2010).

Southern Environmental Law Center. http://www.southernenvironment.org/ (accessed June 7, 2010).

———. "SELC's Greatest Hits." http://www.southernenvironment.org/about/greatest_hits/ (accessed June 7, 2010).

———. "SELC's Long-term Strategic Action Plan." http://www.southernenvironment.org/about/action_plan/ (accessed June 7, 2010).

Stokes-Marshall, Thomasena. Personal blog. "Where I Stand on Important Issues," August 26, 2006. http://thomasenastokes-marshall.blogspot.com/ (accessed July 24, 2009).

Strom Thurmond Institute. "Charleston Urban Growth Project 1973–2030." http://www.strom.clemson.edu/teams/dctech/mapshowB.html (accessed July 8, 2010).

Sweetgrass Festival. "The Festival: Details and Locations." http://www.sweetgrassfestival.org/festival_details.html (accessed April 14, 2011).

TopRetirements.com. "South Carolina Low Country Popular with Boomers." http://www.topretirements.com/tips/Regions/South_Carolina_Low_Country_Popular_with_Boomers.html (accessed June 6, 2010).

Town of Mount Pleasant, South Carolina, website. "Town Co-sponsors Sweetgrass Cultural Event" (May 11, 2005). http://www.townofMountpleasant.com/index.cfm?section=14&page=2&mesg=art426.26737 (accessed November 5, 2010).

Trust for Public Land. "Beaufort County Land Acquisition Program." http://www.tpl.org/tier3_cd.cfm?content_item_id=18762&folder_id=2887 (accessed June 10, 2010).

Vollmer, Paige. "Sustainable Land-Use Planning for the Ashepoo-Combahee-Edisto (ACE) Basin Region: Synthesizing Local Knowledge, Preferences, and Socioeconcomics." http://www.seseagrant.org/pdf_files/cc_sustain.pdf (accessed November 12, 2010.

Page numbers given in *italics* indicate illustrations or material contained in their captions.